VOLUME
11

Silver Spoon

HIROMU ARAKAWA

STORY & CHARACTERS

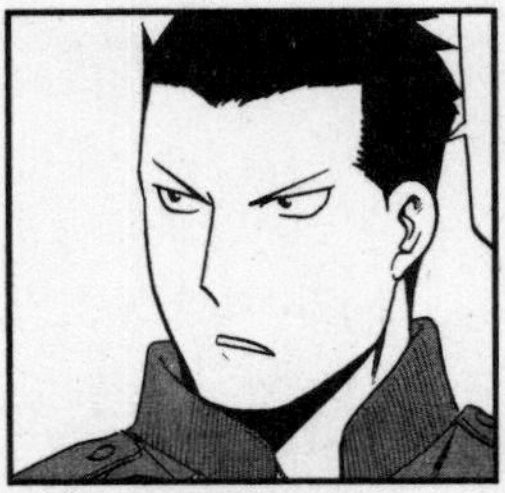

ICHIROU KOMABA

A former first-year student at Ooezo Agricultural High School, enrolled in the Dairy Science Program. He had planned on taking over the family farm after graduation, but it went out of business.

AKI MIKAGE

A first-year student at Ooezo Agricultural High School, enrolled in the Dairy Science Program. Her family keeps cows and horses. While her family has accepted that their only daughter won't carry on the family business, now she has to get into college...

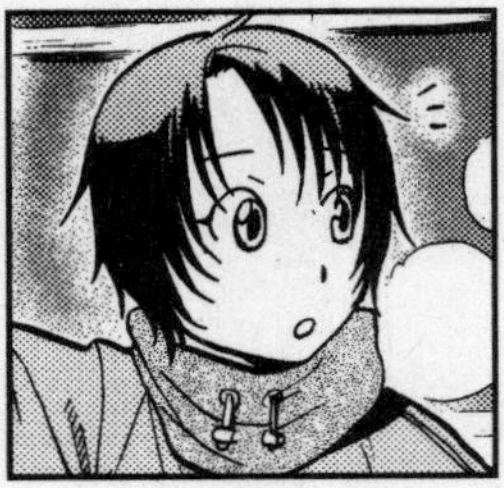

YUUGO HACHIKEN

A first-year student at Ooezo Agricultural High School, enrolled in the Dairy Science Program. A city kid from Sapporo who got in through the general entrance exam. He's finally started to see both the fun and the harshness of the agriculture industry...

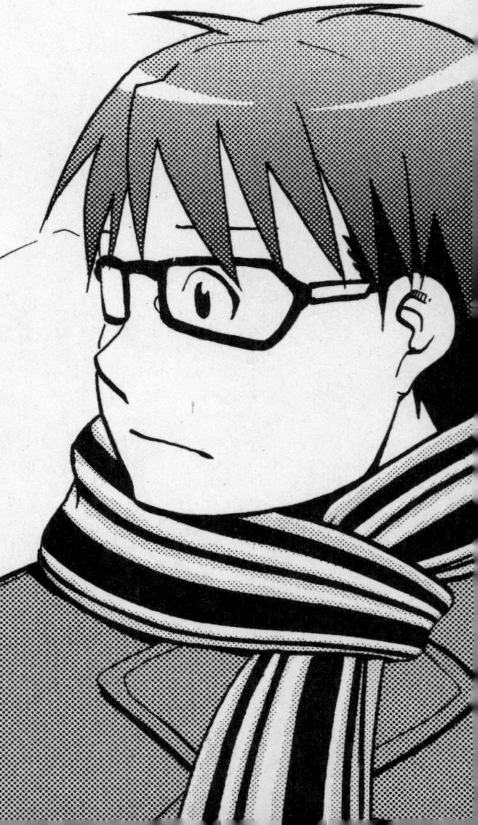

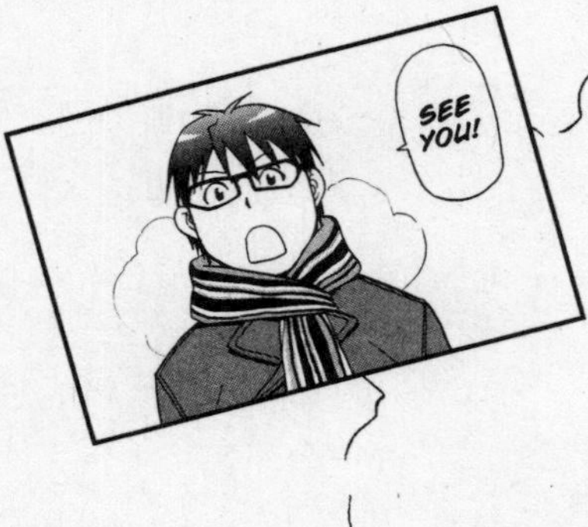
SEE YOU!

TAMAKO INADA

A first-year student at Ooezo Agricultural High School, enrolled in the Dairy Science Program. Her family runs a megafarm. A complete enigma.

SHINNOSUKE AIKAWA

A first-year student at Ooezo Agricultural High School, enrolled in the Dairy Science Program. His dream is to become a veterinarian, but he can't handle blood.

KEIJI TOKIWA

A first-year student at Ooezo Agricultural High School, enrolled in the Dairy Science Program. Son of chicken farmers. Awful at academics.

The Story Thus Far:

When Haciken elects to remain at Ezo Ag for the holidays instead of visiting home, he ends up sampling a flavorful Ezo Ag–style New Year's Eve and shrine visit. And so a new school term begins. The pork purchased through the "Pork Fund" Hachiken organized arrives. The students process the pork into sausage themselves, giving Hachiken his first experience in direct sales. The Ezo Ag market shows Hachiken firsthand the difficulties—but also the rewards and the customer response—of selling a product. Seeing Hachiken's progress begins to influence his friends as well...

CONTENTS

Silver Spoon

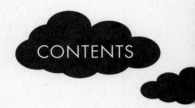

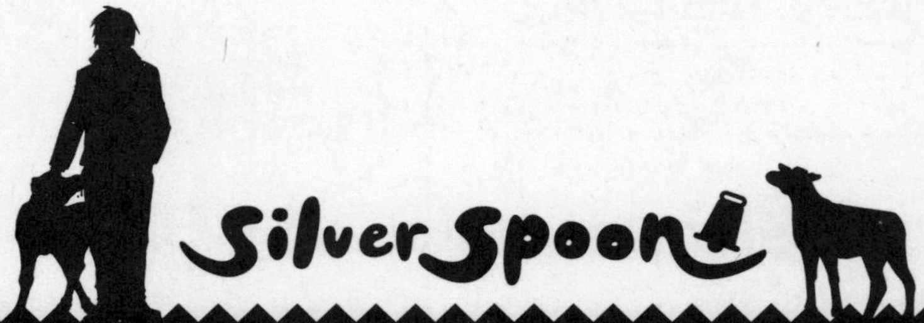

Chapter 89: Tale of Winter ㉖

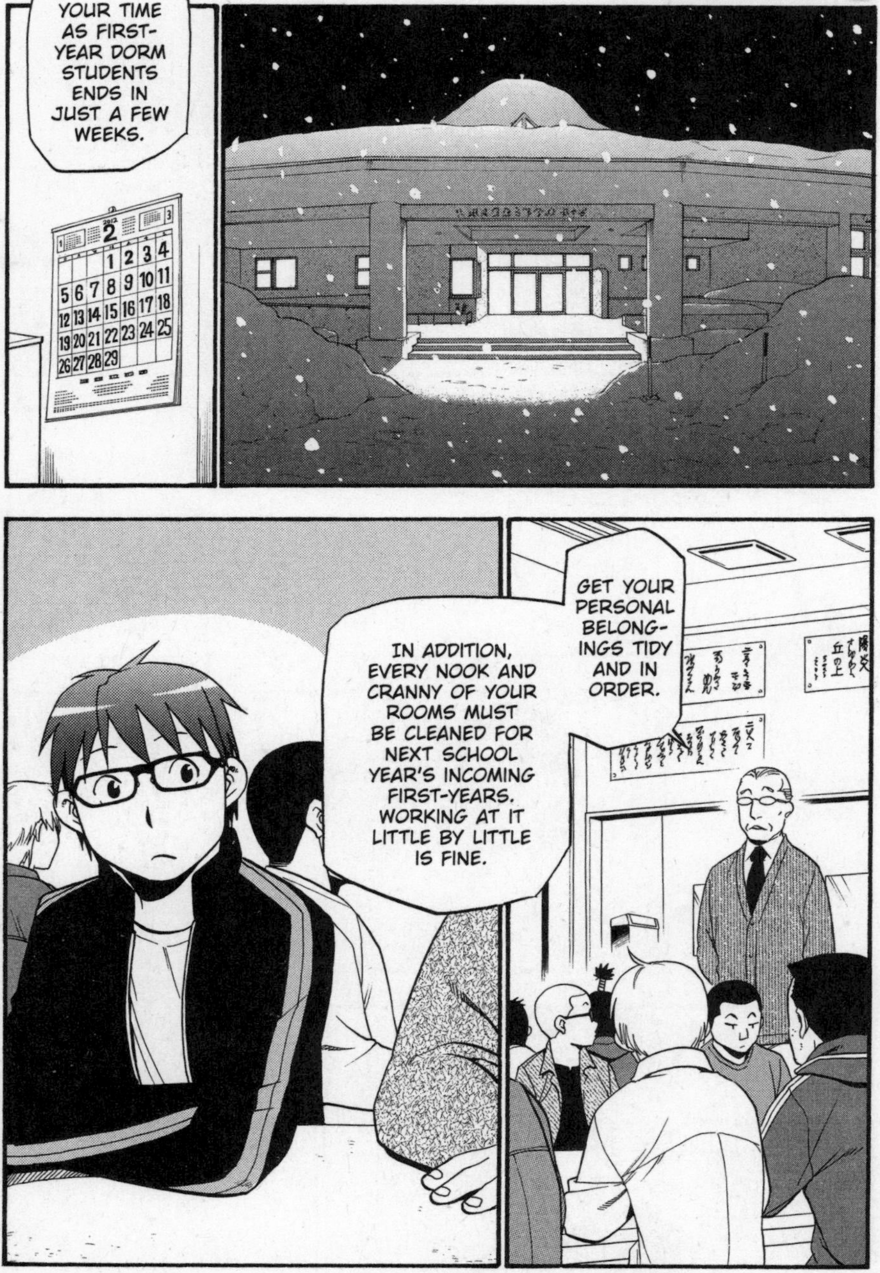
YOUR TIME AS FIRST-YEAR DORM STUDENTS ENDS IN JUST A FEW WEEKS.
GET YOUR PERSONAL BELONGINGS TIDY AND IN ORDER.
IN ADDITION, EVERY NOOK AND CRANNY OF YOUR ROOMS MUST BE CLEANED FOR NEXT SCHOOL YEAR'S INCOMING FIRST-YEARS. WORKING AT IT LITTLE BY LITTLE IS FINE.

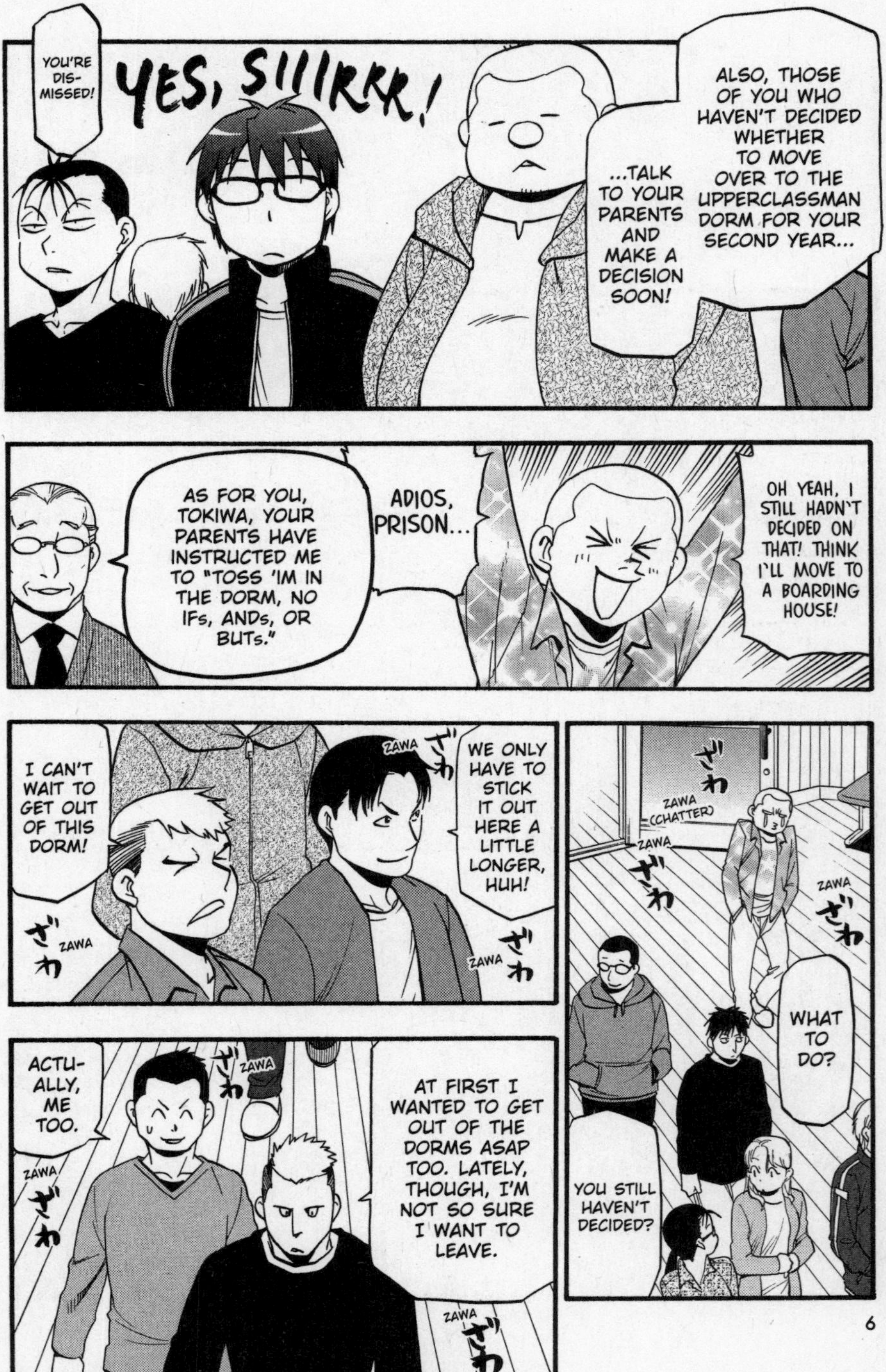
ALSO, THOSE OF YOU WHO HAVEN'T DECIDED WHETHER TO MOVE OVER TO THE UPPERCLASSMAN DORM FOR YOUR SECOND YEAR...
...TALK TO YOUR PARENTS AND MAKE A DECISION SOON!
YOU'RE DIS-MISSED!
YES, SIIIRRRR!
OH YEAH, I STILL HADN'T DECIDED ON THAT! THINK I'LL MOVE TO A BOARDING HOUSE!
ADIOS, PRISON...
AS FOR YOU, TOKIWA, YOUR PARENTS HAVE INSTRUCTED ME TO "TOSS 'IM IN THE DORM, NO IFs, ANDs, OR BUTs."
ざわ ZAWA (CHATTER)
ざわ ZAWA
ざわ ZAWA
WHAT TO DO?
YOU STILL HAVEN'T DECIDED?
ざわ ZAWA
WE ONLY HAVE TO STICK IT OUT HERE A LITTLE LONGER, HUH!
I CAN'T WAIT TO GET OUT OF THIS DORM!
ざわ ZAWA
ざわ ZAWA
ざわ ZAWA
AT FIRST I WANTED TO GET OUT OF THE DORMS ASAP TOO. LATELY, THOUGH, I'M NOT SO SURE I WANT TO LEAVE.
ACTU-ALLY, ME TOO.
ざわ ZAWA
ざわ ZAWA

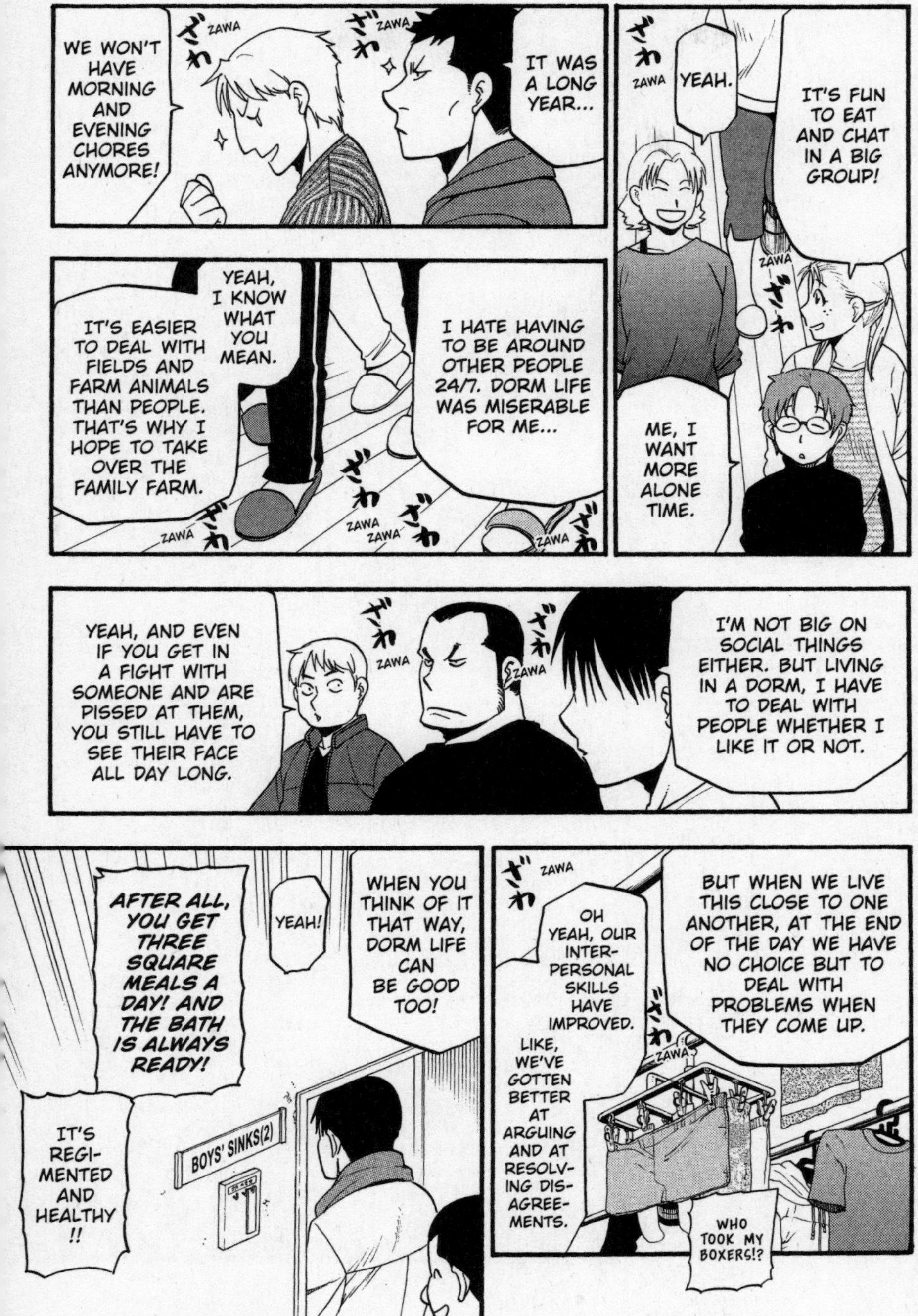
IT'S FUN TO EAT AND CHAT IN A BIG GROUP!
YEAH.
ZAWA
ZAWA
ME, I WANT MORE ALONE TIME.
ZAWA
ZAWA
IT WAS A LONG YEAR...
WE WON'T HAVE MORNING AND EVENING CHORES ANYMORE!
I HATE HAVING TO BE AROUND OTHER PEOPLE 24/7. DORM LIFE WAS MISERABLE FOR ME...
YEAH, I KNOW WHAT YOU MEAN.
IT'S EASIER TO DEAL WITH FIELDS AND FARM ANIMALS THAN PEOPLE. THAT'S WHY I HOPE TO TAKE OVER THE FAMILY FARM.
ZAWA
ZAWA ZAWA
ZAWA
I'M NOT BIG ON SOCIAL THINGS EITHER. BUT LIVING IN A DORM, I HAVE TO DEAL WITH PEOPLE WHETHER I LIKE IT OR NOT.
ZAWA
ZAWA
YEAH, AND EVEN IF YOU GET IN A FIGHT WITH SOMEONE AND ARE PISSED AT THEM, YOU STILL HAVE TO SEE THEIR FACE ALL DAY LONG.
BUT WHEN WE LIVE THIS CLOSE TO ONE ANOTHER, AT THE END OF THE DAY WE HAVE NO CHOICE BUT TO DEAL WITH PROBLEMS WHEN THEY COME UP.
ZAWA
OH YEAH, OUR INTER-PERSONAL SKILLS HAVE IMPROVED.
LIKE, WE'VE GOTTEN BETTER AT ARGUING AND AT RESOLVING DIS-AGREE-MENTS.
ZAWA
WHO TOOK MY BOXERS!?
WHEN YOU THINK OF IT THAT WAY, DORM LIFE CAN BE GOOD TOO!
YEAH!
AFTER ALL, YOU GET THREE SQUARE MEALS A DAY! AND THE BATH IS ALWAYS READY!
BOYS' SINKS(2)
IT'S REGI-MENTED AND HEALTHY!!

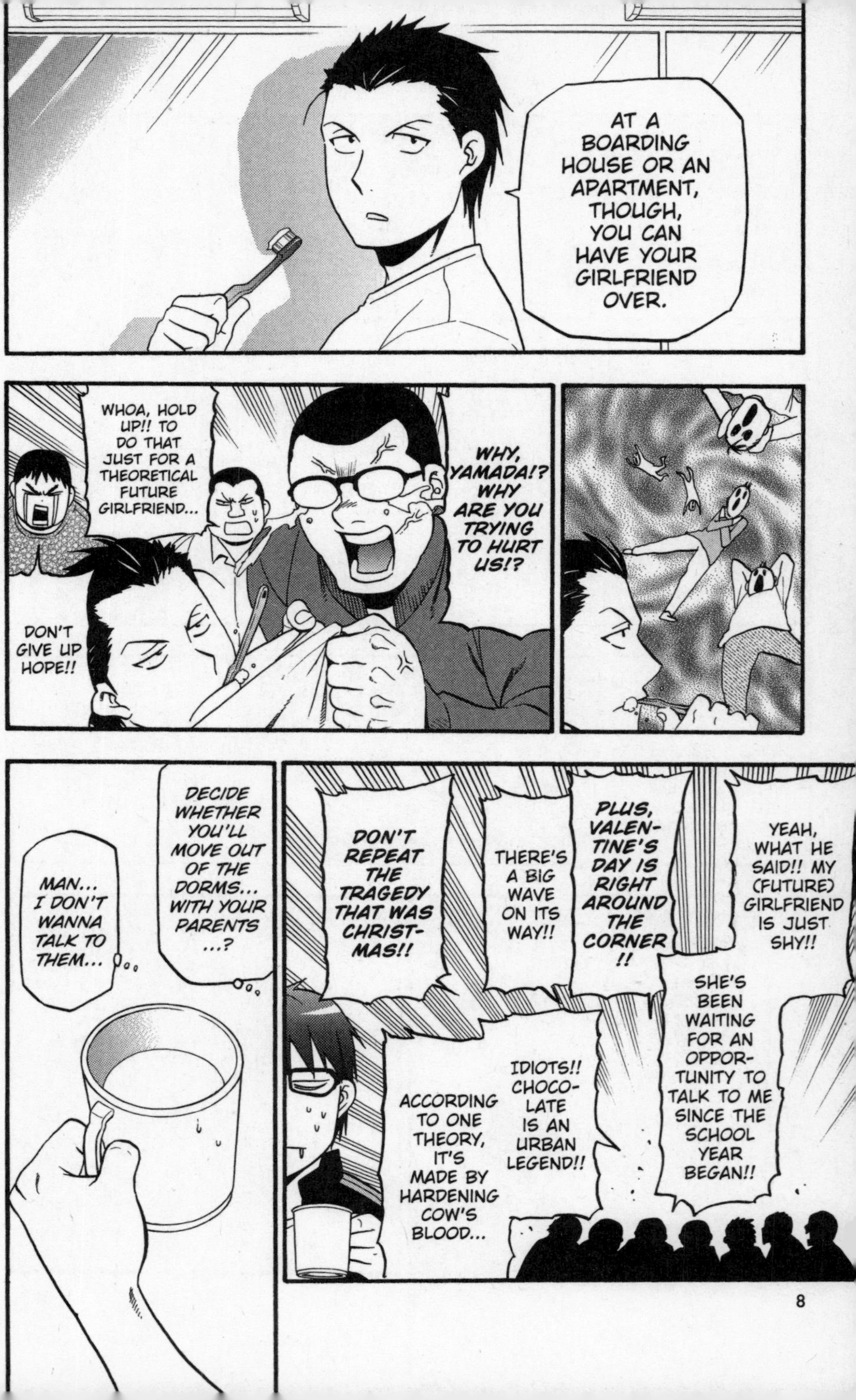
AT A BOARDING HOUSE OR AN APARTMENT, THOUGH, YOU CAN HAVE YOUR GIRLFRIEND OVER.
WHY, YAMADA!? WHY ARE YOU TRYING TO HURT US!?
WHOA, HOLD UP!! TO DO THAT JUST FOR A THEORETICAL FUTURE GIRLFRIEND...
DON'T GIVE UP HOPE!!
YEAH, WHAT HE SAID!! MY (FUTURE) GIRLFRIEND IS JUST SHY!!
PLUS, VALEN-TINE'S DAY IS RIGHT AROUND THE CORNER!!
THERE'S A BIG WAVE ON ITS WAY!!
DON'T REPEAT THE TRAGEDY THAT WAS CHRIST-MAS!!
SHE'S BEEN WAITING FOR AN OPPOR-TUNITY TO TALK TO ME SINCE THE SCHOOL YEAR BEGAN!!
IDIOTS!! CHOCO-LATE IS AN URBAN LEGEND!!
ACCORDING TO ONE THEORY, IT'S MADE BY HARDENING COW'S BLOOD...
DECIDE WHETHER YOU'LL MOVE OUT OF THE DORMS... WITH YOUR PARENTS ...?
MAN... I DON'T WANNA TALK TO THEM...

BOTTLE: NATURAL SPRING WATER, BEAR CREEK
TUB: RICH EZO AG PUDDING

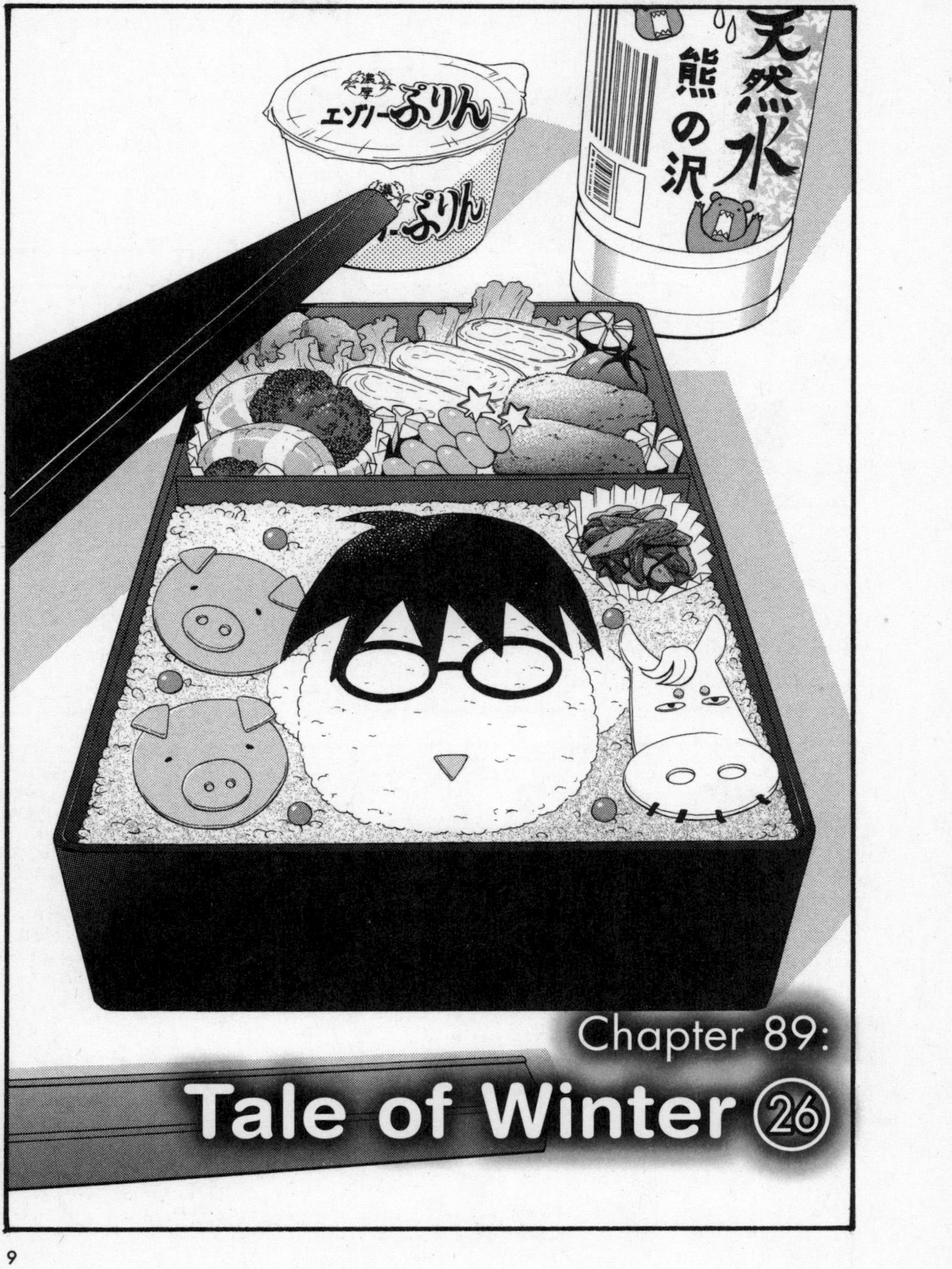
濃厚
エゾノーぷりん
天然水
熊の沢
Chapter 89:
Tale of Winter ㉖

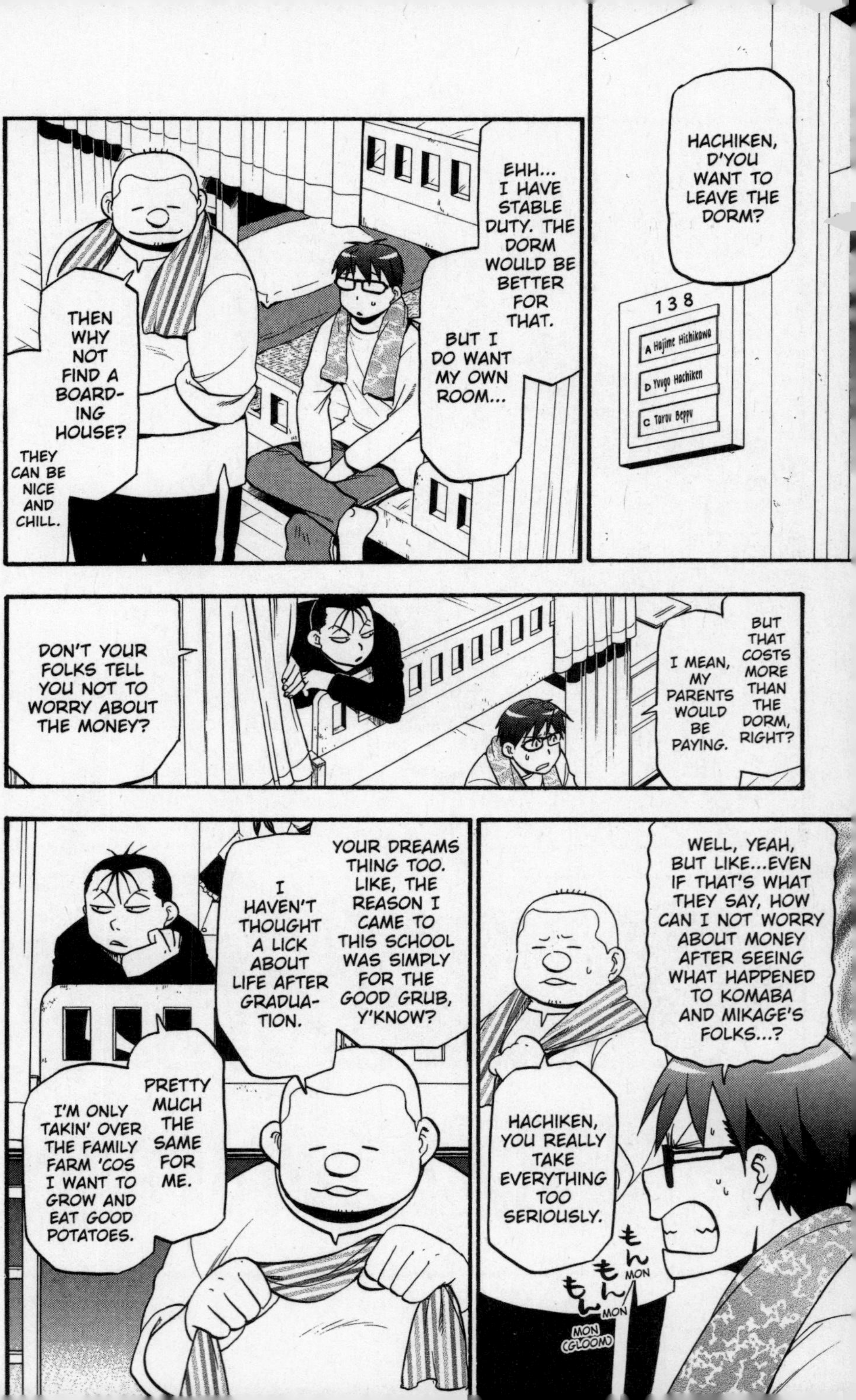
HACHIKEN, D'YOU WANT TO LEAVE THE DORM?
138
A Hajime Hishikawa
D Yuugo Hachiken
C Tarou Beppu
EHH... I HAVE STABLE DUTY. THE DORM WOULD BE BETTER FOR THAT.
BUT I DO WANT MY OWN ROOM...
THEN WHY NOT FIND A BOARDING-HOUSE?
THEY CAN BE NICE AND CHILL.
BUT THAT COSTS MORE THAN THE DORM, RIGHT?
I MEAN, MY PARENTS WOULD BE PAYING.
DON'T YOUR FOLKS TELL YOU NOT TO WORRY ABOUT THE MONEY?
WELL, YEAH, BUT LIKE...EVEN IF THAT'S WHAT THEY SAY, HOW CAN I NOT WORRY ABOUT MONEY AFTER SEEING WHAT HAPPENED TO KOMABA AND MIKAGE'S FOLKS...?
HACHIKEN, YOU REALLY TAKE EVERYTHING TOO SERIOUSLY.
もん MON
もん MON
もん MON (GLOOM)
YOUR DREAMS THING TOO. LIKE, THE REASON I CAME TO THIS SCHOOL WAS SIMPLY FOR THE GOOD GRUB, Y'KNOW?
I HAVEN'T THOUGHT A LICK ABOUT LIFE AFTER GRADUATION.
PRETTY MUCH THE SAME FOR ME.
I'M ONLY TAKIN' OVER THE FAMILY FARM 'COS I WANT TO GROW AND EAT GOOD POTATOES.

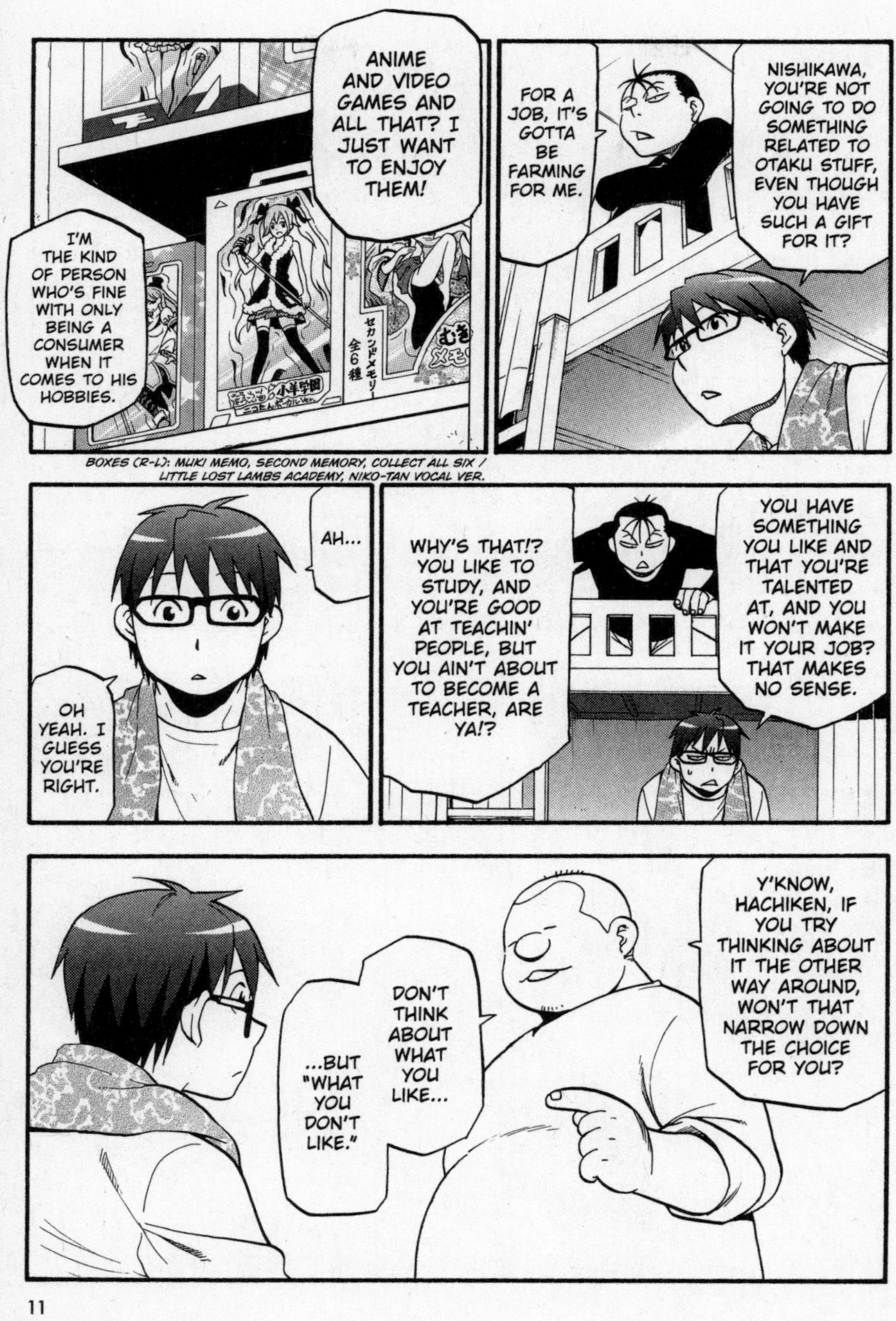
NISHIKAWA, YOU'RE NOT GOING TO DO SOMETHING RELATED TO OTAKU STUFF, EVEN THOUGH YOU HAVE SUCH A GIFT FOR IT?
FOR A JOB, IT'S GOTTA BE FARMING FOR ME.
ANIME AND VIDEO GAMES AND ALL THAT? I JUST WANT TO ENJOY THEM!
I'M THE KIND OF PERSON WHO'S FINE WITH ONLY BEING A CONSUMER WHEN IT COMES TO HIS HOBBIES.
セカンドメモリー 全6種
小羊学園
BOXES (R-L): MUKI MEMO, SECOND MEMORY, COLLECT ALL SIX / LITTLE LOST LAMBS ACADEMY, NIKO-TAN VOCAL VER.
YOU HAVE SOMETHING YOU LIKE AND THAT YOU'RE TALENTED AT, AND YOU WON'T MAKE IT YOUR JOB? THAT MAKES NO SENSE.
WHY'S THAT!? YOU LIKE TO STUDY, AND YOU'RE GOOD AT TEACHIN' PEOPLE, BUT YOU AIN'T ABOUT TO BECOME A TEACHER, ARE YA!?
AH...
OH YEAH. I GUESS YOU'RE RIGHT.
Y'KNOW, HACHIKEN, IF YOU TRY THINKING ABOUT IT THE OTHER WAY AROUND, WON'T THAT NARROW DOWN THE CHOICE FOR YOU?
DON'T THINK ABOUT WHAT YOU LIKE...
...BUT "WHAT YOU DON'T LIKE."

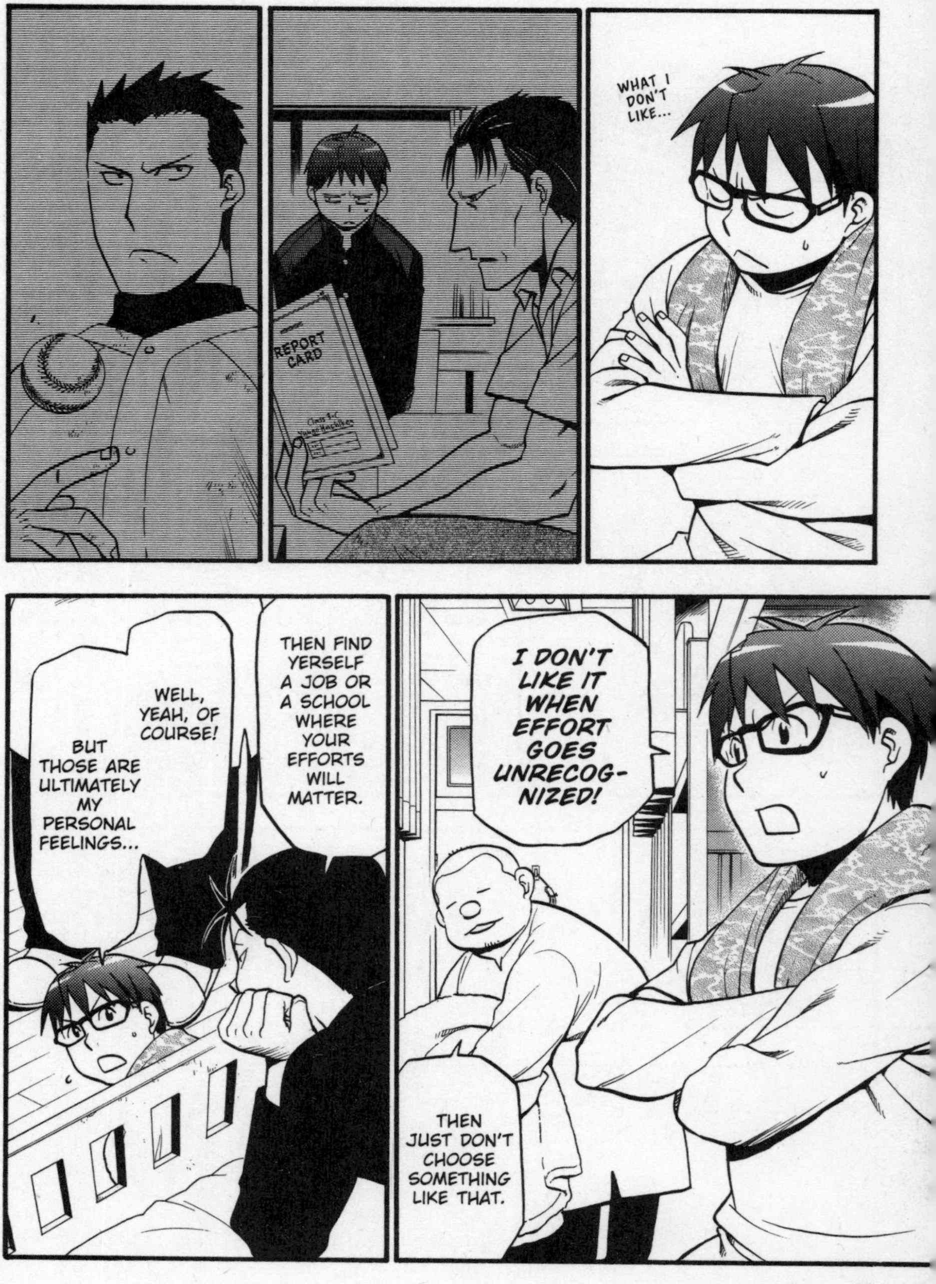
WHAT I DON'T LIKE...
REPORT CARD
I DON'T LIKE IT WHEN EFFORT GOES UNRECOG-NIZED!
THEN JUST DON'T CHOOSE SOMETHING LIKE THAT.
THEN FIND YERSELF A JOB OR A SCHOOL WHERE YOUR EFFORTS WILL MATTER.
WELL, YEAH, OF COURSE!
BUT THOSE ARE ULTIMATELY MY PERSONAL FEELINGS...

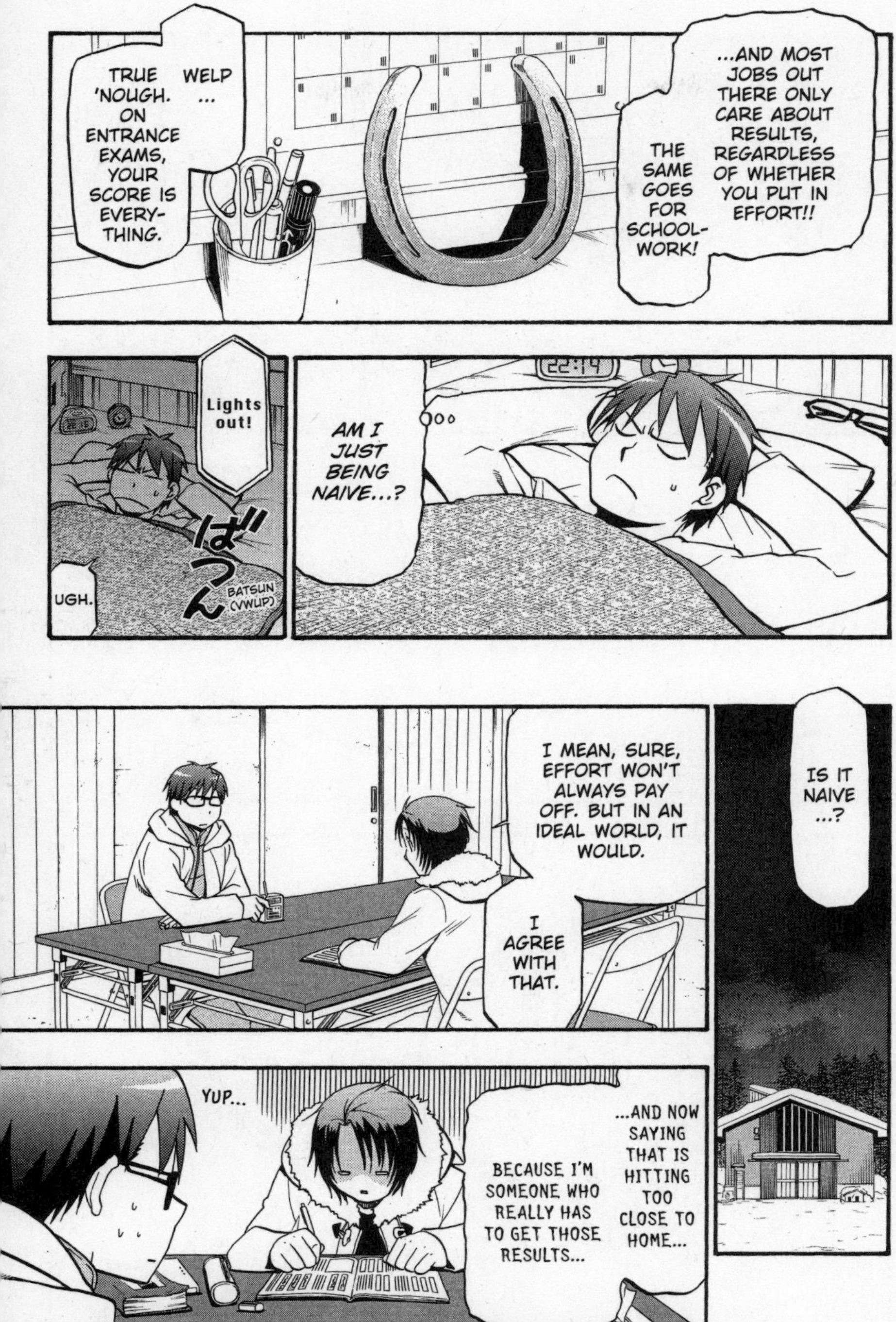
...AND MOST JOBS OUT THERE ONLY CARE ABOUT RESULTS, REGARDLESS OF WHETHER YOU PUT IN EFFORT!!
THE SAME GOES FOR SCHOOLWORK!
WELP ...
TRUE 'NOUGH. ON ENTRANCE EXAMS, YOUR SCORE IS EVERYTHING.
AM I JUST BEING NAIVE...?
Lights out!
ばつん
BATSUN (VWUP)
UGH.
IS IT NAIVE ...?
I MEAN, SURE, EFFORT WON'T ALWAYS PAY OFF. BUT IN AN IDEAL WORLD, IT WOULD.
I AGREE WITH THAT.
...AND NOW SAYING THAT IS HITTING TOO CLOSE TO HOME...
BECAUSE I'M SOMEONE WHO REALLY HAS TO GET THOSE RESULTS...
YUP...

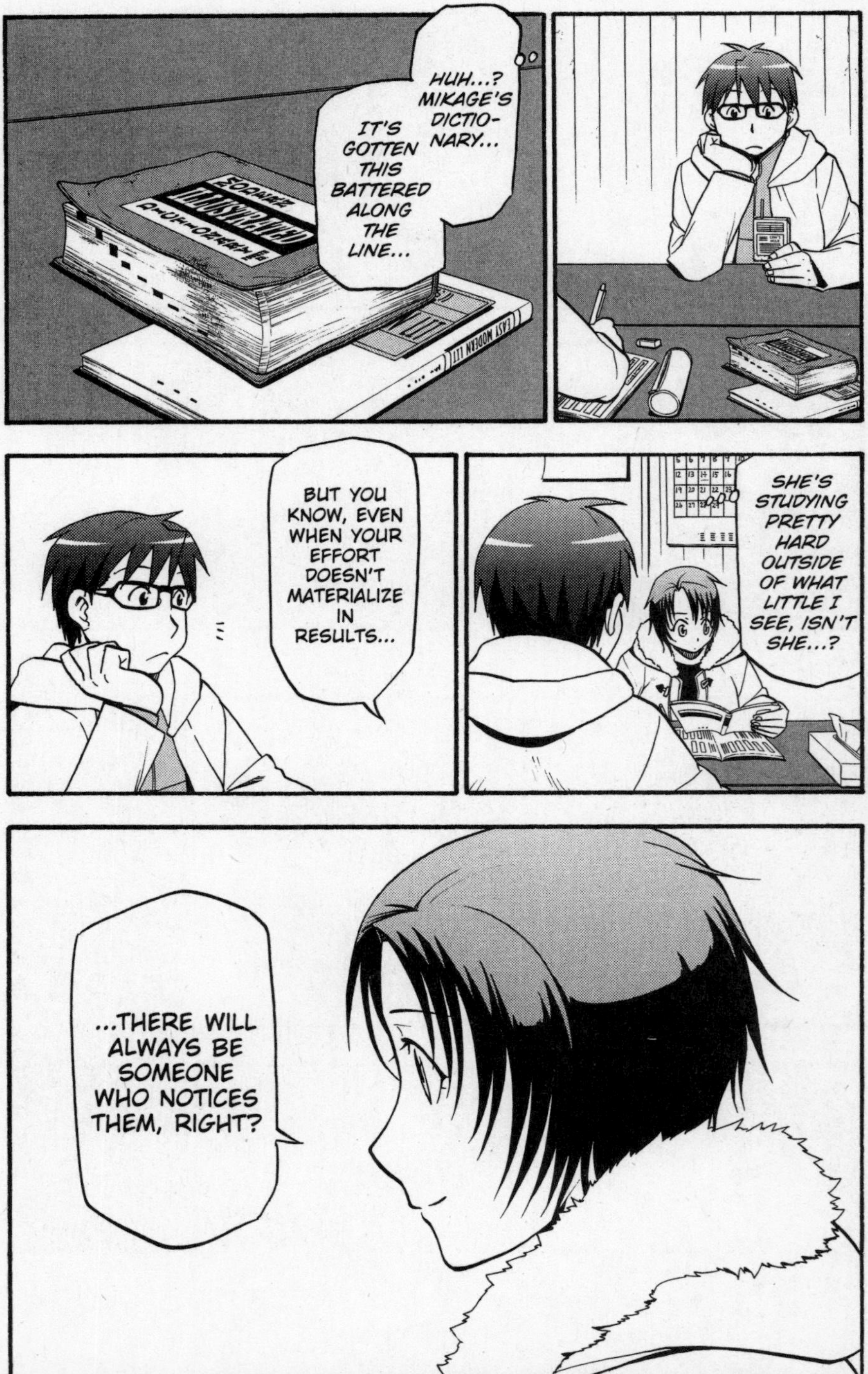
HUH...? MIKAGE'S DICTIONARY...
IT'S GOTTEN THIS BATTERED ALONG THE LINE...
SHE'S STUDYING PRETTY HARD OUTSIDE OF WHAT LITTLE I SEE, ISN'T SHE...?
BUT YOU KNOW, EVEN WHEN YOUR EFFORT DOESN'T MATERIALIZE IN RESULTS...
...THERE WILL ALWAYS BE SOMEONE WHO NOTICES THEM, RIGHT?

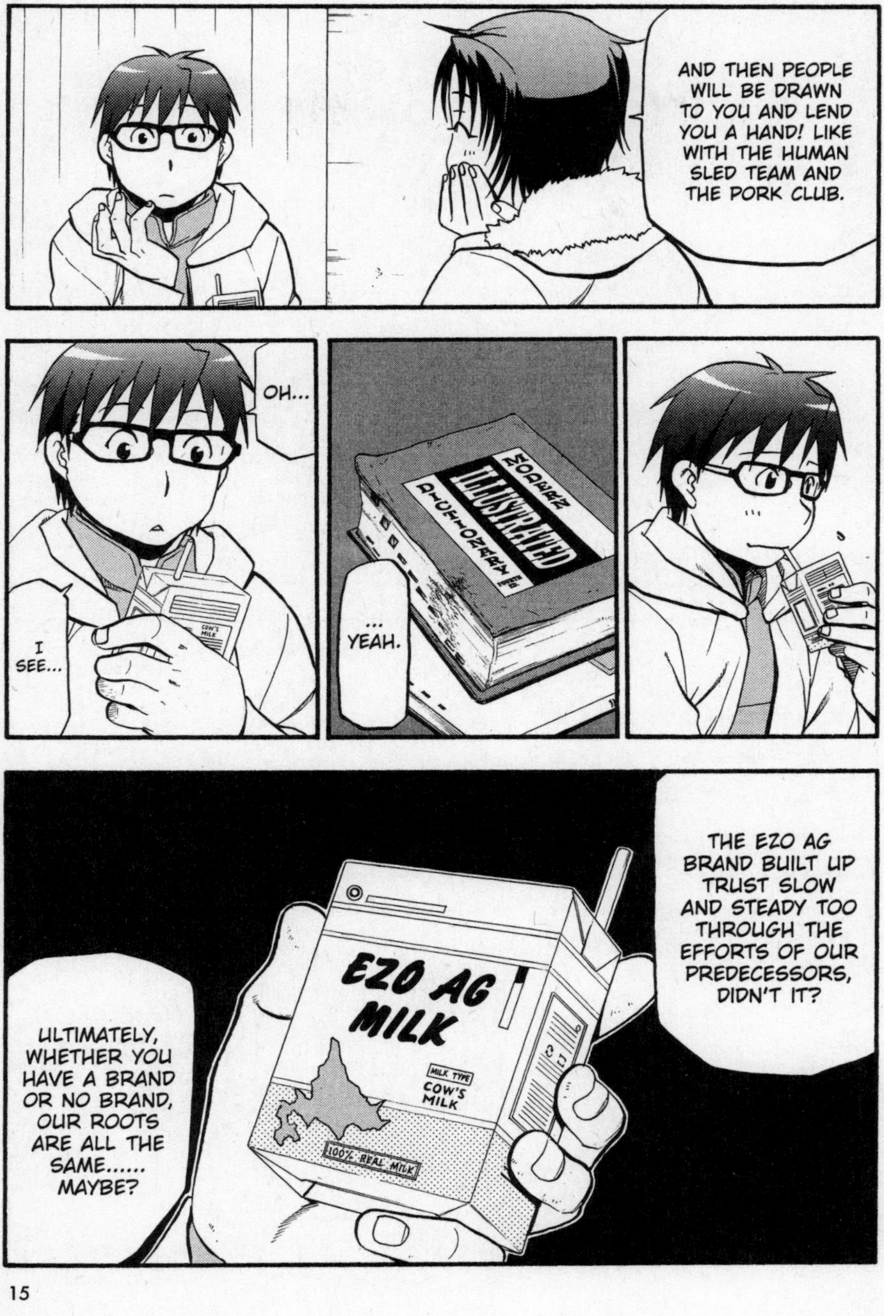
AND THEN PEOPLE WILL BE DRAWN TO YOU AND LEND YOU A HAND! LIKE WITH THE HUMAN SLED TEAM AND THE PORK CLUB.
... YEAH.
OH...
I SEE...
THE EZO AG BRAND BUILT UP TRUST SLOW AND STEADY TOO THROUGH THE EFFORTS OF OUR PREDECESSORS, DIDN'T IT?
EZO AG MILK
MILK TYPE
COW'S MILK
100% REAL MILK
ULTIMATELY, WHETHER YOU HAVE A BRAND OR NO BRAND, OUR ROOTS ARE ALL THE SAME...... MAYBE?

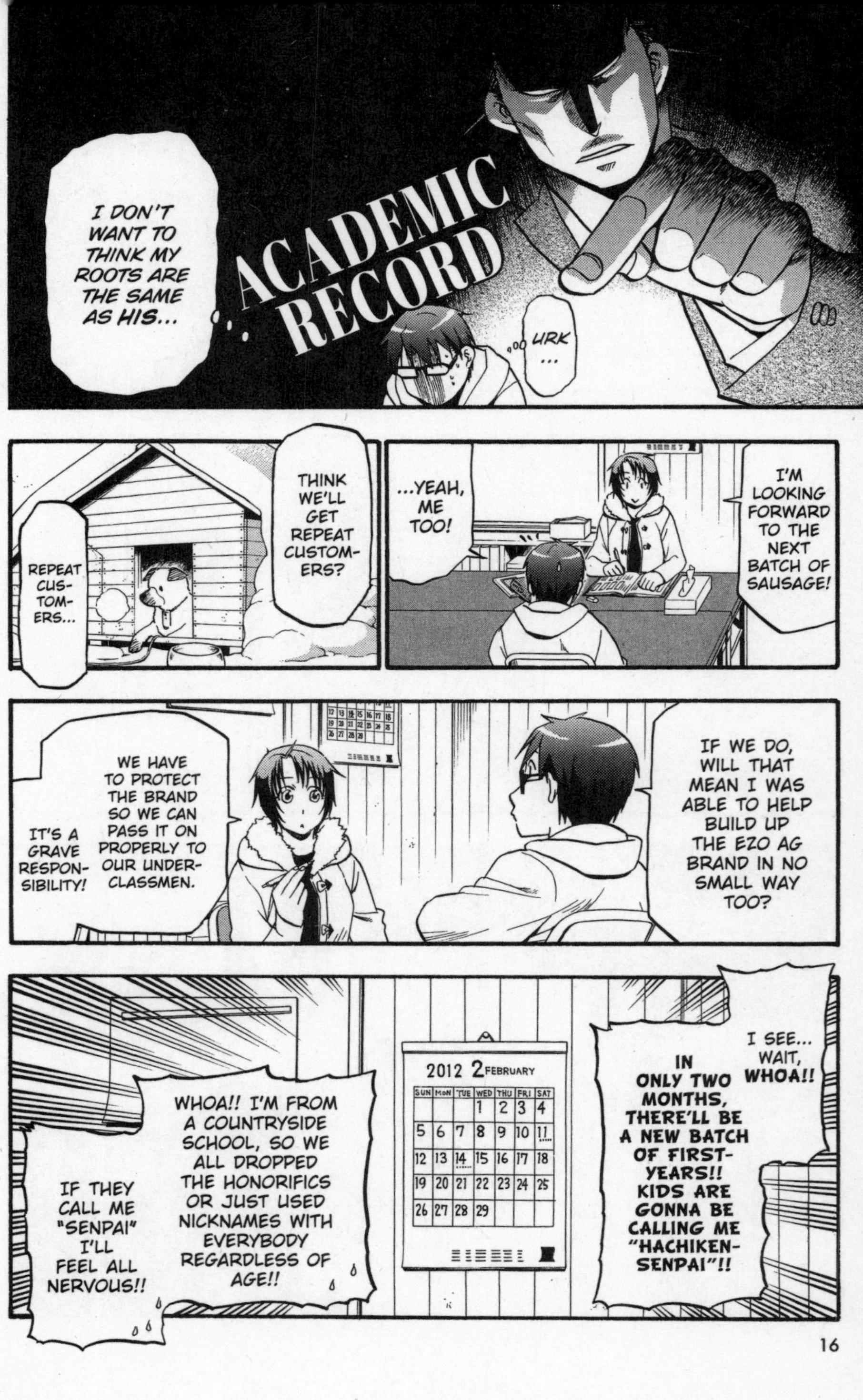
ACADEMIC RECORD
URK...
I DON'T WANT TO THINK MY ROOTS ARE THE SAME AS HIS...
I'M LOOKING FORWARD TO THE NEXT BATCH OF SAUSAGE!
...YEAH, ME TOO!
THINK WE'LL GET REPEAT CUSTOMERS?
REPEAT CUSTOMERS...
IF WE DO, WILL THAT MEAN I WAS ABLE TO HELP BUILD UP THE EZO AG BRAND IN NO SMALL WAY TOO?
WE HAVE TO PROTECT THE BRAND SO WE CAN PASS IT ON PROPERLY TO OUR UNDERCLASSMEN.
IT'S A GRAVE RESPONSIBILITY!
I SEE... WAIT, WHOA!!
IN ONLY TWO MONTHS, THERE'LL BE A NEW BATCH OF FIRST-YEARS!! KIDS ARE GONNA BE CALLING ME "HACHIKEN-SENPAI"!!
2012 2 FEBRUARY
WHOA!! I'M FROM A COUNTRYSIDE SCHOOL, SO WE ALL DROPPED THE HONORIFICS OR JUST USED NICKNAMES WITH EVERYBODY REGARDLESS OF AGE!!
IF THEY CALL ME "SENPAI" I'LL FEEL ALL NERVOUS!!

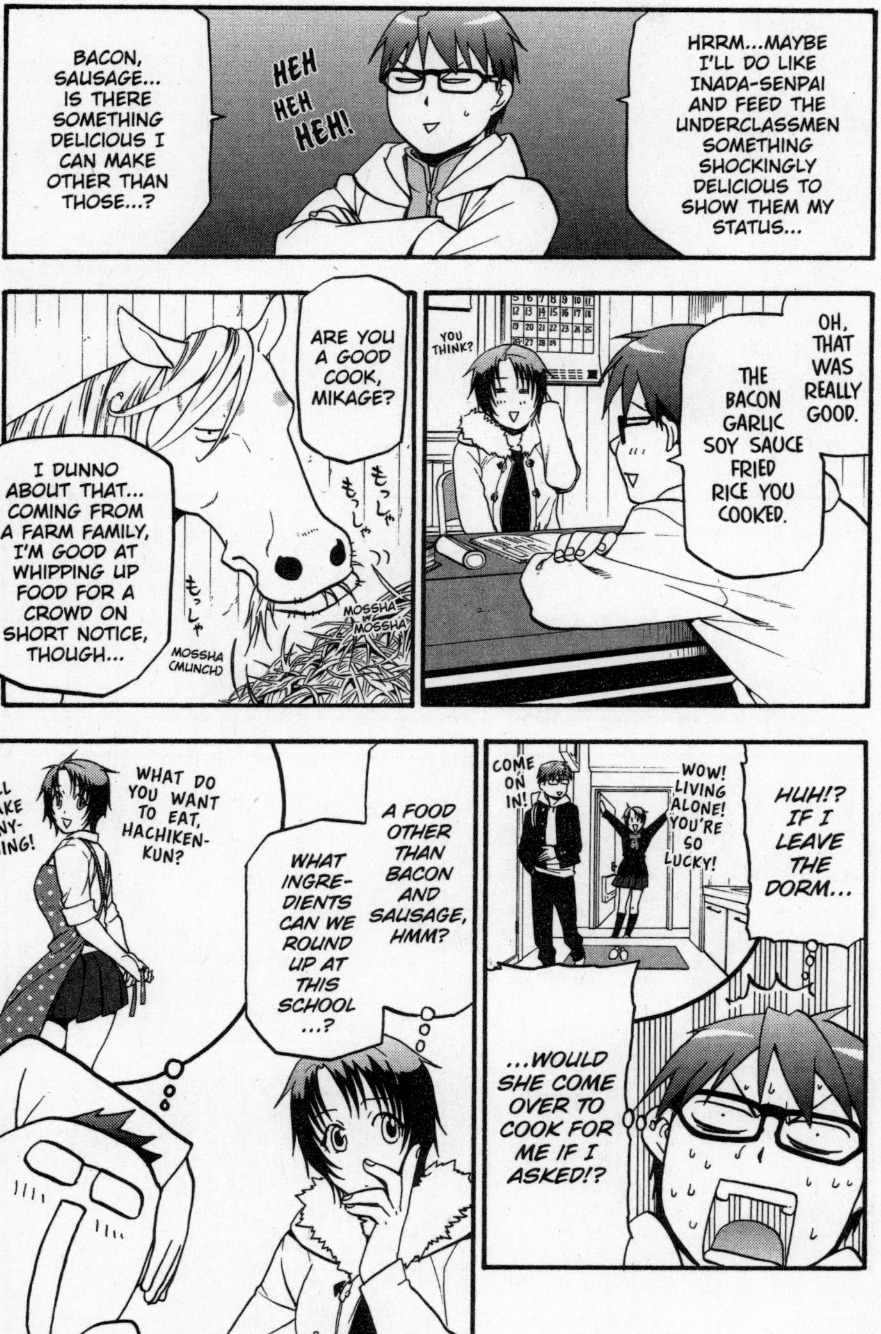
HRRM...MAYBE I'LL DO LIKE INADA-SENPAI AND FEED THE UNDERCLASSMEN SOMETHING SHOCKINGLY DELICIOUS TO SHOW THEM MY STATUS...
HEH HEH HEH!
BACON, SAUSAGE... IS THERE SOMETHING DELICIOUS I CAN MAKE OTHER THAN THOSE...?
OH, THAT WAS REALLY GOOD.
THE BACON GARLIC SOY SAUCE FRIED RICE YOU COOKED.
YOU THINK?
ARE YOU A GOOD COOK, MIKAGE?
もっしゃ もっしゃ
MOSSHA MOSSHA
I DUNNO ABOUT THAT... COMING FROM A FARM FAMILY, I'M GOOD AT WHIPPING UP FOOD FOR A CROWD ON SHORT NOTICE, THOUGH...
もっしゃ
MOSSHA (MUNCH)
HUH!? IF I LEAVE THE DORM...
WOW! LIVING ALONE! YOU'RE SO LUCKY!
COME ON IN!
...WOULD SHE COME OVER TO COOK FOR ME IF I ASKED!?
A FOOD OTHER THAN BACON AND SAUSAGE, HMM?
WHAT INGREDIENTS CAN WE ROUND UP AT THIS SCHOOL...?
WHAT DO YOU WANT TO EAT, HACHIKEN-KUN?
I'LL MAKE ANYTHING!

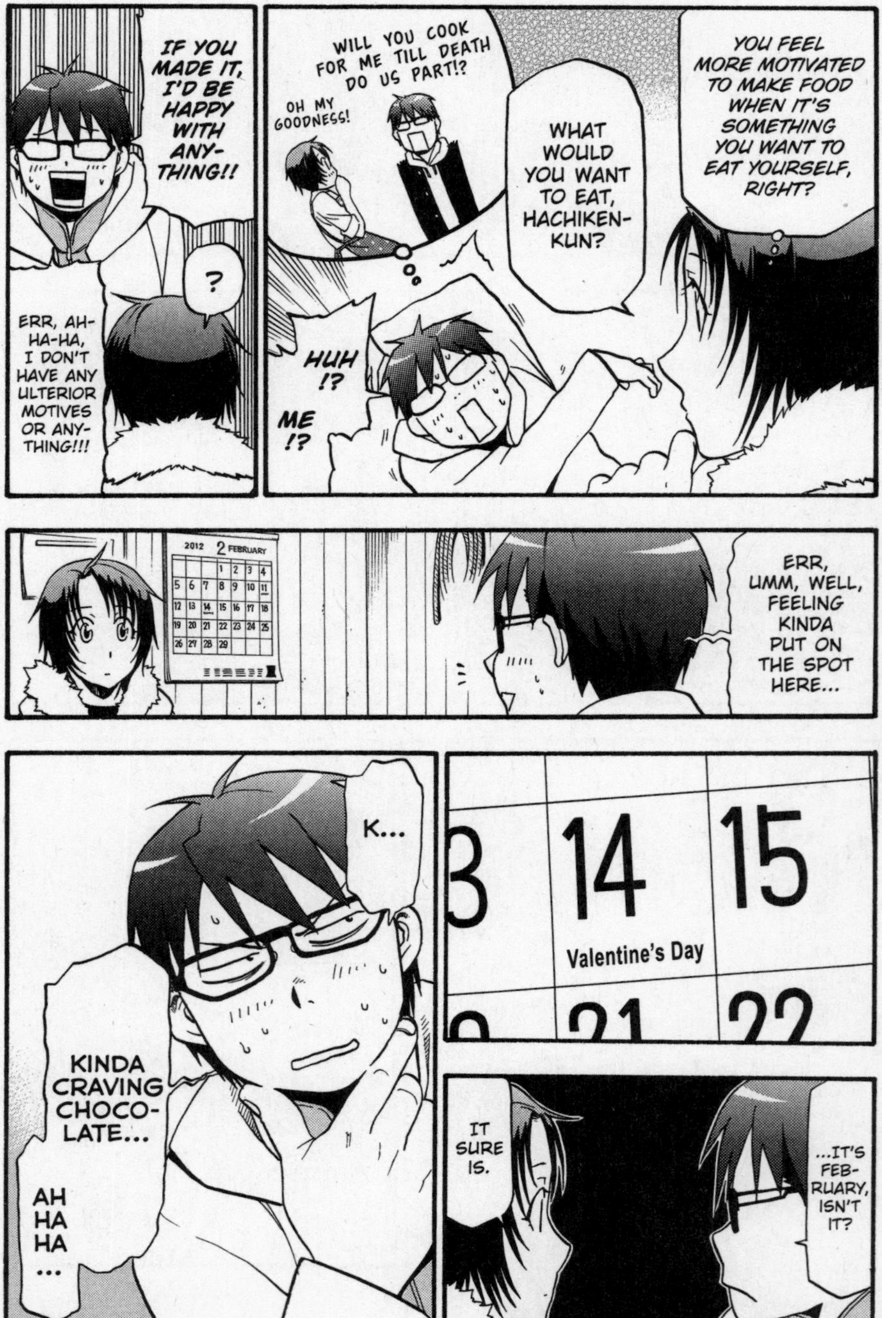
YOU FEEL MORE MOTIVATED TO MAKE FOOD WHEN IT'S SOMETHING YOU WANT TO EAT YOURSELF, RIGHT?
WHAT WOULD YOU WANT TO EAT, HACHIKEN-KUN?
WILL YOU COOK FOR ME TILL DEATH DO US PART!?
OH MY GOODNESS!
HUH !?
ME !?
IF YOU MADE IT, I'D BE HAPPY WITH ANYTHING!!
?
ERR, AH-HA-HA, I DON'T HAVE ANY ULTERIOR MOTIVES OR ANYTHING!!!
ERR, UMM, WELL, FEELING KINDA PUT ON THE SPOT HERE...
2012 2 FEBRUARY
14
15
Valentine's Day
...IT'S FEBRUARY, ISN'T IT?
IT SURE IS.
K...
KINDA CRAVING CHOCOLATE...
AH HA HA ...

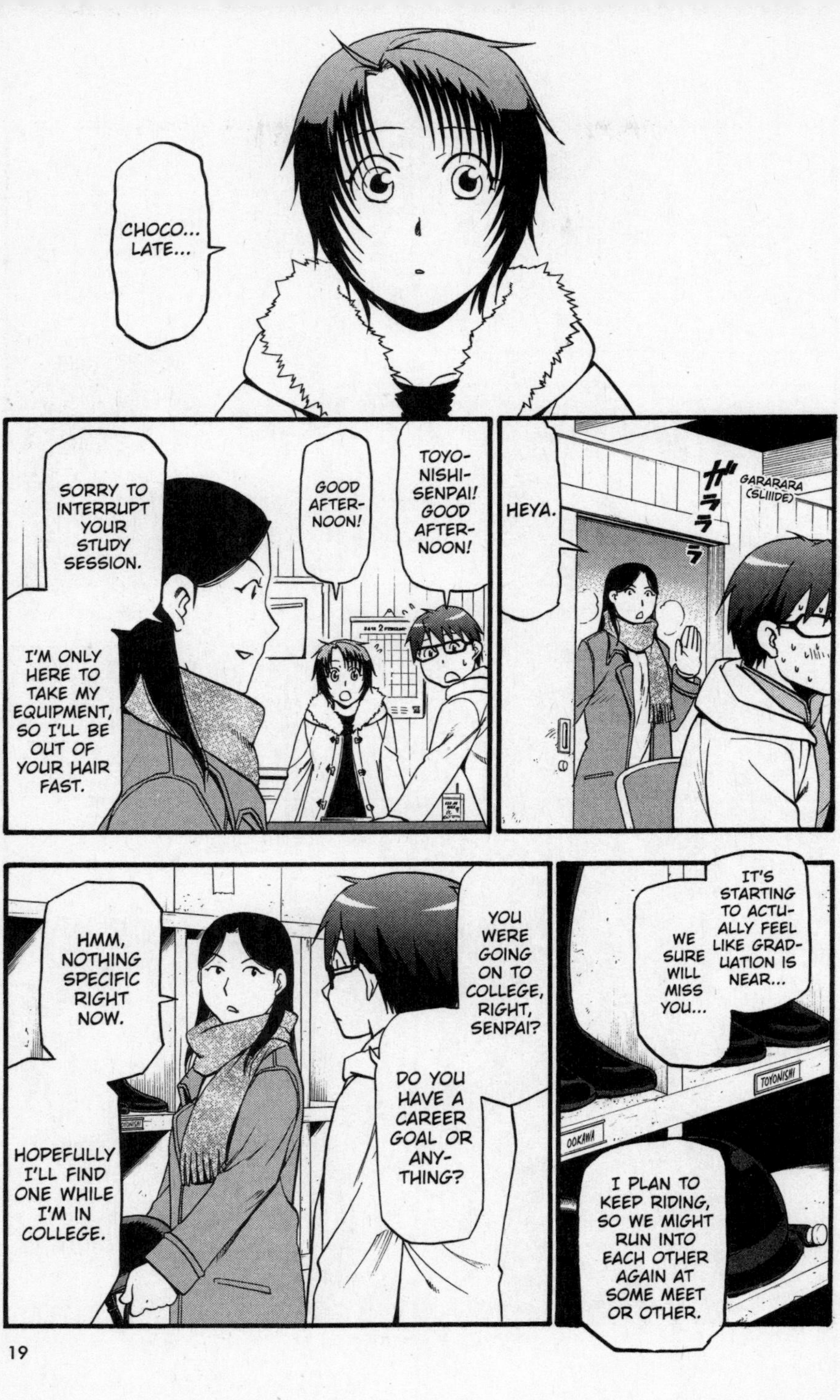
CHOCO... LATE...
ガラララ
GARARARA (SLIIIDE)
HEYA.
TOYO-NISHI-SENPAI! GOOD AFTER-NOON!
GOOD AFTER-NOON!
SORRY TO INTERRUPT YOUR STUDY SESSION.
I'M ONLY HERE TO TAKE MY EQUIPMENT, SO I'LL BE OUT OF YOUR HAIR FAST.
IT'S STARTING TO ACTU-ALLY FEEL LIKE GRAD-UATION IS NEAR...
WE SURE WILL MISS YOU...
TOYONISHI
OOKAWA
I PLAN TO KEEP RIDING, SO WE MIGHT RUN INTO EACH OTHER AGAIN AT SOME MEET OR OTHER.
YOU WERE GOING ON TO COLLEGE, RIGHT, SENPAI?
DO YOU HAVE A CAREER GOAL OR ANY-THING?
HMM, NOTHING SPECIFIC RIGHT NOW.
HOPEFULLY I'LL FIND ONE WHILE I'M IN COLLEGE.

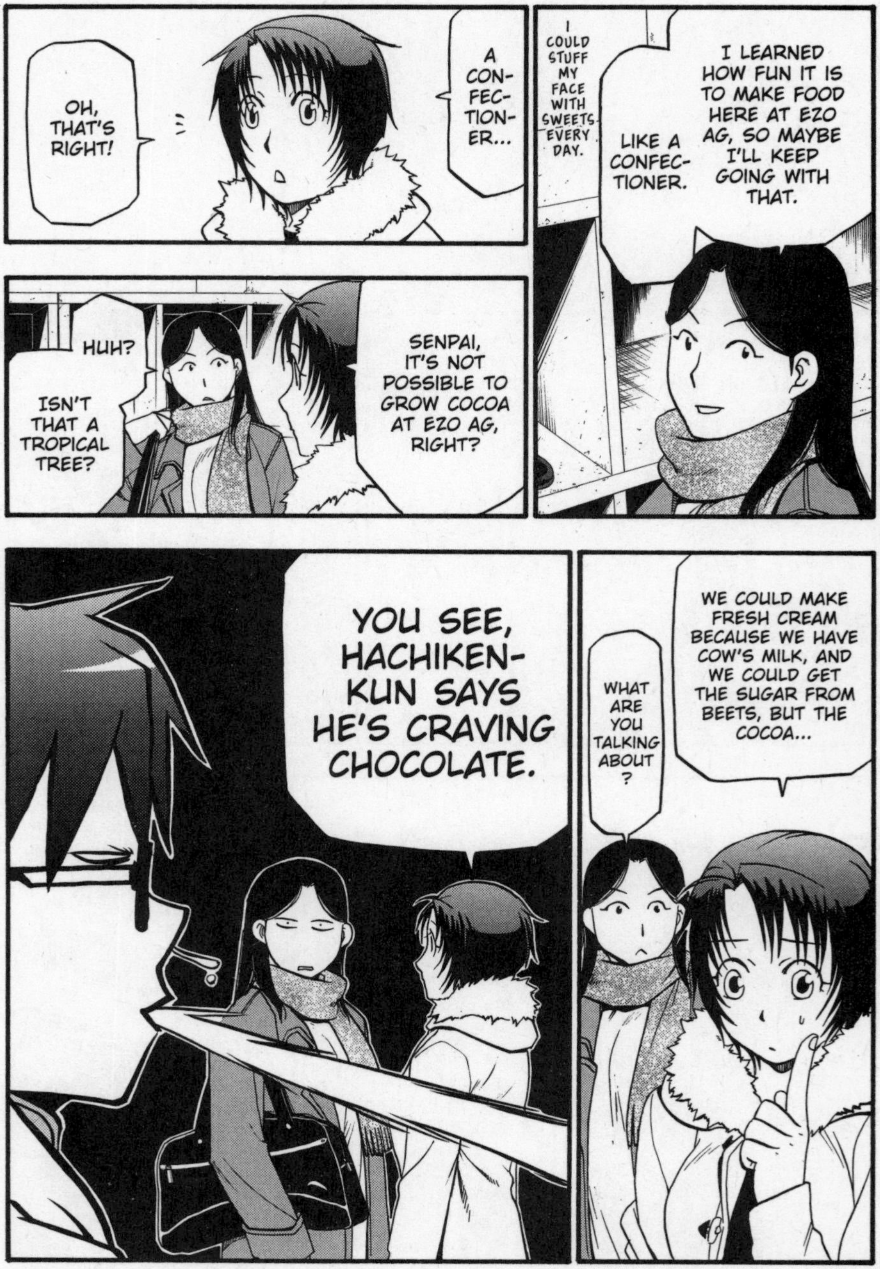
I LEARNED HOW FUN IT IS TO MAKE FOOD HERE AT EZO AG, SO MAYBE I'LL KEEP GOING WITH THAT.
LIKE A CONFECTIONER.
I COULD STUFF MY FACE WITH SWEETS EVERY DAY.
A CONFECTIONER...
OH, THAT'S RIGHT!
SENPAI, IT'S NOT POSSIBLE TO GROW COCOA AT EZO AG, RIGHT?
HUH?
ISN'T THAT A TROPICAL TREE?
WE COULD MAKE FRESH CREAM BECAUSE WE HAVE COW'S MILK, AND WE COULD GET THE SUGAR FROM BEETS, BUT THE COCOA...
WHAT ARE YOU TALKING ABOUT?
YOU SEE, HACHIKEN-KUN SAYS HE'S CRAVING CHOCOLATE.

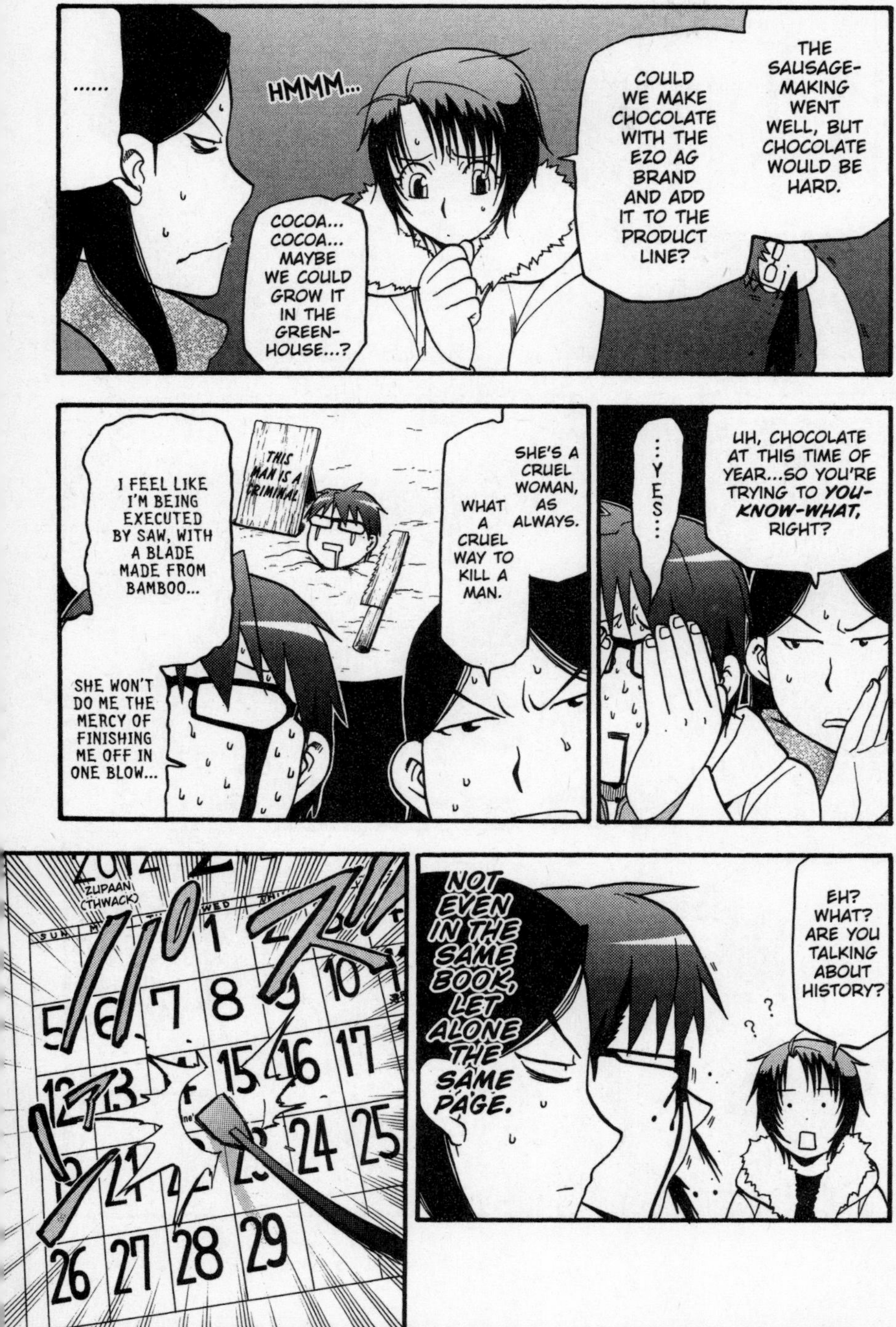
THE SAUSAGE-MAKING WENT WELL, BUT CHOCOLATE WOULD BE HARD.
COULD WE MAKE CHOCOLATE WITH THE EZO AG BRAND AND ADD IT TO THE PRODUCT LINE?
HMMM...
COCOA... COCOA... MAYBE WE COULD GROW IT IN THE GREEN-HOUSE...?
......
UH, CHOCOLATE AT THIS TIME OF YEAR...SO YOU'RE TRYING TO *YOU-KNOW-WHAT*, RIGHT?
...YES...
SHE'S A CRUEL WOMAN, AS ALWAYS.
WHAT A CRUEL WAY TO KILL A MAN.
THIS MAN IS A CRIMINAL
I FEEL LIKE I'M BEING EXECUTED BY SAW, WITH A BLADE MADE FROM BAMBOO...
SHE WON'T DO ME THE MERCY OF FINISHING ME OFF IN ONE BLOW...
EH? WHAT? ARE YOU TALKING ABOUT HISTORY?
NOT EVEN IN THE SAME BOOK, LET ALONE THE SAME PAGE.
ZUPAAN (THWACK)

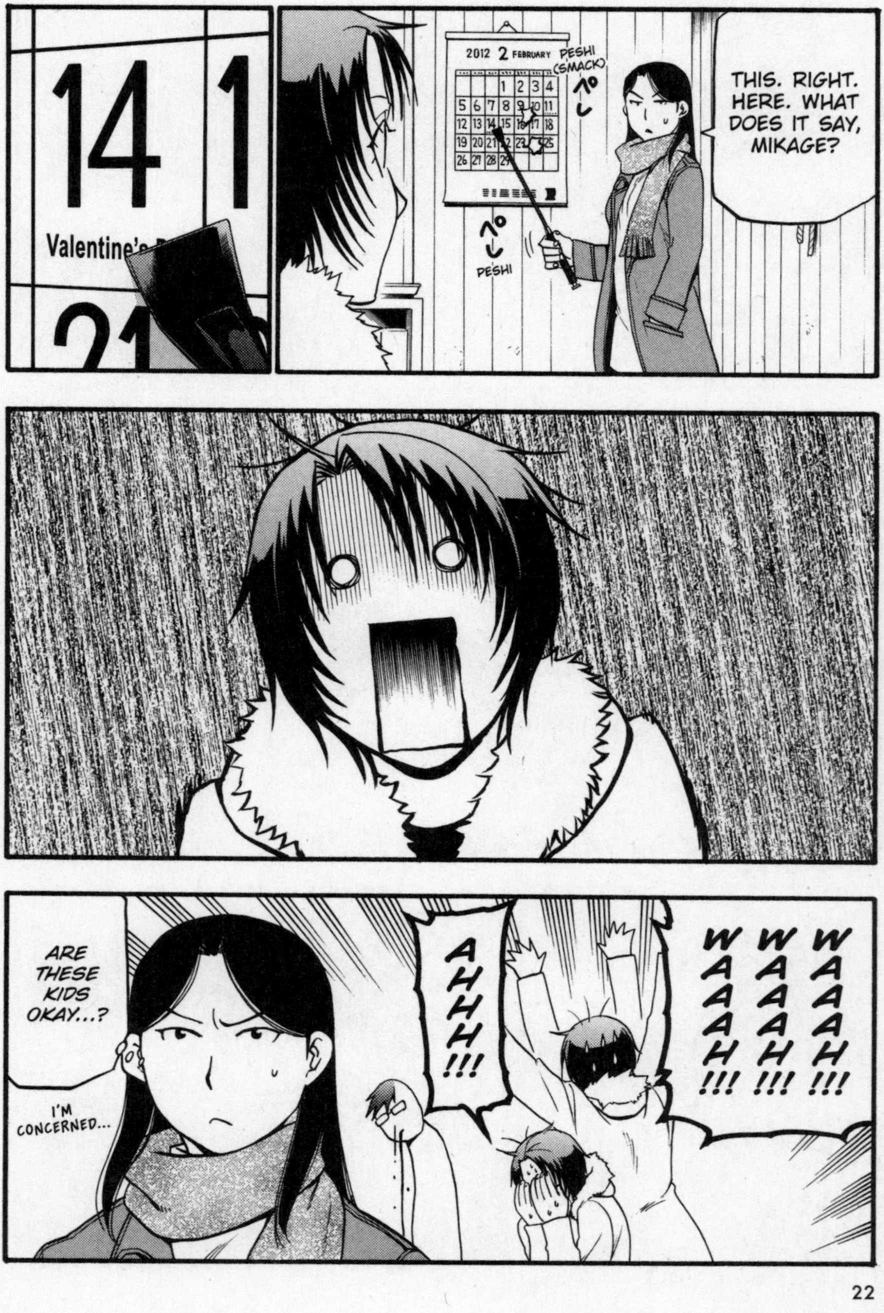
THIS. RIGHT. HERE. WHAT DOES IT SAY, MIKAGE?
PESHI (SMACK)
2012 2 FEBRUARY
PESHI
14
1
Valentine's D
21
WAAAAH!!!
WAAAAH!!!
WAAAAH!!!
AHHHH!!!
ARE THESE KIDS OKAY...?
I'M CONCERNED...

Silver Spoon

Chapter 90:

Tale of Winter ㉗

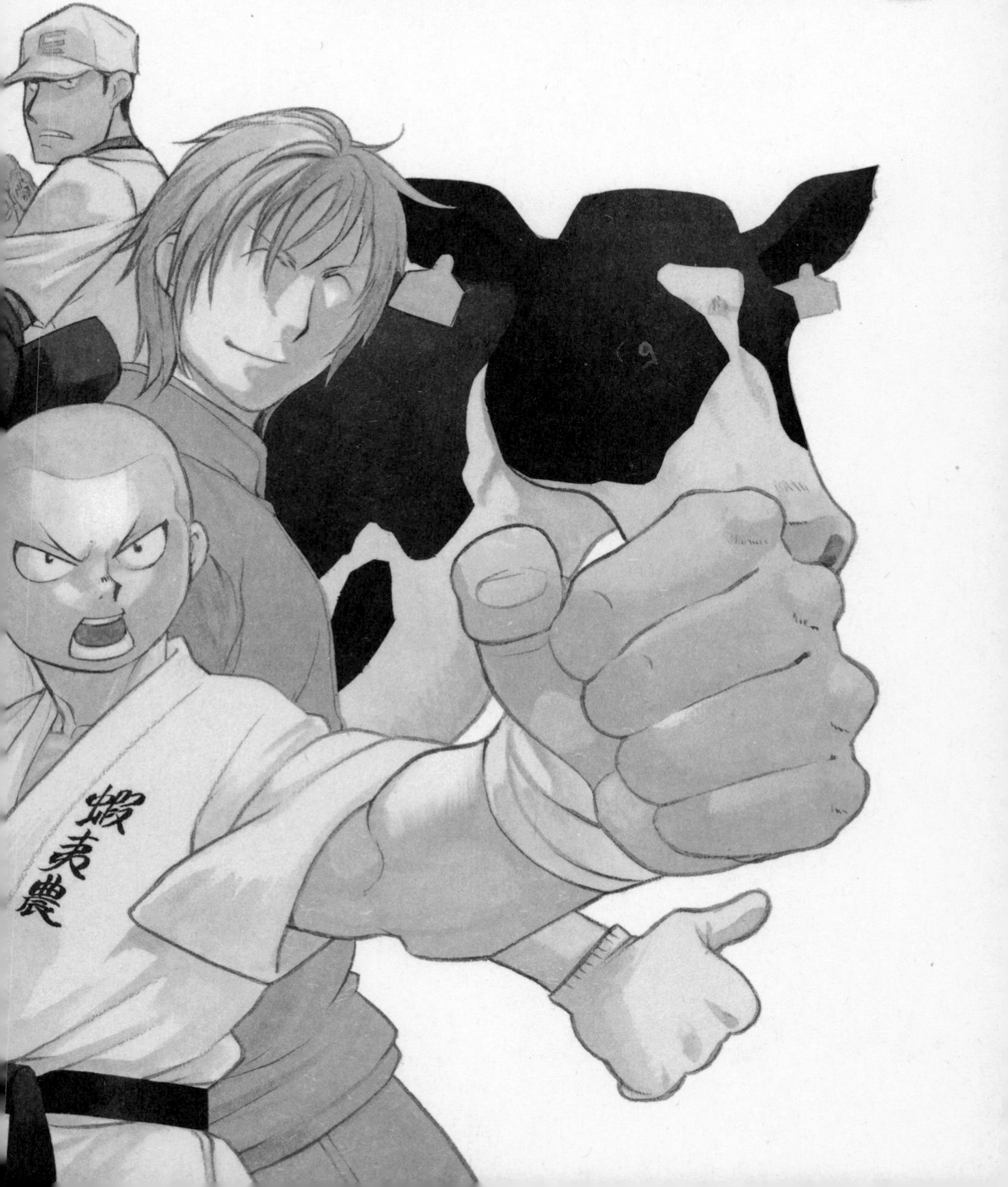
蝦夷農

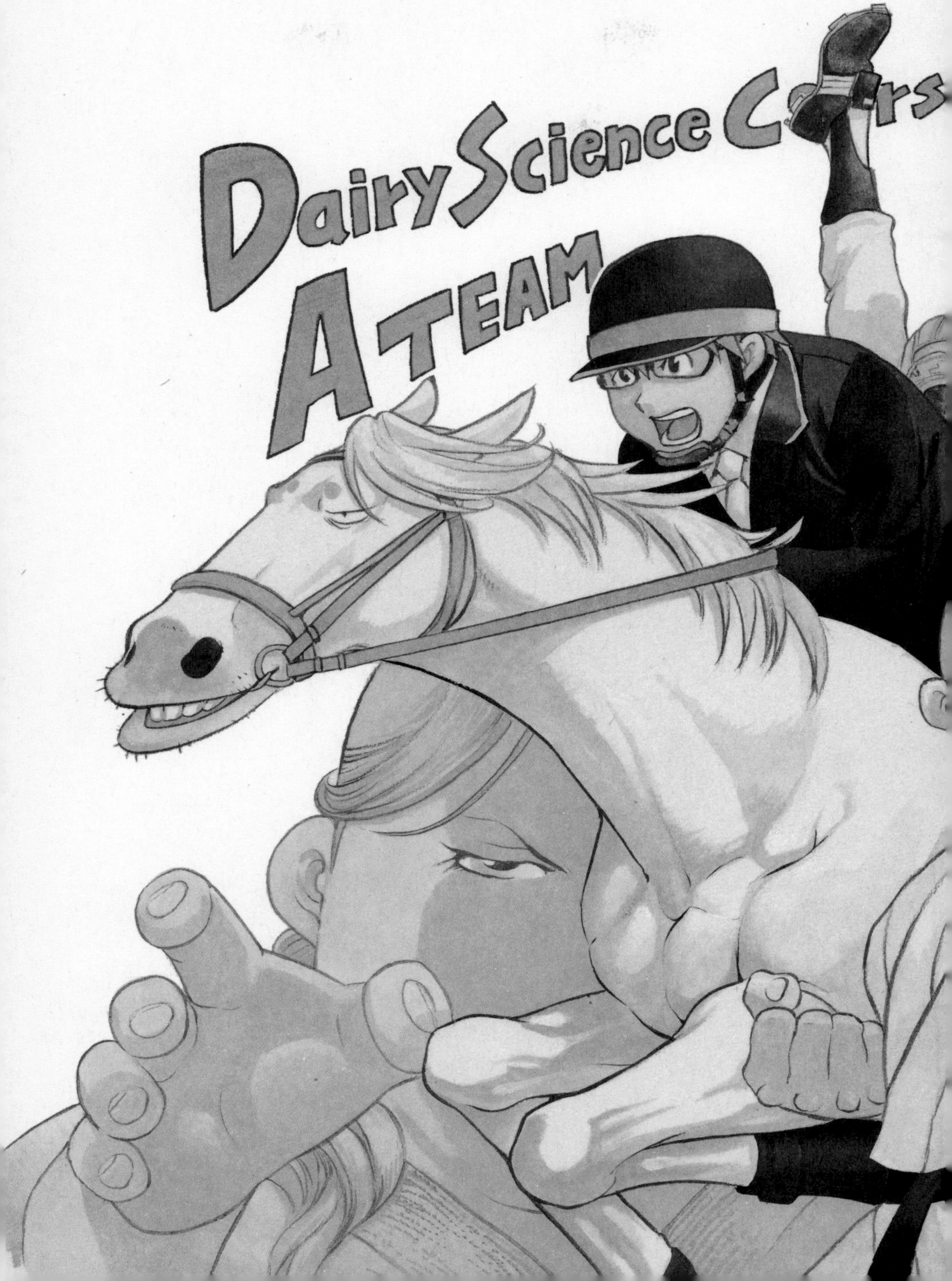
Dairy Science
A TEAM

DAI OOMORI

AGRICULTURAL
SCIENCE PROGRAM
THIRD-YEAR

GOING ON TO
COLLEGE.

STINKY FEET.

JUDO TEAM

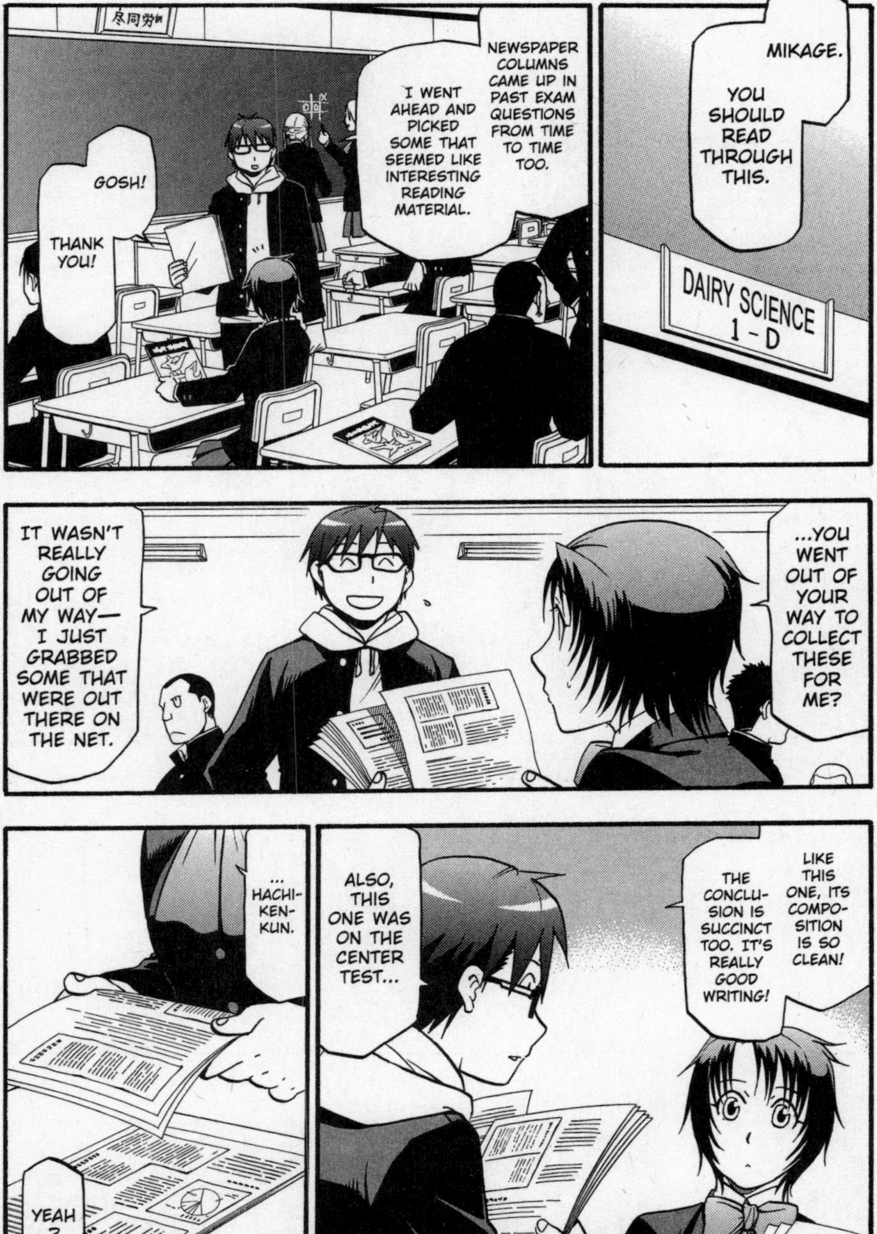
MIKAGE.
YOU SHOULD READ THROUGH THIS.
DAIRY SCIENCE 1 - D
NEWSPAPER COLUMNS CAME UP IN PAST EXAM QUESTIONS FROM TIME TO TIME TOO.
I WENT AHEAD AND PICKED SOME THAT SEEMED LIKE INTERESTING READING MATERIAL.
GOSH!
THANK YOU!
...YOU WENT OUT OF YOUR WAY TO COLLECT THESE FOR ME?
IT WASN'T REALLY GOING OUT OF MY WAY— I JUST GRABBED SOME THAT WERE OUT THERE ON THE NET.
LIKE THIS ONE, ITS COMPOSITION IS SO CLEAN!
THE CONCLUSION IS SUCCINCT TOO. IT'S REALLY GOOD WRITING!
ALSO, THIS ONE WAS ON THE CENTER TEST...
...HACHIKEN-KUN.
YEAH?

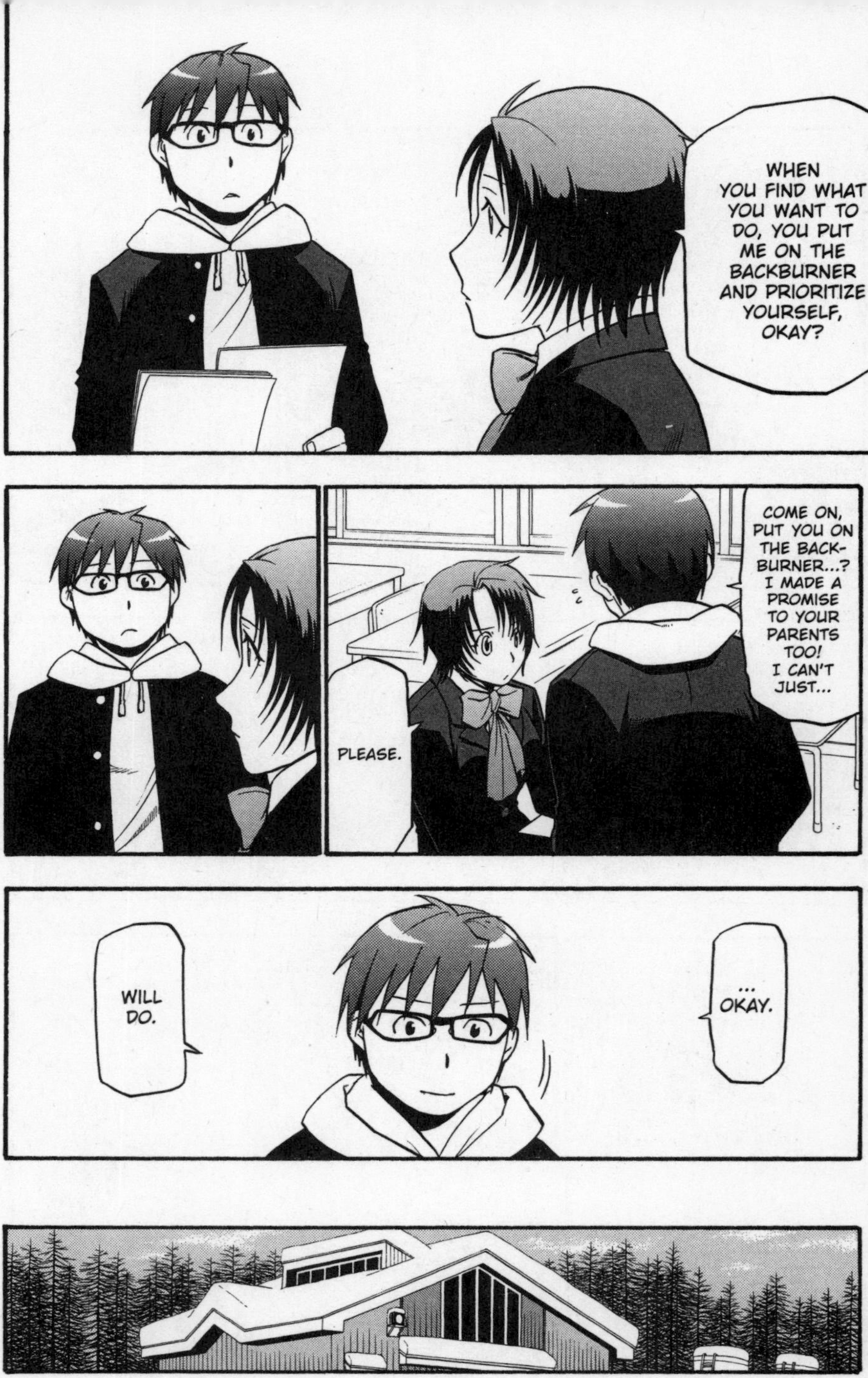
WHEN YOU FIND WHAT YOU WANT TO DO, YOU PUT ME ON THE BACKBURNER AND PRIORITIZE YOURSELF, OKAY?
COME ON, PUT YOU ON THE BACK-BURNER...? I MADE A PROMISE TO YOUR PARENTS TOO! I CAN'T JUST...
PLEASE.
...OKAY.
WILL DO.

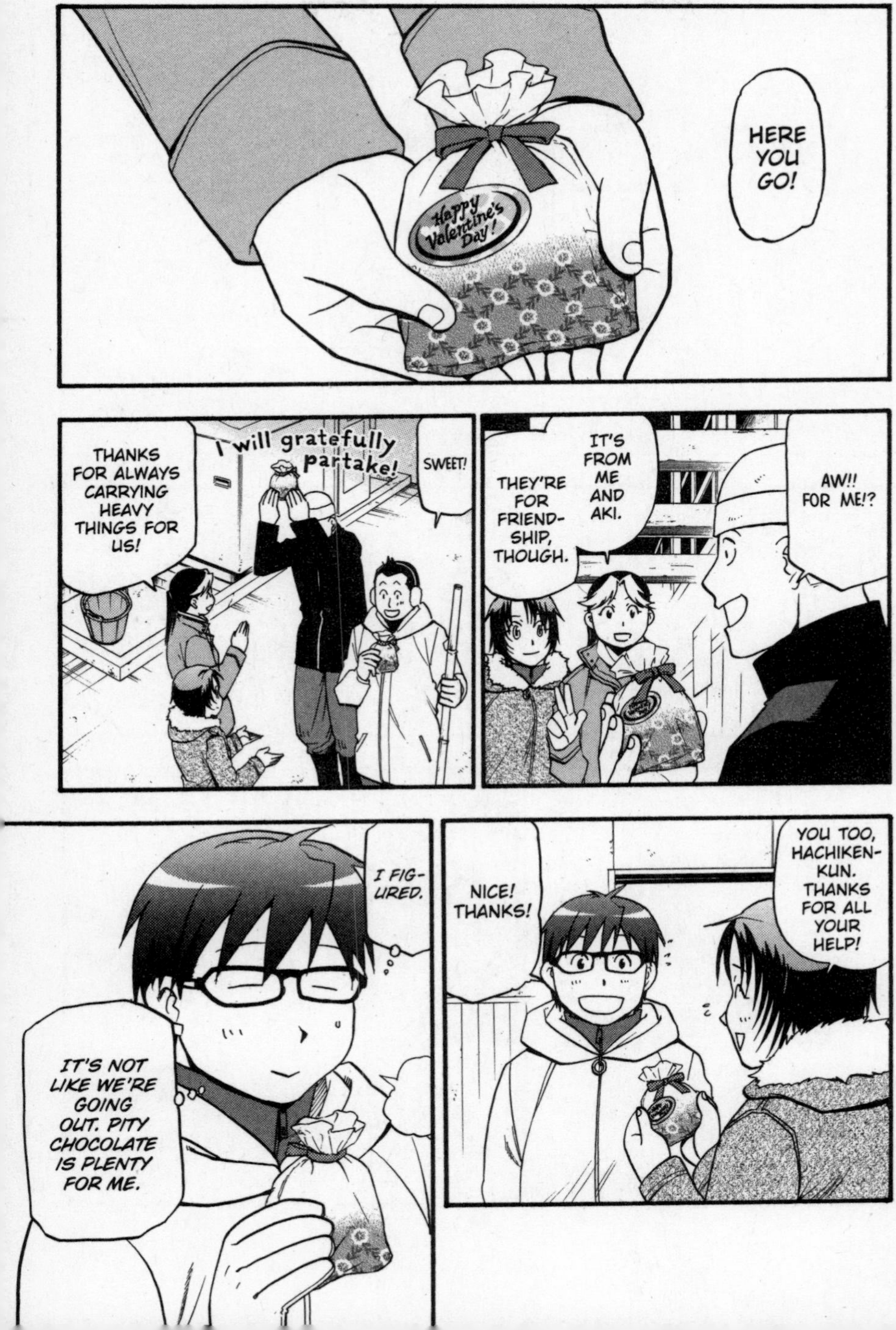
Happy Valentine's Day!
HERE YOU GO!
AW!! FOR ME!?
IT'S FROM ME AND AKI.
THEY'RE FOR FRIEND-SHIP, THOUGH.
SWEET!
I will gratefully partake!
THANKS FOR ALWAYS CARRYING HEAVY THINGS FOR US!
YOU TOO, HACHIKEN-KUN. THANKS FOR ALL YOUR HELP!
NICE! THANKS!
I FIG-URED.
IT'S NOT LIKE WE'RE GOING OUT. PITY CHOCOLATE IS PLENTY FOR ME.

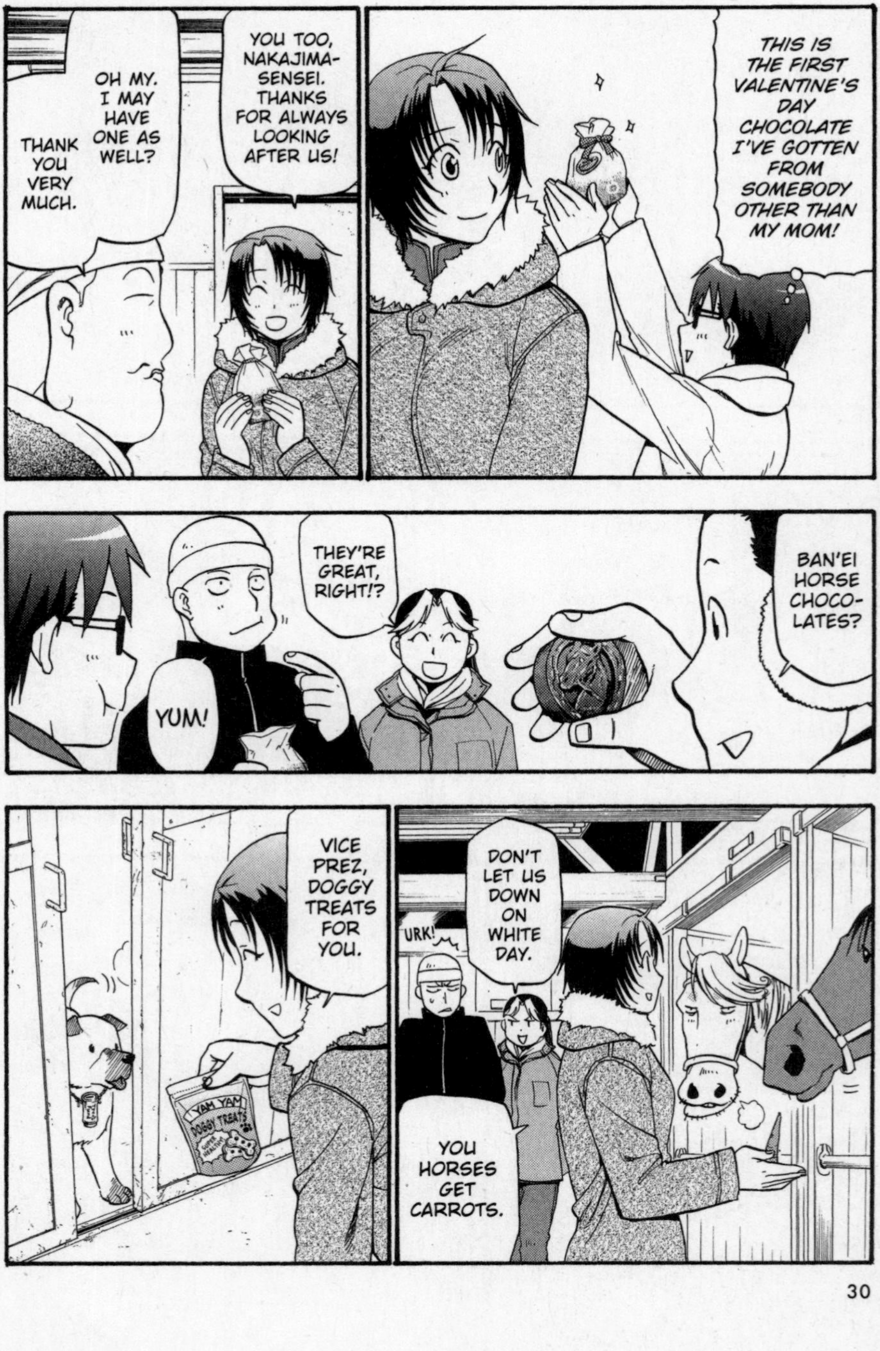
THIS IS THE FIRST VALENTINE'S DAY CHOCOLATE I'VE GOTTEN FROM SOMEBODY OTHER THAN MY MOM!
YOU TOO, NAKAJIMA-SENSEI. THANKS FOR ALWAYS LOOKING AFTER US!
OH MY. I MAY HAVE ONE AS WELL?
THANK YOU VERY MUCH.
BAN'EI HORSE CHOCOLATES?
THEY'RE GREAT, RIGHT!?
YUM!
DON'T LET US DOWN ON WHITE DAY.
URK!
YOU HORSES GET CARROTS.
VICE PREZ, DOGGY TREATS FOR YOU.
YAM YAM
DOGGY TREATS

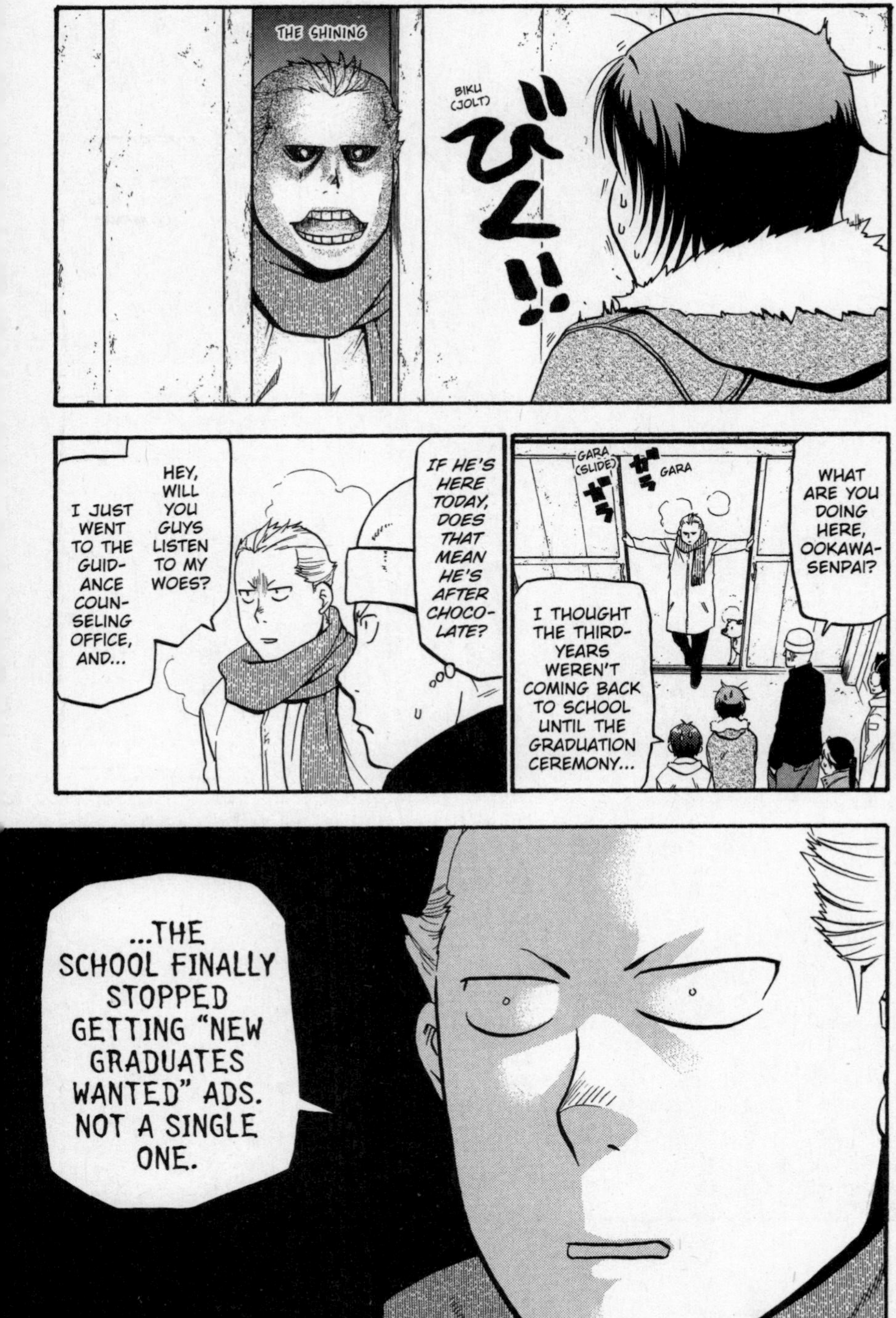
THE SHINING
BIKU (JOLT)
びく!!
GARA (SLIDE)
GARA
WHAT ARE YOU DOING HERE, OOKAWA-SENPAI?
I THOUGHT THE THIRD-YEARS WEREN'T COMING BACK TO SCHOOL UNTIL THE GRADUATION CEREMONY...
IF HE'S HERE TODAY, DOES THAT MEAN HE'S AFTER CHOCOLATE?
HEY, WILL YOU GUYS LISTEN TO MY WOES?
I JUST WENT TO THE GUIDANCE COUNSELING OFFICE, AND...
...THE SCHOOL FINALLY STOPPED GETTING "NEW GRADUATES WANTED" ADS. NOT A SINGLE ONE.

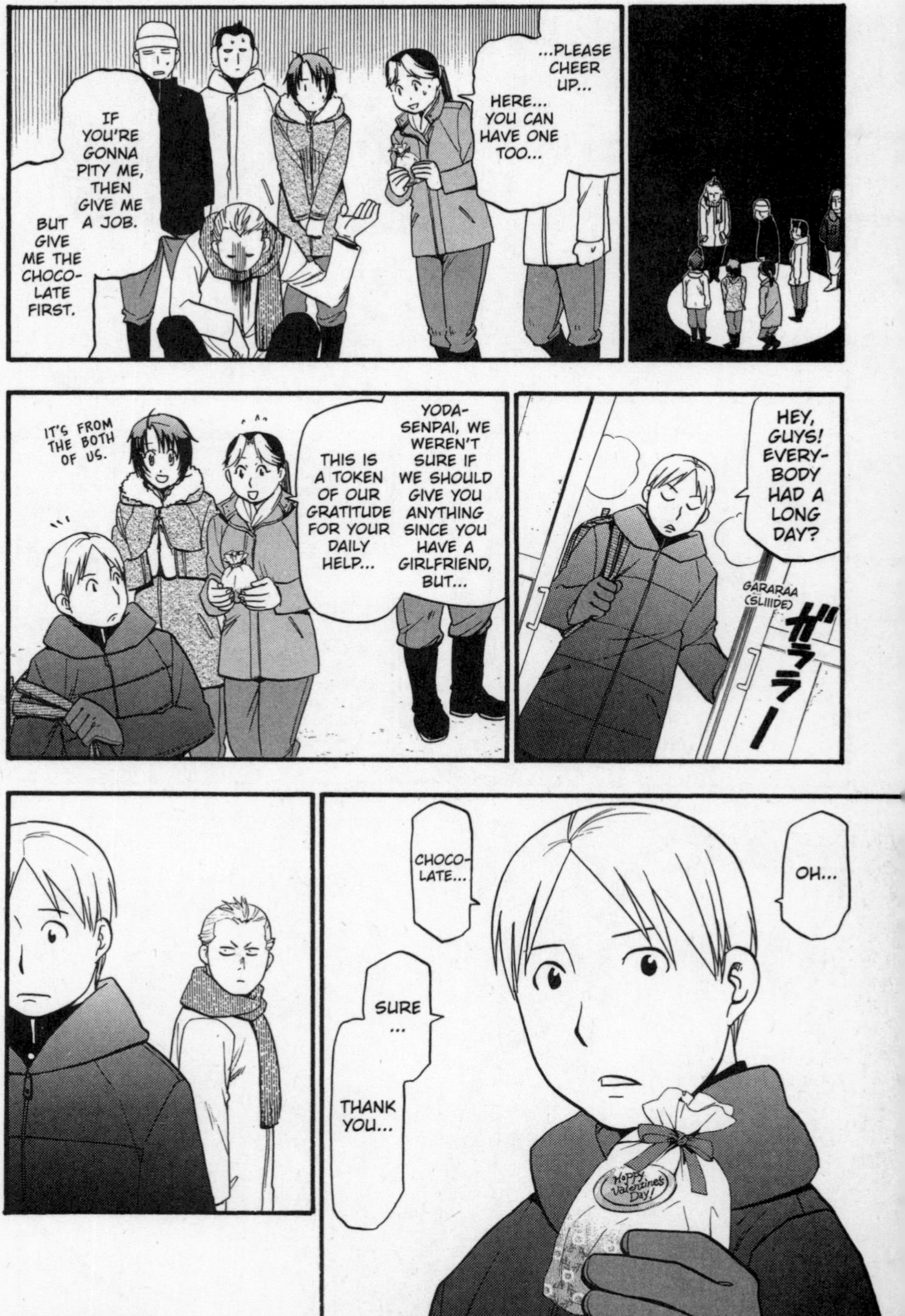
...PLEASE CHEER UP...
HERE... YOU CAN HAVE ONE TOO...
IF YOU'RE GONNA PITY ME, THEN GIVE ME A JOB.
BUT GIVE ME THE CHOCOLATE FIRST.
HEY, GUYS! EVERYBODY HAD A LONG DAY?
GARARAA (SLIIIDE)
ガララー
YODA-SENPAI, WE WEREN'T SURE IF WE SHOULD GIVE YOU ANYTHING SINCE YOU HAVE A GIRLFRIEND, BUT...
THIS IS A TOKEN OF OUR GRATITUDE FOR YOUR DAILY HELP...
IT'S FROM THE BOTH OF US.
OH...
CHOCOLATE...
SURE...
THANK YOU...
Happy Valentine's Day!

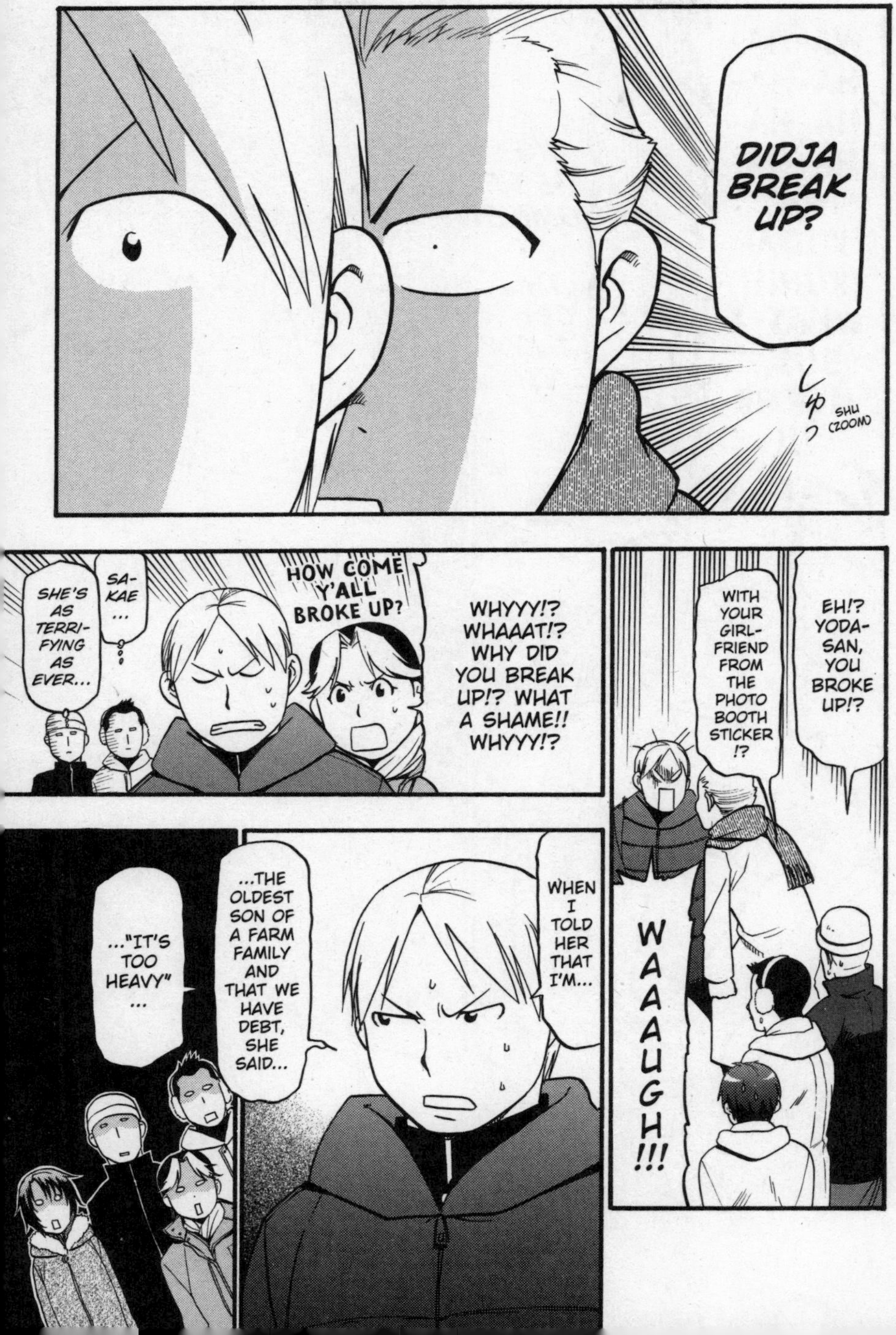
DIDJA BREAK UP?
しゅっ
SHU (ZOOM)
EH!? YODA-SAN, YOU BROKE UP!?
WITH YOUR GIRL-FRIEND FROM THE PHOTO BOOTH STICKER!?
WAAAUGH!!!
WHYYY!? WHAAAT!? WHY DID YOU BREAK UP!? WHAT A SHAME!! WHYYY!?
HOW COME Y'ALL BROKE UP?
SA-KAE...
SHE'S AS TERRI-FYING AS EVER...
WHEN I TOLD HER THAT I'M...
...THE OLDEST SON OF A FARM FAMILY AND THAT WE HAVE DEBT, SHE SAID...
..."IT'S TOO HEAVY"...

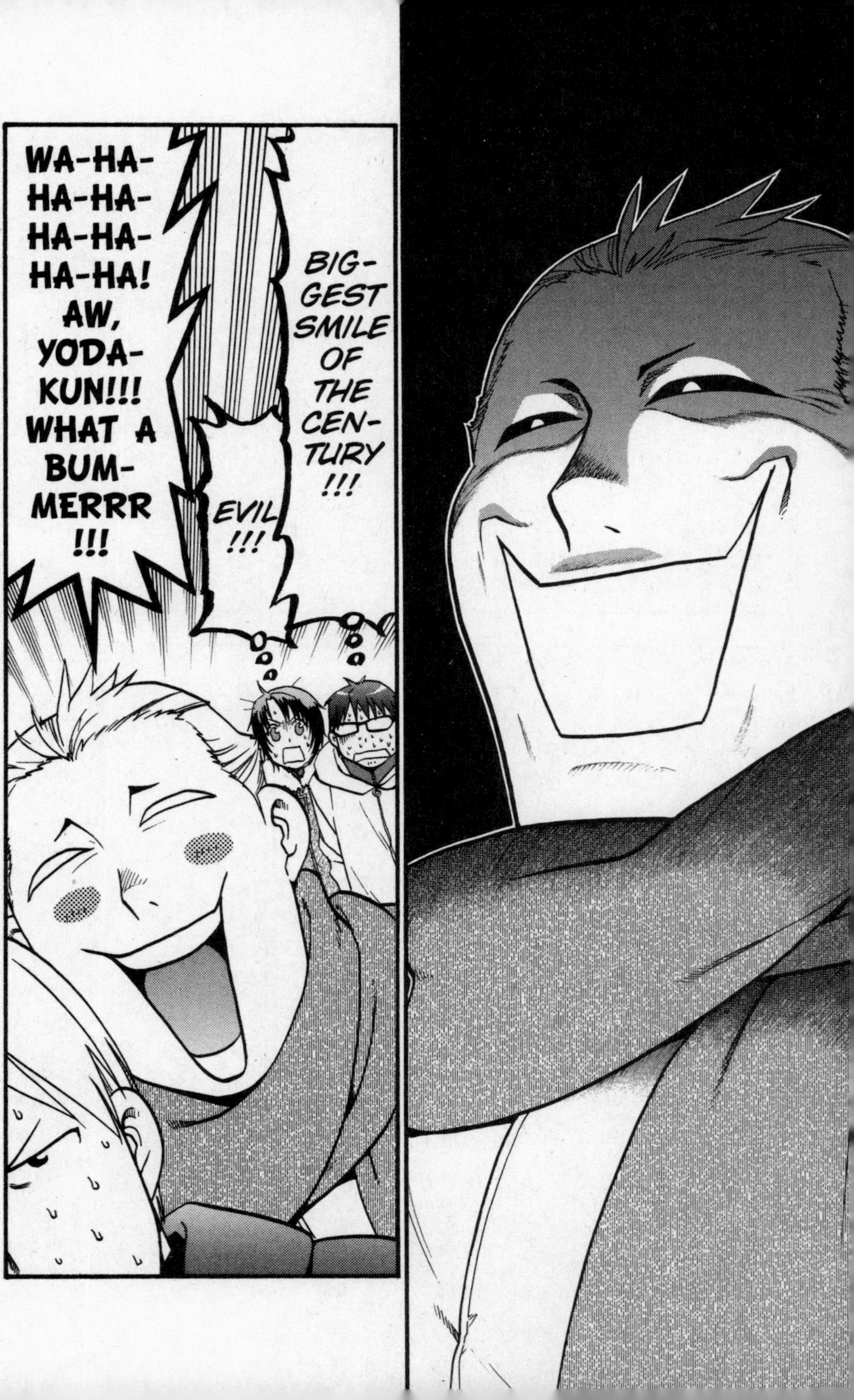
BIG-GEST SMILE OF THE CEN-TURY!!!
WA-HA-HA-HA-HA-HA-HA-HA! AW, YODA-KUN!!! WHAT A BUM-MERRR!!!
EVIL!!!

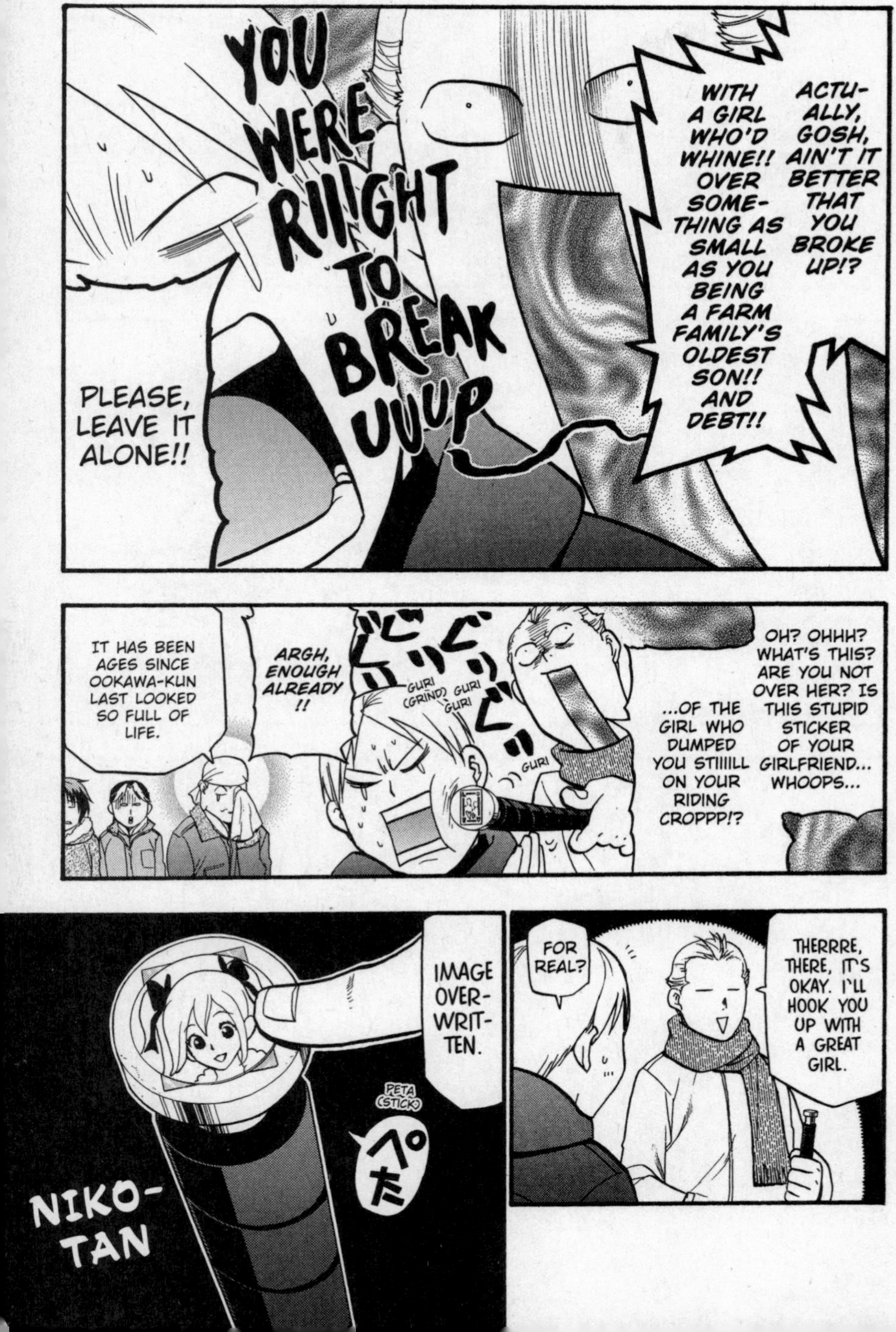
ACTUALLY, GOSH, AIN'T IT BETTER THAT YOU BROKE UP!?
WITH A GIRL WHO'D WHINE!! OVER SOMETHING AS SMALL AS YOU BEING A FARM FAMILY'S OLDEST SON!! AND DEBT!!
YOU WERE RIIIGHT TO BREAK UUUP
PLEASE, LEAVE IT ALONE!!
OH? OHHH? WHAT'S THIS? ARE YOU NOT OVER HER? IS THIS STUPID STICKER OF YOUR GIRLFRIEND... WHOOPS...
...OF THE GIRL WHO DUMPED YOU STIIIILL ON YOUR RIDING CROPPP!?
GURI (GRIND) GURI GURI
GURI
ARGH, ENOUGH ALREADY!!
IT HAS BEEN AGES SINCE OOKAWA-KUN LAST LOOKED SO FULL OF LIFE.
THERRRE, THERE, IT'S OKAY. I'LL HOOK YOU UP WITH A GREAT GIRL.
FOR REAL?
IMAGE OVER-WRITTEN.
PETA (STICK)
NIKO-TAN

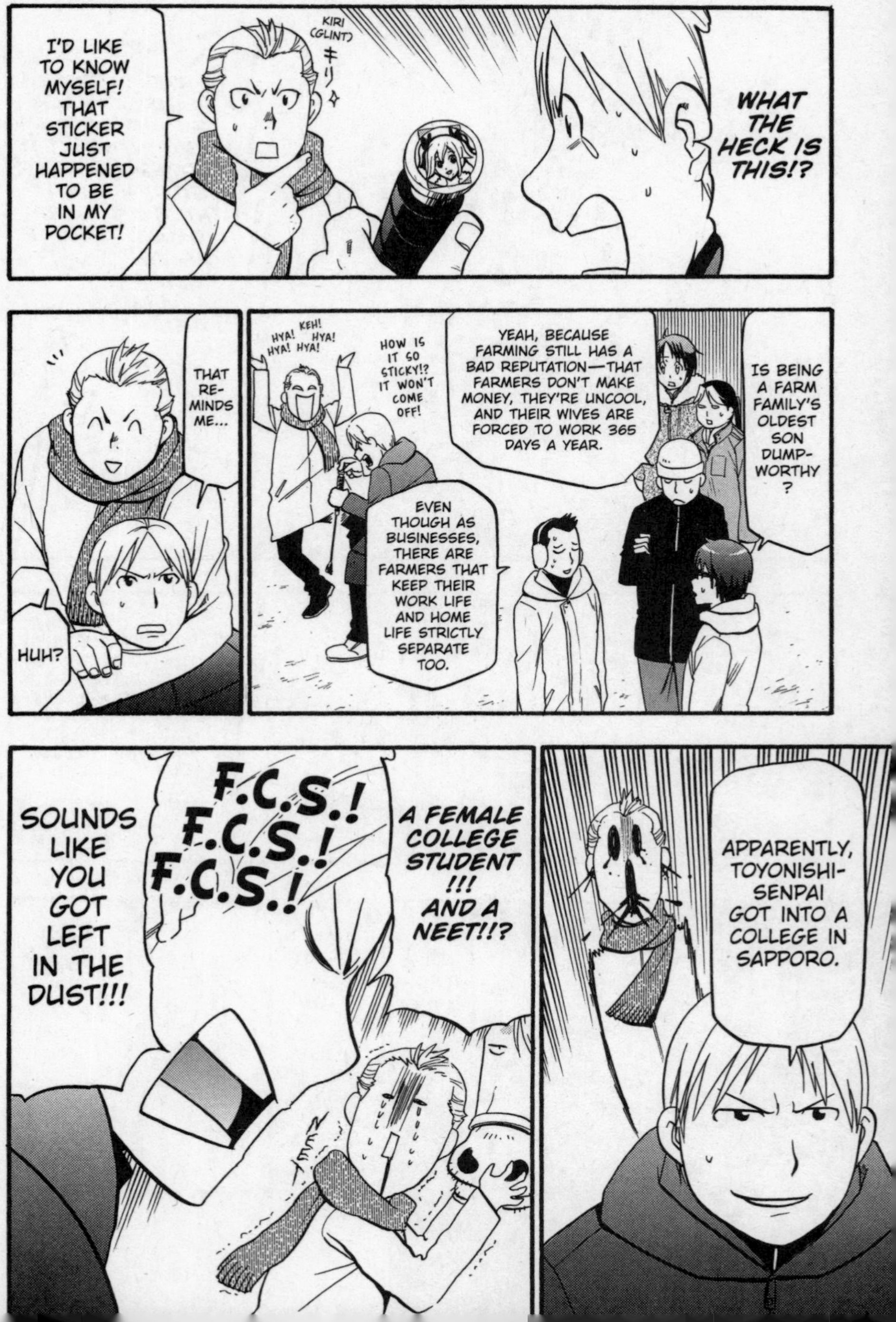
WHAT THE HECK IS THIS!?
KIRI (GLINT)
キリ
I'D LIKE TO KNOW MYSELF! THAT STICKER JUST HAPPENED TO BE IN MY POCKET!
IS BEING A FARM FAMILY'S OLDEST SON DUMP-WORTHY?
YEAH, BECAUSE FARMING STILL HAS A BAD REPUTATION—THAT FARMERS DON'T MAKE MONEY, THEY'RE UNCOOL, AND THEIR WIVES ARE FORCED TO WORK 365 DAYS A YEAR.
HOW IS IT SO STICKY!? IT WON'T COME OFF!
KEH! HYA! HYA! HYA! HYA!
EVEN THOUGH AS BUSINESSES, THERE ARE FARMERS THAT KEEP THEIR WORK LIFE AND HOME LIFE STRICTLY SEPARATE TOO.
THAT RE-MINDS ME...
HUH?
APPARENTLY, TOYONISHI-SENPAI GOT INTO A COLLEGE IN SAPPORO.
A FEMALE COLLEGE STUDENT!!! AND A NEET!!?
F.C.S.!
F.C.S.!
F.C.S.!
SOUNDS LIKE YOU GOT LEFT IN THE DUST!!!

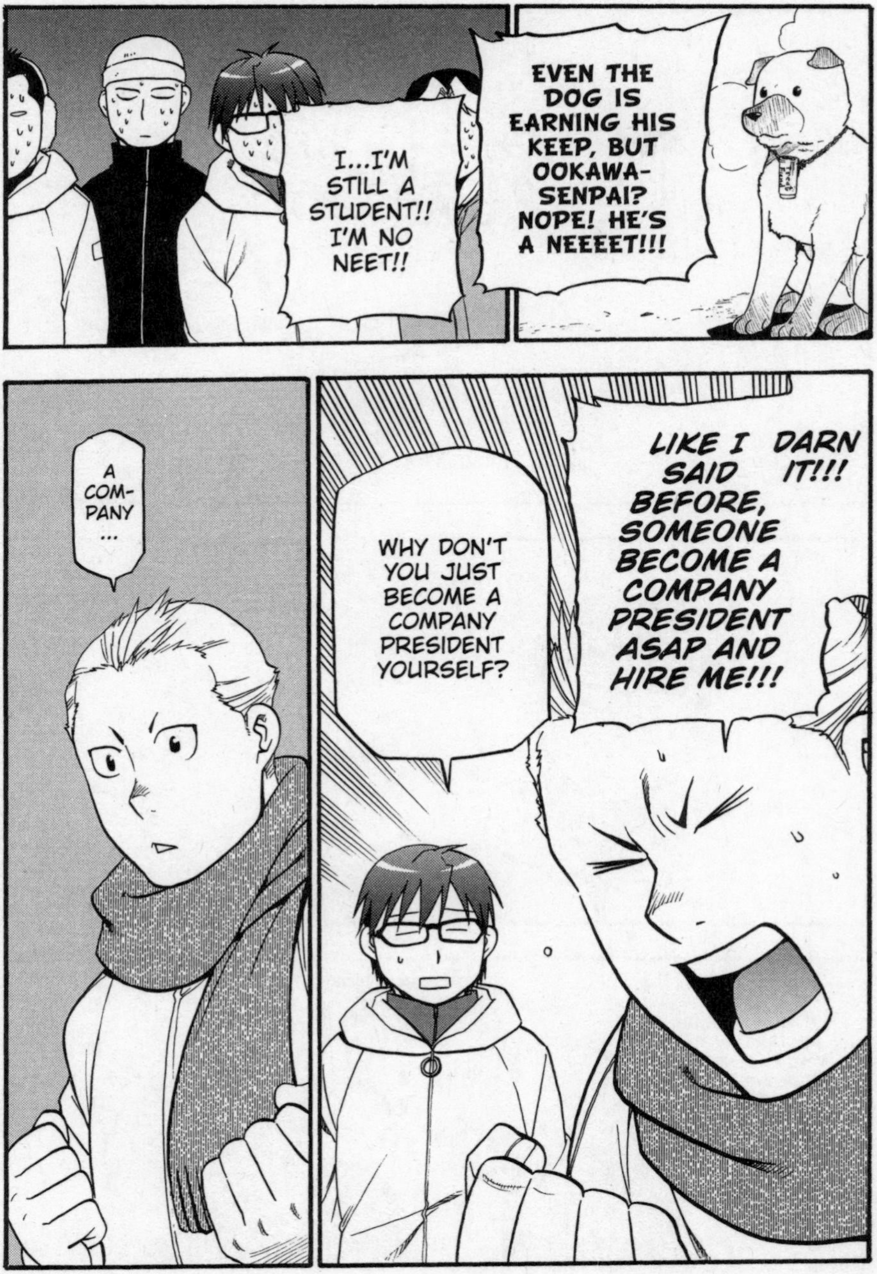
EVEN THE DOG IS EARNING HIS KEEP, BUT OOKAWA-SENPAI? NOPE! HE'S A NEEEET!!!
I...I'M STILL A STUDENT!! I'M NO NEET!!
DARN IT!!!
LIKE I SAID BEFORE, SOMEONE BECOME A COMPANY PRESIDENT ASAP AND HIRE ME!!!
WHY DON'T YOU JUST BECOME A COMPANY PRESIDENT YOURSELF?
A COMPANY...

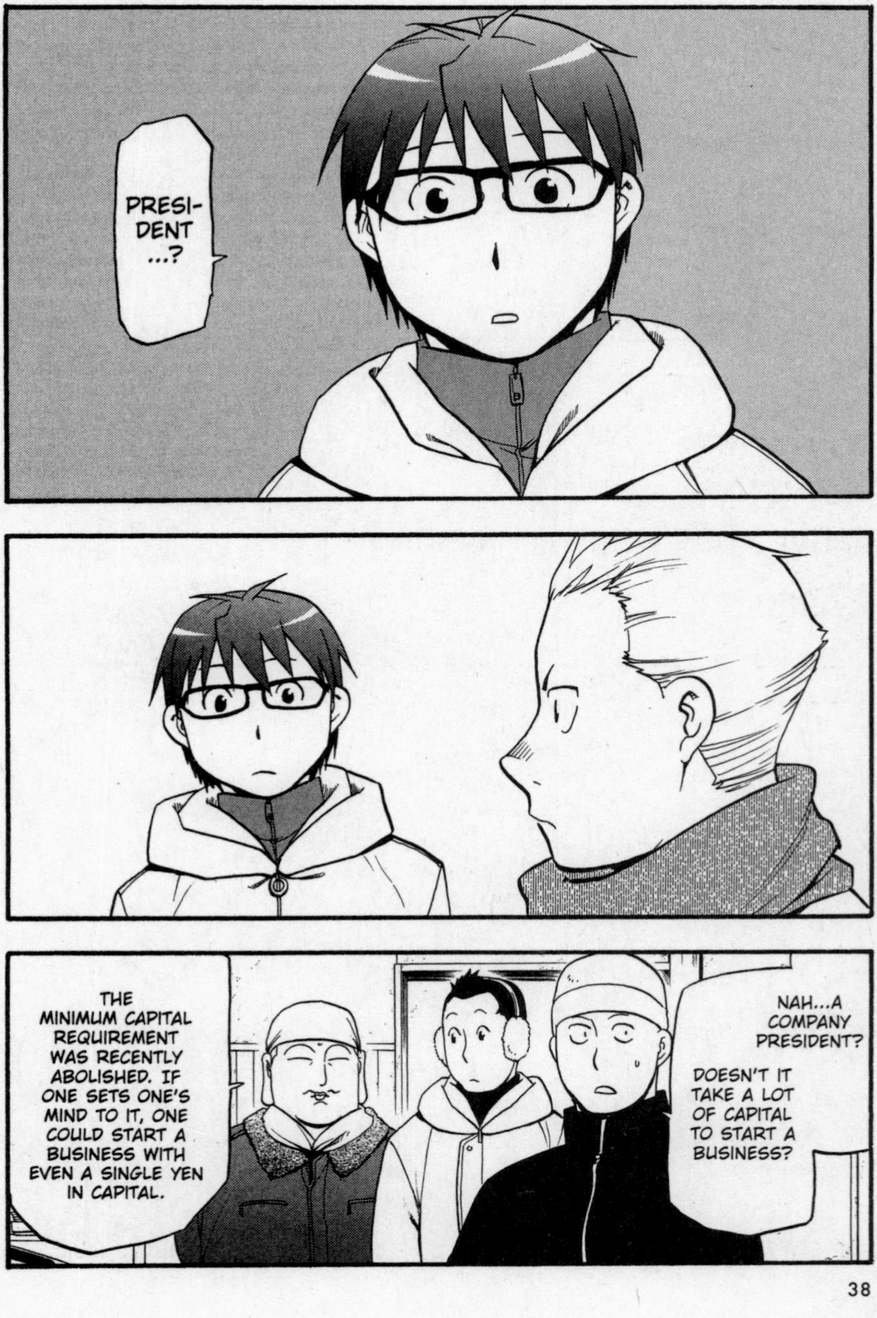
PRESI-DENT ...?
NAH...A COMPANY PRESIDENT?
DOESN'T IT TAKE A LOT OF CAPITAL TO START A BUSINESS?
THE MINIMUM CAPITAL REQUIREMENT WAS RECENTLY ABOLISHED. IF ONE SETS ONE'S MIND TO IT, ONE COULD START A BUSINESS WITH EVEN A SINGLE YEN IN CAPITAL.

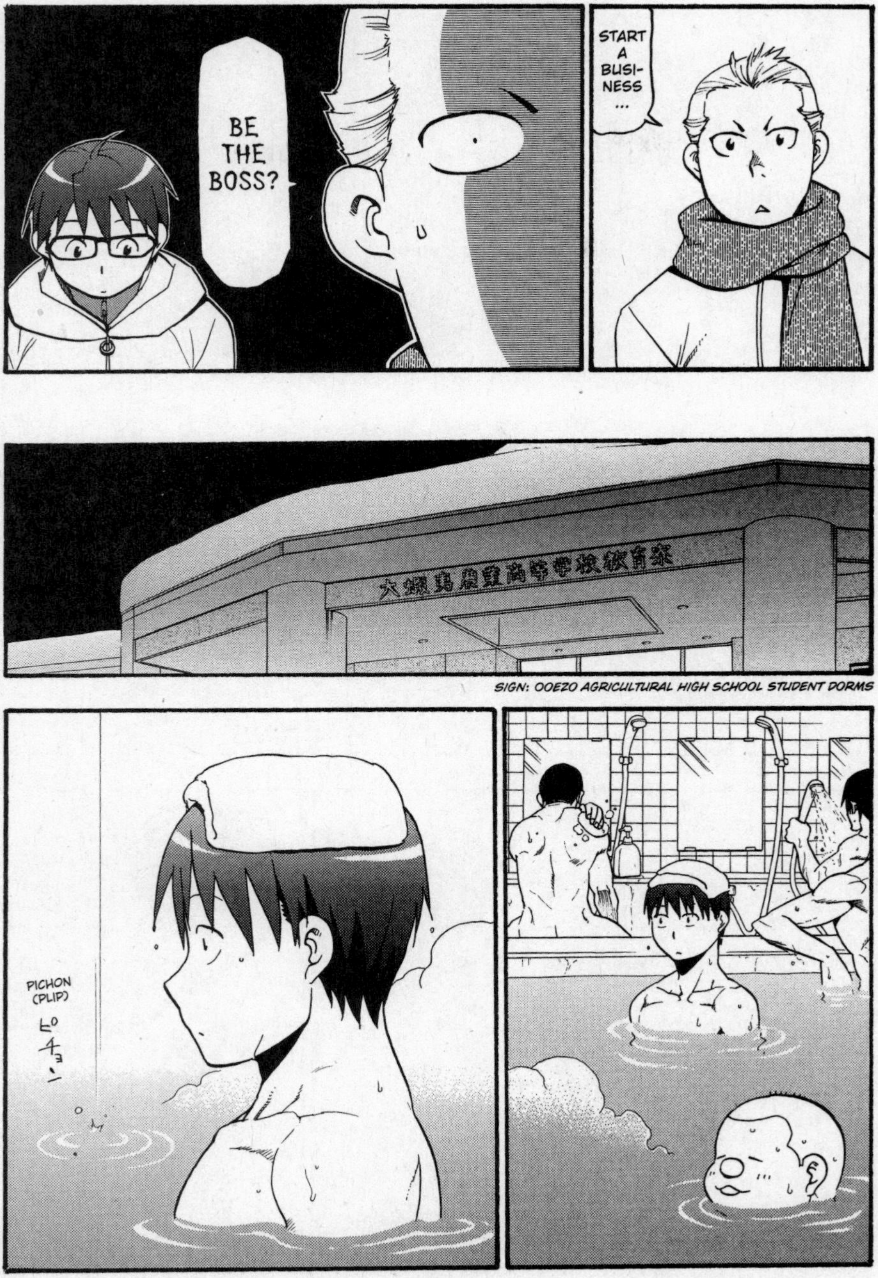
START A BUSINESS...
BE THE BOSS?
SIGN: OOEZO AGRICULTURAL HIGH SCHOOL STUDENT DORMS
PICHON (PLIP)
ピチョン

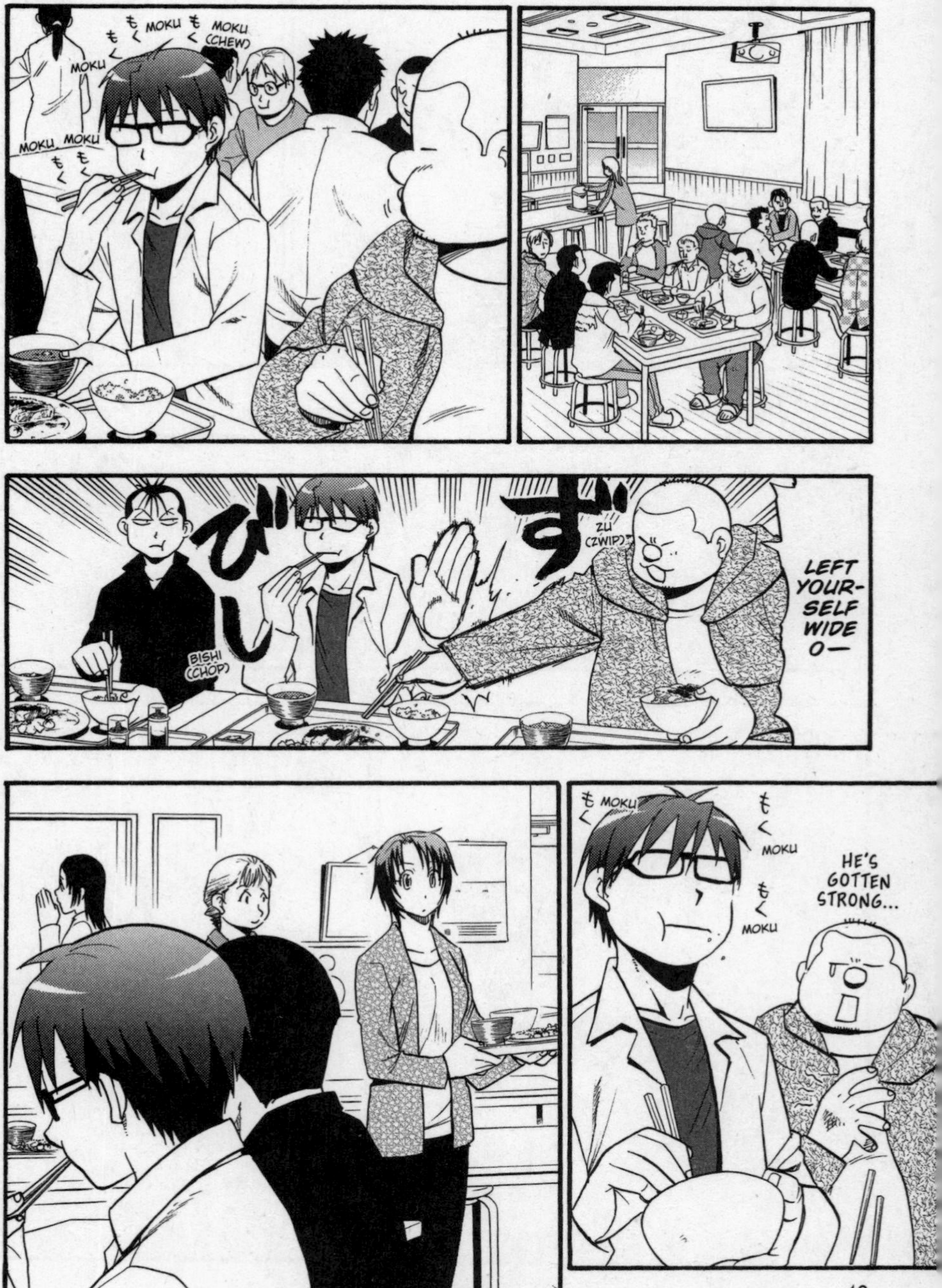

もく
MOKU
もく
MOKU (CHEW)
MOKU
MOKU MOKU
もく もく
LEFT YOURSELF WIDE O—
ず
ZU (ZWIP)
びし
BISHI (CHOP)
HE'S GOTTEN STRONG...
もく
MOKU
もく
MOKU
もく
MOKU

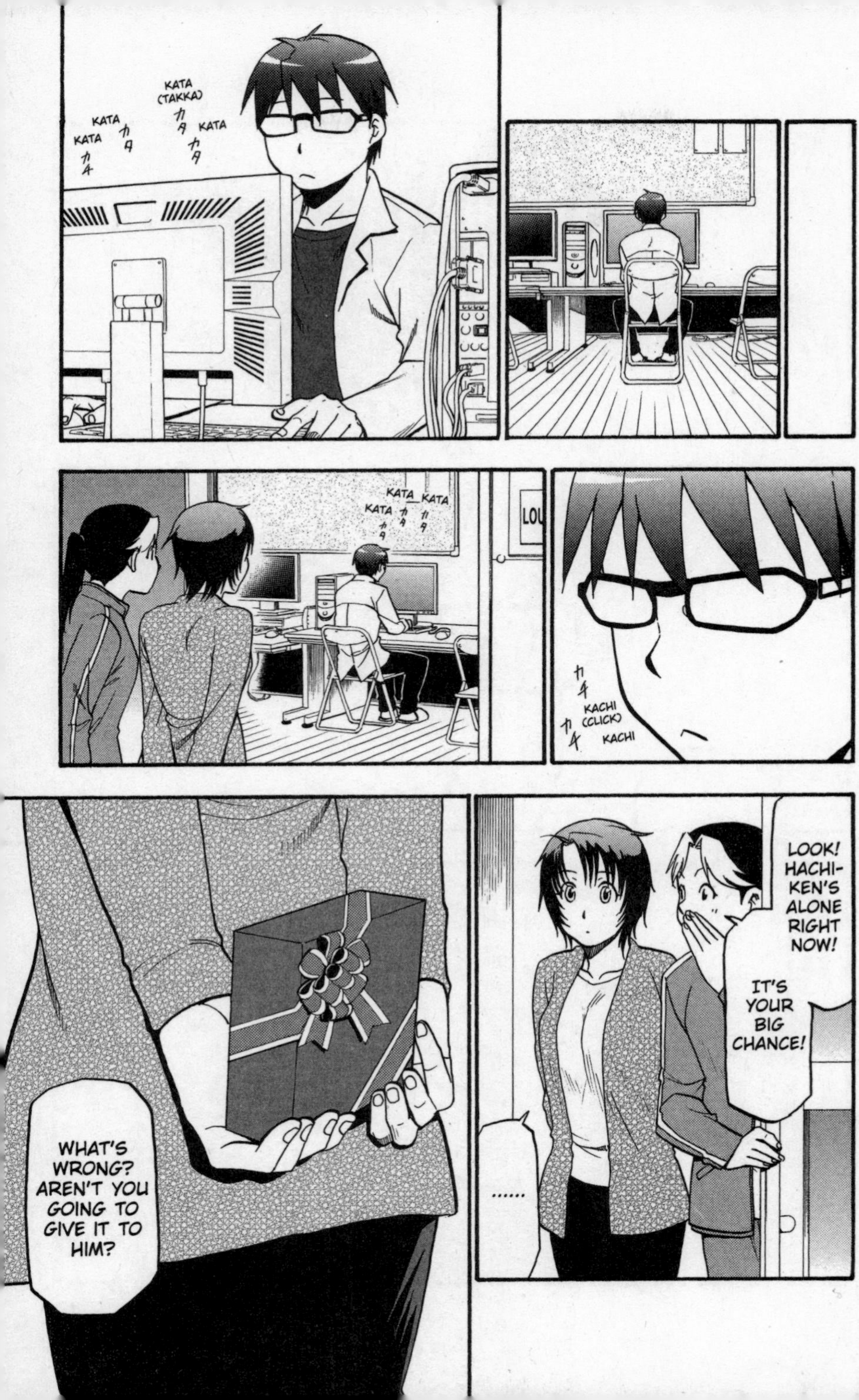
KATA (TAKKA) KATA
KATA KATA
カタ カタ
カタ カタ
KACHI (CLICK) KACHI
カチ カチ
KATA KATA KATA
カタ カタ カタ
LOOK! HACHI-KEN'S ALONE RIGHT NOW!
IT'S YOUR BIG CHANCE!
......
WHAT'S WRONG? AREN'T YOU GOING TO GIVE IT TO HIM?

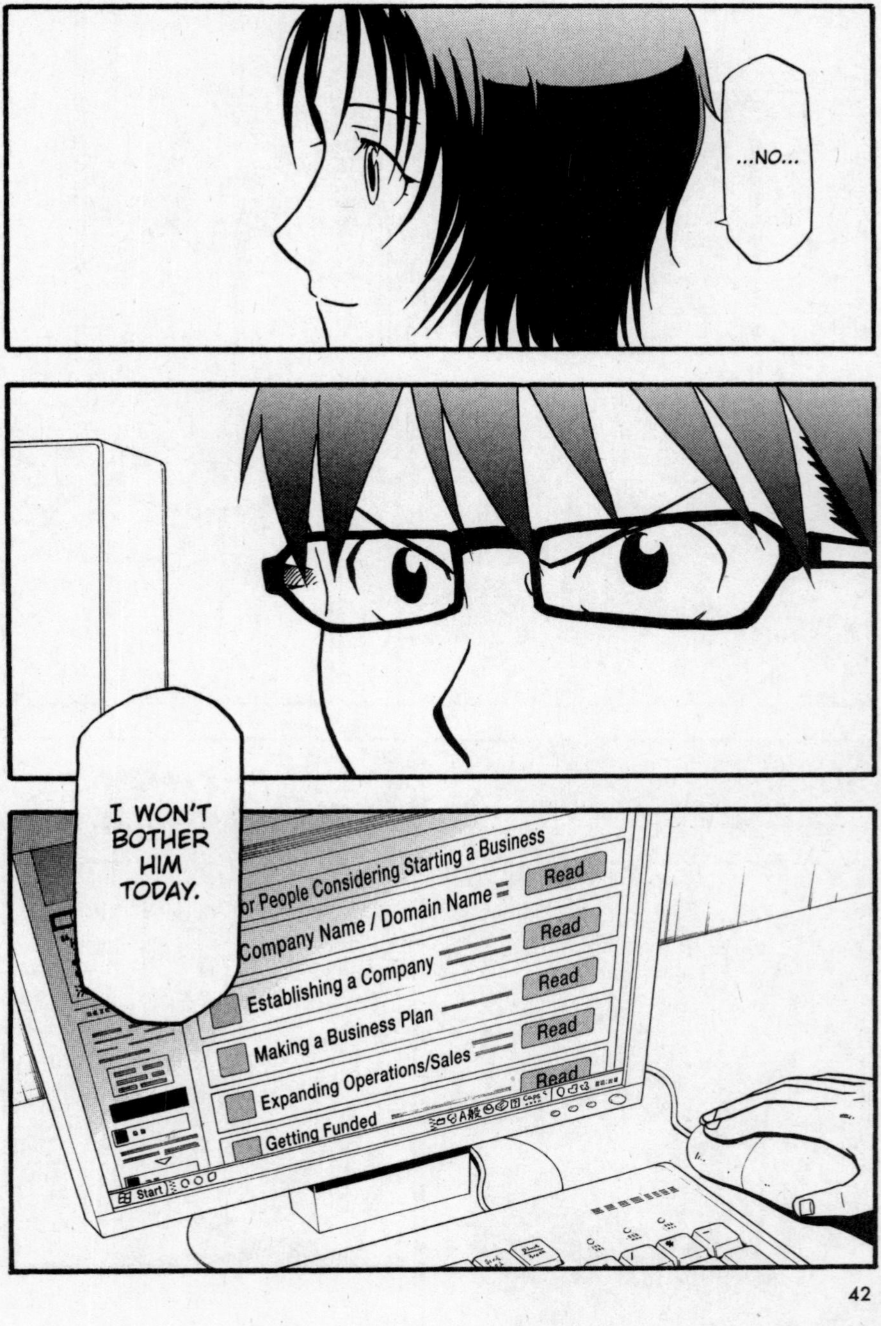
...NO...
I WON'T BOTHER HIM TODAY.
or People Considering Starting a Business
Read
Company Name / Domain Name
Read
Establishing a Company
Read
Making a Business Plan
Read
Expanding Operations/Sales
Read
Getting Funded
Start

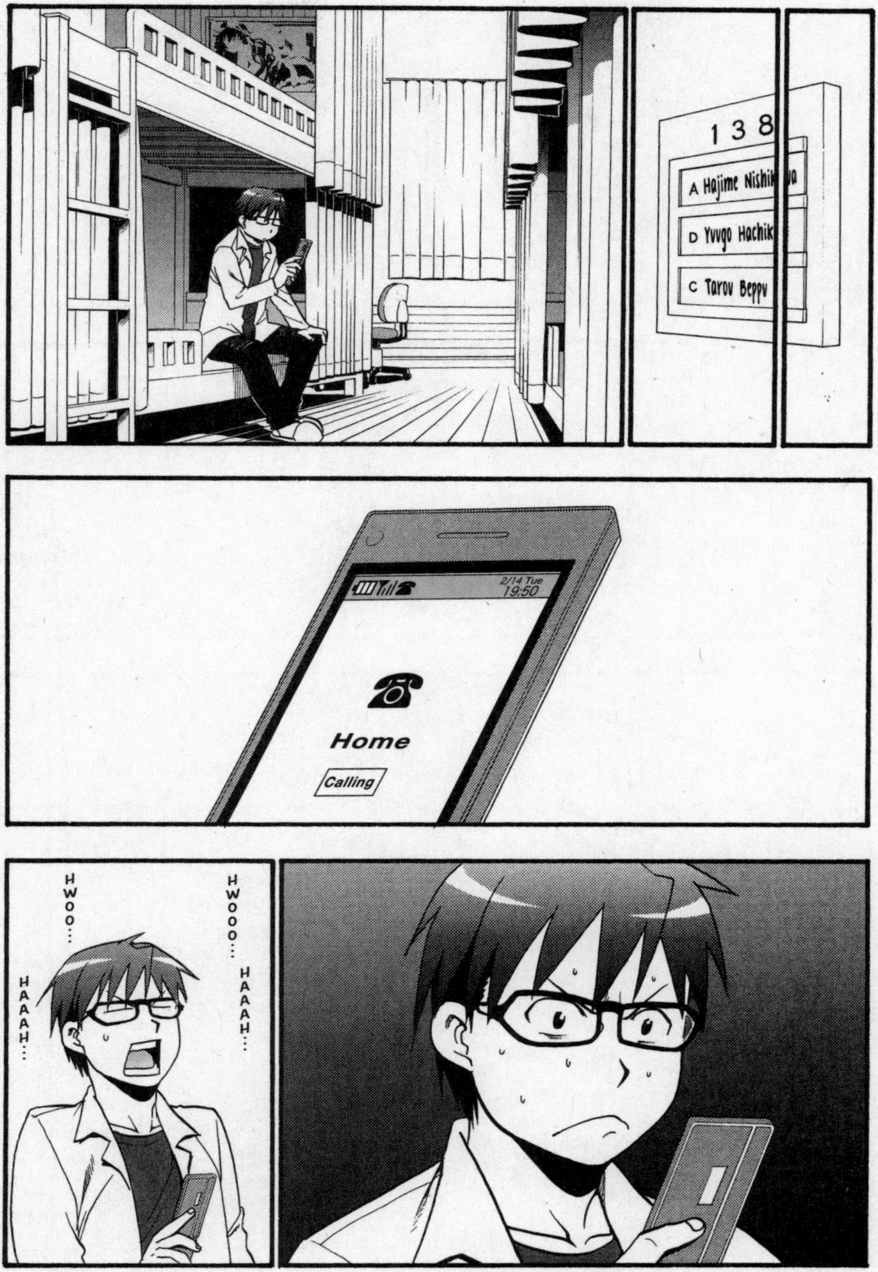
138
A Hajime Nishik va
D Yvugo Hachik
C Tarov Beppv
2/14 Tue 19:50
Home
Calling
HWOOOO… HAAAH…
HWOO… HAAAH…

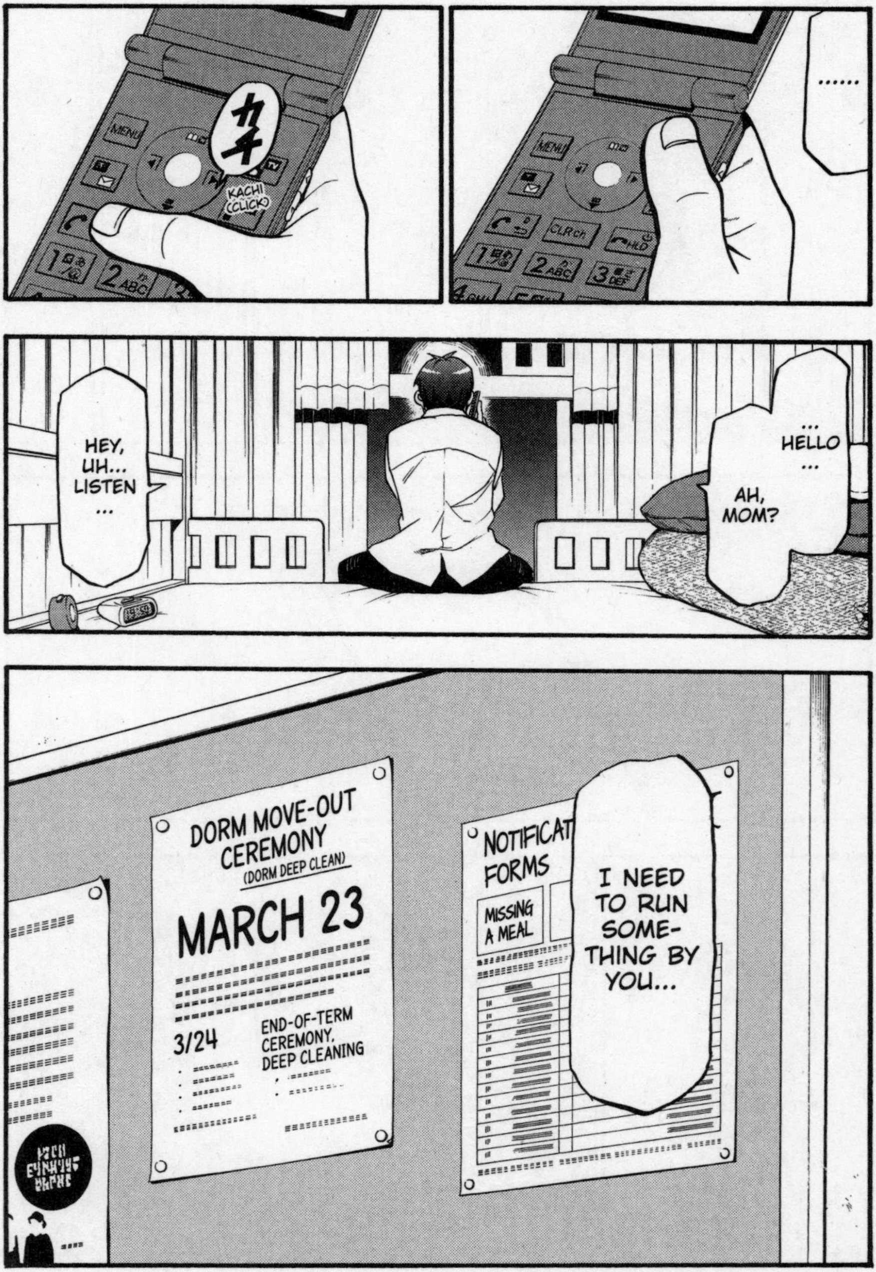
......
カチ
KACHI (CLICK)
... HELLO ... AH, MOM?
HEY, UH... LISTEN ...
NOTIFICAT FORMS
MISSING A MEAL
DORM MOVE-OUT CEREMONY
(DORM DEEP CLEAN)
MARCH 23
3/24
END-OF-TERM CEREMONY, DEEP CLEANING
I NEED TO RUN SOME-THING BY YOU...

Silver Spoon

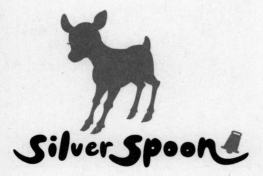

DAISAKU MIKAGE

AKI'S GRANDPA

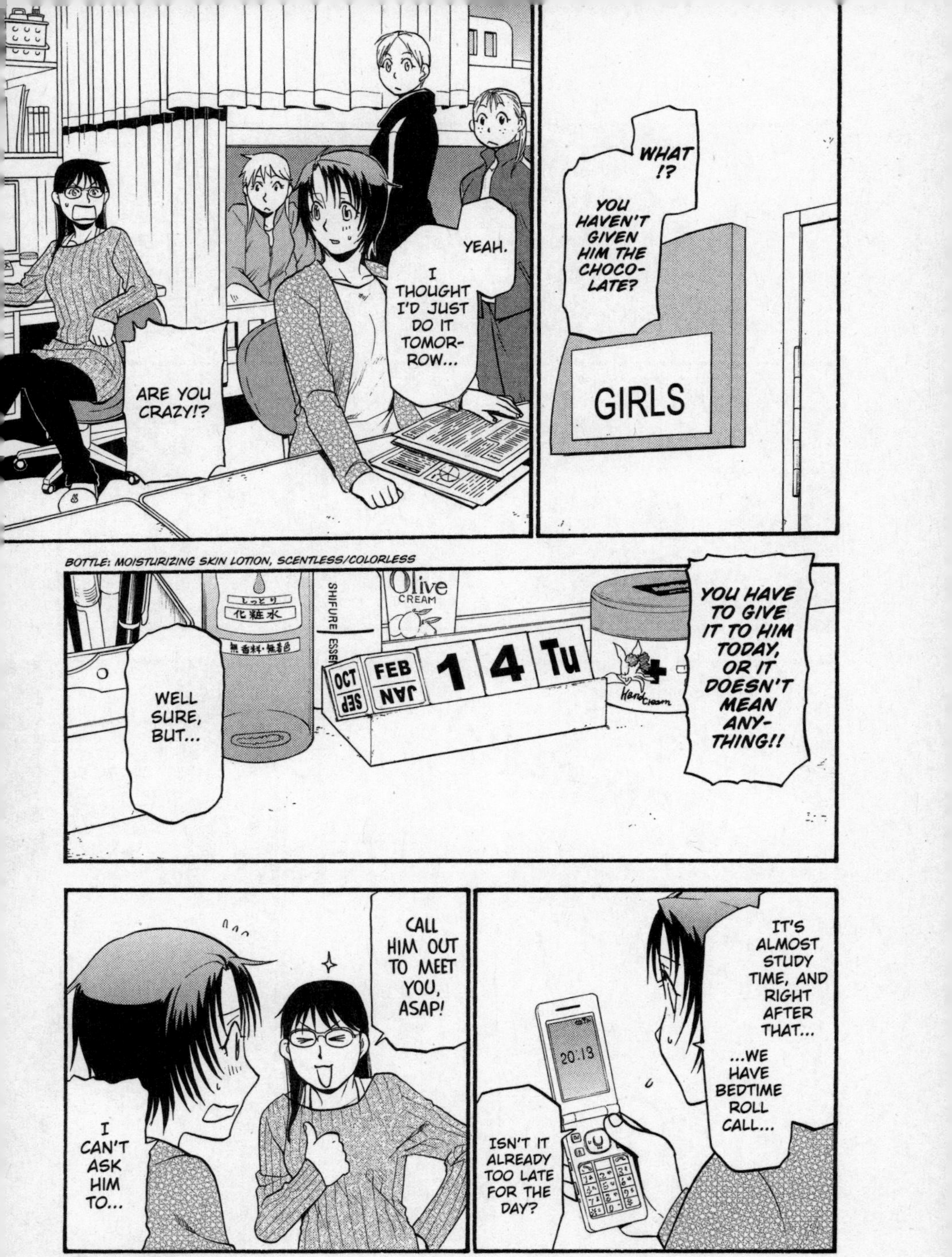
WHAT !?
YOU HAVEN'T GIVEN HIM THE CHOCO-LATE?
GIRLS
YEAH.
I THOUGHT I'D JUST DO IT TOMOR-ROW...
ARE YOU CRAZY!?
BOTTLE: MOISTURIZING SKIN LOTION, SCENTLESS/COLORLESS
YOU HAVE TO GIVE IT TO HIM TODAY, OR IT DOESN'T MEAN ANY-THING!!
Olive CREAM
SHIFURE
しっとり
化粧水
無香料・無着色
OCT
FEB
JAN
SEP
14
Tu
Hand Cream
WELL SURE, BUT...
IT'S ALMOST STUDY TIME, AND RIGHT AFTER THAT...
...WE HAVE BEDTIME ROLL CALL...
20:13
ISN'T IT ALREADY TOO LATE FOR THE DAY?
CALL HIM OUT TO MEET YOU, ASAP!
I CAN'T ASK HIM TO...

Chapter 91:
Tale of Winter ㉘

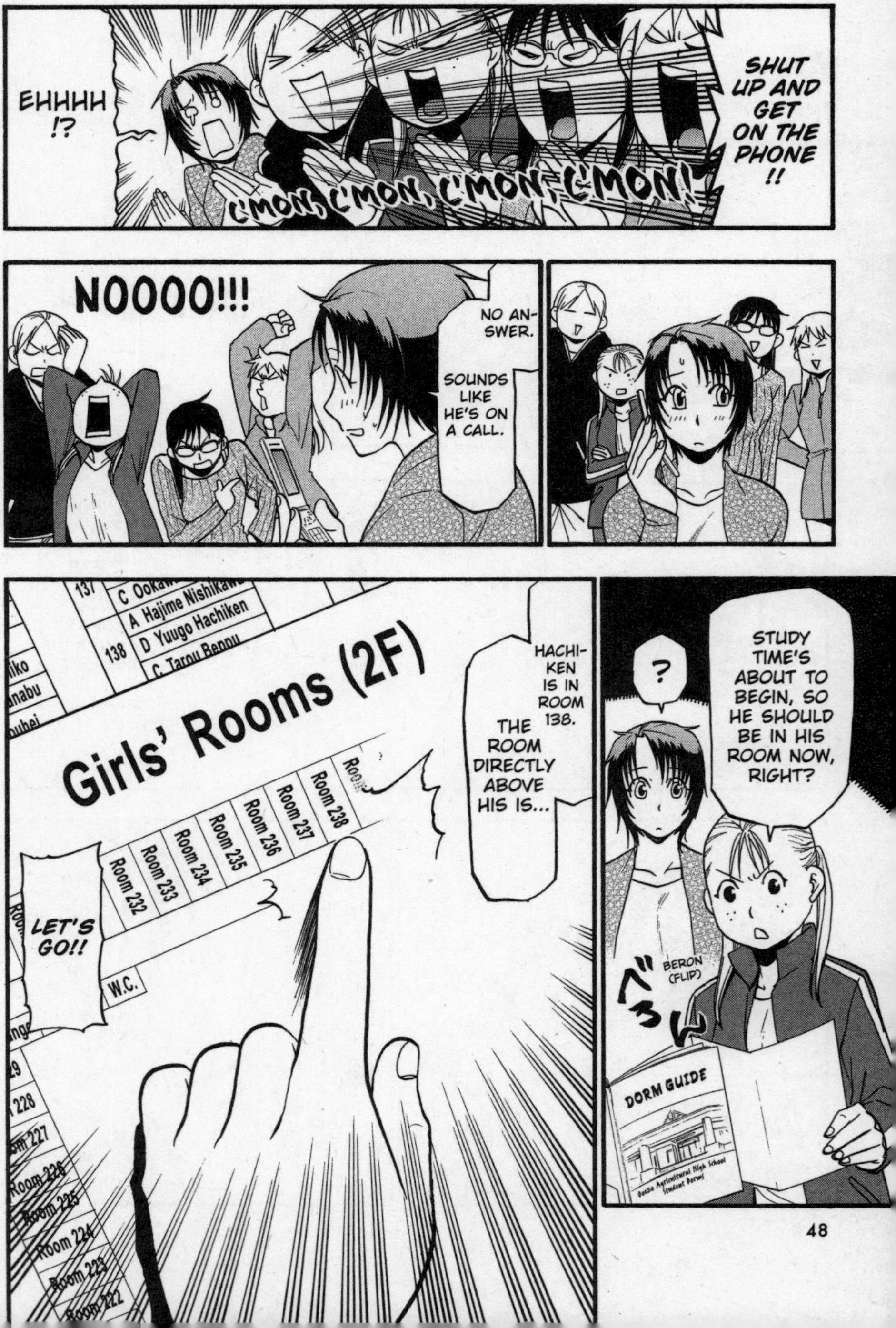
SHUT UP AND GET ON THE PHONE!!
C'MON, C'MON, C'MON, C'MON!
EHHHH!?
NO ANSWER.
SOUNDS LIKE HE'S ON A CALL.
NOOOO!!!
STUDY TIME'S ABOUT TO BEGIN, SO HE SHOULD BE IN HIS ROOM NOW, RIGHT?
?
BERON (FLIP)
DORM GUIDE
HACHIKEN IS IN ROOM 138.
THE ROOM DIRECTLY ABOVE HIS IS...
137 C Ookawa
A Hajime Nishikawa
138 D Yuugo Hachiken
C Tarou Beppu
Girls' Rooms (2F)
Room 232
Room 233
Room 234
Room 235
Room 236
Room 237
Room 238
W.C.
Room 227
Room 226
Room 225
Room 224
Room 223
Room 222
LET'S GO!!

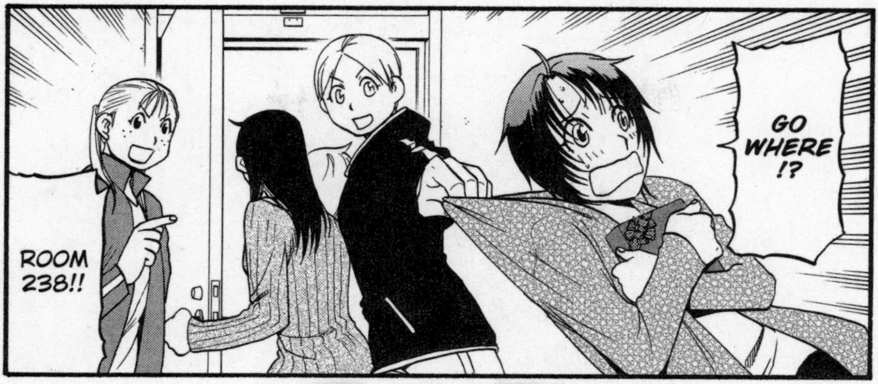
ROOM 238!!
GO WHERE !?

Chapter 91: Tale of Winter ㉘

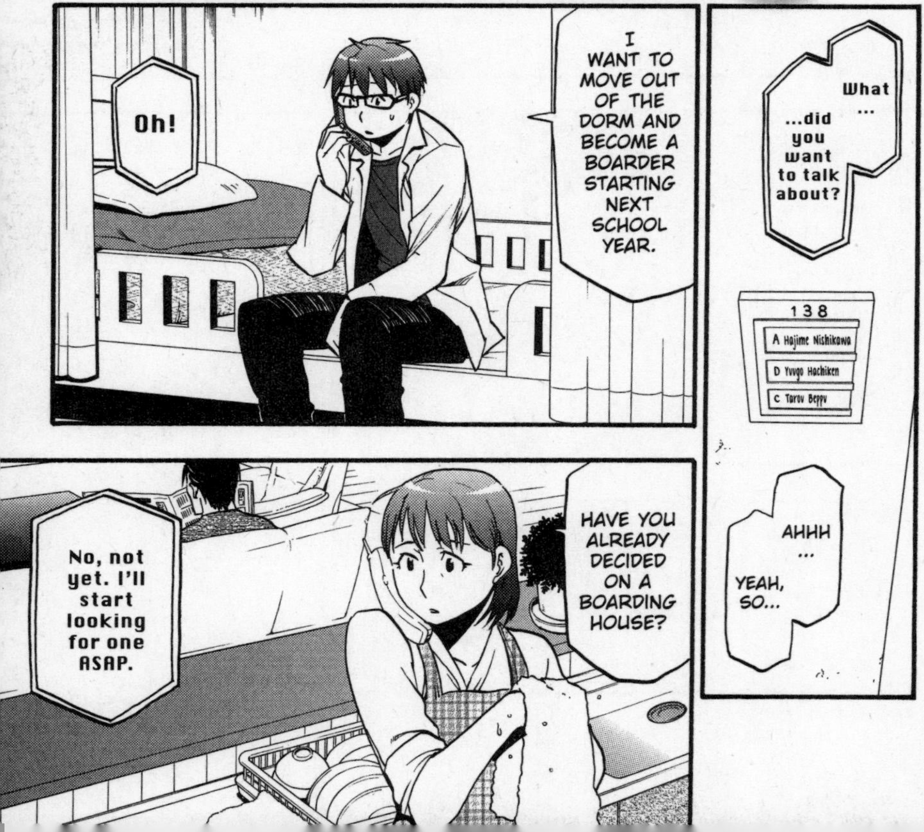
What ... ...did you want to talk about?
138
A Hajime Nishikawa
D Yuugo Hachiken
C Tarou Beppu
AHHH ... YEAH, SO...
I WANT TO MOVE OUT OF THE DORM AND BECOME A BOARDER STARTING NEXT SCHOOL YEAR.
Oh!
HAVE YOU ALREADY DECIDED ON A BOARDING HOUSE?
No, not yet. I'll start looking for one ASAP.

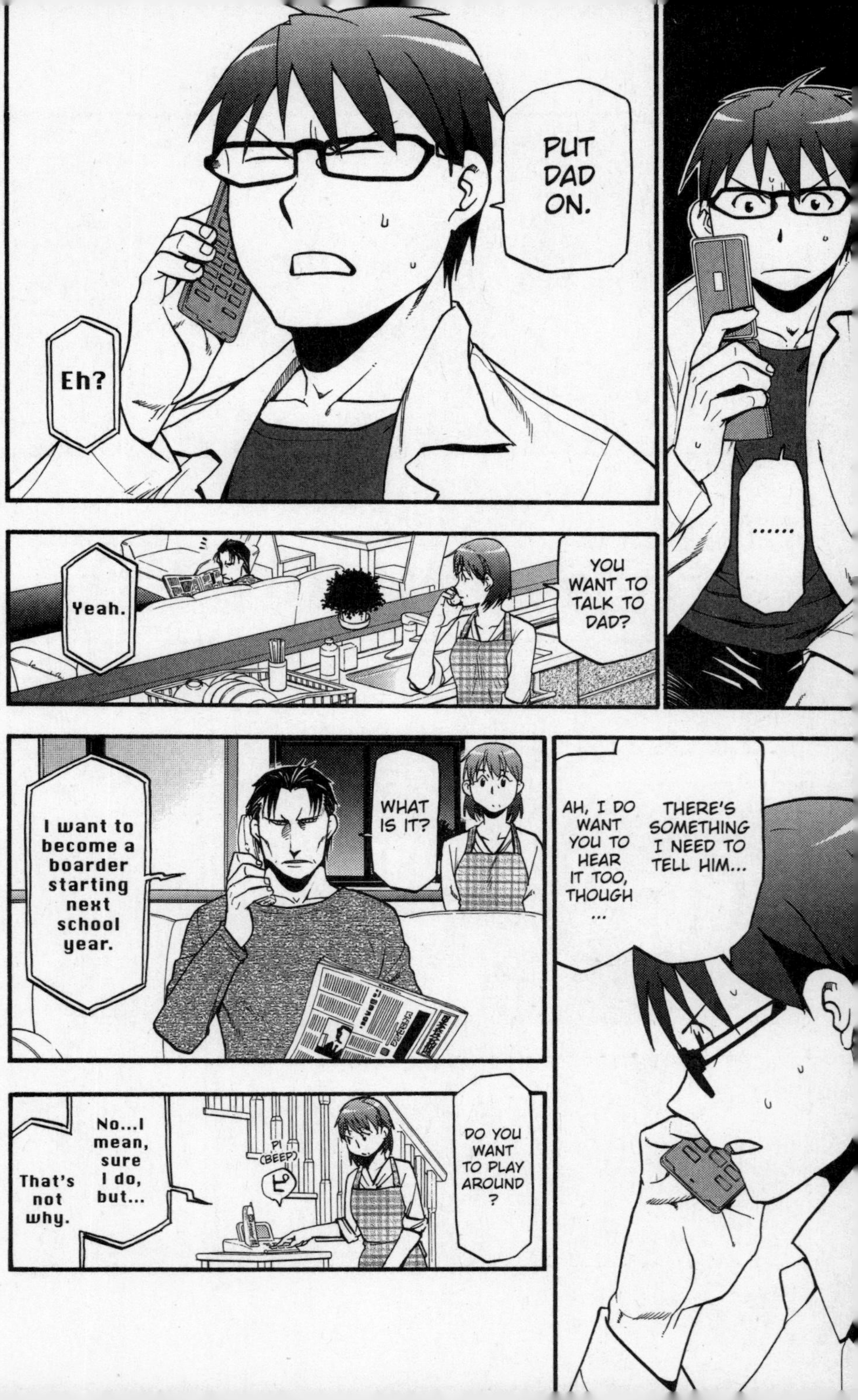
......
PUT DAD ON.
Eh?
YOU WANT TO TALK TO DAD?
Yeah.
THERE'S SOMETHING I NEED TO TELL HIM...
AH, I DO WANT YOU TO HEAR IT TOO, THOUGH...
WHAT IS IT?
I want to become a boarder starting next school year.
DO YOU WANT TO PLAY AROUND?
PI (BEEP)
ピ
No...I mean, sure I do, but...
That's not why.

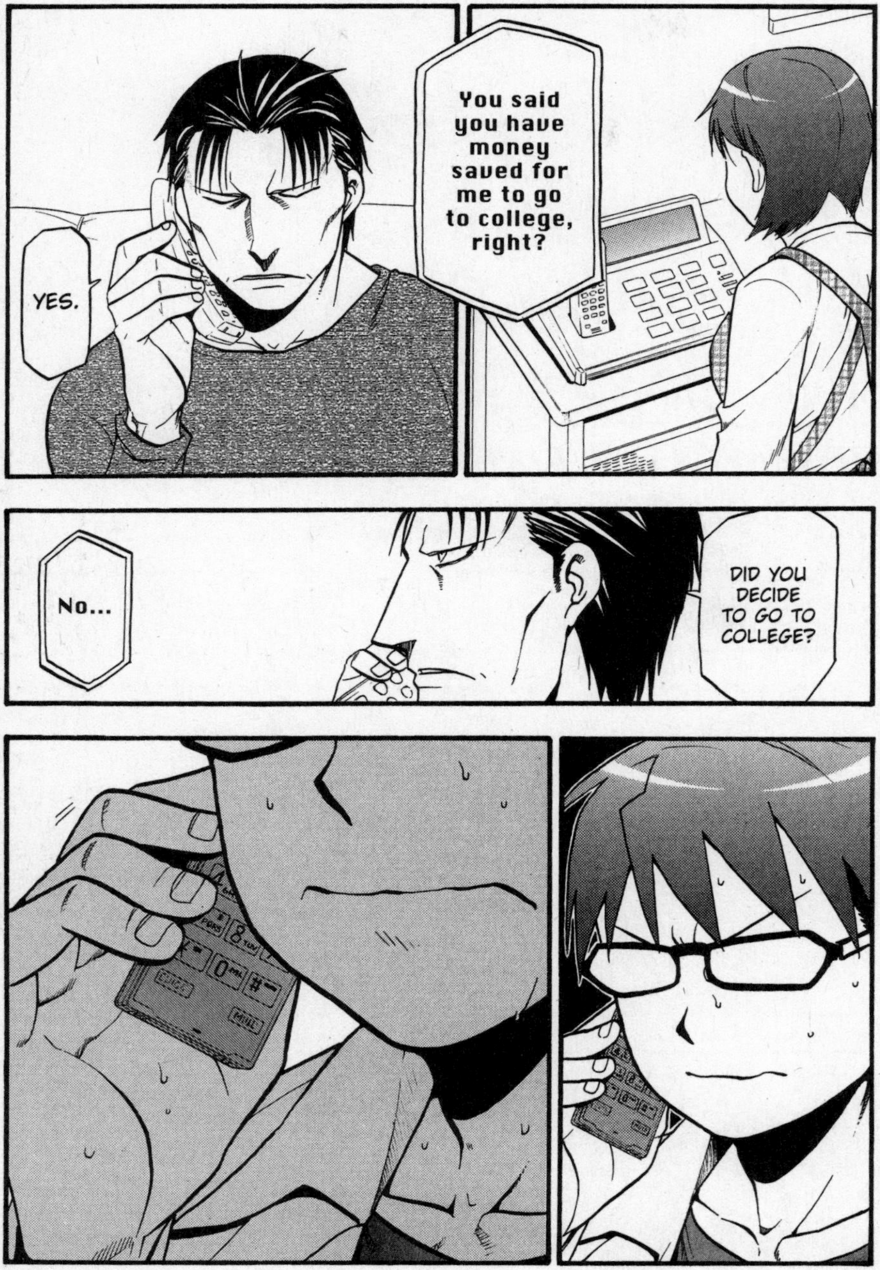
You said you have money saved for me to go to college, right?
YES.
DID YOU DECIDE TO GO TO COLLEGE?
No...

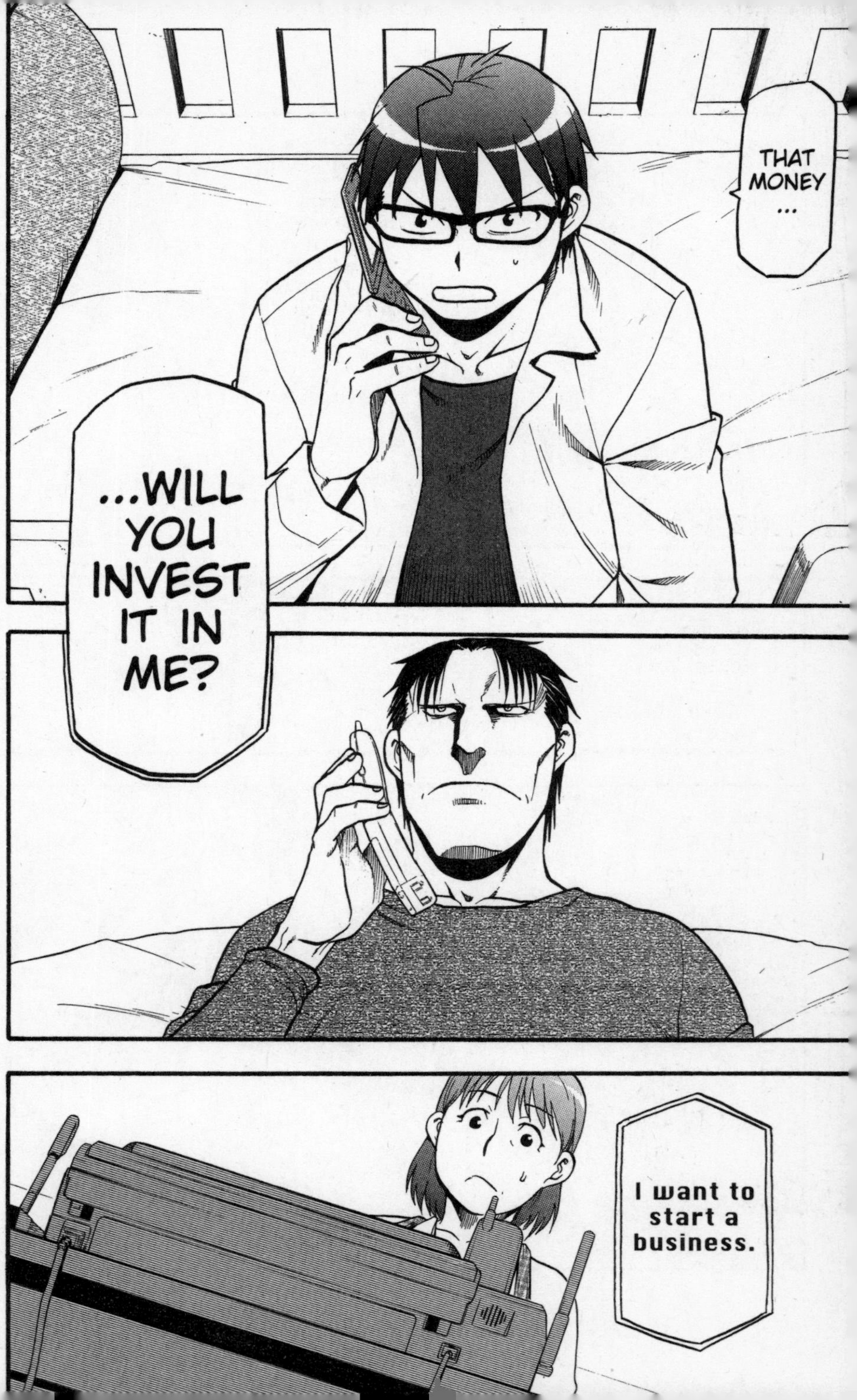
THAT MONEY ...
...WILL YOU INVEST IT IN ME?
I want to start a business.

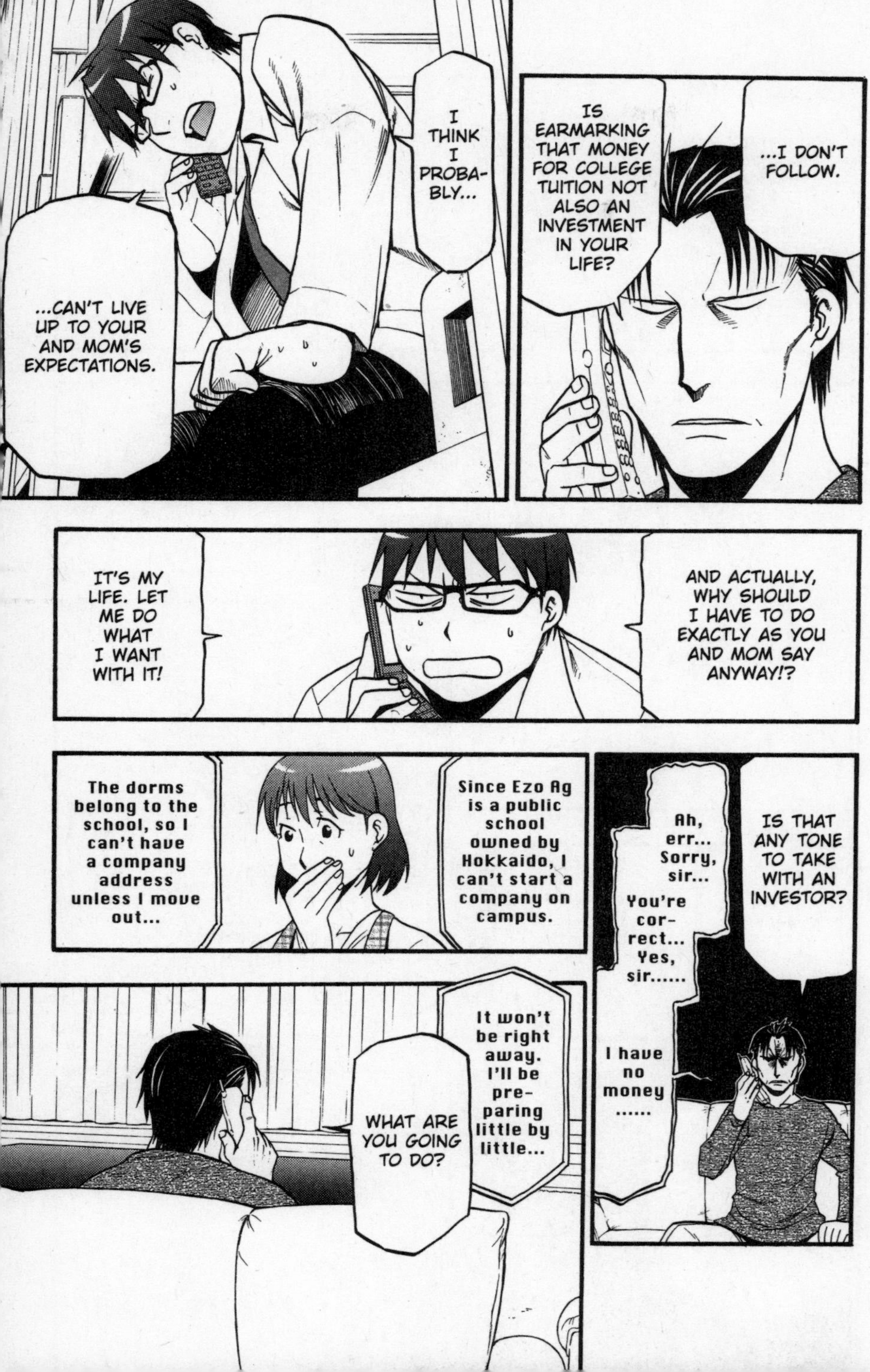
...I DON'T FOLLOW.
IS EARMARKING THAT MONEY FOR COLLEGE TUITION NOT ALSO AN INVESTMENT IN YOUR LIFE?
I THINK I PROBA-BLY...
...CAN'T LIVE UP TO YOUR AND MOM'S EXPECTATIONS.
AND ACTUALLY, WHY SHOULD I HAVE TO DO EXACTLY AS YOU AND MOM SAY ANYWAY!?
IT'S MY LIFE. LET ME DO WHAT I WANT WITH IT!
IS THAT ANY TONE TO TAKE WITH AN INVESTOR?
Ah, err... Sorry, sir...
You're cor-rect... Yes, sir......
I have no money ......
Since Ezo Ag is a public school owned by Hokkaido, I can't start a company on campus.
The dorms belong to the school, so I can't have a company address unless I move out...
It won't be right away. I'll be pre-paring little by little...
WHAT ARE YOU GOING TO DO?

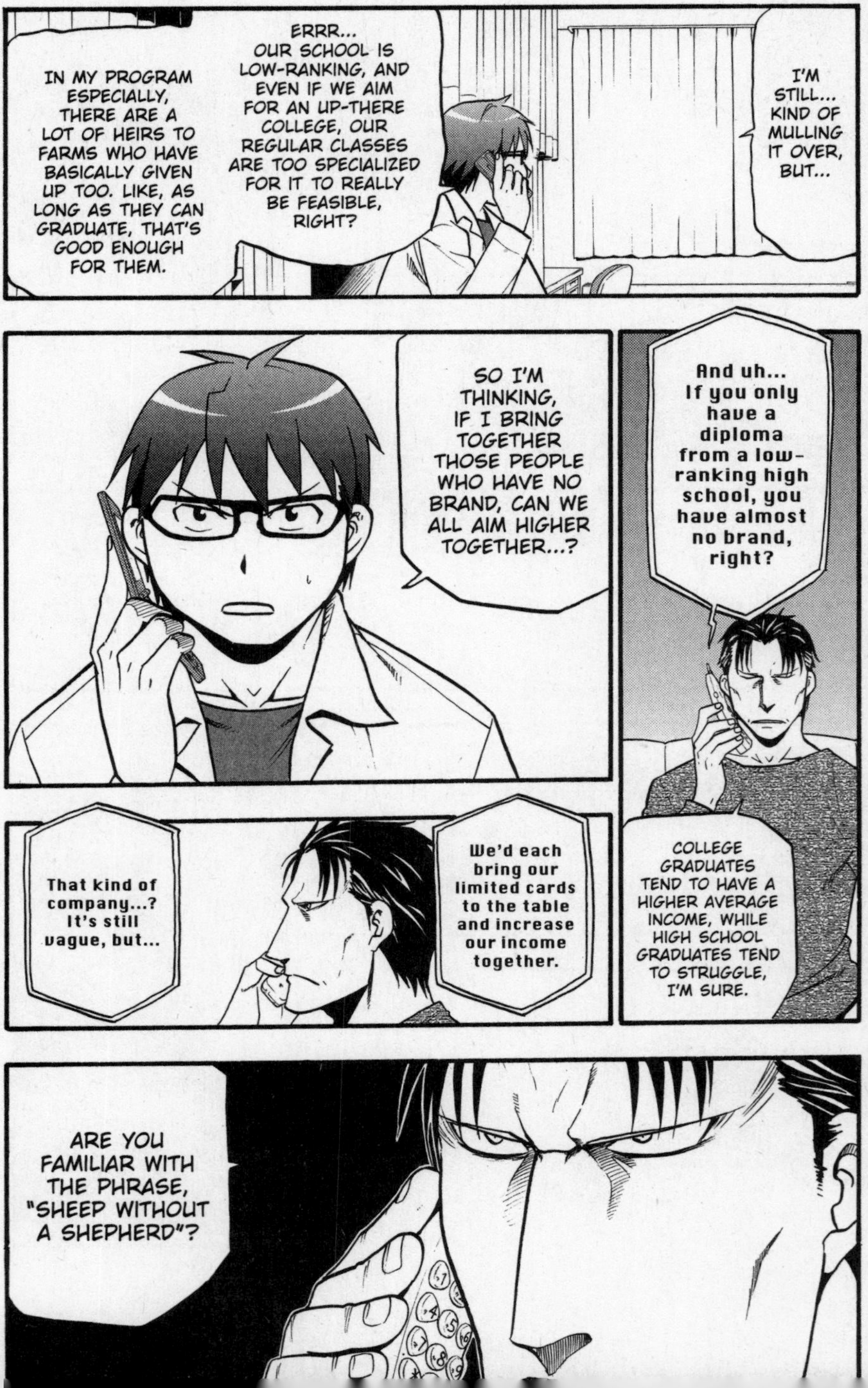
I'M STILL... KIND OF MULLING IT OVER, BUT...
ERRR... OUR SCHOOL IS LOW-RANKING, AND EVEN IF WE AIM FOR AN UP-THERE COLLEGE, OUR REGULAR CLASSES ARE TOO SPECIALIZED FOR IT TO REALLY BE FEASIBLE, RIGHT?
IN MY PROGRAM ESPECIALLY, THERE ARE A LOT OF HEIRS TO FARMS WHO HAVE BASICALLY GIVEN UP TOO. LIKE, AS LONG AS THEY CAN GRADUATE, THAT'S GOOD ENOUGH FOR THEM.
And uh... If you only have a diploma from a low-ranking high school, you have almost no brand, right?
COLLEGE GRADUATES TEND TO HAVE A HIGHER AVERAGE INCOME, WHILE HIGH SCHOOL GRADUATES TEND TO STRUGGLE, I'M SURE.
SO I'M THINKING, IF I BRING TOGETHER THOSE PEOPLE WHO HAVE NO BRAND, CAN WE ALL AIM HIGHER TOGETHER...?
We'd each bring our limited cards to the table and increase our income together.
That kind of company...? It's still vague, but...
ARE YOU FAMILIAR WITH THE PHRASE, "SHEEP WITHOUT A SHEPHERD"?

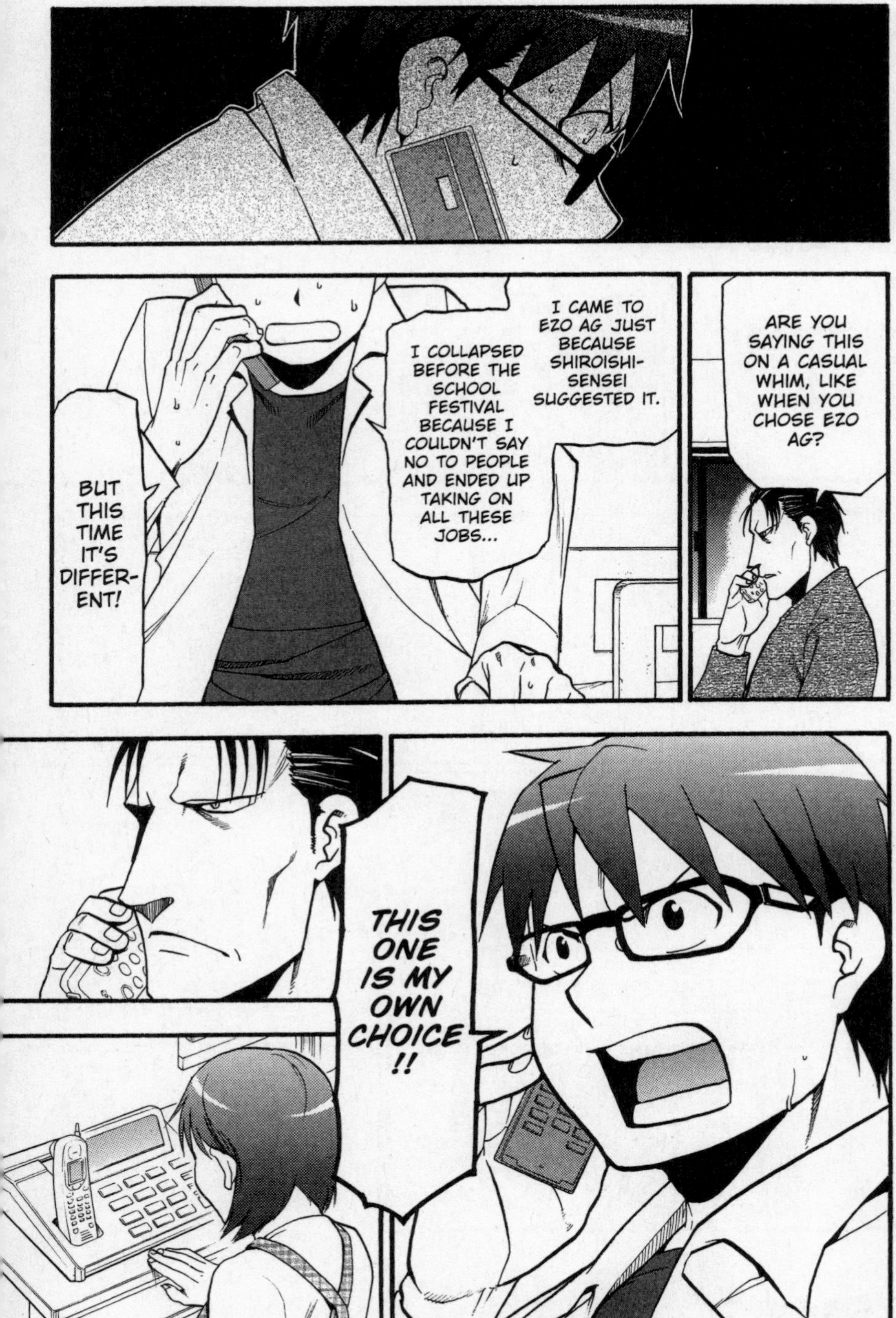
ARE YOU SAYING THIS ON A CASUAL WHIM, LIKE WHEN YOU CHOSE EZO AG?
I CAME TO EZO AG JUST BECAUSE SHIROISHI-SENSEI SUGGESTED IT.
I COLLAPSED BEFORE THE SCHOOL FESTIVAL BECAUSE I COULDN'T SAY NO TO PEOPLE AND ENDED UP TAKING ON ALL THESE JOBS...
BUT THIS TIME IT'S DIFFER-ENT!
THIS ONE IS MY OWN CHOICE!!

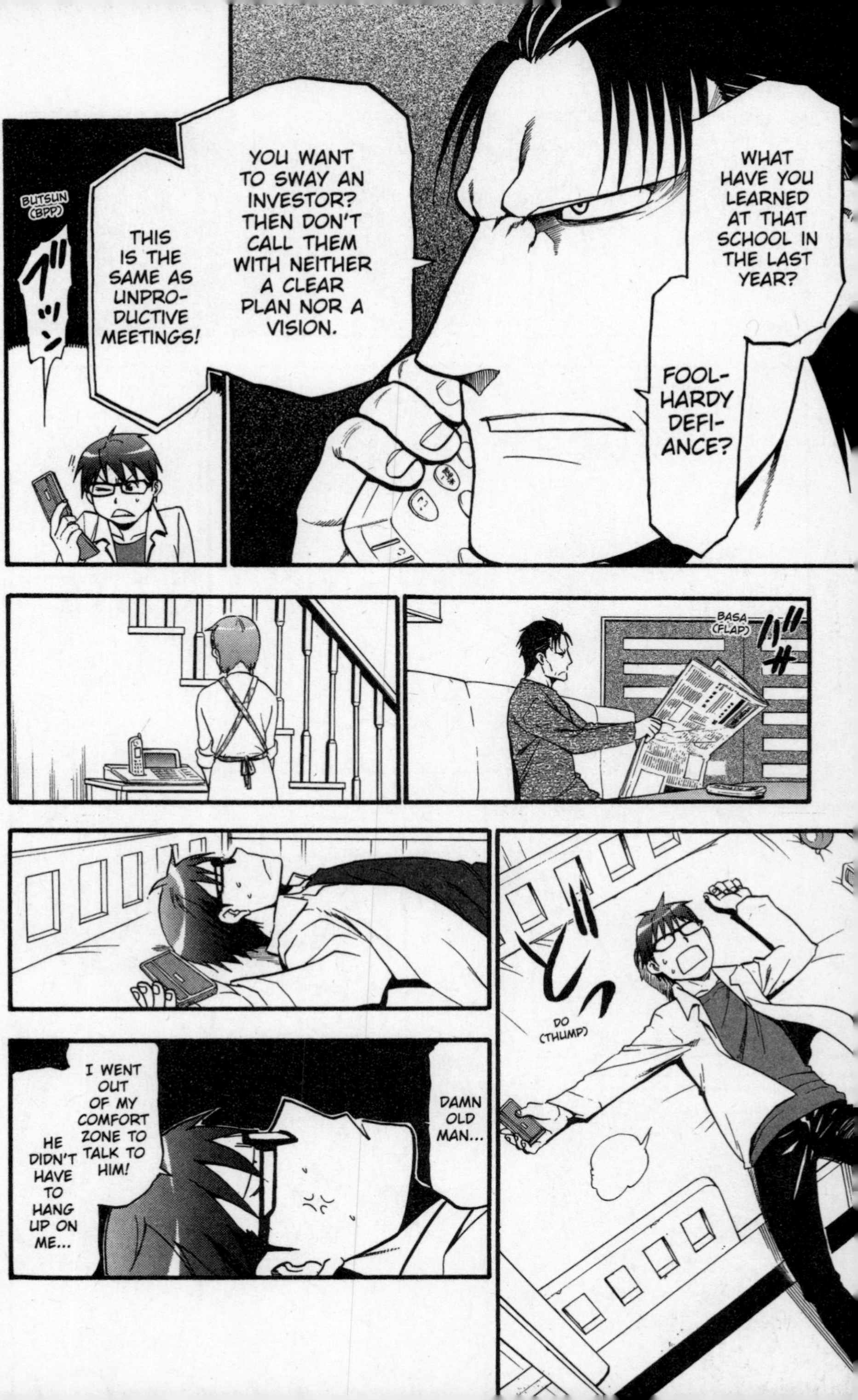
WHAT HAVE YOU LEARNED AT THAT SCHOOL IN THE LAST YEAR?
FOOL-HARDY DEFI-ANCE?
YOU WANT TO SWAY AN INVESTOR? THEN DON'T CALL THEM WITH NEITHER A CLEAR PLAN NOR A VISION.
THIS IS THE SAME AS UNPRO-DUCTIVE MEETINGS!
BUTSUN (BPP)
BASA (FLAP)
DO (THUMP)
DAMN OLD MAN...
I WENT OUT OF MY COMFORT ZONE TO TALK TO HIM!
HE DIDN'T HAVE TO HANG UP ON ME...

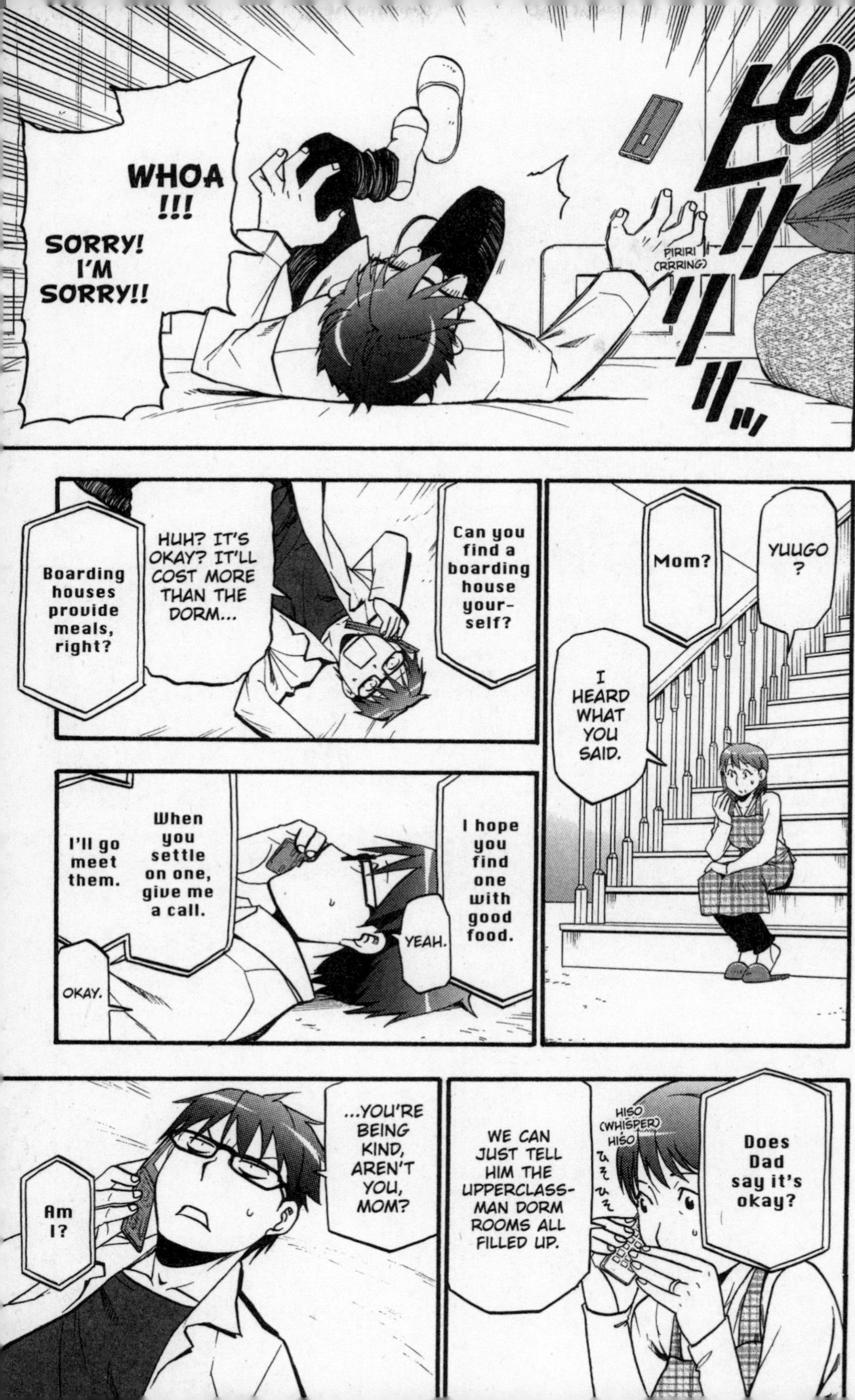
PIRIRI (RRRING)
WHOA!!!
SORRY! I'M SORRY!!
YUUGO?
Mom?
I HEARD WHAT YOU SAID.
Can you find a boarding house yourself?
HUH? IT'S OKAY? IT'LL COST MORE THAN THE DORM...
Boarding houses provide meals, right?
I hope you find one with good food.
YEAH.
When you settle on one, give me a call.
I'll go meet them.
OKAY.
Does Dad say it's okay?
HISO (WHISPER) HISO
WE CAN JUST TELL HIM THE UPPERCLASSMAN DORM ROOMS ALL FILLED UP.
...YOU'RE BEING KIND, AREN'T YOU, MOM?
Am I?

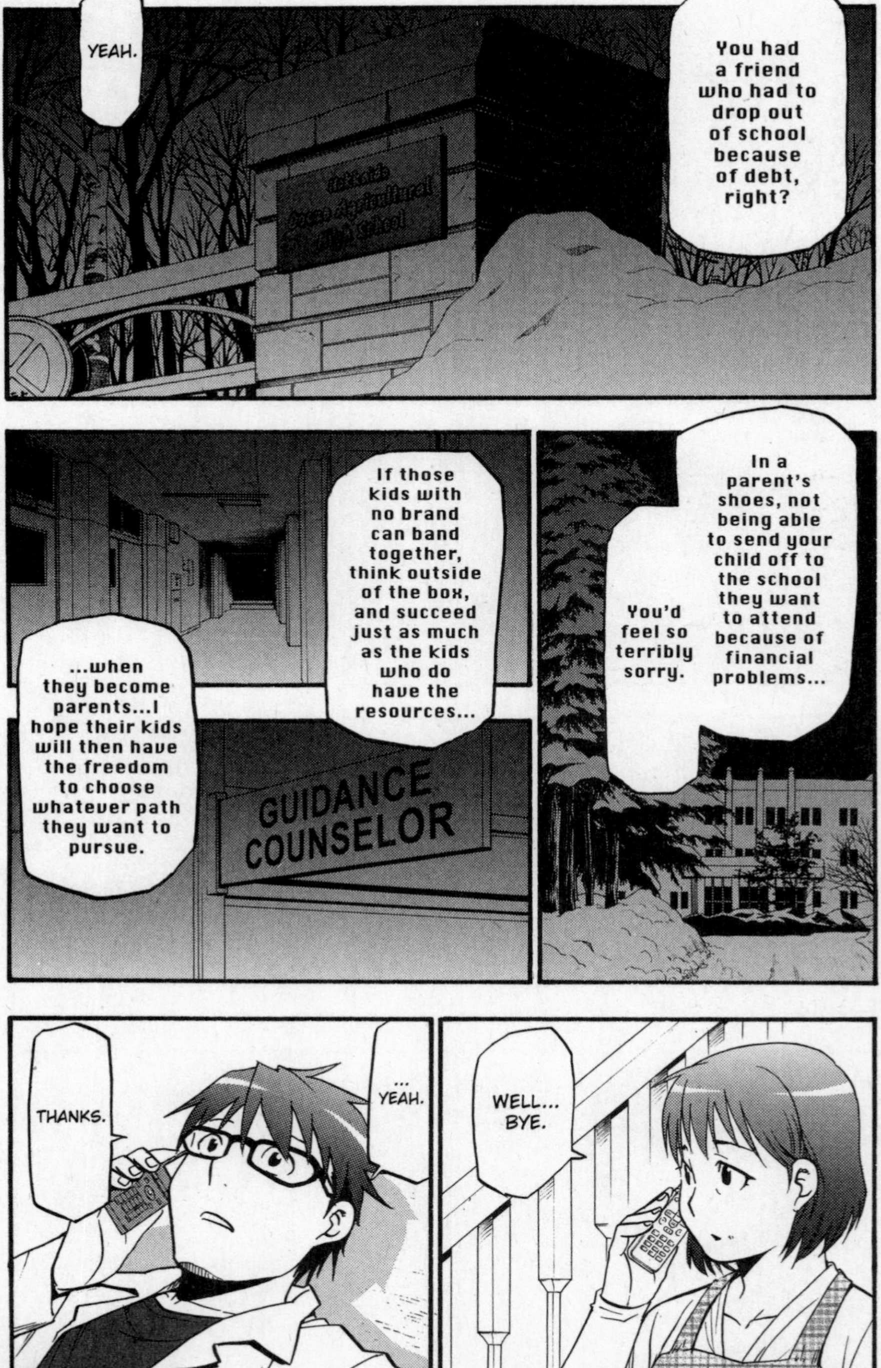
You had a friend who had to drop out of school because of debt, right?
YEAH.
In a parent's shoes, not being able to send your child off to the school they want to attend because of financial problems...
You'd feel so terribly sorry.
If those kids with no brand can band together, think outside of the box, and succeed just as much as the kids who do have the resources...
...when they become parents...I hope their kids will then have the freedom to choose whatever path they want to pursue.
GUIDANCE COUNSELOR
WELL... BYE.
... YEAH.
THANKS.

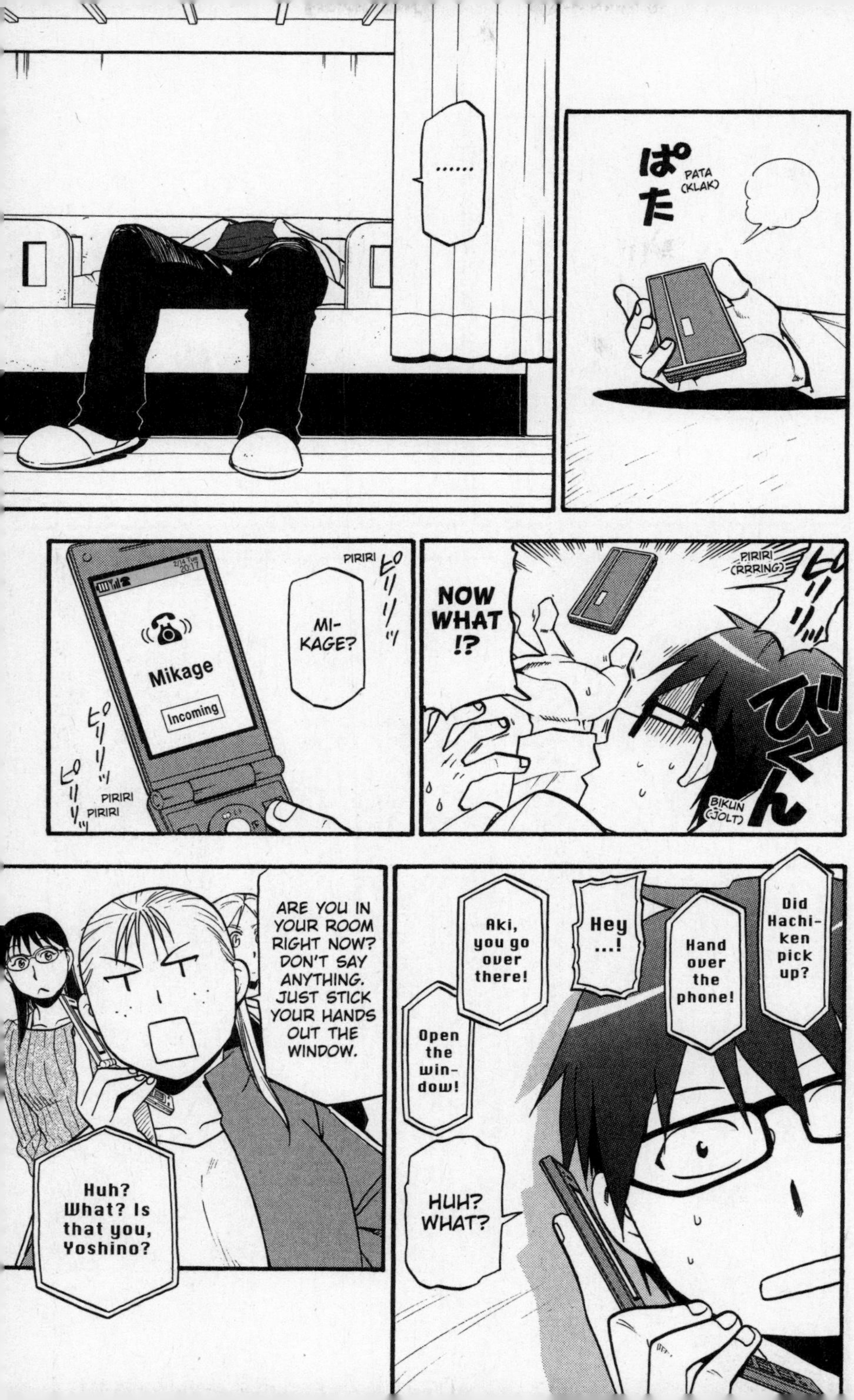
ぱた
PATA (KLAK)
......
ぴりりっ
PIRIRI (RRRING)
NOW WHAT !?
びくん
BIKUN (JOLT)
PIRIRI
ピリリリッ
MI-KAGE?
2/14 Tue 20:17
Mikage
Incoming
ピリリリッ
ピリリッ
PIRIRI
PIRIRI
Did Hachi-ken pick up?
Hand over the phone!
Hey ...!
Aki, you go over there!
Open the win-dow!
HUH? WHAT?
ARE YOU IN YOUR ROOM RIGHT NOW? DON'T SAY ANYTHING. JUST STICK YOUR HANDS OUT THE WINDOW.
Huh? What? Is that you, Yoshino?

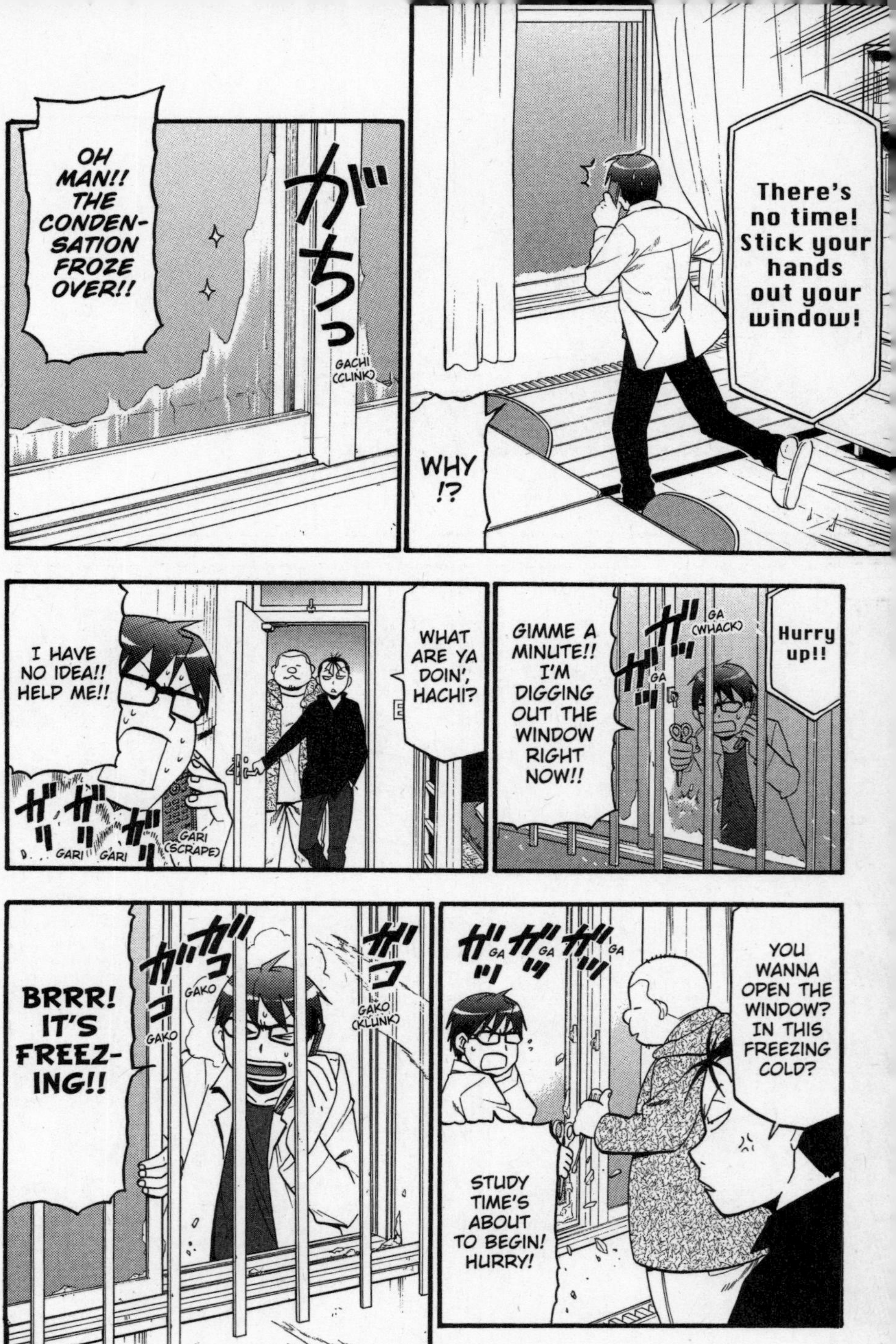
There's no time! Stick your hands out your window!
WHY !?
がちっ
GACHI (CLINK)
OH MAN!! THE CONDEN- SATION FROZE OVER!!
Hurry up!!
GIMME A MINUTE!! I'M DIGGING OUT THE WINDOW RIGHT NOW!!
GA (WHACK)
GA
WHAT ARE YA DOIN', HACHI?
I HAVE NO IDEA!! HELP ME!!
GARI GARI GARI (SCRAPE)
YOU WANNA OPEN THE WINDOW? IN THIS FREEZING COLD?
GA GA GA
STUDY TIME'S ABOUT TO BEGIN! HURRY!
GAKO (KLUNK)
GAKO
GAKO
BRRR! IT'S FREEZ- ING!!

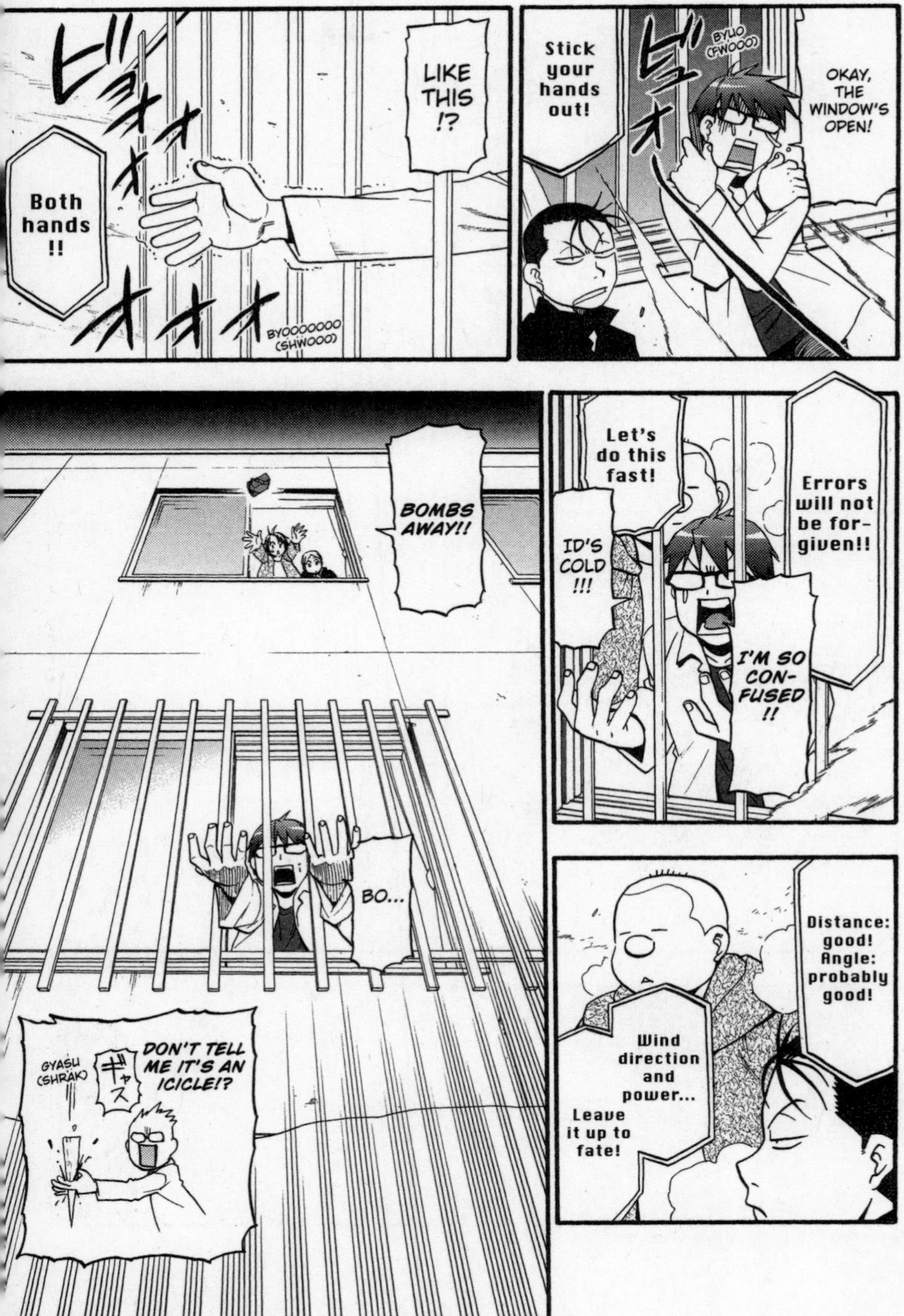
OKAY, THE WINDOW'S OPEN!
ビュオ
BYUO (FWOOO)
Stick your hands out!
LIKE THIS !?
ビョオオオオオオオ
Both hands !!
BYOOOOOOO (SHWOOO)
Errors will not be for-given!!
Let's do this fast!
ID'S COLD !!!
I'M SO CON-FUSED !!
Distance: good! Angle: probably good!
Wind direction and power...
Leave it up to fate!
BOMBS AWAY!!
BO...
DON'T TELL ME IT'S AN ICICLE!?
ギャス
GYASU (SHRAK)

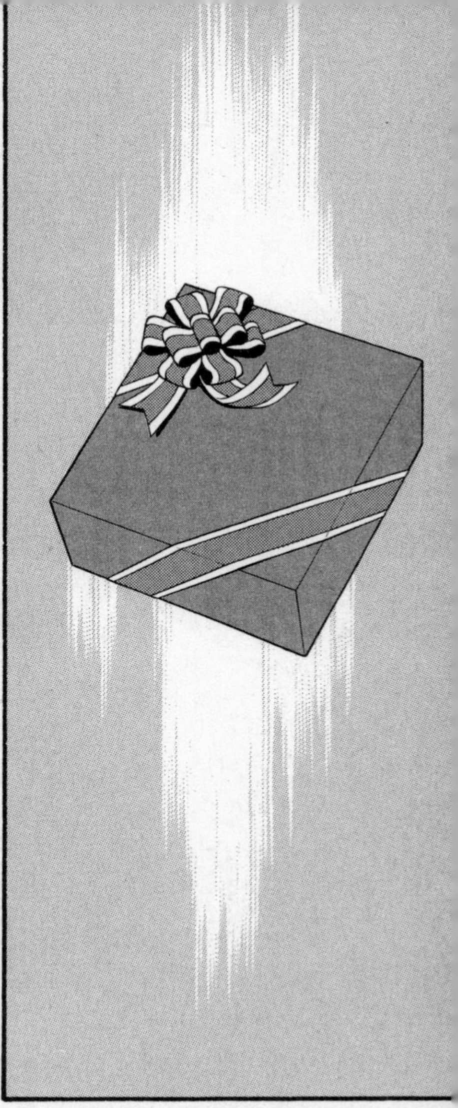

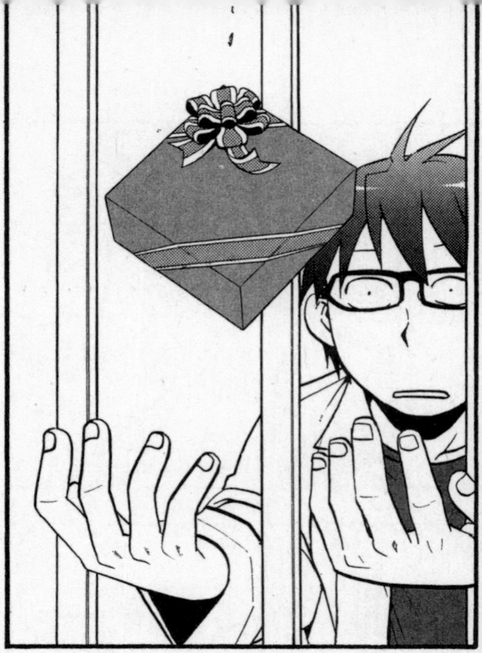

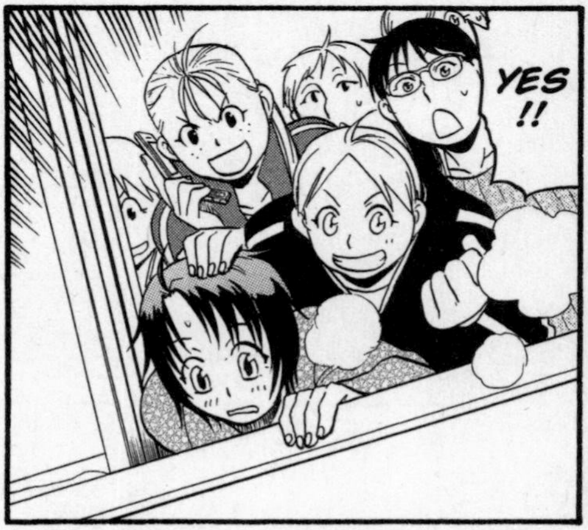
YES!!

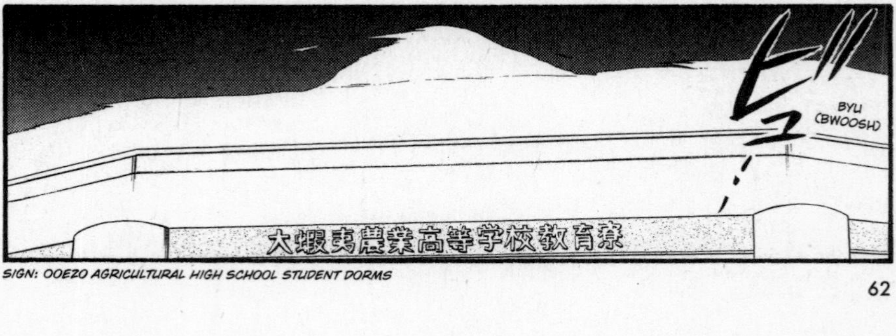
BYU (BWOOSH)
大蝦夷農業高等学校教育寮

SIGN: OOEZO AGRICULTURAL HIGH SCHOOL STUDENT DORMS

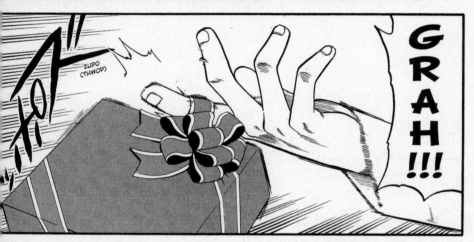

ZUPO
(THWOP)

GRAH!!!

I SAW URYUU-SAN'S FACE FOR AN INSTANT THERE...

プル
PURU

プル
PURU

プル
PURU (TRMBL)

プル
PURU

HR RR IHNR

NICE CATCH!

63

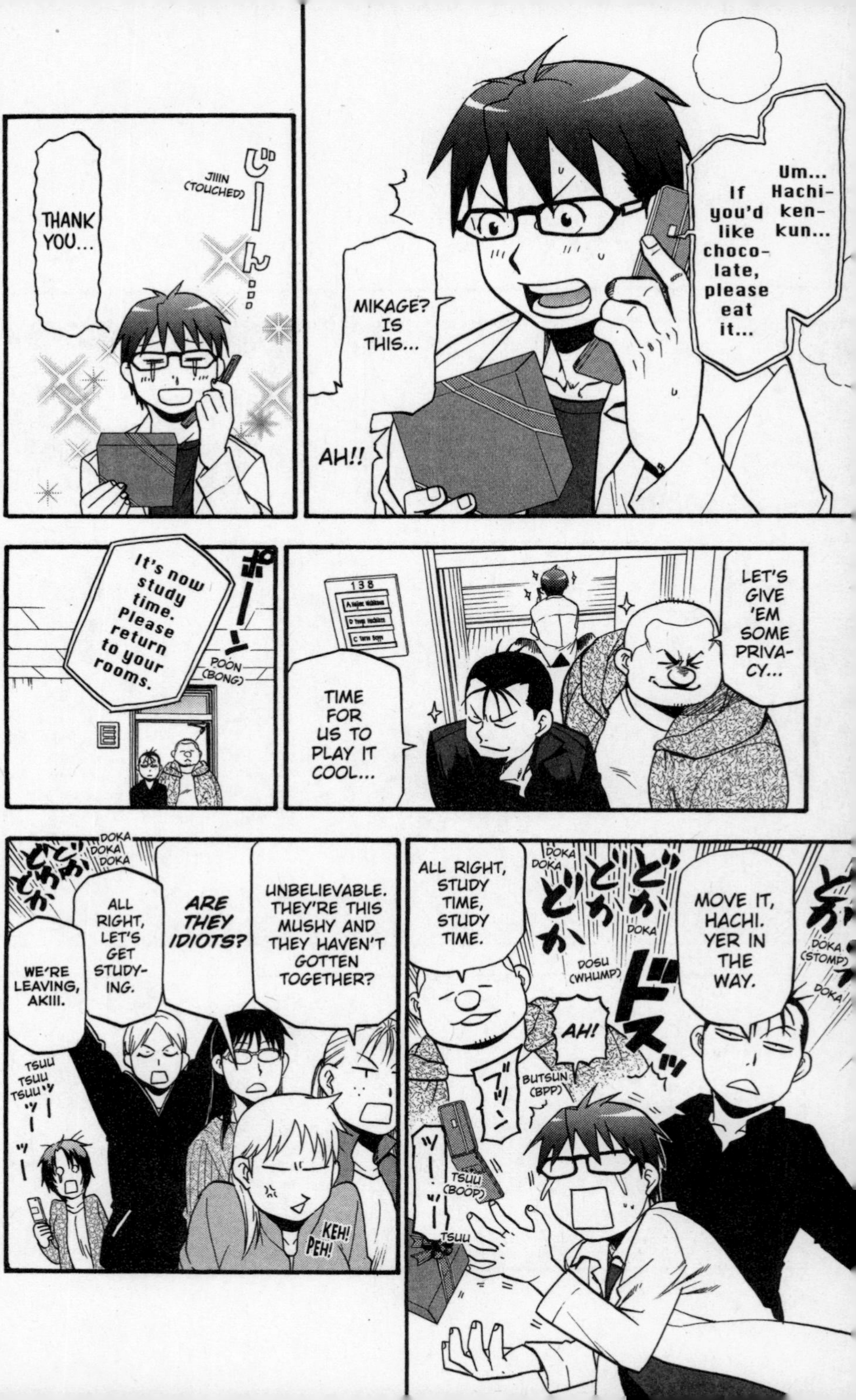
Um... Hachi-ken-kun... If you'd like chocolate, please eat it...
MIKAGE? IS THIS...
AH!!
JIIN (TOUCHED)
THANK YOU...
LET'S GIVE 'EM SOME PRIVACY...
TIME FOR US TO PLAY IT COOL...
It's now study time. Please return to your rooms.
POON (BONG)
MOVE IT, HACHI. YER IN THE WAY.
DOKA (STOMP)
DOKA
ALL RIGHT, STUDY TIME, STUDY TIME.
DOKA DOKA
DOKA
DOSU (WHUMP)
AH!
BUTSUN (BPP)
TSUU (BOOP)
TSUU
UNBELIEVABLE. THEY'RE THIS MUSHY AND THEY HAVEN'T GOTTEN TOGETHER?
ARE THEY IDIOTS?
ALL RIGHT, LET'S GET STUDYING.
DOKA DOKA DOKA
WE'RE LEAVING, AKIII.
TSUU TSUU TSUU
KEH! PEH!

Silver Spoon

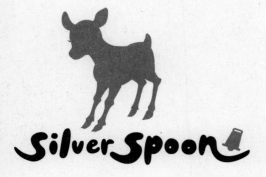

SATO MIKAGE

AKI'S GRANDMA

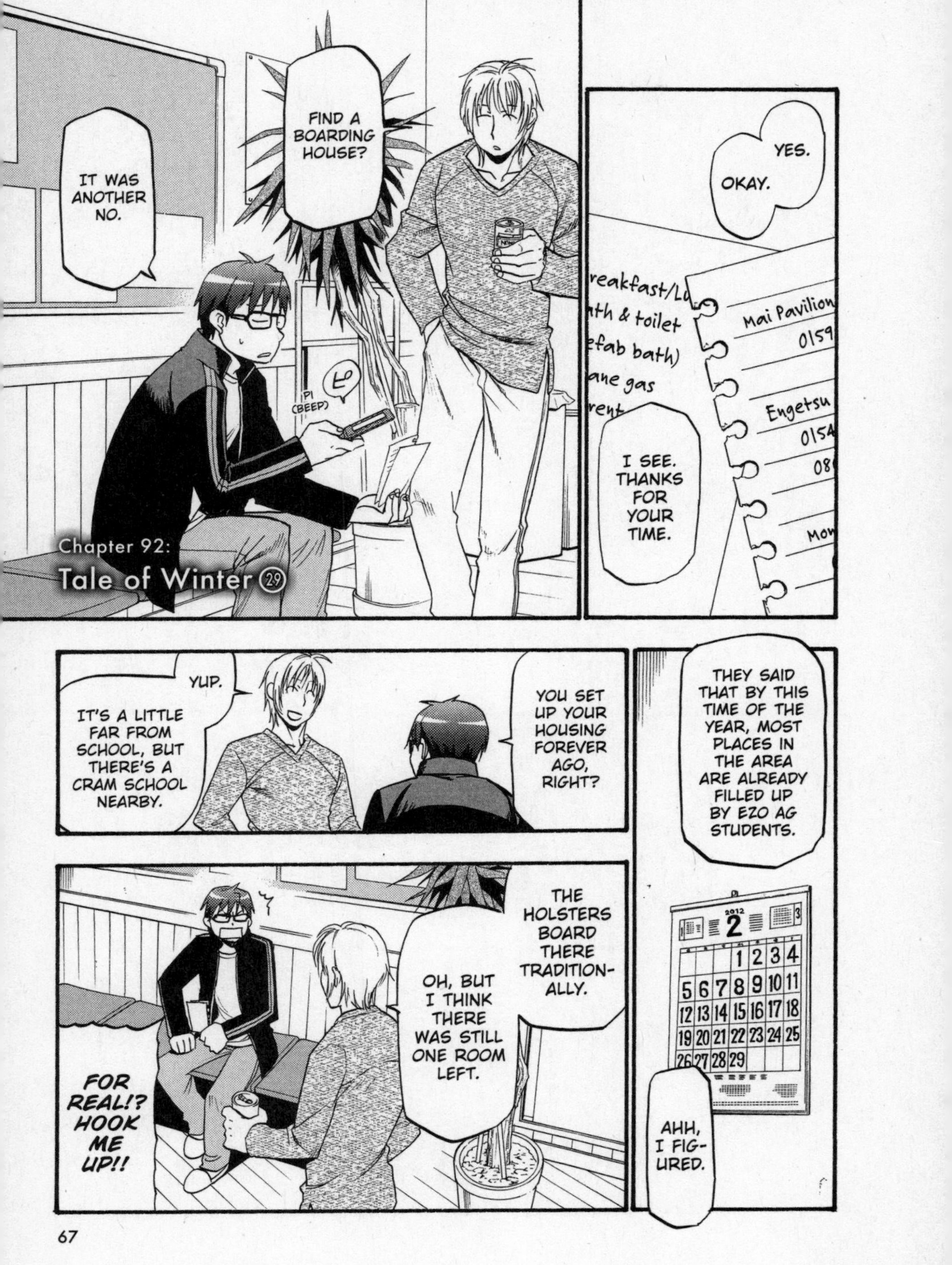
YES.
OKAY.
Mai Pavilion
Engetsu
I SEE. THANKS FOR YOUR TIME.
FIND A BOARDING HOUSE?
IT WAS ANOTHER NO.
ピ
PI (BEEP)
Chapter 92:
Tale of Winter ㉙
THEY SAID THAT BY THIS TIME OF THE YEAR, MOST PLACES IN THE AREA ARE ALREADY FILLED UP BY EZO AG STUDENTS.
YOU SET UP YOUR HOUSING FOREVER AGO, RIGHT?
YUP.
IT'S A LITTLE FAR FROM SCHOOL, BUT THERE'S A CRAM SCHOOL NEARBY.
AHH, I FIG-URED.
THE HOLSTERS BOARD THERE TRADITION-ALLY.
OH, BUT I THINK THERE WAS STILL ONE ROOM LEFT.
FOR REAL!? HOOK ME UP!!

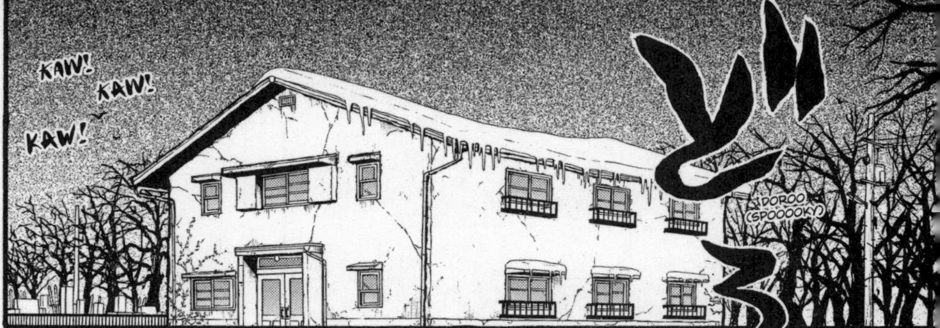
KAW! KAW!
KAW!
DOROO (SPOOOOKY)

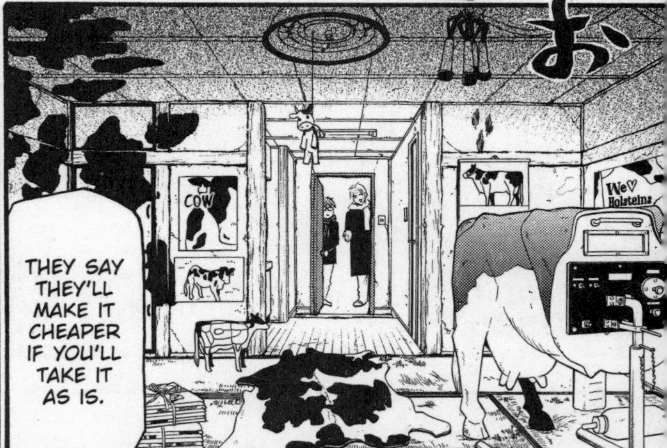
THEY SAY THEY'LL MAKE IT CHEAPER IF YOU'LL TAKE IT AS IS.
COW
We♥ Holsteins

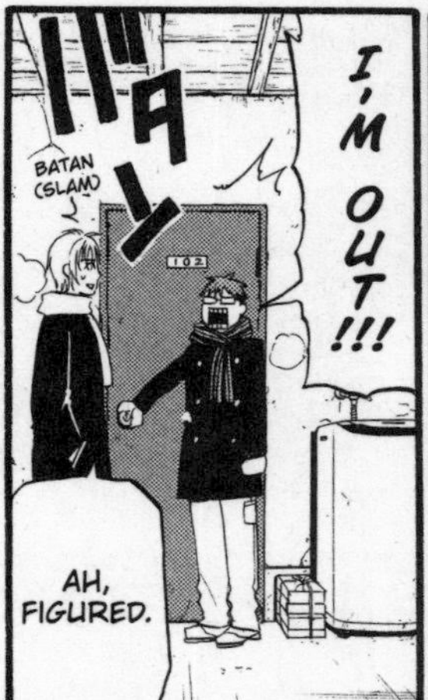
I'M OUT!!!
BATAN (SLAM)
102
AH, FIGURED.

Chapter 92:

Tale of Winter ㉙

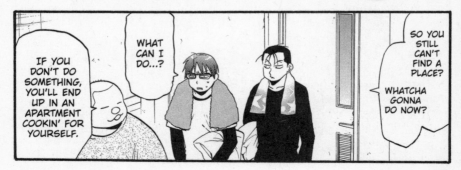

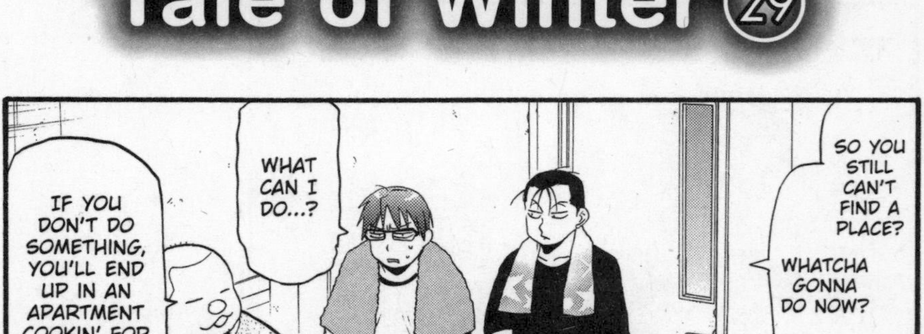
SO YOU STILL CAN'T FIND A PLACE?
WHATCHA GONNA DO NOW?
WHAT CAN I DO...?
IF YOU DON'T DO SOMETHING, YOU'LL END UP IN AN APARTMENT COOKIN' FOR YOURSELF.

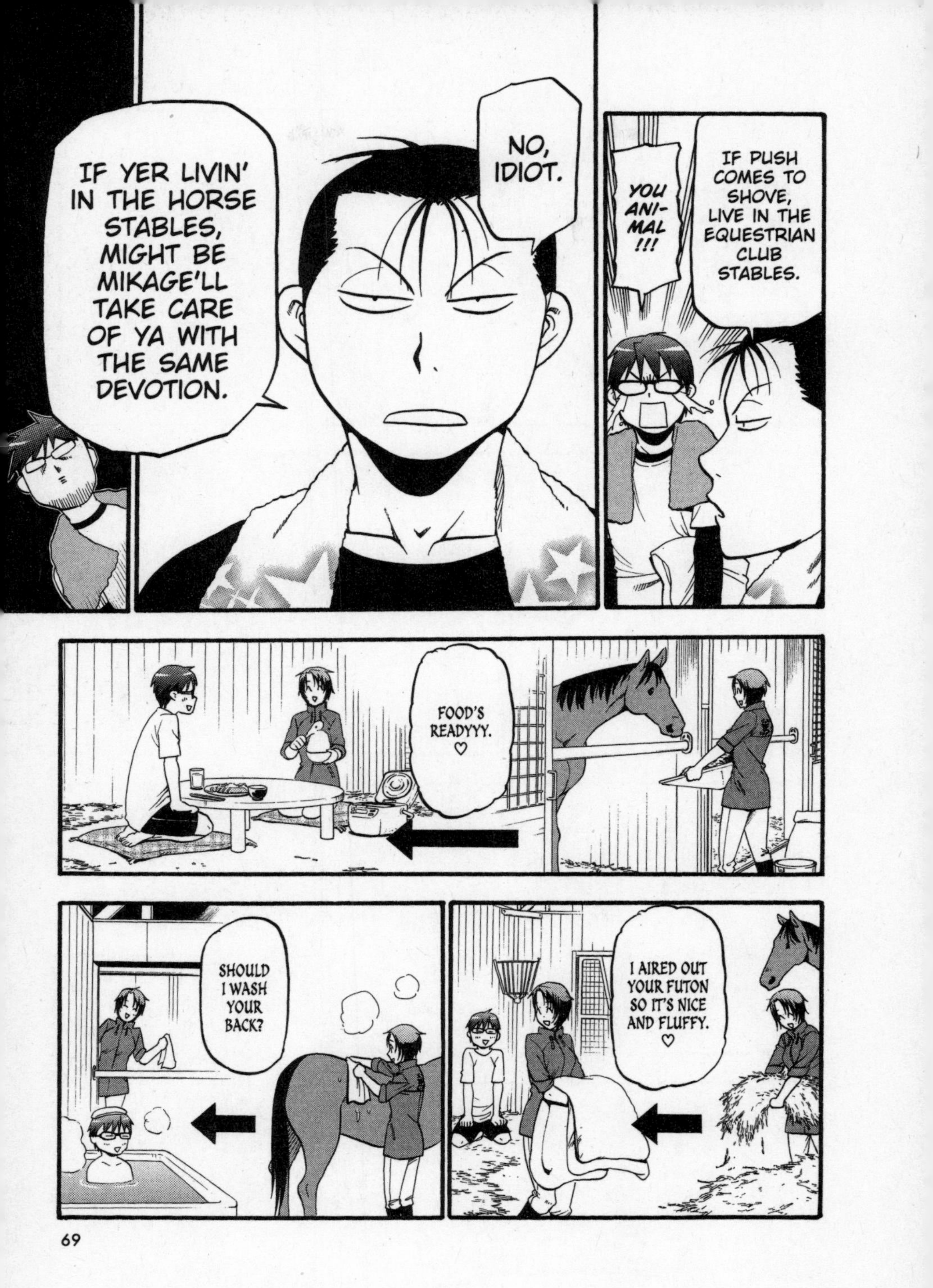
IF PUSH COMES TO SHOVE, LIVE IN THE EQUESTRIAN CLUB STABLES.
YOU ANI-MAL!!!
NO, IDIOT.
IF YER LIVIN' IN THE HORSE STABLES, MIGHT BE MIKAGE'LL TAKE CARE OF YA WITH THE SAME DEVOTION.
FOOD'S READYYY. ♡
I AIRED OUT YOUR FUTON SO IT'S NICE AND FLUFFY. ♡
SHOULD I WASH YOUR BACK?

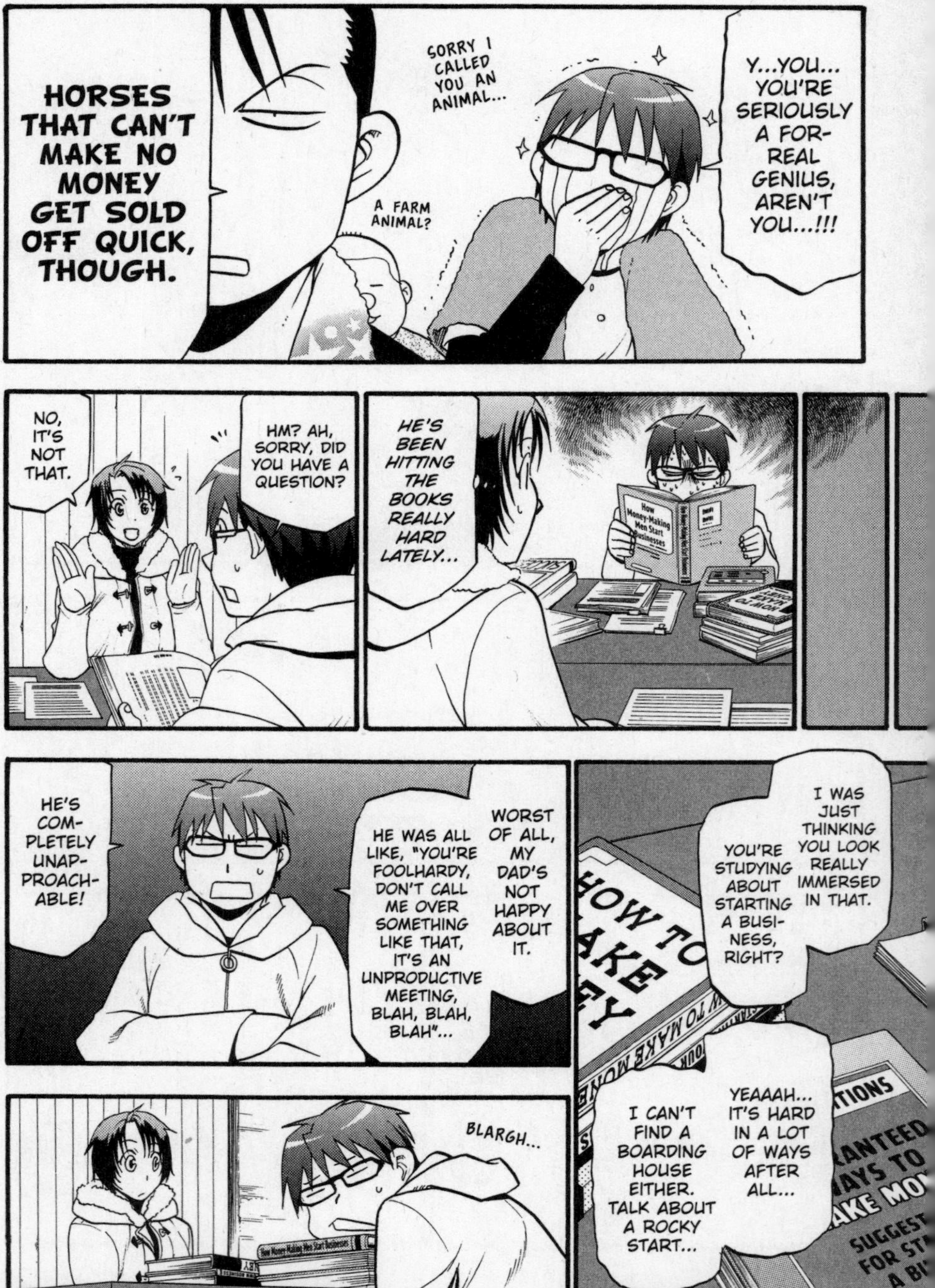
Y...YOU... YOU'RE SERIOUSLY A FOR-REAL GENIUS, AREN'T YOU...!!!
SORRY I CALLED YOU AN ANIMAL...
A FARM ANIMAL?
HORSES THAT CAN'T MAKE NO MONEY GET SOLD OFF QUICK, THOUGH.
HE'S BEEN HITTING THE BOOKS REALLY HARD LATELY...
How Money-Making Men Start Businesses
HM? AH, SORRY, DID YOU HAVE A QUESTION?
NO, IT'S NOT THAT.
I WAS JUST THINKING YOU LOOK REALLY IMMERSED IN THAT.
YOU'RE STUDYING ABOUT STARTING A BUSINESS, RIGHT?
YEAAAH... IT'S HARD IN A LOT OF WAYS AFTER ALL...
I CAN'T FIND A BOARDING HOUSE EITHER. TALK ABOUT A ROCKY START...
THIRD REVISED EDITION
WORST OF ALL, MY DAD'S NOT HAPPY ABOUT IT.
HE WAS ALL LIKE, "YOU'RE FOOLHARDY, DON'T CALL ME OVER SOMETHING LIKE THAT, IT'S AN UNPRODUCTIVE MEETING, BLAH, BLAH, BLAH"...
HE'S COMPLETELY UNAPPROACHABLE!
BLARGH...

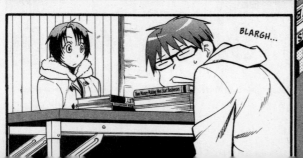

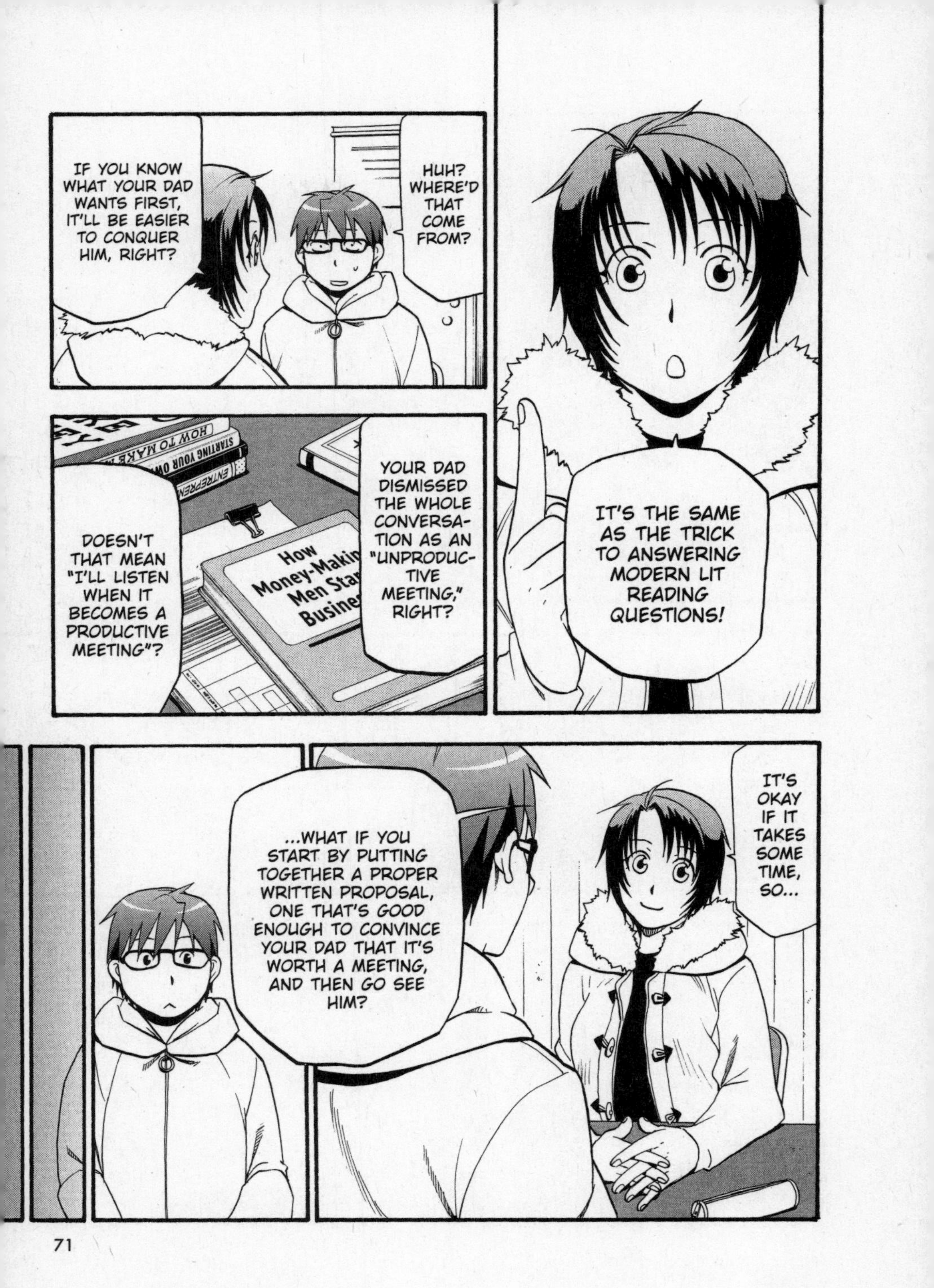
IT'S THE SAME AS THE TRICK TO ANSWERING MODERN LIT READING QUESTIONS!
IF YOU KNOW WHAT YOUR DAD WANTS FIRST, IT'LL BE EASIER TO CONQUER HIM, RIGHT?
HUH? WHERE'D THAT COME FROM?
YOUR DAD DISMISSED THE WHOLE CONVERSA-TION AS AN "UNPRODUC-TIVE MEETING," RIGHT?
DOESN'T THAT MEAN "I'LL LISTEN WHEN IT BECOMES A PRODUCTIVE MEETING"?
IT'S OKAY IF IT TAKES SOME TIME, SO...
...WHAT IF YOU START BY PUTTING TOGETHER A PROPER WRITTEN PROPOSAL, ONE THAT'S GOOD ENOUGH TO CONVINCE YOUR DAD THAT IT'S WORTH A MEETING, AND THEN GO SEE HIM?

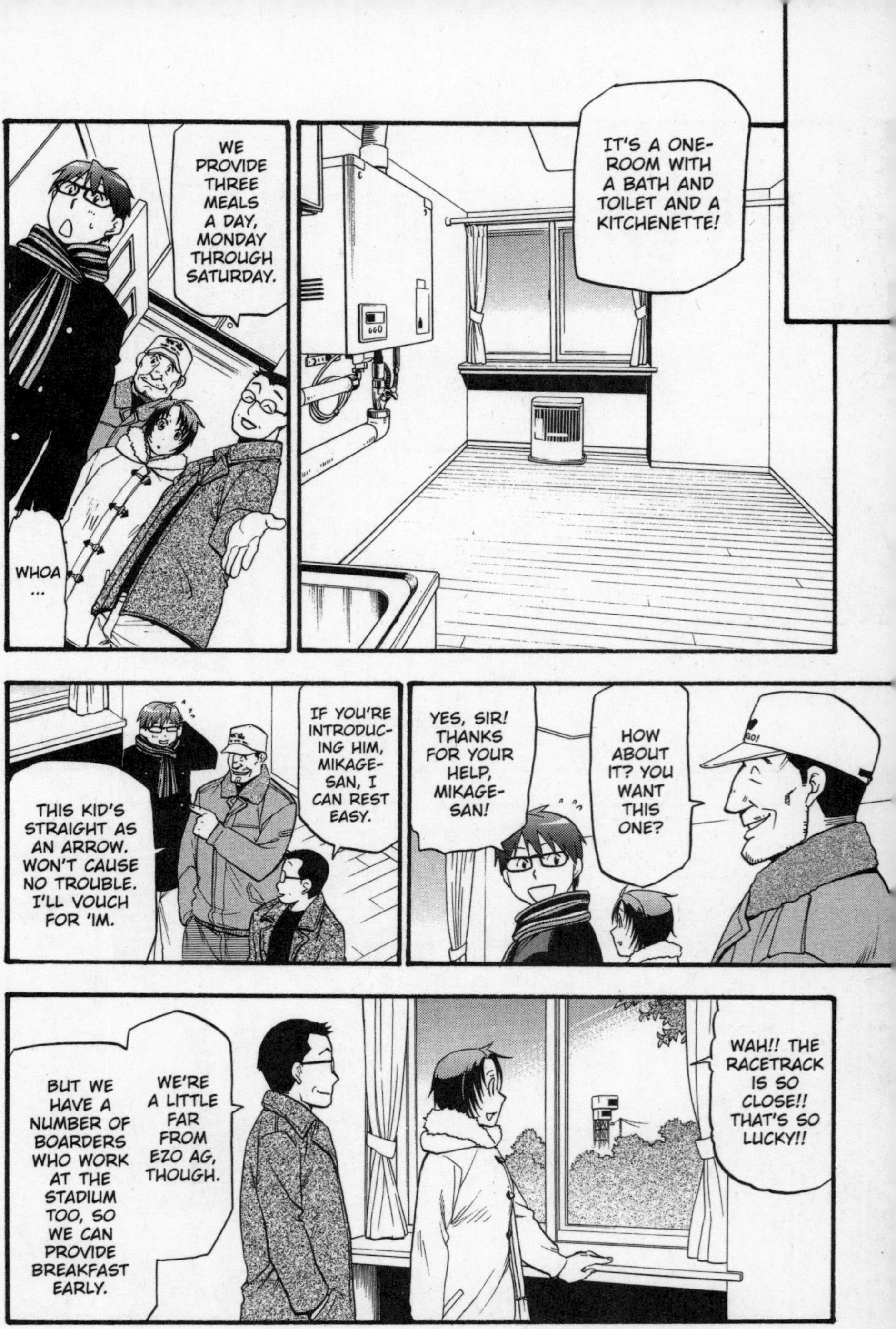
IT'S A ONE-ROOM WITH A BATH AND TOILET AND A KITCHENETTE!
WE PROVIDE THREE MEALS A DAY, MONDAY THROUGH SATURDAY.
WHOA ...
HOW ABOUT IT? YOU WANT THIS ONE?
YES, SIR! THANKS FOR YOUR HELP, MIKAGE-SAN!
IF YOU'RE INTRODUCING HIM, MIKAGE-SAN, I CAN REST EASY.
THIS KID'S STRAIGHT AS AN ARROW. WON'T CAUSE NO TROUBLE. I'LL VOUCH FOR 'IM.
WAH!! THE RACETRACK IS SO CLOSE!! THAT'S SO LUCKY!!
WE'RE A LITTLE FAR FROM EZO AG, THOUGH.
BUT WE HAVE A NUMBER OF BOARDERS WHO WORK AT THE STADIUM TOO, SO WE CAN PROVIDE BREAKFAST EARLY.

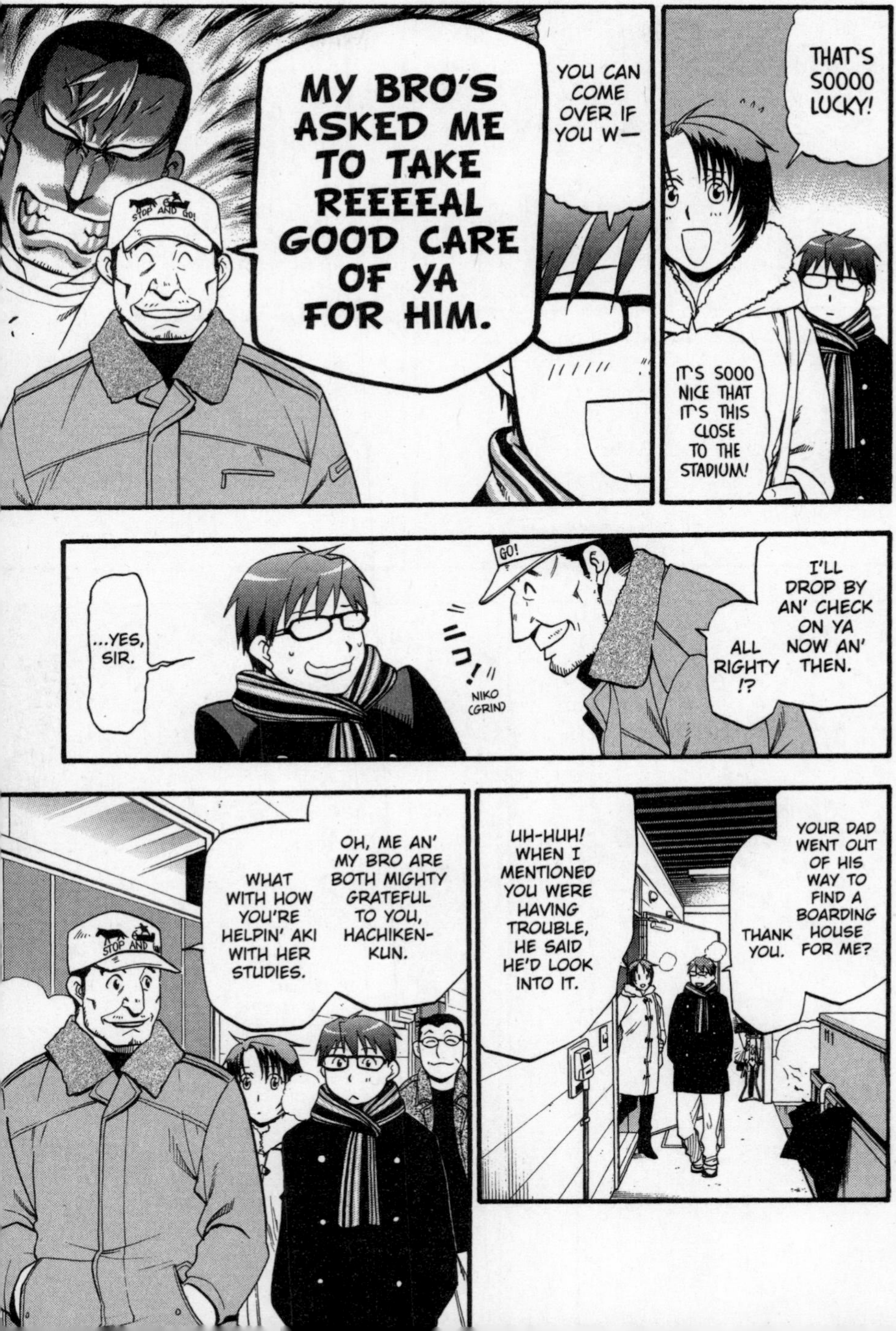
THAT'S SOOOO LUCKY!
IT'S SOOO NICE THAT IT'S THIS CLOSE TO THE STADIUM!
YOU CAN COME OVER IF YOU W—
MY BRO'S ASKED ME TO TAKE REEEEAL GOOD CARE OF YA FOR HIM.
STOP AND GO!
I'LL DROP BY AN' CHECK ON YA NOW AN' THEN.
ALL RIGHTY !?
NIKO (GRIN)
...YES, SIR.
YOUR DAD WENT OUT OF HIS WAY TO FIND A BOARDING HOUSE FOR ME?
THANK YOU.
UH-HUH! WHEN I MENTIONED YOU WERE HAVING TROUBLE, HE SAID HE'D LOOK INTO IT.
OH, ME AN' MY BRO ARE BOTH MIGHTY GRATEFUL TO YOU, HACHIKEN-KUN.
WHAT WITH HOW YOU'RE HELPIN' AKI WITH HER STUDIES.

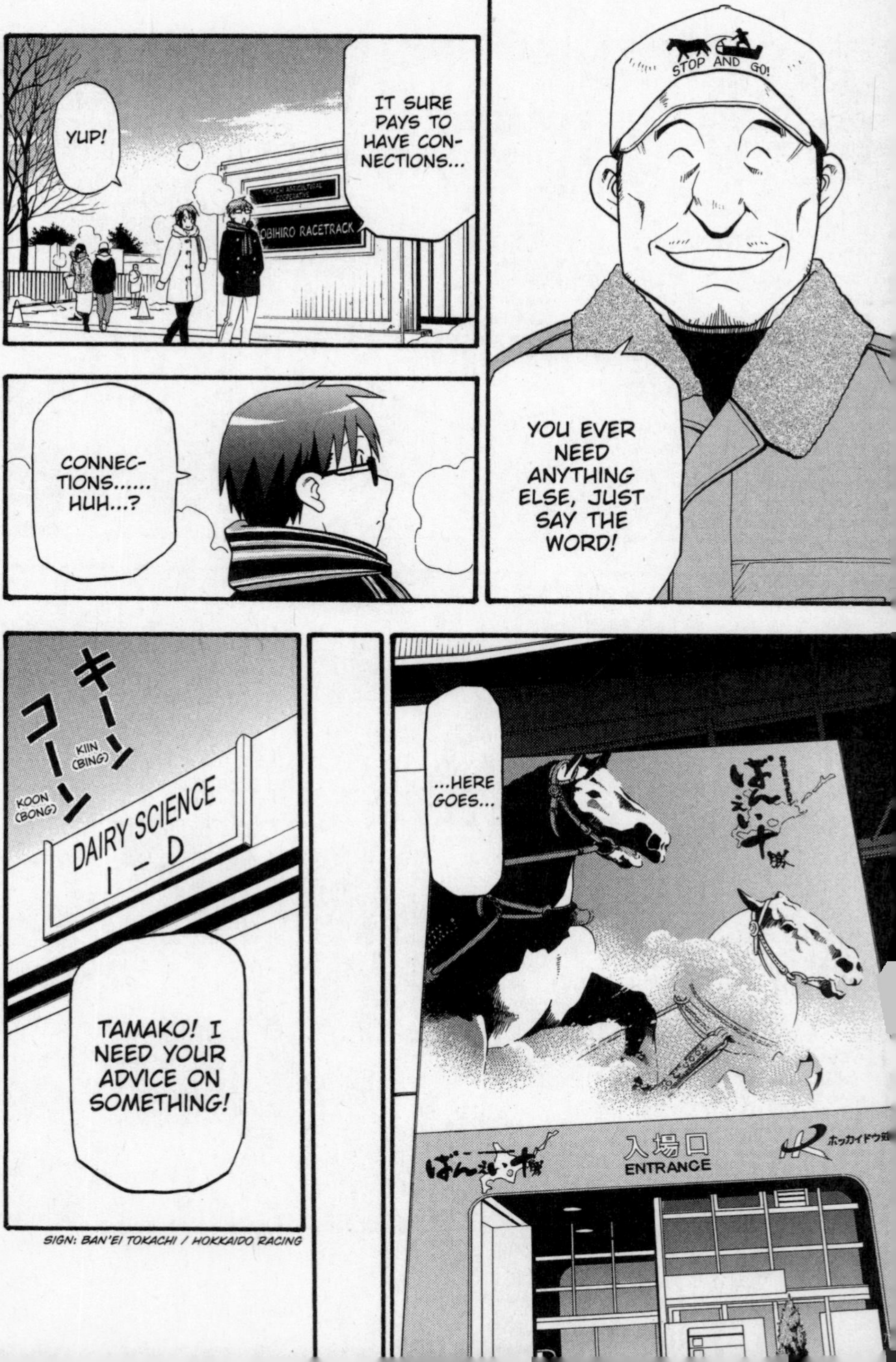
STOP AND GO!
YOU EVER NEED ANYTHING ELSE, JUST SAY THE WORD!
OBIHIRO RACETRACK
IT SURE PAYS TO HAVE CON- NECTIONS...
YUP!
CONNEC- TIONS...... HUH...?
入場口
ENTRANCE
...HERE GOES...
キーンコーン
KIIN (BING)
KOON (BONG)
DAIRY SCIENCE
1 - D
TAMAKO! I NEED YOUR ADVICE ON SOMETHING!
SIGN: BAN'EI TOKACHI / HOKKAIDO RACING

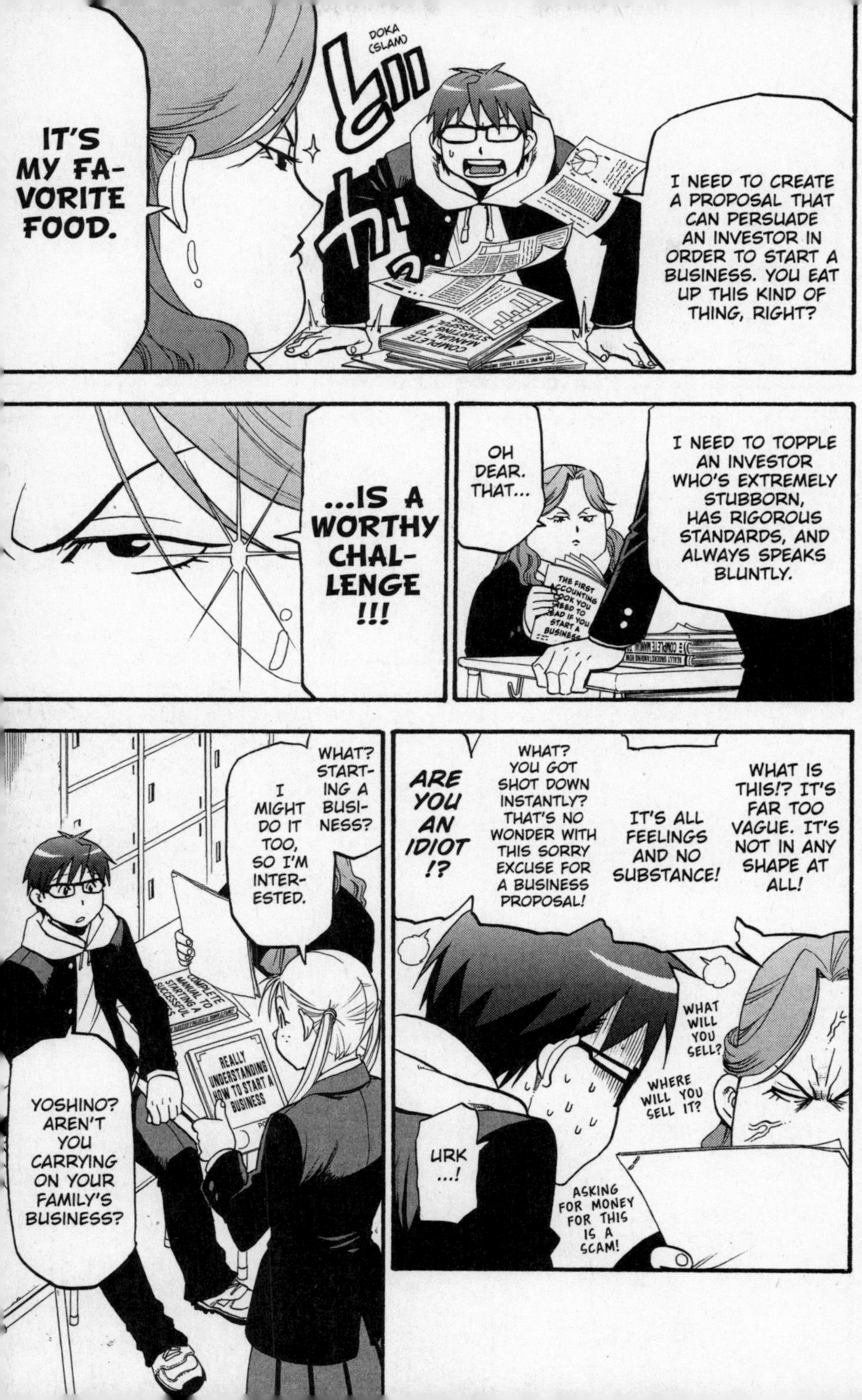
DOKA (SLAM)
I NEED TO CREATE A PROPOSAL THAT CAN PERSUADE AN INVESTOR IN ORDER TO START A BUSINESS. YOU EAT UP THIS KIND OF THING, RIGHT?
IT'S MY FA-VORITE FOOD.
I NEED TO TOPPLE AN INVESTOR WHO'S EXTREMELY STUBBORN, HAS RIGOROUS STANDARDS, AND ALWAYS SPEAKS BLUNTLY.
OH DEAR. THAT...
...IS A WORTHY CHAL-LENGE!!!
WHAT IS THIS!? IT'S FAR TOO VAGUE. IT'S NOT IN ANY SHAPE AT ALL!
IT'S ALL FEELINGS AND NO SUBSTANCE!
WHAT? YOU GOT SHOT DOWN INSTANTLY? THAT'S NO WONDER WITH THIS SORRY EXCUSE FOR A BUSINESS PROPOSAL!
ARE YOU AN IDIOT!?
WHAT WILL YOU SELL?
WHERE WILL YOU SELL IT?
URK ...!
ASKING FOR MONEY FOR THIS IS A SCAM!
WHAT? STARTING A BUSI-NESS?
I MIGHT DO IT TOO, SO I'M INTER-ESTED.
REALLY UNDERSTANDING HOW TO START A BUSINESS
YOSHINO? AREN'T YOU CARRYING ON YOUR FAMILY'S BUSINESS?

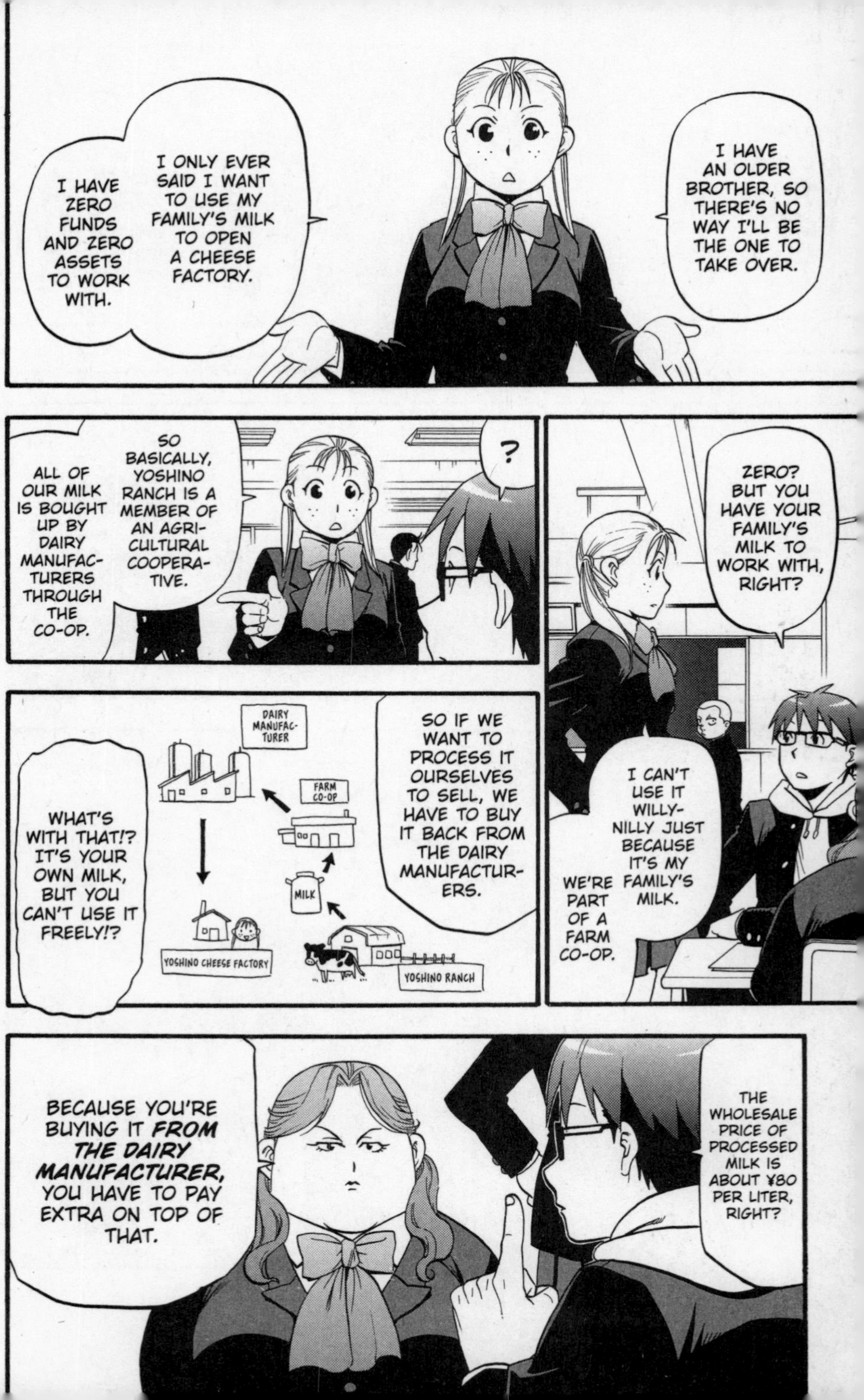
I HAVE AN OLDER BROTHER, SO THERE'S NO WAY I'LL BE THE ONE TO TAKE OVER.
I ONLY EVER SAID I WANT TO USE MY FAMILY'S MILK TO OPEN A CHEESE FACTORY.
I HAVE ZERO FUNDS AND ZERO ASSETS TO WORK WITH.
ZERO? BUT YOU HAVE YOUR FAMILY'S MILK TO WORK WITH, RIGHT?
I CAN'T USE IT WILLY-NILLY JUST BECAUSE IT'S MY FAMILY'S MILK.
WE'RE PART OF A FARM CO-OP.
?
SO BASICALLY, YOSHINO RANCH IS A MEMBER OF AN AGRICULTURAL COOPERATIVE.
ALL OF OUR MILK IS BOUGHT UP BY DAIRY MANUFACTURERS THROUGH THE CO-OP.
SO IF WE WANT TO PROCESS IT OURSELVES TO SELL, WE HAVE TO BUY IT BACK FROM THE DAIRY MANUFACTURERS.
DAIRY MANUFACTURER
FARM CO-OP
MILK
YOSHINO RANCH
YOSHINO CHEESE FACTORY
WHAT'S WITH THAT!? IT'S YOUR OWN MILK, BUT YOU CAN'T USE IT FREELY!?
THE WHOLESALE PRICE OF PROCESSED MILK IS ABOUT ¥80 PER LITER, RIGHT?
BECAUSE YOU'RE BUYING IT *FROM THE DAIRY MANUFACTURER*, YOU HAVE TO PAY EXTRA ON TOP OF THAT.

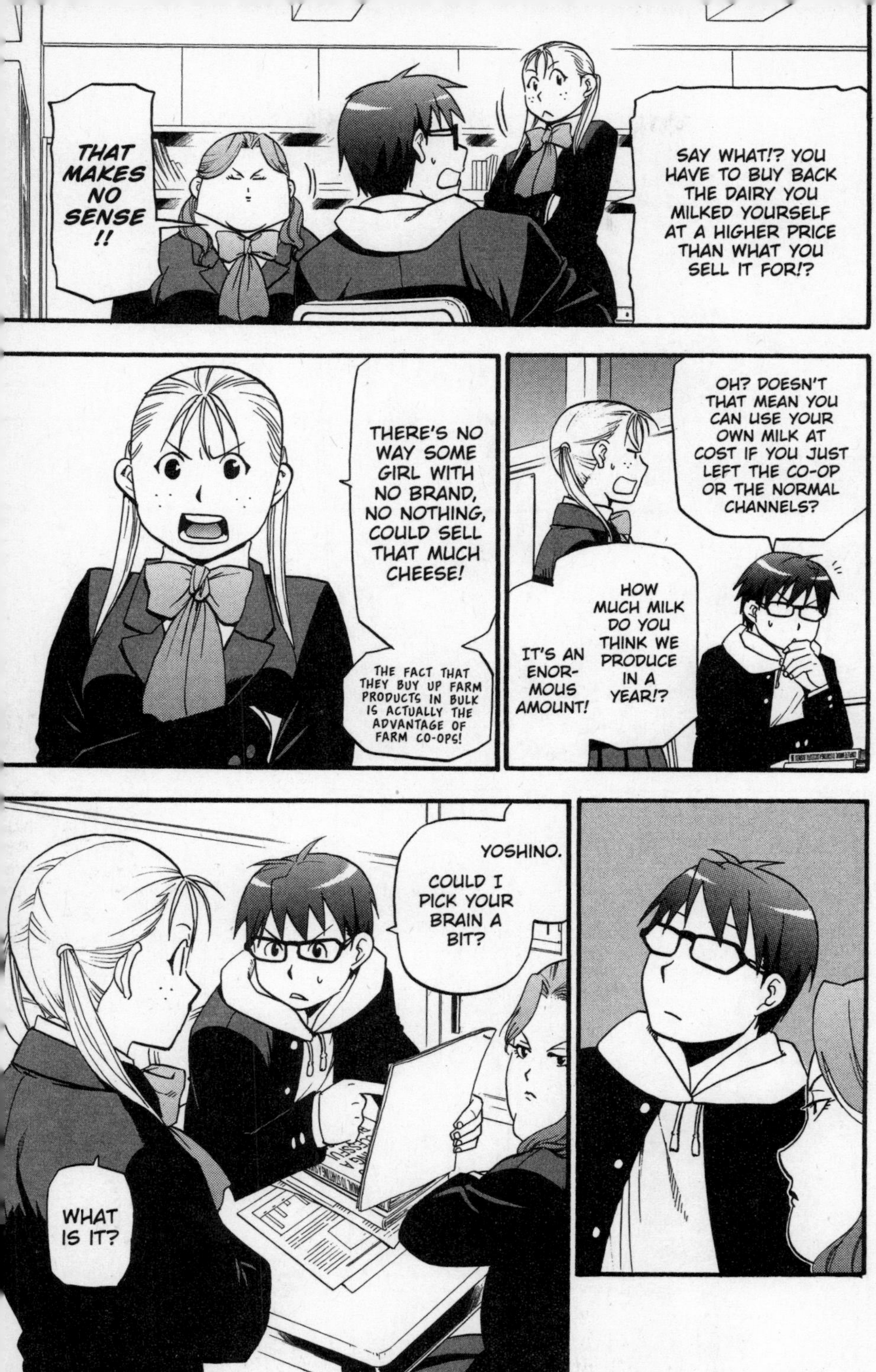
SAY WHAT!? YOU HAVE TO BUY BACK THE DAIRY YOU MILKED YOURSELF AT A HIGHER PRICE THAN WHAT YOU SELL IT FOR!?
THAT MAKES NO SENSE !!
OH? DOESN'T THAT MEAN YOU CAN USE YOUR OWN MILK AT COST IF YOU JUST LEFT THE CO-OP OR THE NORMAL CHANNELS?
HOW MUCH MILK DO YOU THINK WE PRODUCE IN A YEAR!?
IT'S AN ENOR-MOUS AMOUNT!
THERE'S NO WAY SOME GIRL WITH NO BRAND, NO NOTHING, COULD SELL THAT MUCH CHEESE!
THE FACT THAT THEY BUY UP FARM PRODUCTS IN BULK IS ACTUALLY THE ADVANTAGE OF FARM CO-OPS!
YOSHINO.
COULD I PICK YOUR BRAIN A BIT?
WHAT IS IT?

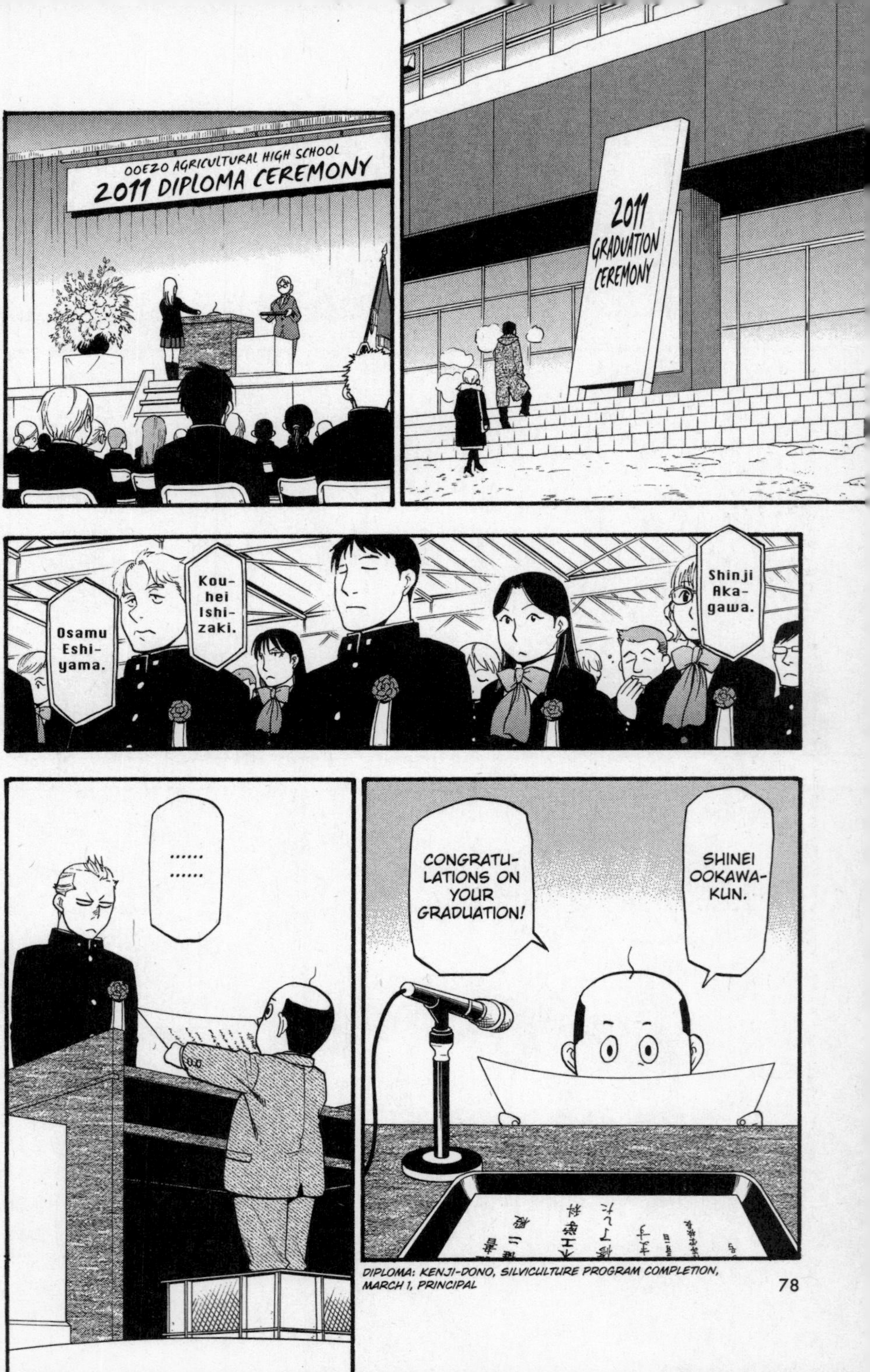
2011 GRADUATION CEREMONY
OOEZO AGRICULTURAL HIGH SCHOOL
2011 DIPLOMA CEREMONY
Shinji Akagawa.
Kouhei Ishizaki.
Osamu Eshiyama.
SHINEI OOKAWA-KUN.
CONGRATULATIONS ON YOUR GRADUATION!
......
......

DIPLOMA: KENJI-DONO, SILVICULTURE PROGRAM COMPLETION, MARCH 1, PRINCIPAL

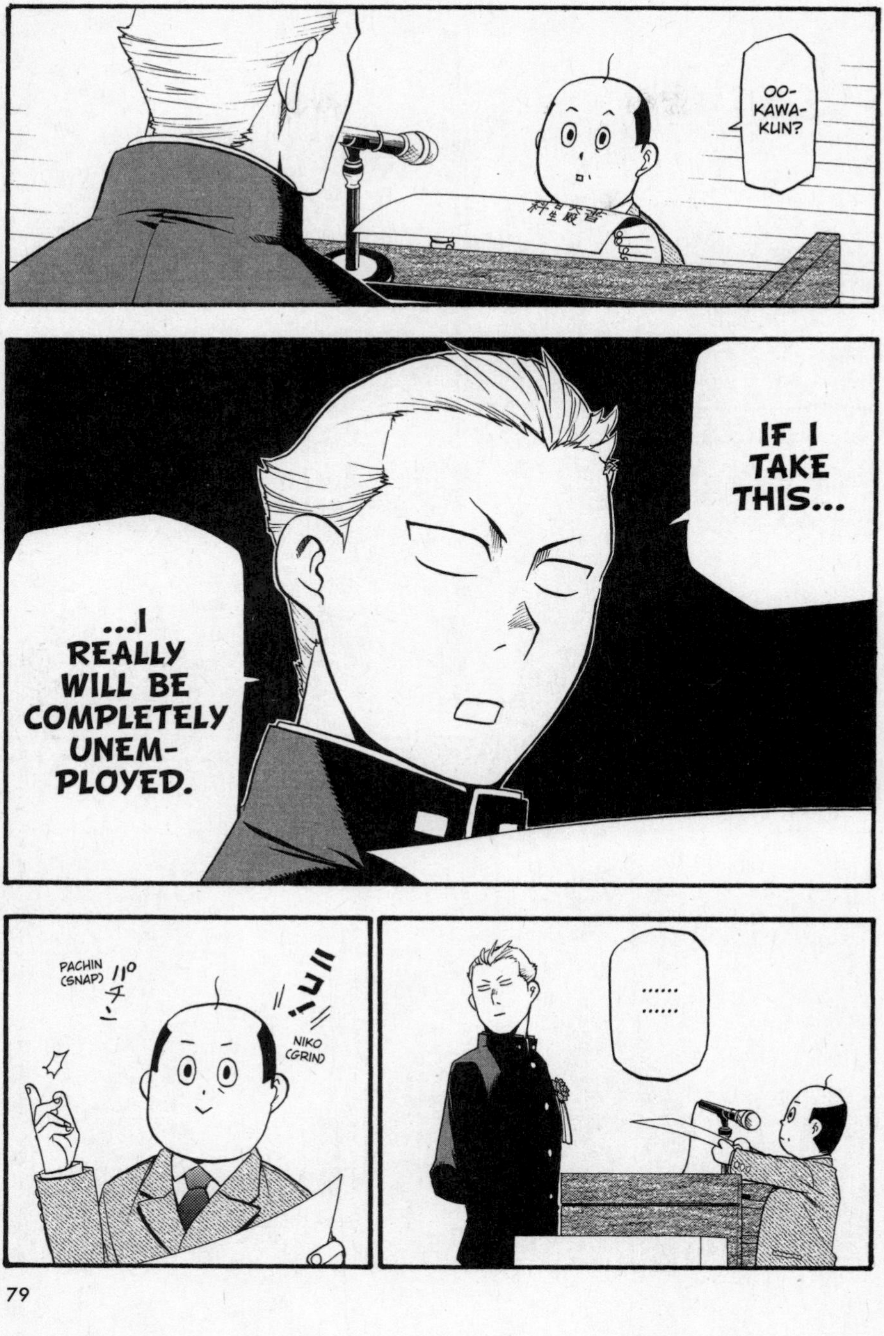
OO-KAWA-KUN?
IF I TAKE THIS...
...I REALLY WILL BE COMPLETELY UNEMPLOYED.
......
......
PACHIN (SNAP)
パチン
NIKO (GRIN
ニコッ!

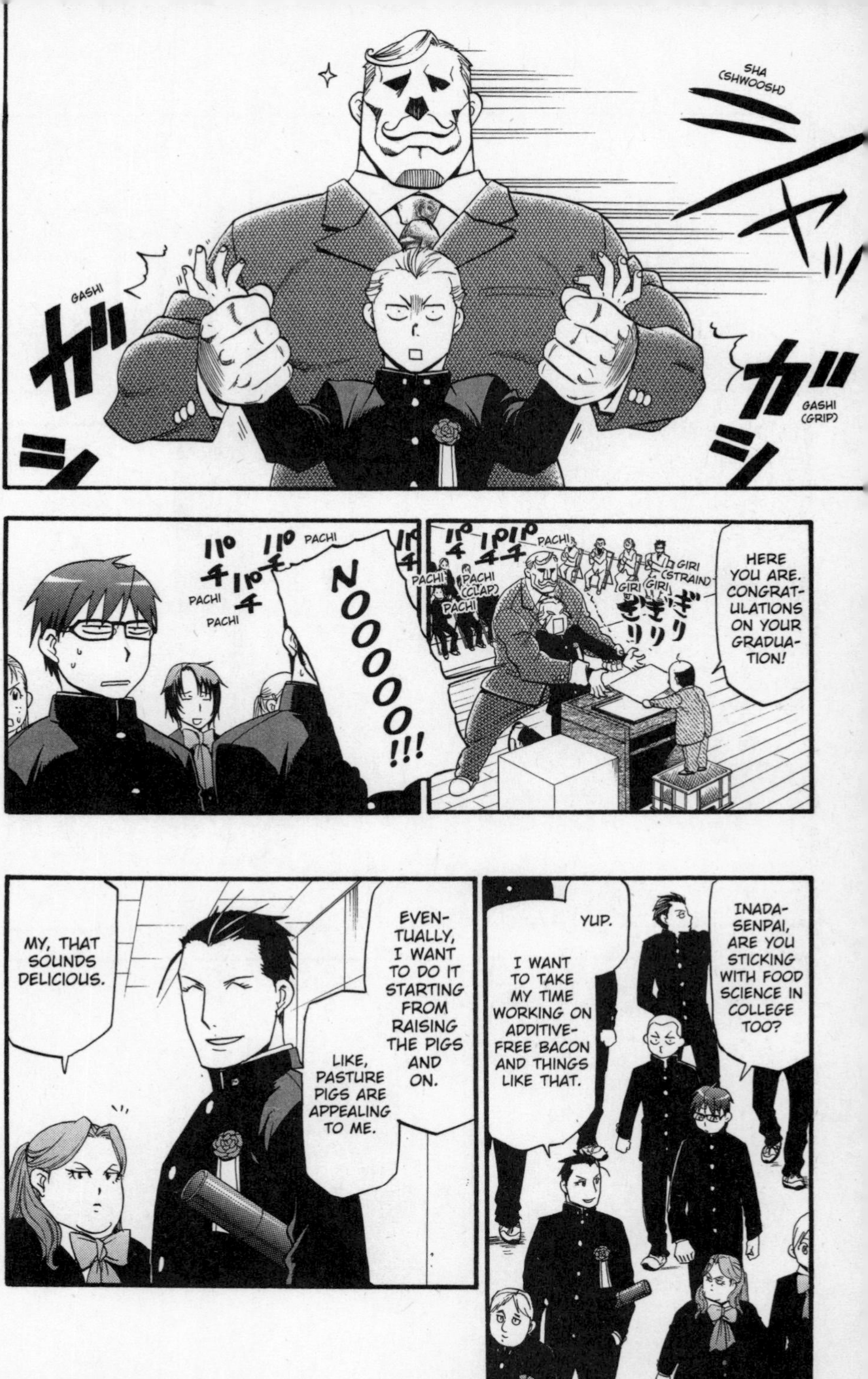

シャッ
SHA (SHWOOSH)
ガシ
GASHI (GRIP)
ガシ
GASHI
HERE YOU ARE. CONGRATULATIONS ON YOUR GRADUATION!
ぎりぎり
GIRI (STRAIN)
GIRI
PACHI (CLAP)
PACHI
PACHI
NOOOOOO!!!
PACHI
PACHI
PACHI
INADA-SENPAI, ARE YOU STICKING WITH FOOD SCIENCE IN COLLEGE TOO?
YUP.
I WANT TO TAKE MY TIME WORKING ON ADDITIVE-FREE BACON AND THINGS LIKE THAT.
EVENTUALLY, I WANT TO DO IT STARTING FROM RAISING THE PIGS AND ON.
LIKE, PASTURE PIGS ARE APPEALING TO ME.
MY, THAT SOUNDS DELICIOUS.

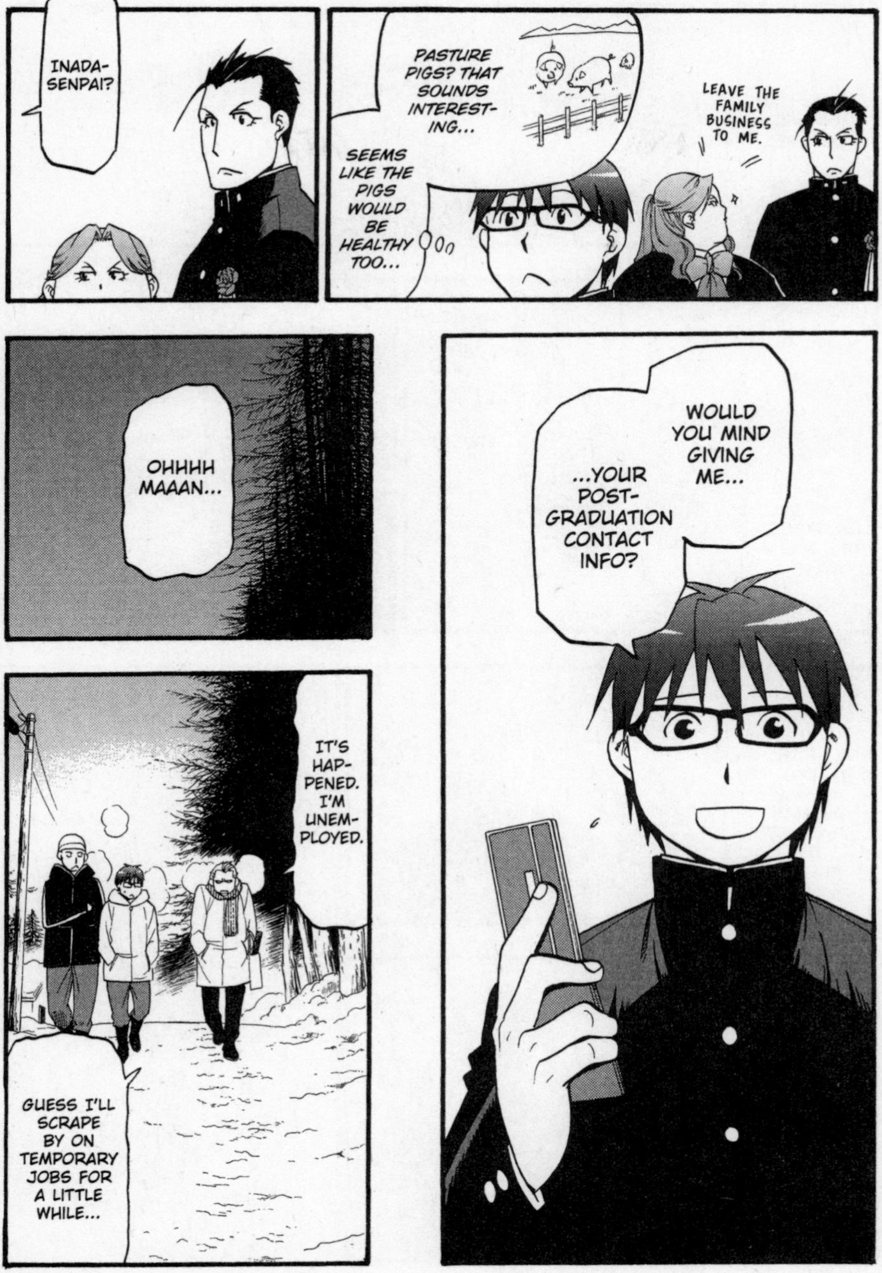
LEAVE THE FAMILY BUSINESS TO ME.
PASTURE PIGS? THAT SOUNDS INTERESTING...
SEEMS LIKE THE PIGS WOULD BE HEALTHY TOO...
INADA-SENPAI?
WOULD YOU MIND GIVING ME...
...YOUR POST-GRADUATION CONTACT INFO?
OHHHH MAAAN...
IT'S HAPPENED. I'M UNEMPLOYED.
GUESS I'LL SCRAPE BY ON TEMPORARY JOBS FOR A LITTLE WHILE...

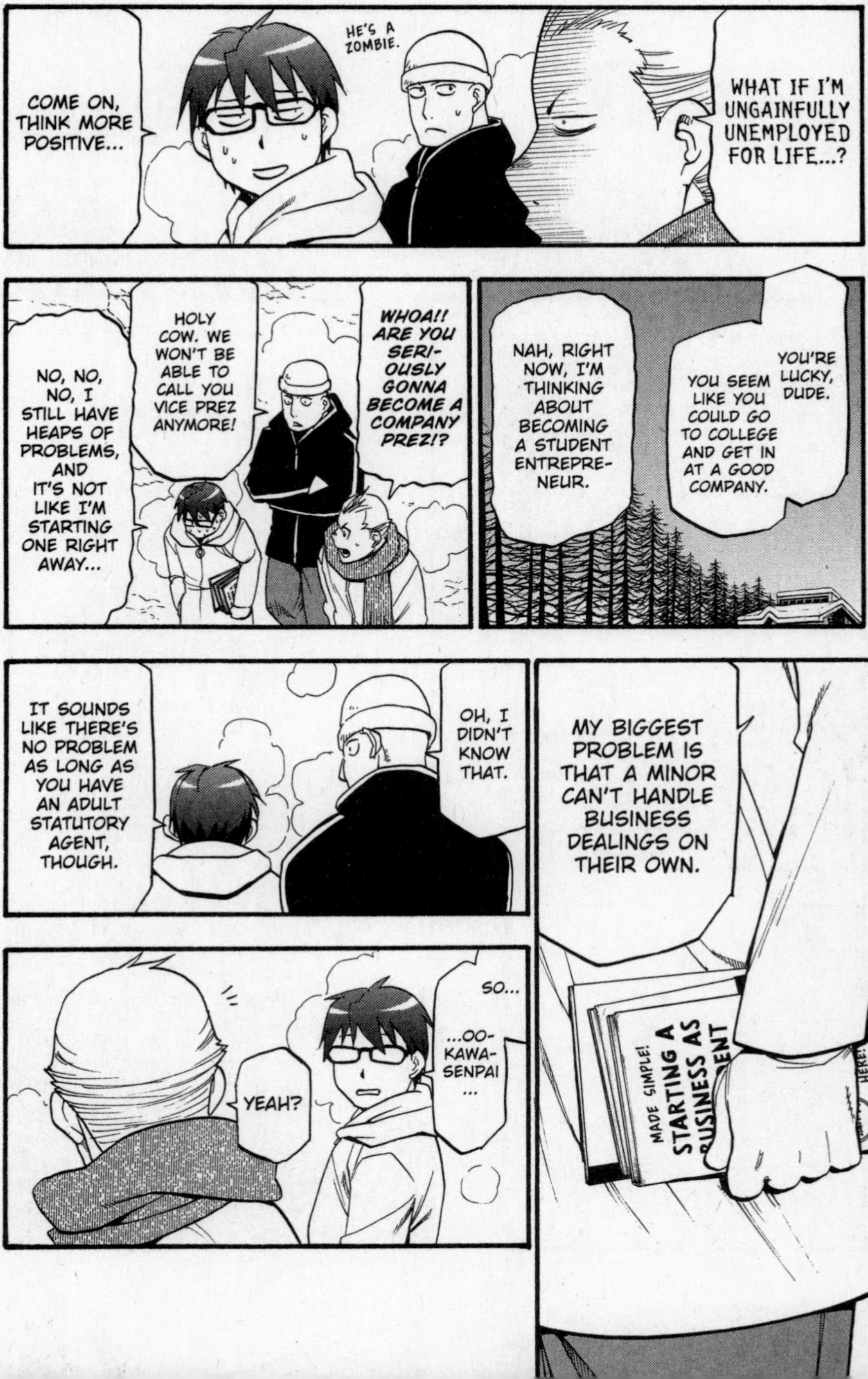
WHAT IF I'M UNGAINFULLY UNEMPLOYED FOR LIFE...?
HE'S A ZOMBIE.
COME ON, THINK MORE POSITIVE...
YOU'RE LUCKY, DUDE.
YOU SEEM LIKE YOU COULD GO TO COLLEGE AND GET IN AT A GOOD COMPANY.
NAH, RIGHT NOW, I'M THINKING ABOUT BECOMING A STUDENT ENTREPRENEUR.
WHOA!! ARE YOU SERIOUSLY GONNA BECOME A COMPANY PREZ!?
HOLY COW. WE WON'T BE ABLE TO CALL YOU VICE PREZ ANYMORE!
NO, NO, NO, I STILL HAVE HEAPS OF PROBLEMS, AND IT'S NOT LIKE I'M STARTING ONE RIGHT AWAY...
MY BIGGEST PROBLEM IS THAT A MINOR CAN'T HANDLE BUSINESS DEALINGS ON THEIR OWN.
OH, I DIDN'T KNOW THAT.
IT SOUNDS LIKE THERE'S NO PROBLEM AS LONG AS YOU HAVE AN ADULT STATUTORY AGENT, THOUGH.
SO...
...OO-KAWA-SENPAI...
YEAH?

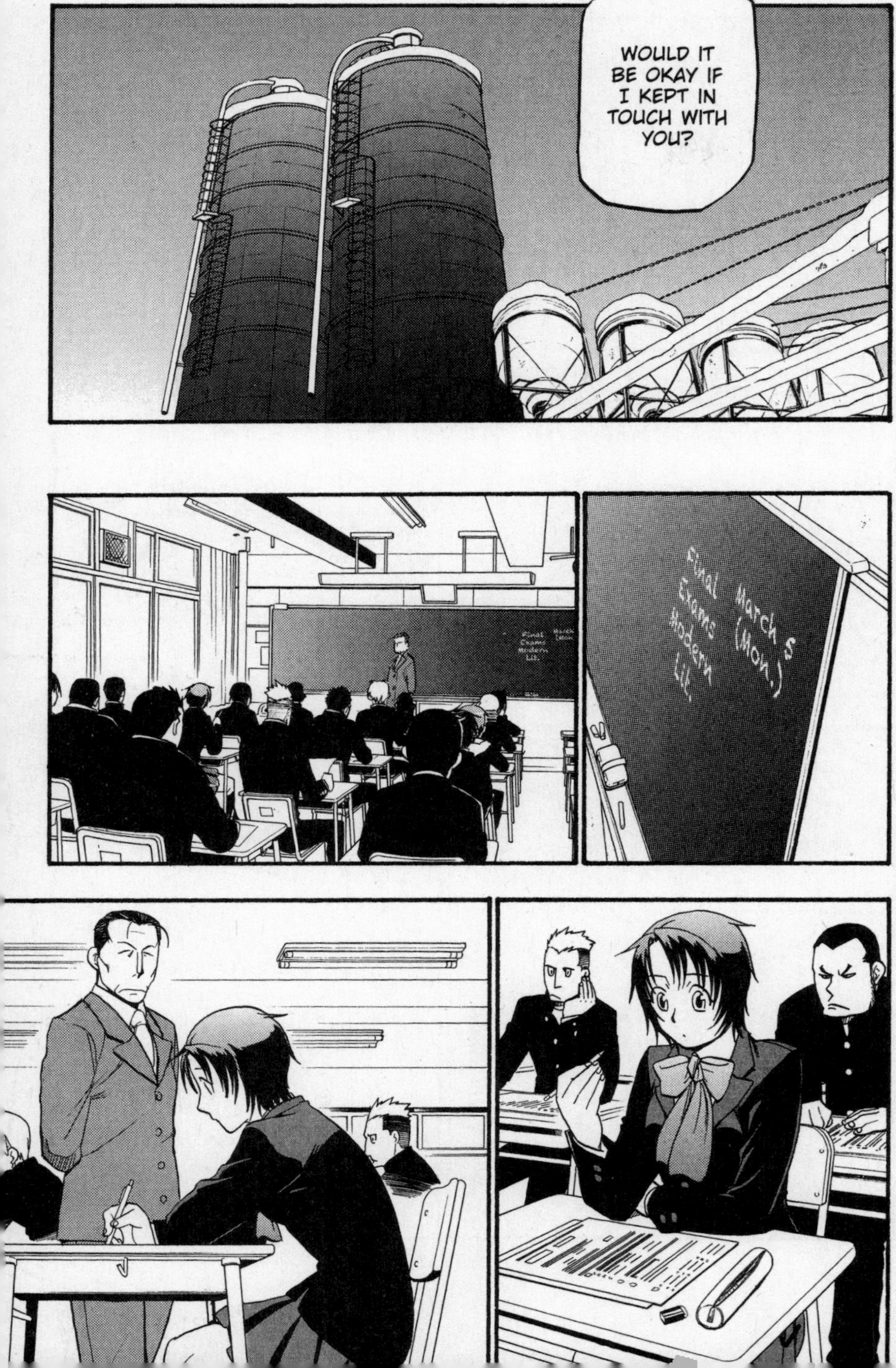
WOULD IT BE OKAY IF I KEPT IN TOUCH WITH YOU?
Final Exams Modern Lit.
March 5 (Mon.)

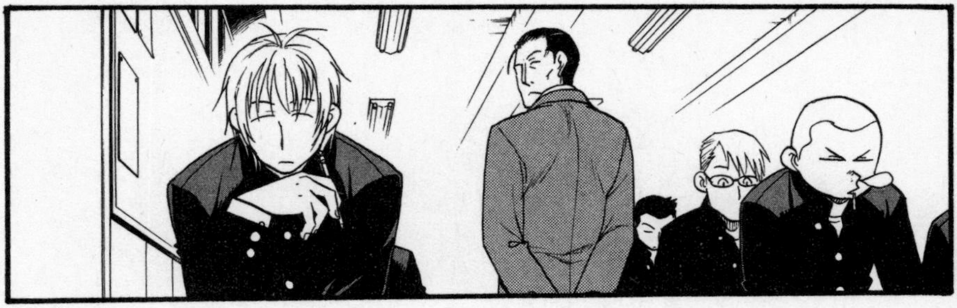

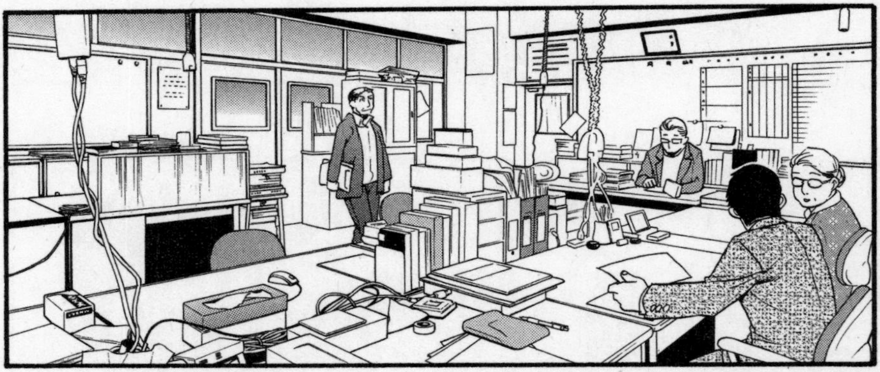

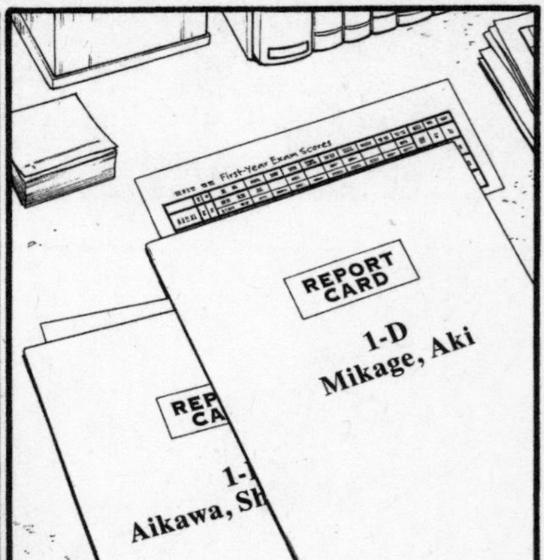
First-Year Exam Scores
REPORT CARD
1-D
Mikage, Aki

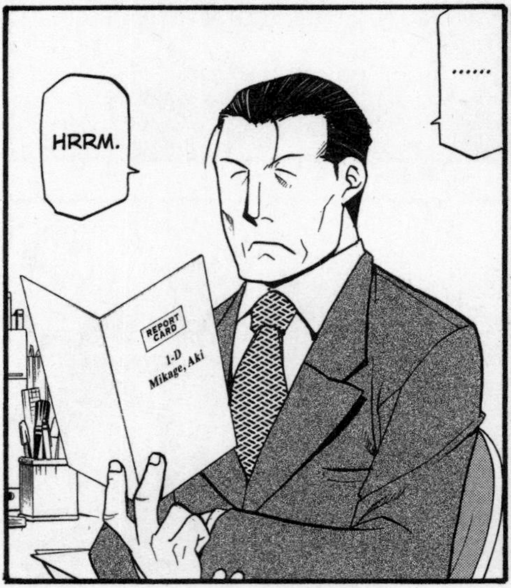
……
HRRM.
REPORT CARD
1-D
Mikage, Aki

Silver Spoon

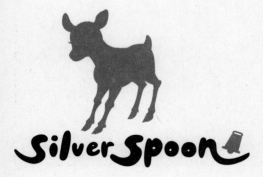

GOUSHI MIKAGE

AKI'S DAD

Chapter 93:

Tale of Winter ㉚

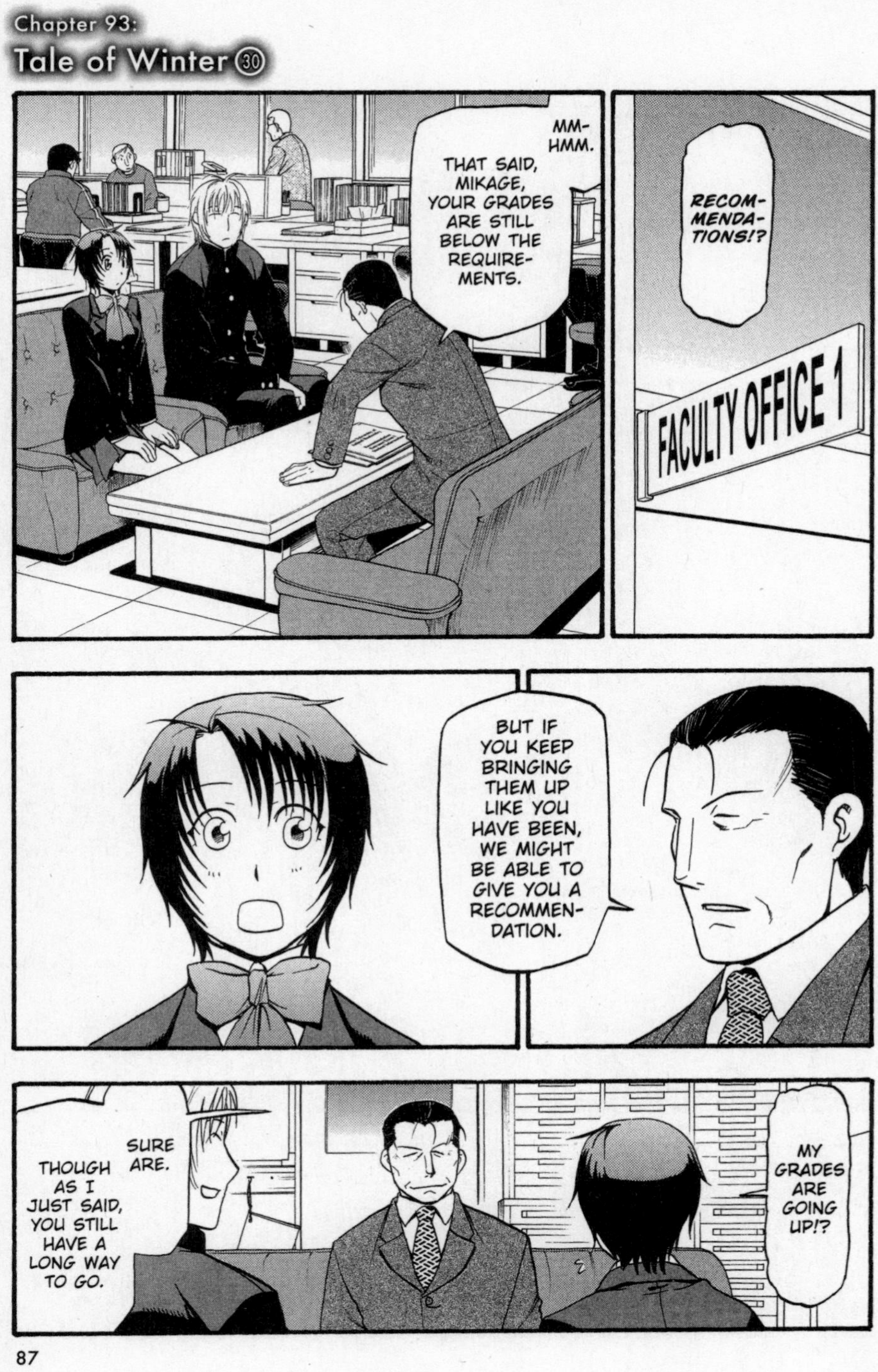

RECOMMENDATIONS!?
FACULTY OFFICE 1
MM-HMM.
THAT SAID, MIKAGE, YOUR GRADES ARE STILL BELOW THE REQUIREMENTS.
BUT IF YOU KEEP BRINGING THEM UP LIKE YOU HAVE BEEN, WE MIGHT BE ABLE TO GIVE YOU A RECOMMENDATION.
MY GRADES ARE GOING UP!?
SURE ARE.
THOUGH AS I JUST SAID, YOU STILL HAVE A LONG WAY TO GO.

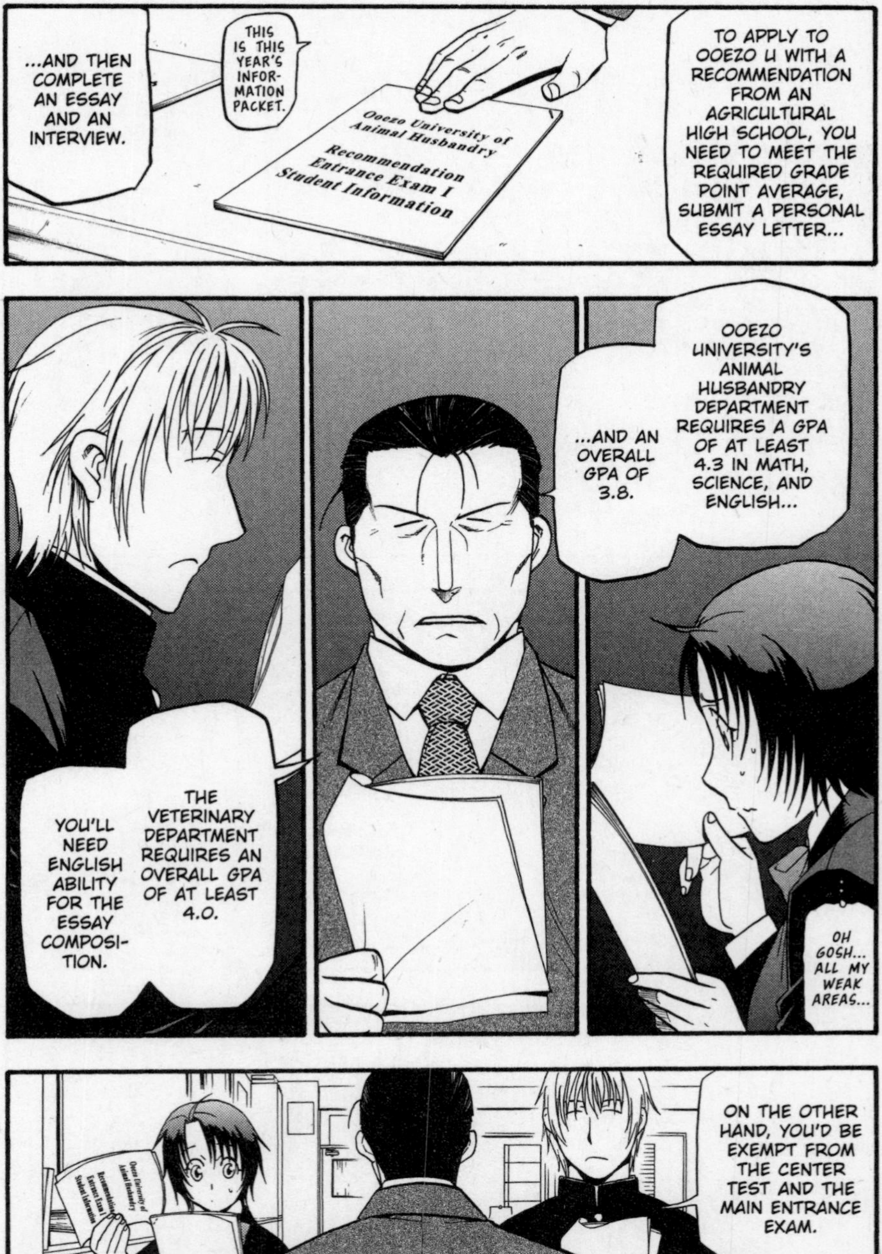
TO APPLY TO OOEZO U WITH A RECOMMENDATION FROM AN AGRICULTURAL HIGH SCHOOL, YOU NEED TO MEET THE REQUIRED GRADE POINT AVERAGE, SUBMIT A PERSONAL ESSAY LETTER...
THIS IS THIS YEAR'S INFORMATION PACKET.
Ooezo University of Animal Husbandry
Recommendation Entrance Exam I Student Information
...AND THEN COMPLETE AN ESSAY AND AN INTERVIEW.
OOEZO UNIVERSITY'S ANIMAL HUSBANDRY DEPARTMENT REQUIRES A GPA OF AT LEAST 4.3 IN MATH, SCIENCE, AND ENGLISH...
...AND AN OVERALL GPA OF 3.8.
OH GOSH... ALL MY WEAK AREAS...
THE VETERINARY DEPARTMENT REQUIRES AN OVERALL GPA OF AT LEAST 4.0.
YOU'LL NEED ENGLISH ABILITY FOR THE ESSAY COMPOSITION.
ON THE OTHER HAND, YOU'D BE EXEMPT FROM THE CENTER TEST AND THE MAIN ENTRANCE EXAM.

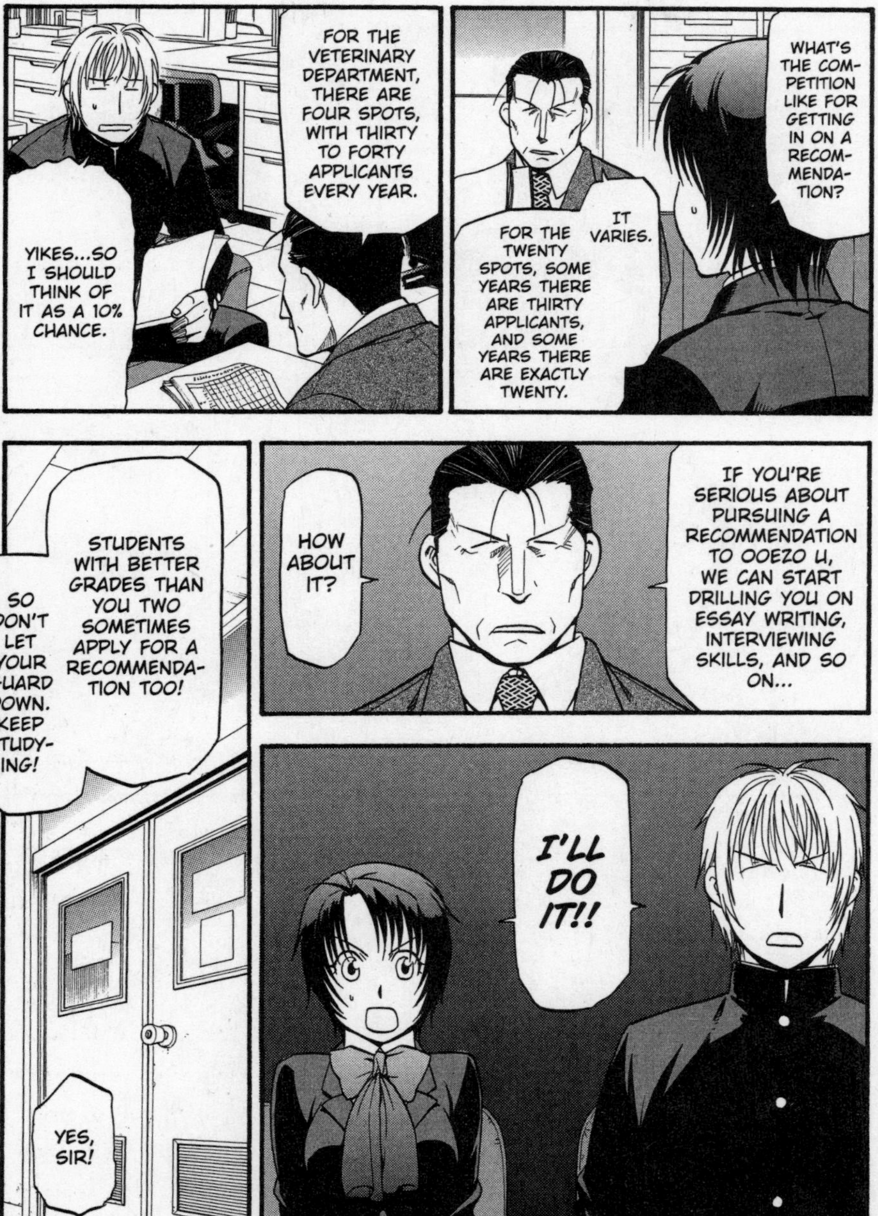
WHAT'S THE COMPETITION LIKE FOR GETTING IN ON A RECOMMENDATION?
IT VARIES.
FOR THE TWENTY SPOTS, SOME YEARS THERE ARE THIRTY APPLICANTS, AND SOME YEARS THERE ARE EXACTLY TWENTY.
FOR THE VETERINARY DEPARTMENT, THERE ARE FOUR SPOTS, WITH THIRTY TO FORTY APPLICANTS EVERY YEAR.
YIKES...SO I SHOULD THINK OF IT AS A 10% CHANCE.
IF YOU'RE SERIOUS ABOUT PURSUING A RECOMMENDATION TO OOEZO U, WE CAN START DRILLING YOU ON ESSAY WRITING, INTERVIEWING SKILLS, AND SO ON...
HOW ABOUT IT?
I'LL DO IT!!
STUDENTS WITH BETTER GRADES THAN YOU TWO SOMETIMES APPLY FOR A RECOMMENDATION TOO!
SO DON'T LET YOUR GUARD DOWN. KEEP STUDYING!
YES, SIR!

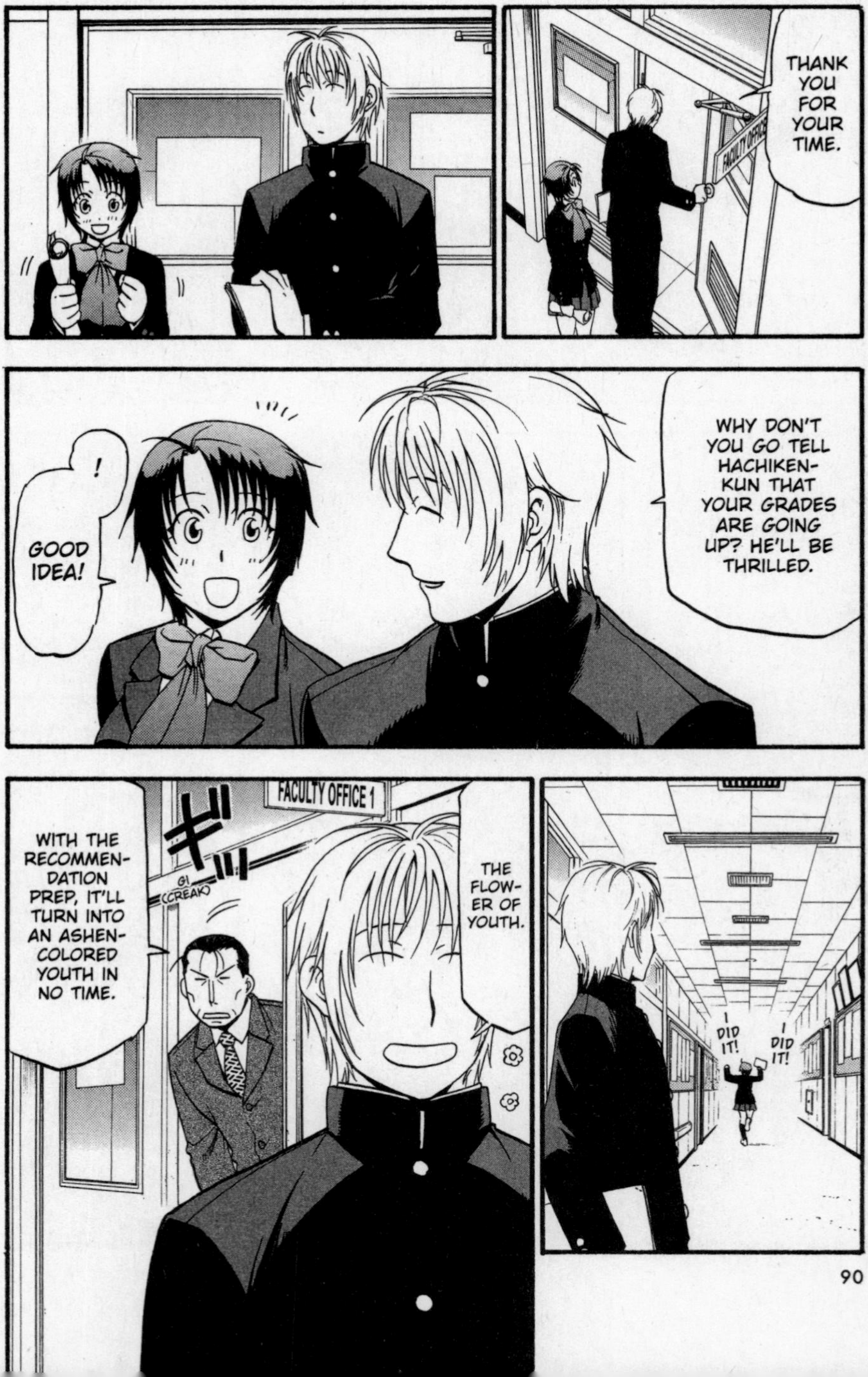
THANK YOU FOR YOUR TIME.
FACULTY OFFICE
WHY DON'T YOU GO TELL HACHIKEN-KUN THAT YOUR GRADES ARE GOING UP? HE'LL BE THRILLED.
!
GOOD IDEA!
I DID IT!
I DID IT!
THE FLOWER OF YOUTH.
FACULTY OFFICE 1
GI (CREAK)
WITH THE RECOMMENDATION PREP, IT'LL TURN INTO AN ASHEN-COLORED YOUTH IN NO TIME.

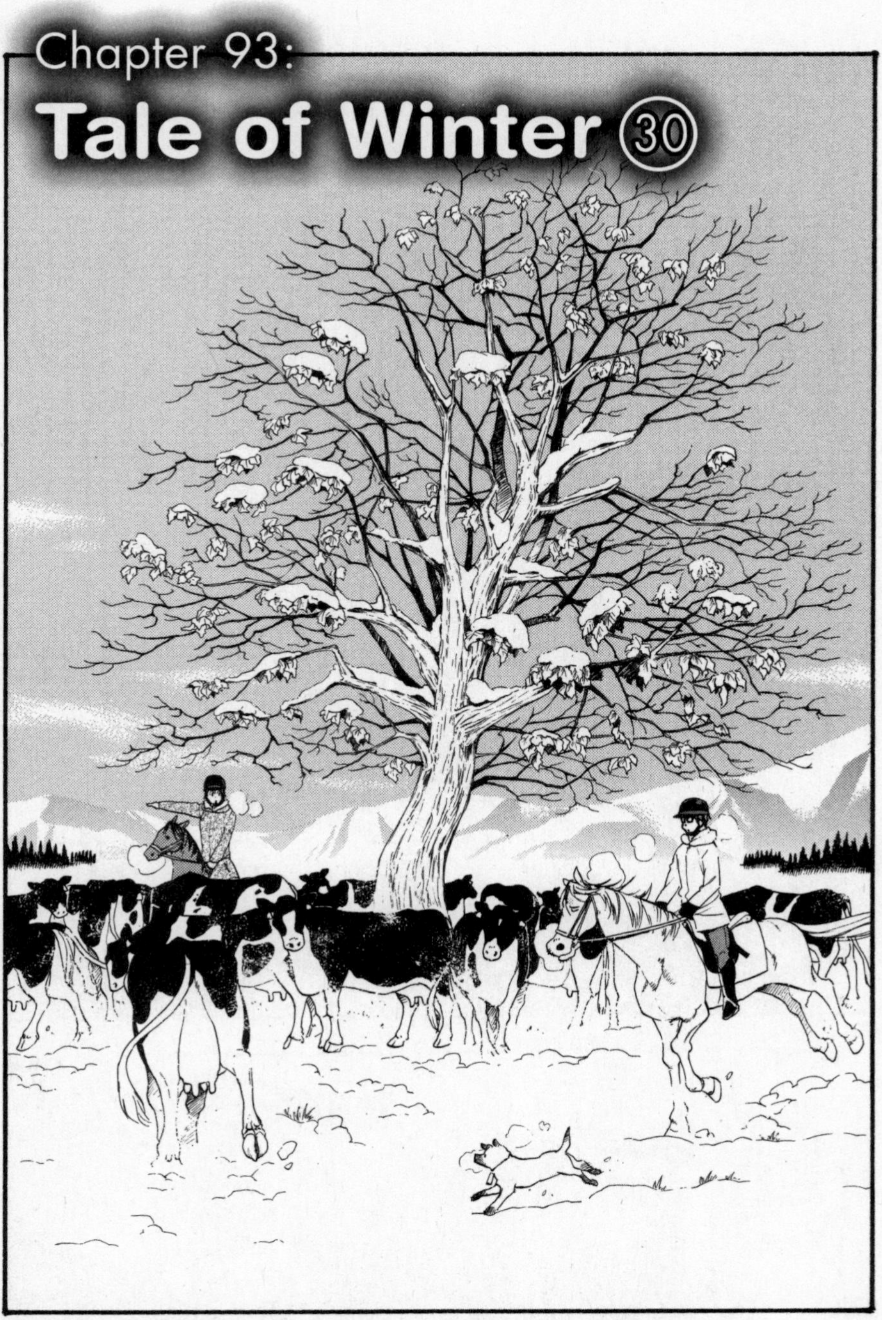
Chapter 93:
Tale of Winter ㉚

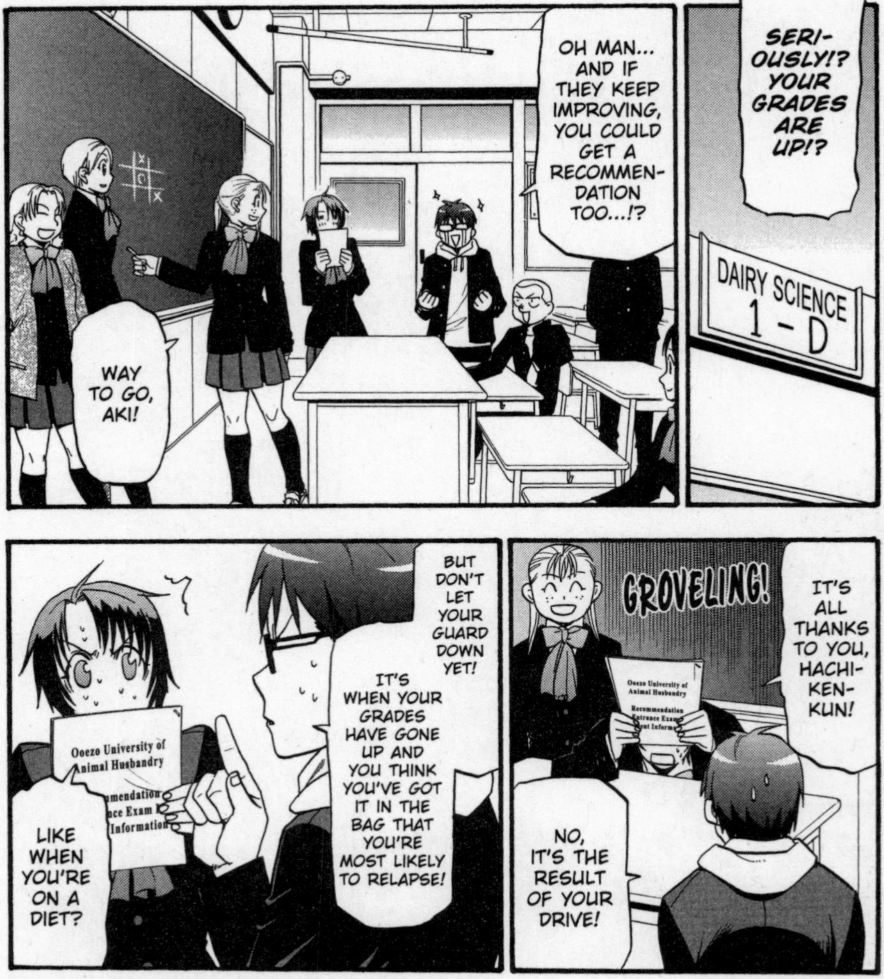
SERI-OUSLY!? YOUR GRADES ARE UP!?
DAIRY SCIENCE 1 - D
OH MAN... AND IF THEY KEEP IMPROVING, YOU COULD GET A RECOMMEN-DATION TOO...!?
WAY TO GO, AKI!
GROVELING!
IT'S ALL THANKS TO YOU, HACHI-KEN-KUN!
Ooezo University of Animal Husbandry
NO, IT'S THE RESULT OF YOUR DRIVE!
BUT DON'T LET YOUR GUARD DOWN YET!
IT'S WHEN YOUR GRADES HAVE GONE UP AND YOU THINK YOU'VE GOT IT IN THE BAG THAT YOU'RE MOST LIKELY TO RELAPSE!
Ooezo University of Animal Husbandry
LIKE WHEN YOU'RE ON A DIET?

SIGN: SCHOOL PRECEPTS / WORK, COLLABORATE, DEFY LOGIC

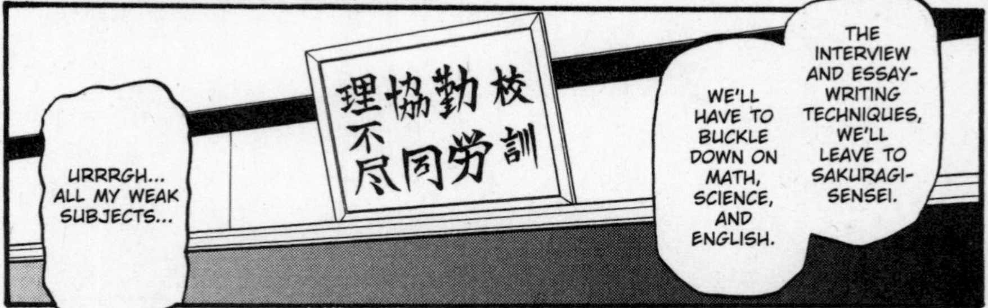
THE INTERVIEW AND ESSAY-WRITING TECHNIQUES, WE'LL LEAVE TO SAKURAGI-SENSEI.
WE'LL HAVE TO BUCKLE DOWN ON MATH, SCIENCE, AND ENGLISH.
校訓 勤労 協同 理不尽
URRRGH... ALL MY WEAK SUBJECTS...

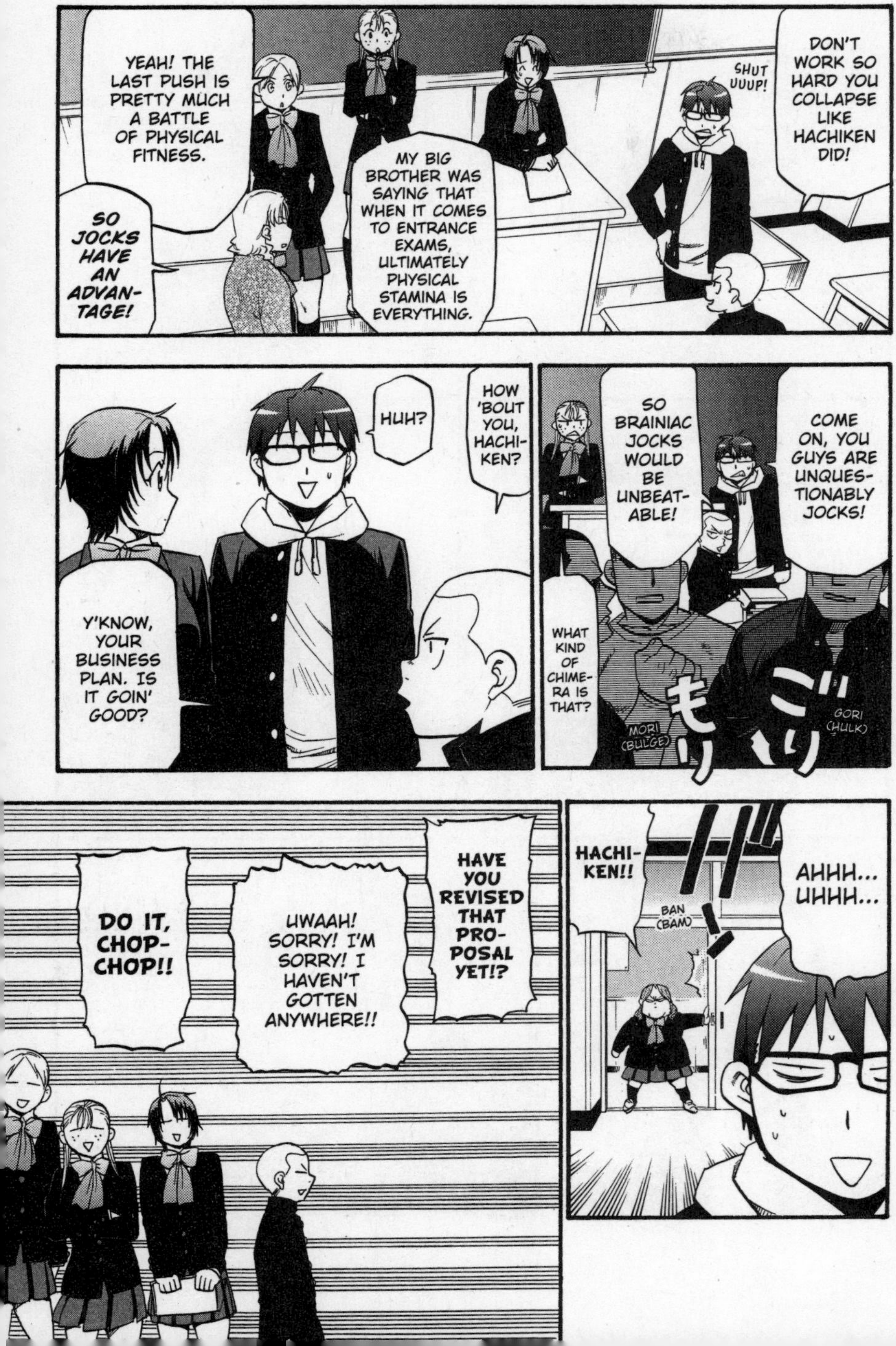
DON'T WORK SO HARD YOU COLLAPSE LIKE HACHIKEN DID!
SHUT UUUP!
MY BIG BROTHER WAS SAYING THAT WHEN IT COMES TO ENTRANCE EXAMS, ULTIMATELY PHYSICAL STAMINA IS EVERYTHING.
YEAH! THE LAST PUSH IS PRETTY MUCH A BATTLE OF PHYSICAL FITNESS.
SO JOCKS HAVE AN ADVAN-TAGE!
COME ON, YOU GUYS ARE UNQUES-TIONABLY JOCKS!
SO BRAINIAC JOCKS WOULD BE UNBEAT-ABLE!
WHAT KIND OF CHIME-RA IS THAT?
GORI (HULK)
MORI (BULGE)
HOW 'BOUT YOU, HACHI-KEN?
HUH?
Y'KNOW, YOUR BUSINESS PLAN. IS IT GOIN' GOOD?
AHHH... UHHH...
HACHI-KEN!!
BAN (BAM)
HAVE YOU REVISED THAT PRO-POSAL YET!?
UWAAH! SORRY! I'M SORRY! I HAVEN'T GOTTEN ANYWHERE!!
DO IT, CHOP-CHOP!!

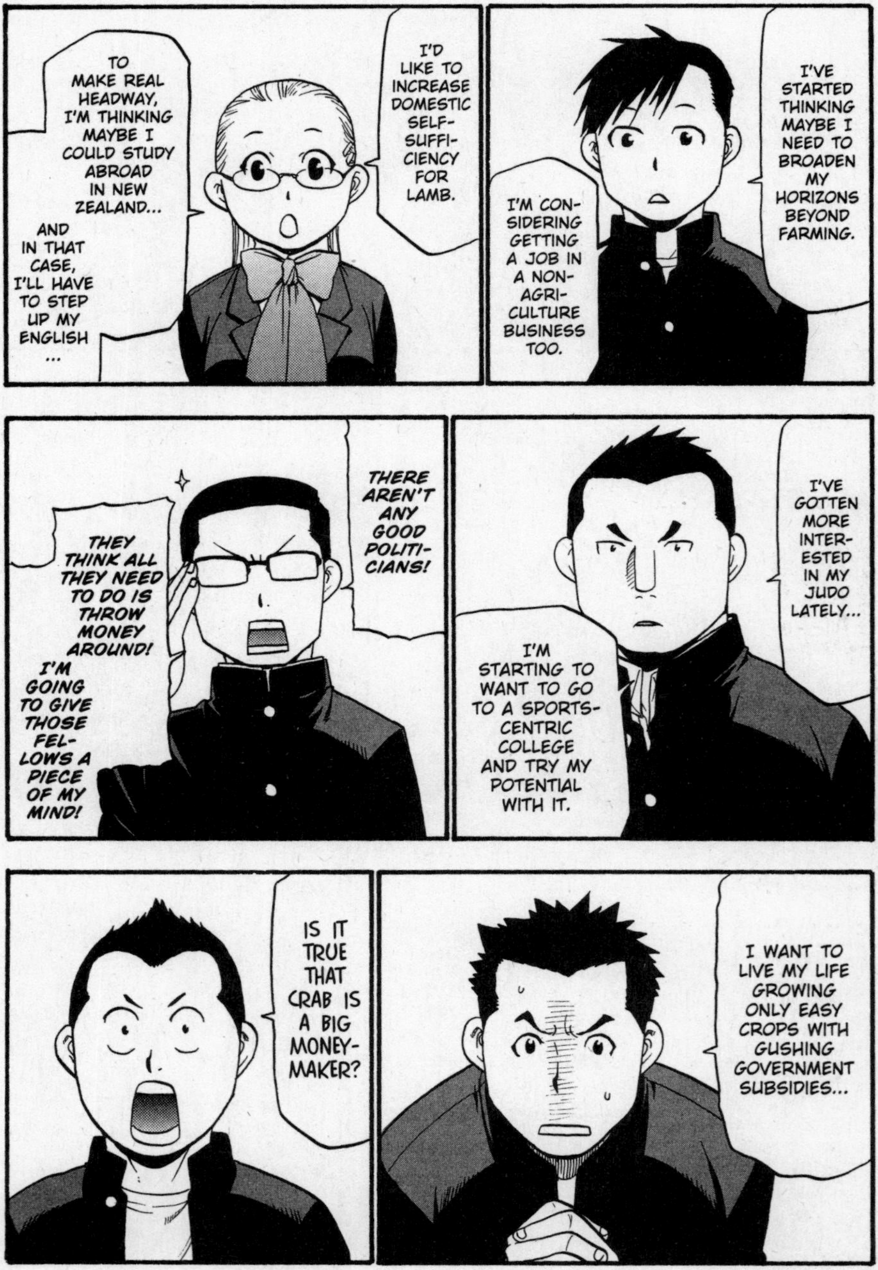
I'VE STARTED THINKING MAYBE I NEED TO BROADEN MY HORIZONS BEYOND FARMING.
I'M CONSIDERING GETTING A JOB IN A NON-AGRICULTURE BUSINESS TOO.
I'D LIKE TO INCREASE DOMESTIC SELF-SUFFICIENCY FOR LAMB.
TO MAKE REAL HEADWAY, I'M THINKING MAYBE I COULD STUDY ABROAD IN NEW ZEALAND...
AND IN THAT CASE, I'LL HAVE TO STEP UP MY ENGLISH...
I'VE GOTTEN MORE INTERESTED IN MY JUDO LATELY...
I'M STARTING TO WANT TO GO TO A SPORTS-CENTRIC COLLEGE AND TRY MY POTENTIAL WITH IT.
THERE AREN'T ANY GOOD POLITICIANS!
THEY THINK ALL THEY NEED TO DO IS THROW MONEY AROUND!
I'M GOING TO GIVE THOSE FELLOWS A PIECE OF MY MIND!
I WANT TO LIVE MY LIFE GROWING ONLY EASY CROPS WITH GUSHING GOVERNMENT SUBSIDIES...
IS IT TRUE THAT CRAB IS A BIG MONEYMAKER?

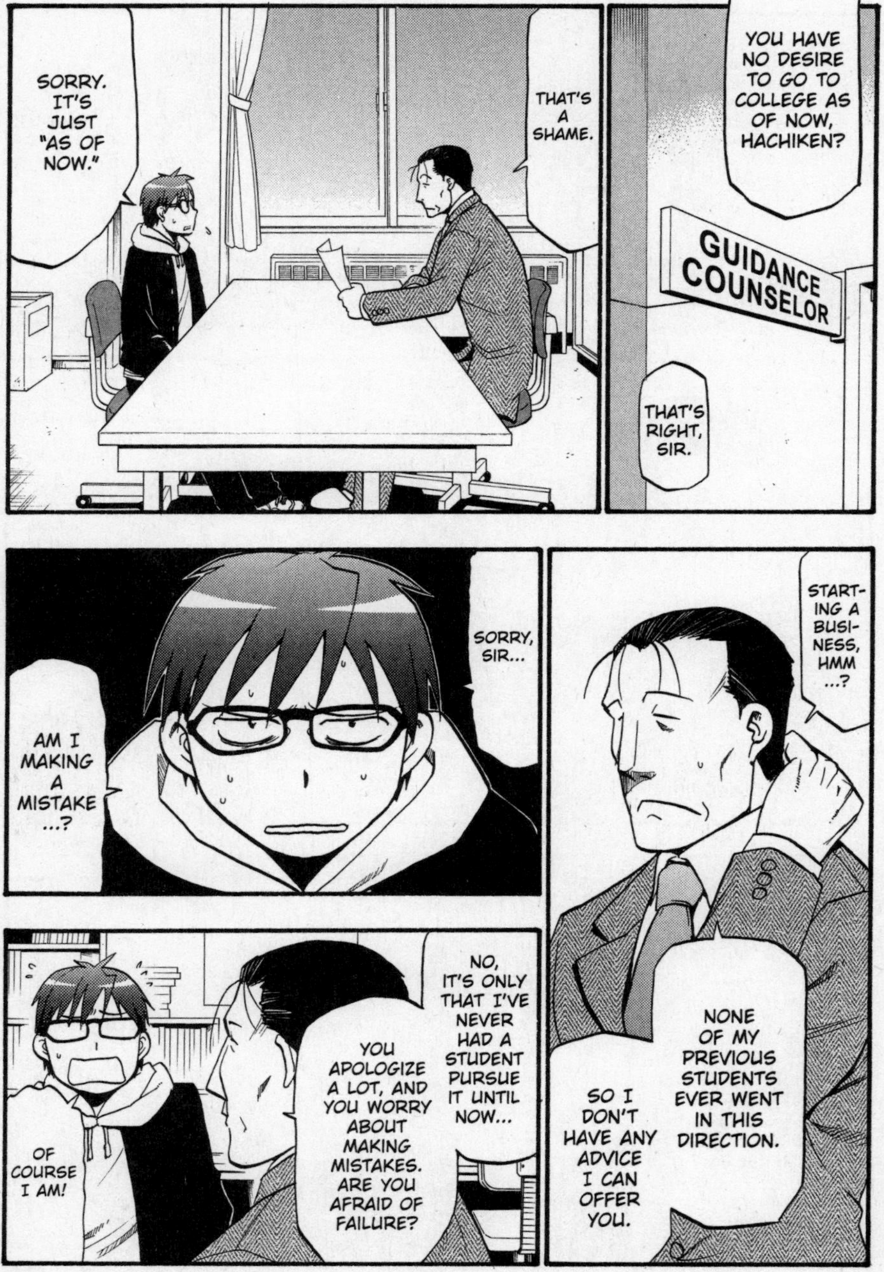
YOU HAVE NO DESIRE TO GO TO COLLEGE AS OF NOW, HACHIKEN?
GUIDANCE COUNSELOR
THAT'S RIGHT, SIR.
THAT'S A SHAME.
SORRY. IT'S JUST "AS OF NOW."
STARTING A BUSINESS, HMM ...?
NONE OF MY PREVIOUS STUDENTS EVER WENT IN THIS DIRECTION.
SO I DON'T HAVE ANY ADVICE I CAN OFFER YOU.
SORRY, SIR...
AM I MAKING A MISTAKE ...?
NO, IT'S ONLY THAT I'VE NEVER HAD A STUDENT PURSUE IT UNTIL NOW...
YOU APOLOGIZE A LOT, AND YOU WORRY ABOUT MAKING MISTAKES. ARE YOU AFRAID OF FAILURE?
OF COURSE I AM!

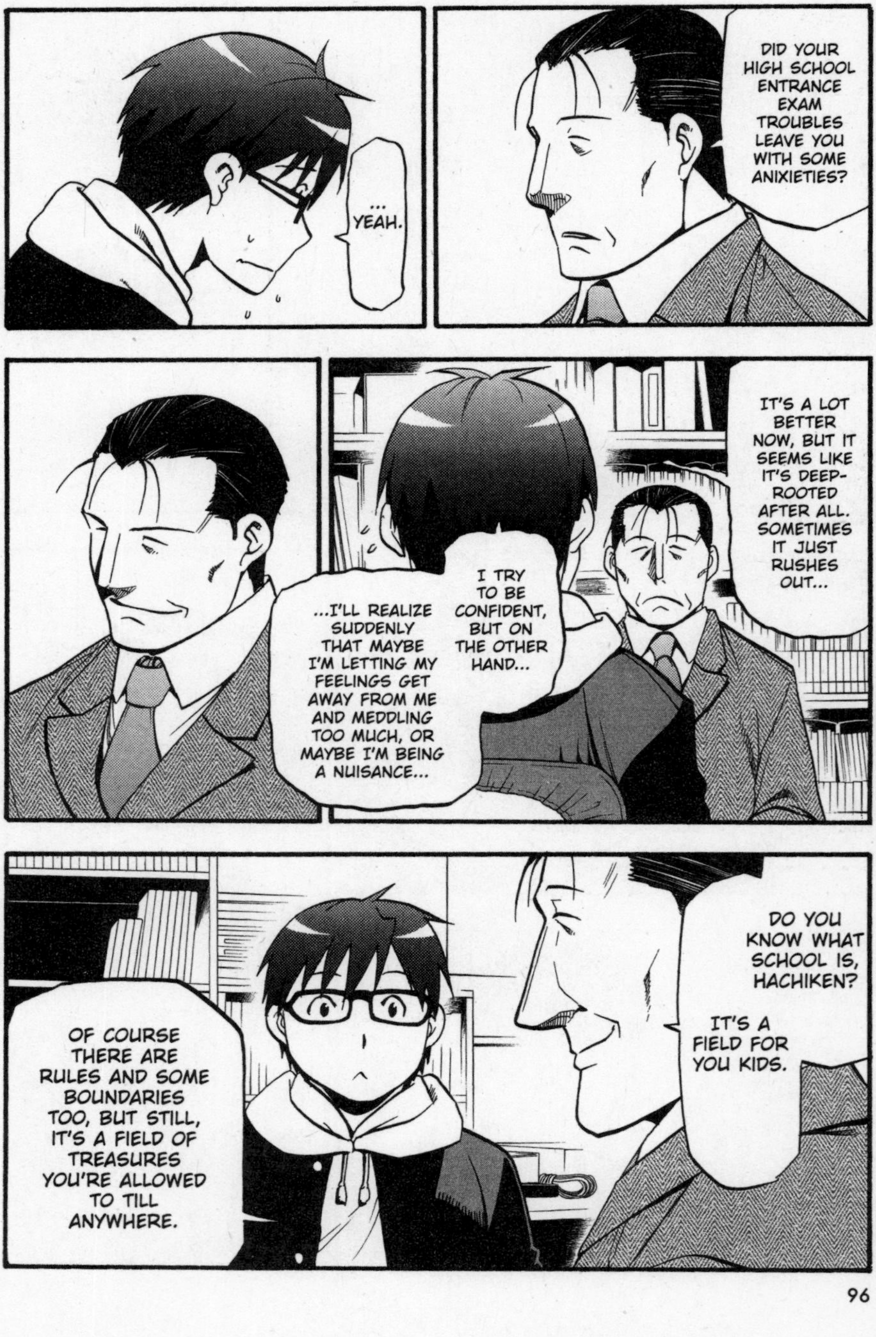
DID YOUR HIGH SCHOOL ENTRANCE EXAM TROUBLES LEAVE YOU WITH SOME ANIXIETIES?
... YEAH.
IT'S A LOT BETTER NOW, BUT IT SEEMS LIKE IT'S DEEP-ROOTED AFTER ALL. SOMETIMES IT JUST RUSHES OUT...
I TRY TO BE CONFIDENT, BUT ON THE OTHER HAND...
...I'LL REALIZE SUDDENLY THAT MAYBE I'M LETTING MY FEELINGS GET AWAY FROM ME AND MEDDLING TOO MUCH, OR MAYBE I'M BEING A NUISANCE...
DO YOU KNOW WHAT SCHOOL IS, HACHIKEN?
IT'S A FIELD FOR YOU KIDS.
OF COURSE THERE ARE RULES AND SOME BOUNDARIES TOO, BUT STILL, IT'S A FIELD OF TREASURES YOU'RE ALLOWED TO TILL ANYWHERE.

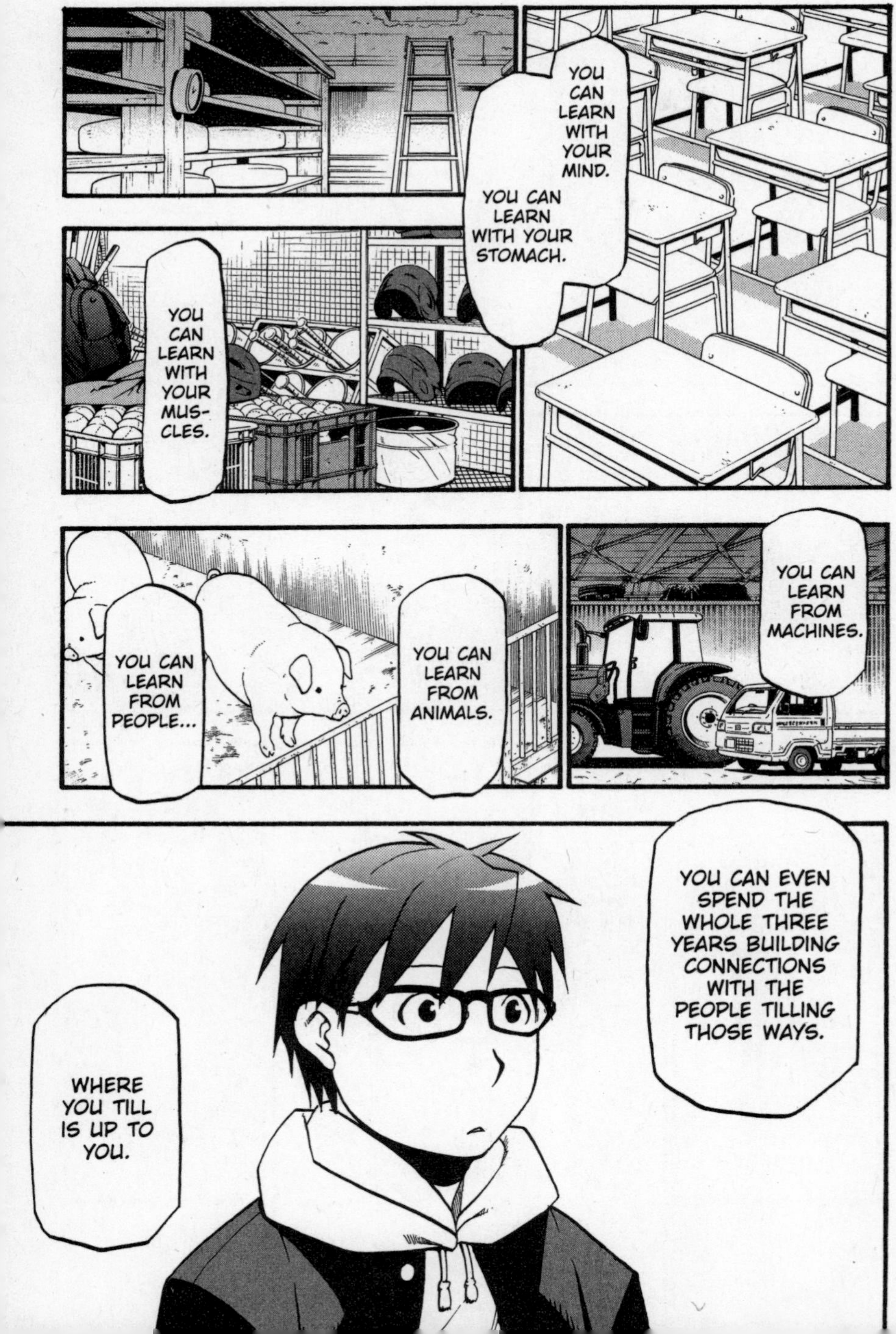
YOU CAN LEARN WITH YOUR MIND.
YOU CAN LEARN WITH YOUR STOMACH.
YOU CAN LEARN WITH YOUR MUS-CLES.
YOU CAN LEARN FROM MACHINES.
YOU CAN LEARN FROM ANIMALS.
YOU CAN LEARN FROM PEOPLE...
YOU CAN EVEN SPEND THE WHOLE THREE YEARS BUILDING CONNECTIONS WITH THE PEOPLE TILLING THOSE WAYS.
WHERE YOU TILL IS UP TO YOU.

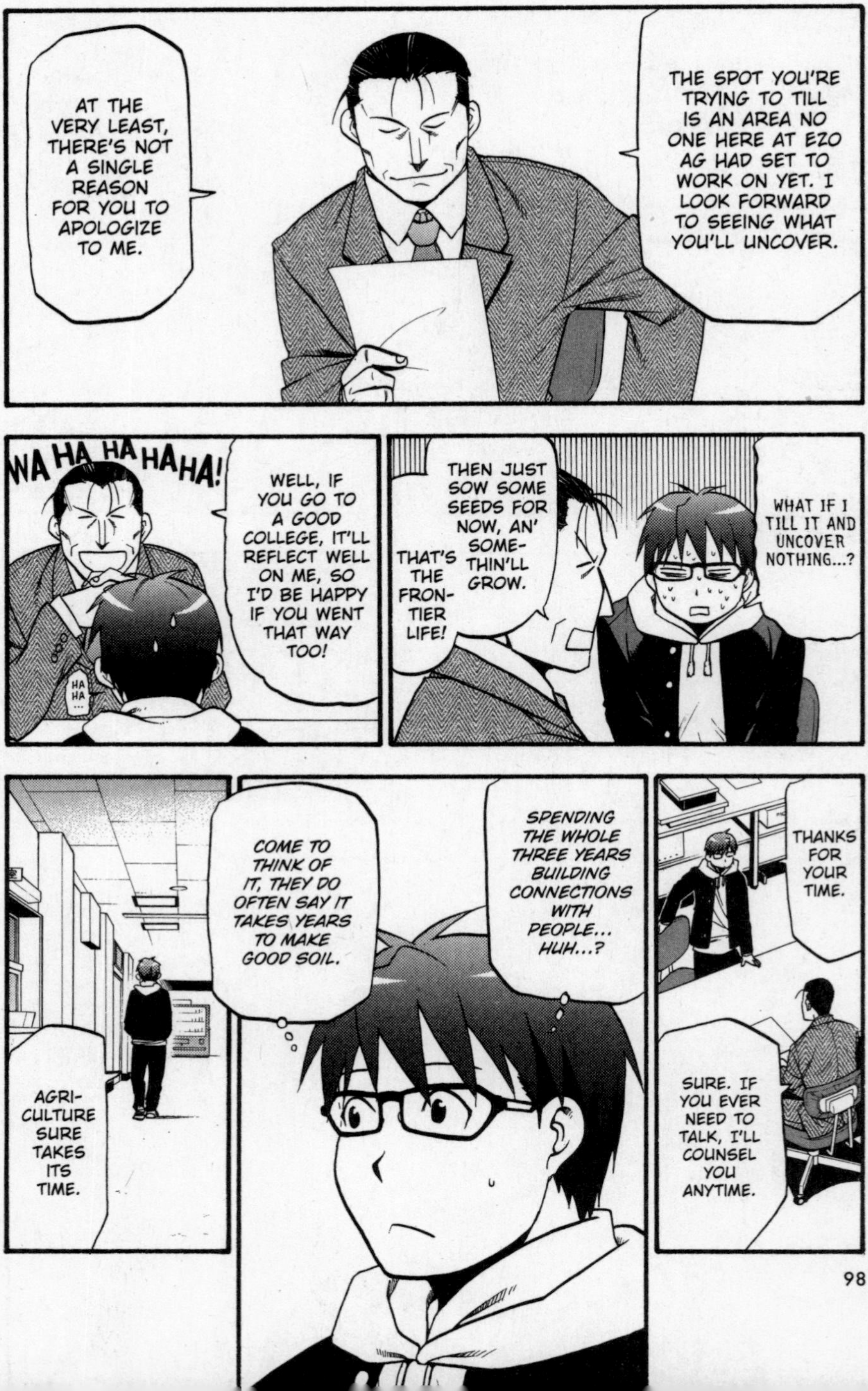
THE SPOT YOU'RE TRYING TO TILL IS AN AREA NO ONE HERE AT EZO AG HAD SET TO WORK ON YET. I LOOK FORWARD TO SEEING WHAT YOU'LL UNCOVER.
AT THE VERY LEAST, THERE'S NOT A SINGLE REASON FOR YOU TO APOLOGIZE TO ME.
WHAT IF I TILL IT AND UNCOVER NOTHING...?
THEN JUST SOW SOME SEEDS FOR NOW, AN' SOME-THIN'LL GROW.
THAT'S THE FRON-TIER LIFE!
WA HA HA HA HA!
WELL, IF YOU GO TO A GOOD COLLEGE, IT'LL REFLECT WELL ON ME, SO I'D BE HAPPY IF YOU WENT THAT WAY TOO!
HA HA...
THANKS FOR YOUR TIME.
SURE. IF YOU EVER NEED TO TALK, I'LL COUNSEL YOU ANYTIME.
SPENDING THE WHOLE THREE YEARS BUILDING CONNECTIONS WITH PEOPLE... HUH...?
COME TO THINK OF IT, THEY DO OFTEN SAY IT TAKES YEARS TO MAKE GOOD SOIL.
AGRI-CULTURE SURE TAKES ITS TIME.

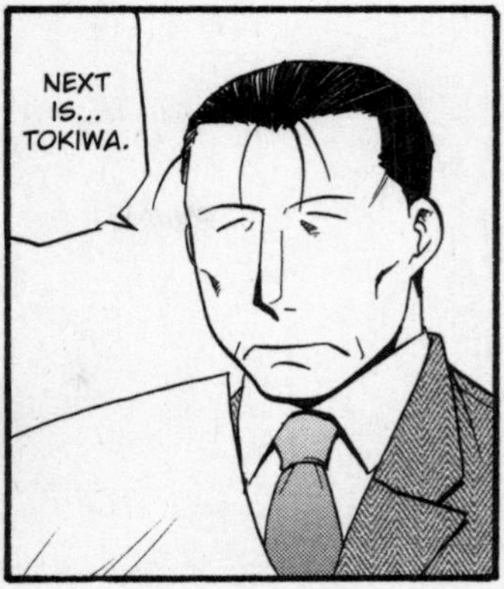
NEXT IS... TOKIWA.
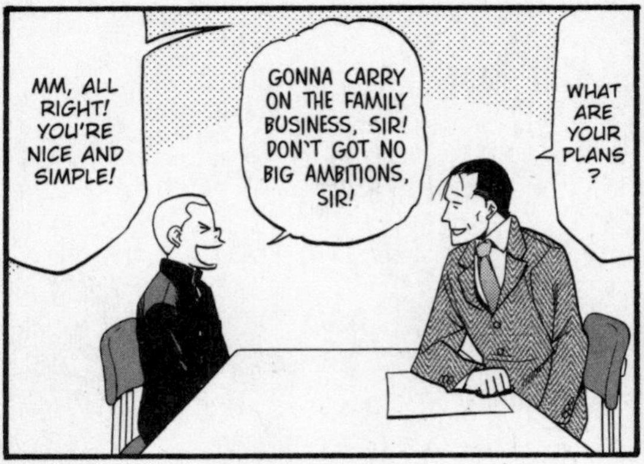
WHAT ARE YOUR PLANS?
GONNA CARRY ON THE FAMILY BUSINESS, SIR! DON'T GOT NO BIG AMBITIONS, SIR!
MM, ALL RIGHT! YOU'RE NICE AND SIMPLE!
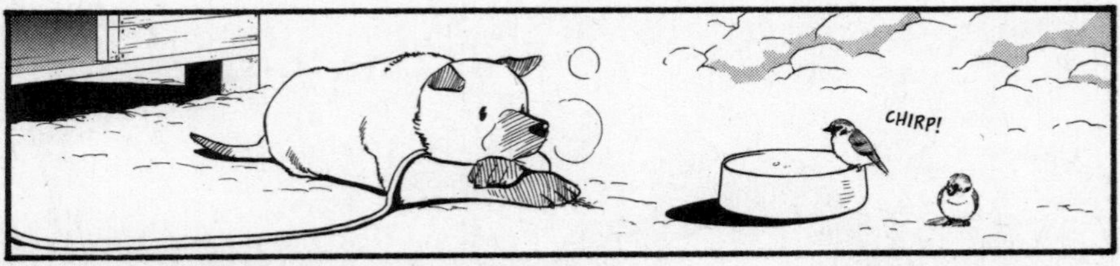
CHIRP!

JACKETS: OOEZO AGRICULTURAL HIGH SCHOOL EQUESTRIAN CLUB

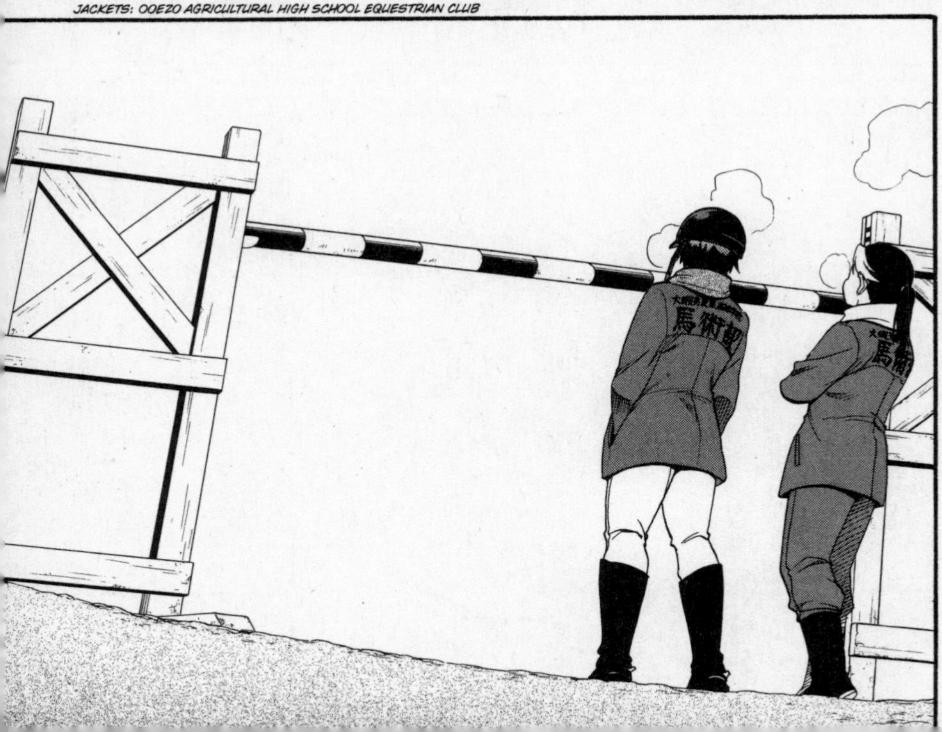

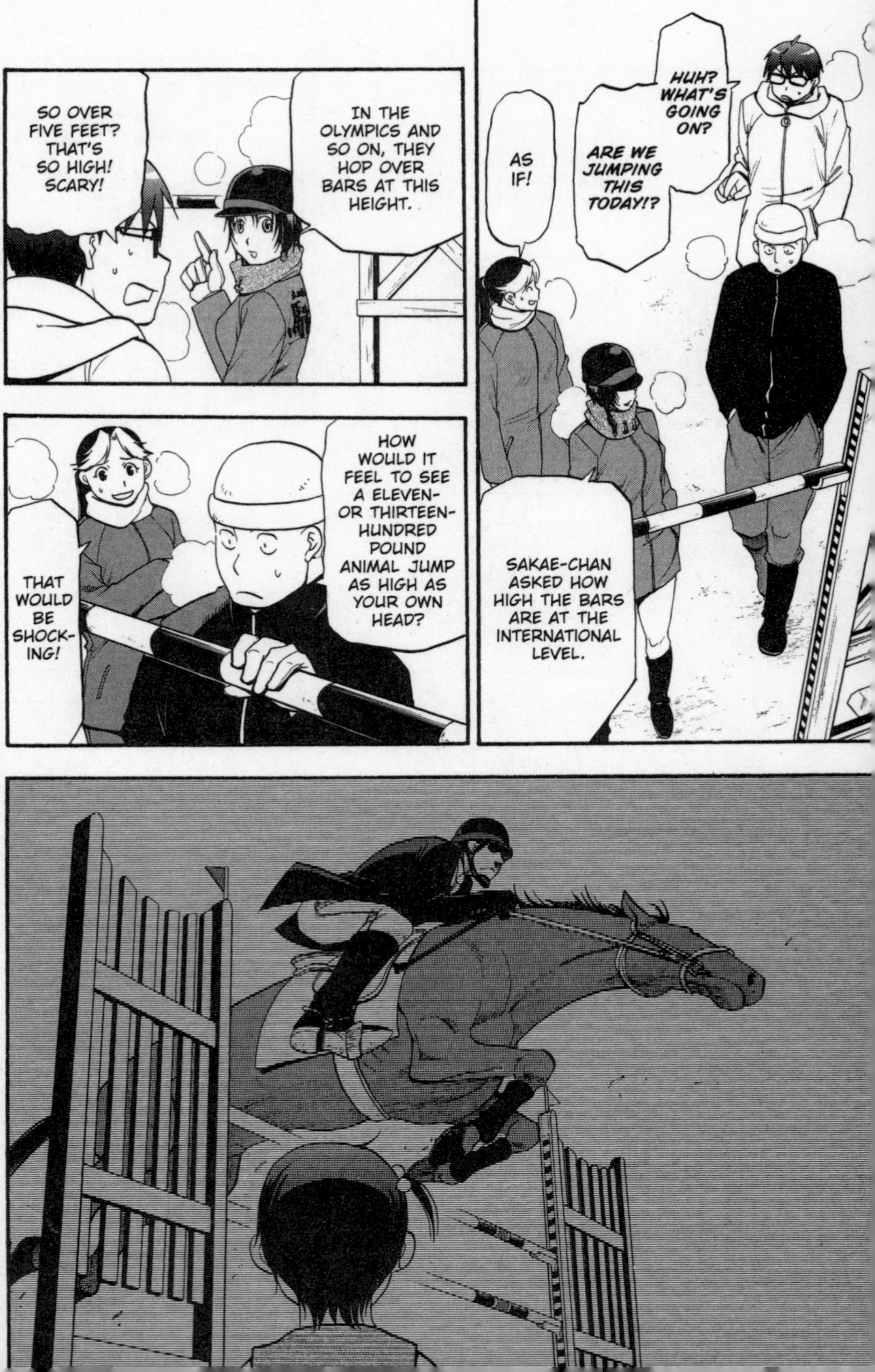
HUH? WHAT'S GOING ON?
ARE WE JUMPING THIS TODAY!?
AS IF!
SAKAE-CHAN ASKED HOW HIGH THE BARS ARE AT THE INTERNATIONAL LEVEL.
IN THE OLYMPICS AND SO ON, THEY HOP OVER BARS AT THIS HEIGHT.
SO OVER FIVE FEET? THAT'S SO HIGH! SCARY!
HOW WOULD IT FEEL TO SEE A ELEVEN- OR THIRTEEN-HUNDRED POUND ANIMAL JUMP AS HIGH AS YOUR OWN HEAD?
THAT WOULD BE SHOCKING!

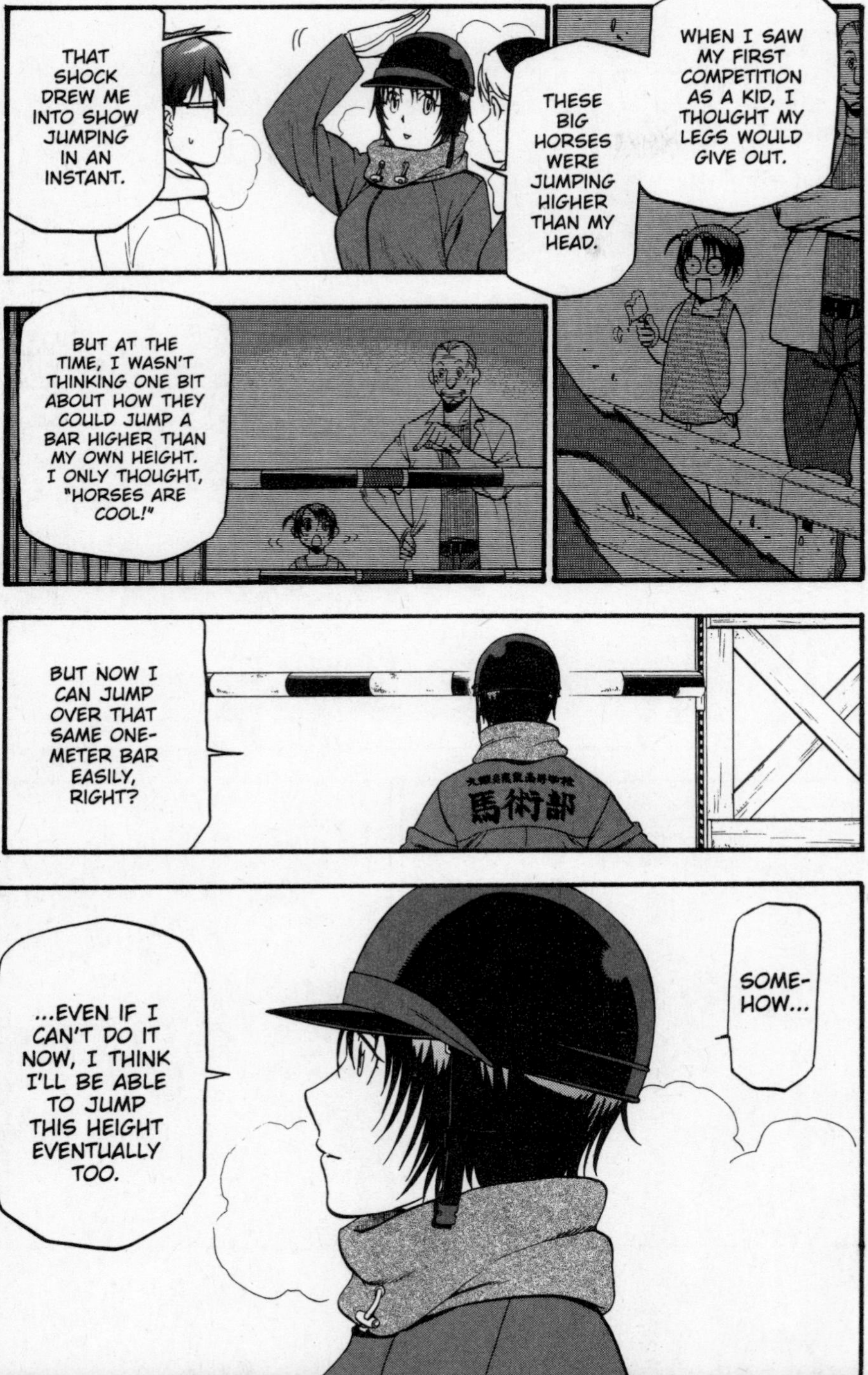
WHEN I SAW MY FIRST COMPETITION AS A KID, I THOUGHT MY LEGS WOULD GIVE OUT.
THESE BIG HORSES WERE JUMPING HIGHER THAN MY HEAD.
THAT SHOCK DREW ME INTO SHOW JUMPING IN AN INSTANT.
BUT AT THE TIME, I WASN'T THINKING ONE BIT ABOUT HOW THEY COULD JUMP A BAR HIGHER THAN MY OWN HEIGHT. I ONLY THOUGHT, "HORSES ARE COOL!"
BUT NOW I CAN JUMP OVER THAT SAME ONE-METER BAR EASILY, RIGHT?
馬術部
SOME-HOW...
...EVEN IF I CAN'T DO IT NOW, I THINK I'LL BE ABLE TO JUMP THIS HEIGHT EVENTUALLY TOO.

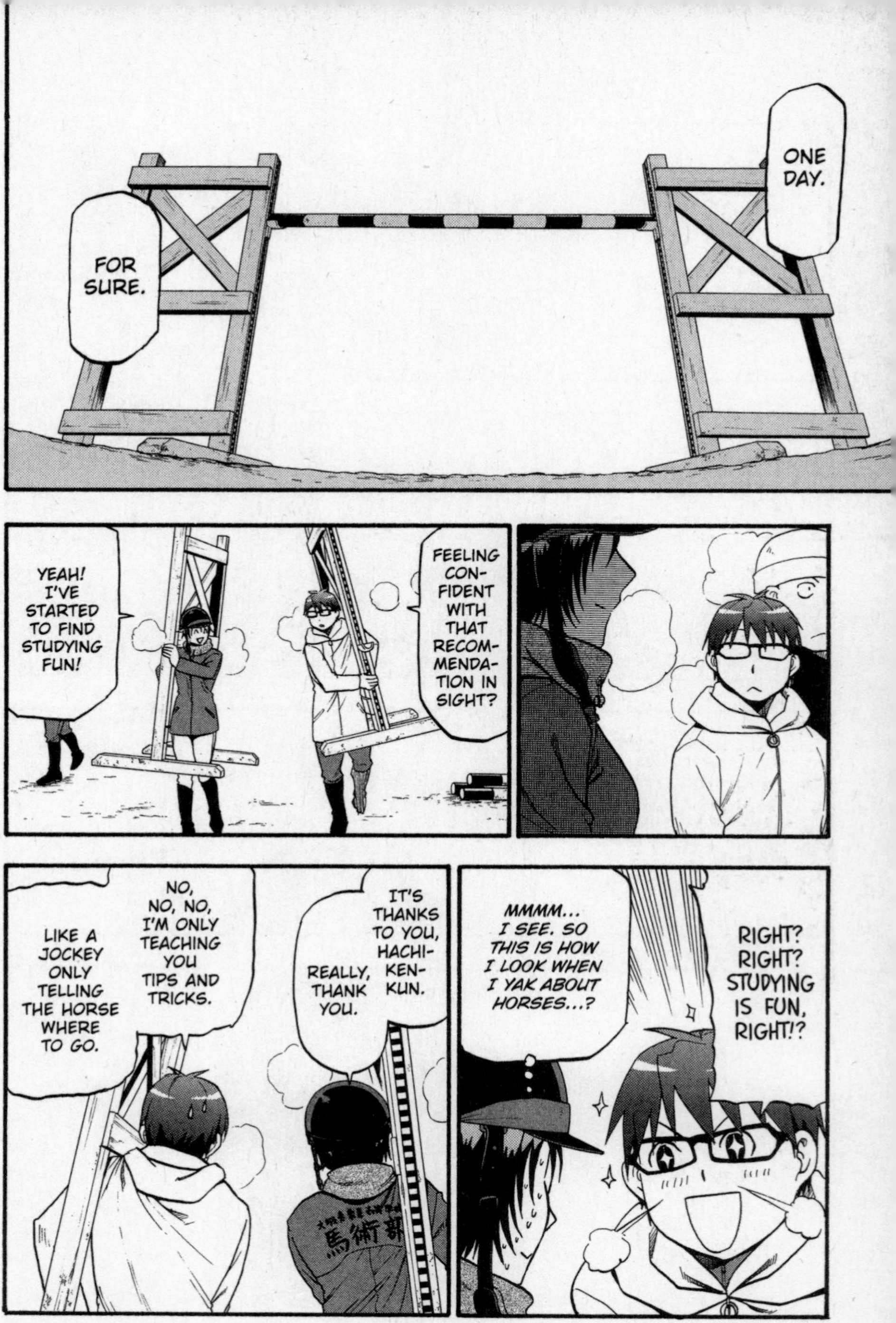
ONE DAY.
FOR SURE.
FEELING CONFIDENT WITH THAT RECOMMENDATION IN SIGHT?
YEAH! I'VE STARTED TO FIND STUDYING FUN!
RIGHT? RIGHT? STUDYING IS FUN, RIGHT!?
MMMM... I SEE. SO THIS IS HOW I LOOK WHEN I YAK ABOUT HORSES...?
IT'S THANKS TO YOU, HACHIKEN-KUN.
REALLY, THANK YOU.
馬術部
NO, NO, NO, I'M ONLY TEACHING YOU TIPS AND TRICKS.
LIKE A JOCKEY ONLY TELLING THE HORSE WHERE TO GO.

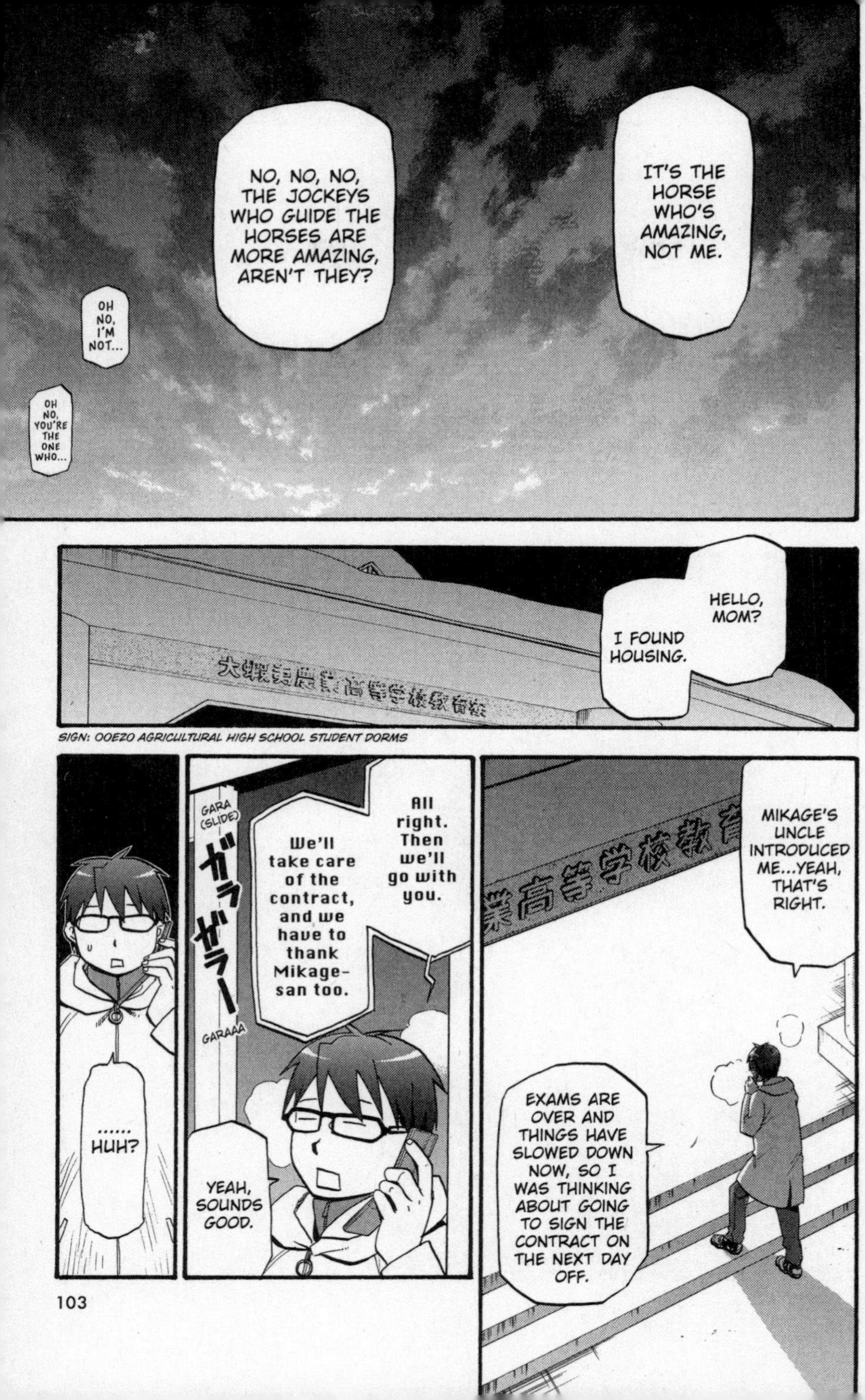
IT'S THE HORSE WHO'S AMAZING, NOT ME.
NO, NO, NO, THE JOCKEYS WHO GUIDE THE HORSES ARE MORE AMAZING, AREN'T THEY?
OH NO, I'M NOT...
OH NO, YOU'RE THE ONE WHO...
HELLO, MOM?
I FOUND HOUSING.
大蝦夷農業高等学校教育寮
SIGN: OOEZO AGRICULTURAL HIGH SCHOOL STUDENT DORMS
MIKAGE'S UNCLE INTRODUCED ME...YEAH, THAT'S RIGHT.
EXAMS ARE OVER AND THINGS HAVE SLOWED DOWN NOW, SO I WAS THINKING ABOUT GOING TO SIGN THE CONTRACT ON THE NEXT DAY OFF.
All right. Then we'll go with you.
We'll take care of the contract, and we have to thank Mikage-san too.
YEAH, SOUNDS GOOD.
GARA (SLIDE)
ガラガラー
GARAAA
...... HUH?

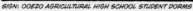

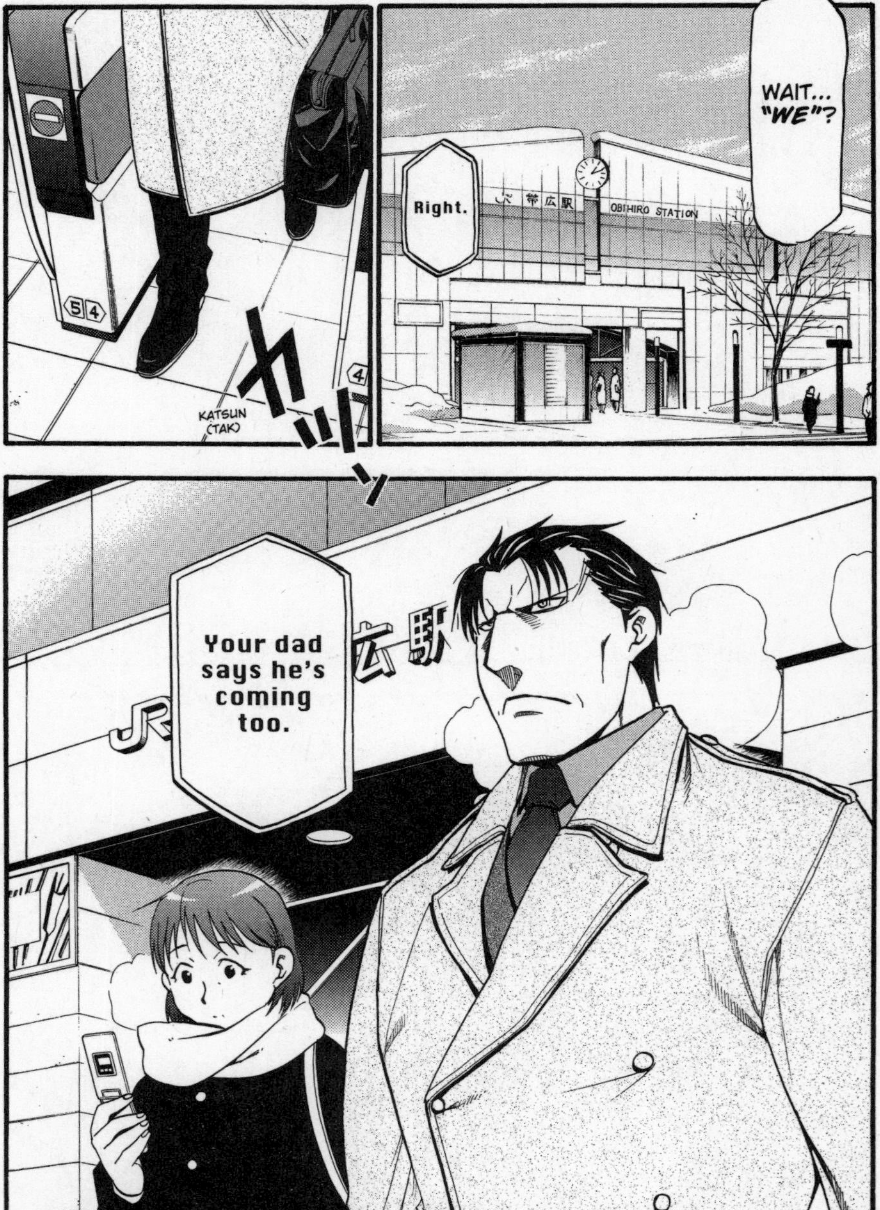
WAIT... "WE"?
Right.
OBIHIRO STATION
KATSUN (TAK)
Your dad says he's coming too.

Silver Spoon

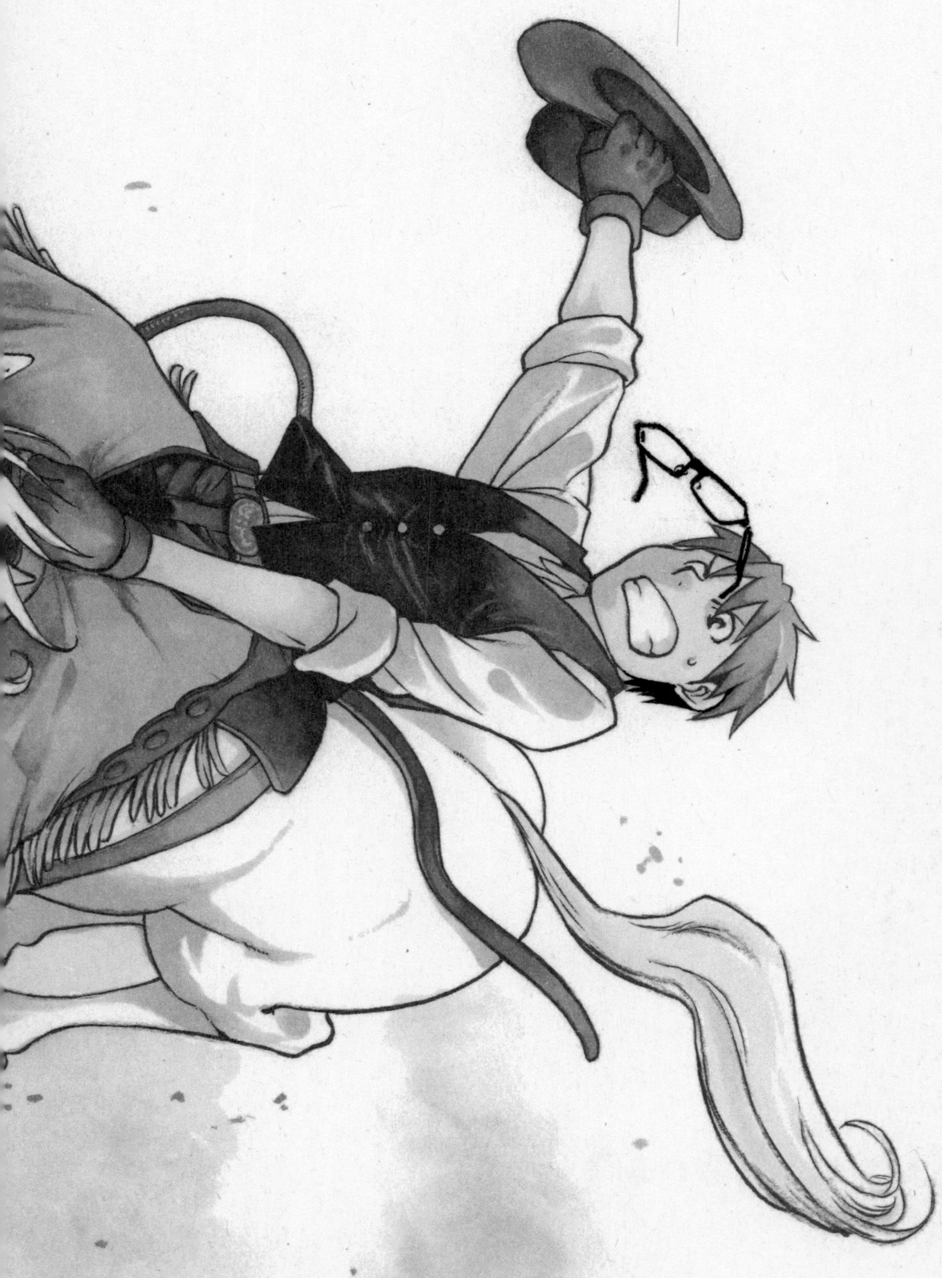

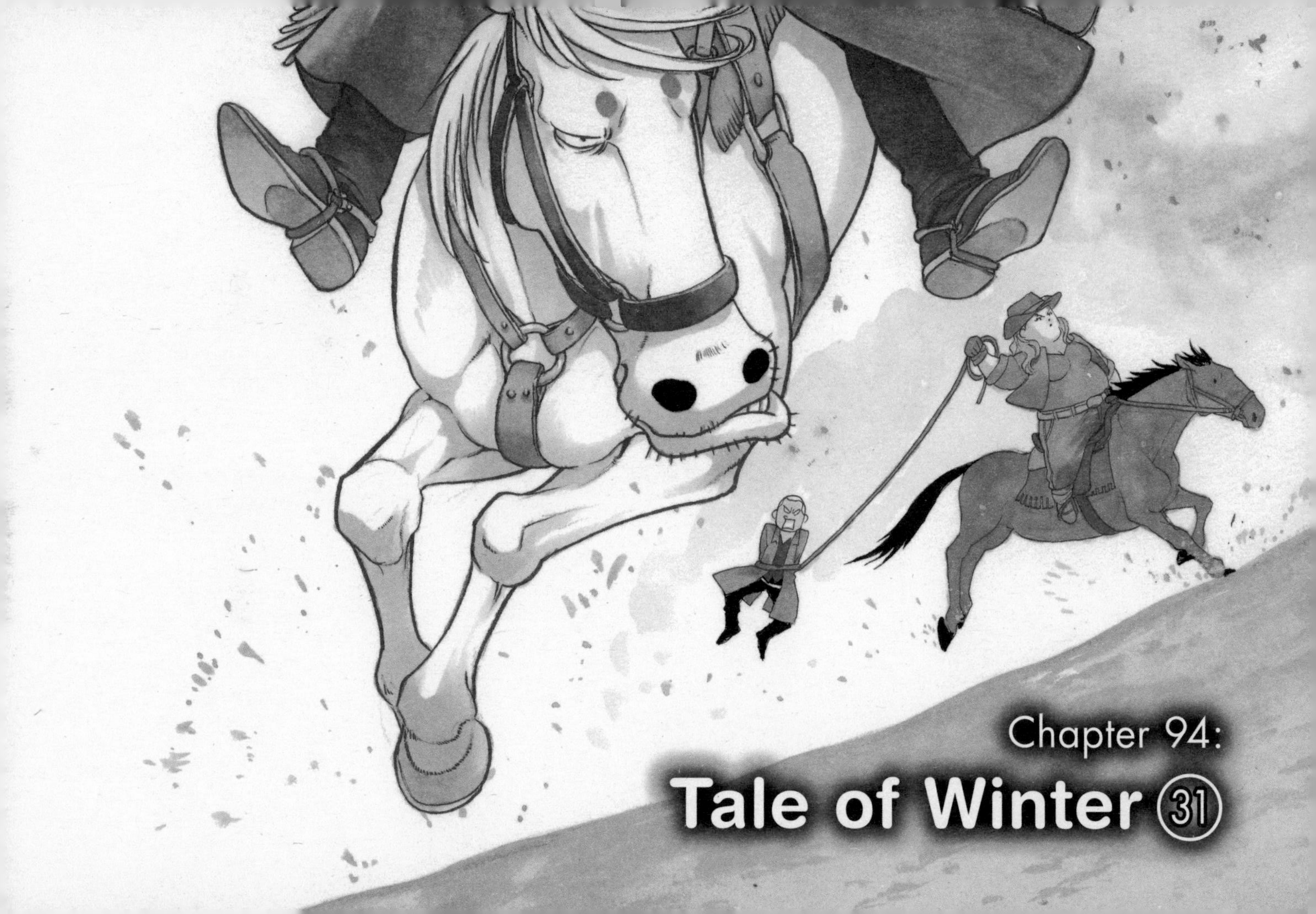
Chapter 94:
Tale of Winter ㉛

MASAKO MIKAGE

AKI'S MOM

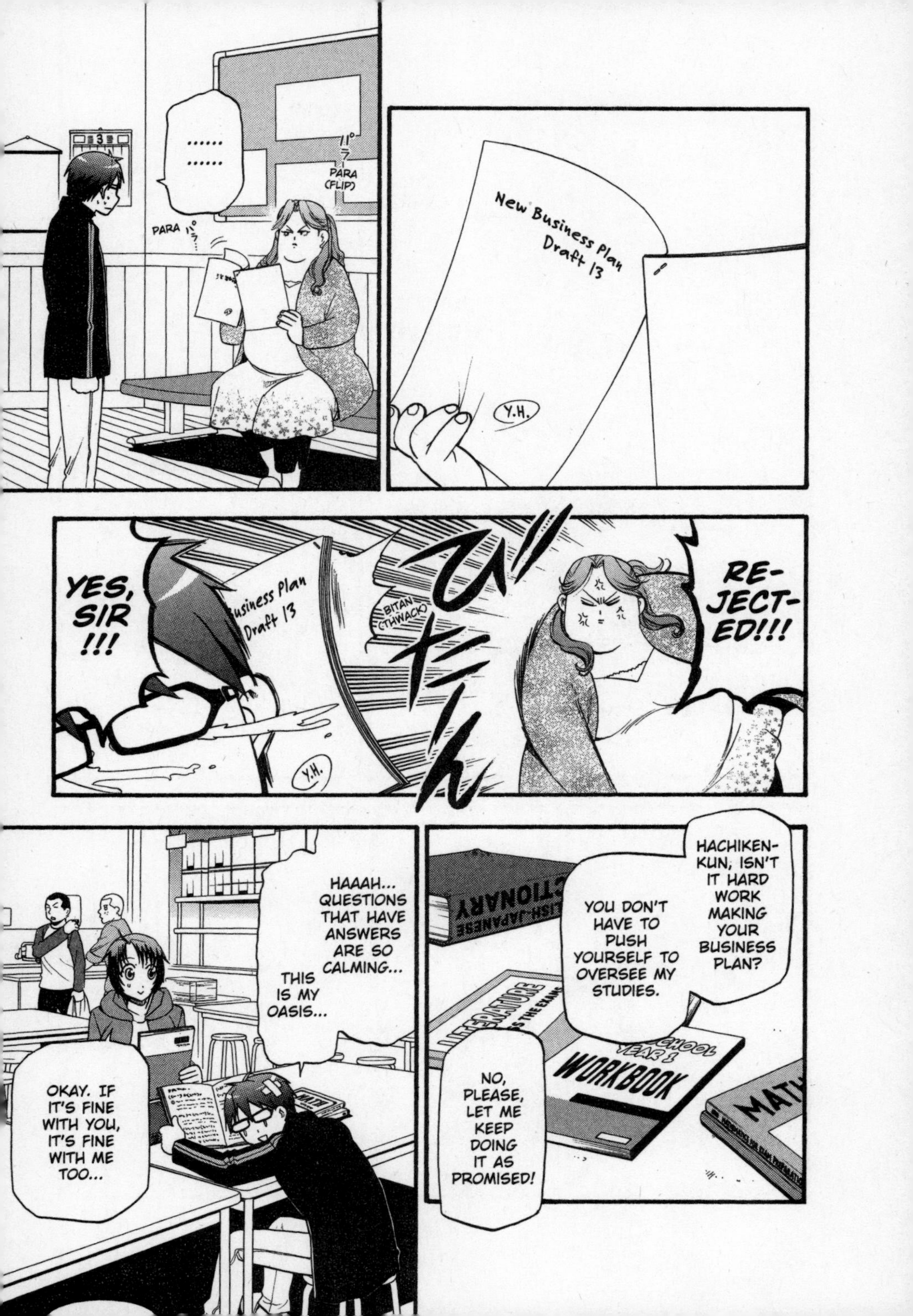
New Business Plan Draft 13
Y.H.
PARA (FLIP)
PARA
......
......
RE-JECT-ED!!!
BITAN (THWACK)
Business Plan Draft 13
Y.H.
YES, SIR!!!
HACHIKEN-KUN, ISN'T IT HARD WORK MAKING YOUR BUSINESS PLAN?
YOU DON'T HAVE TO PUSH YOURSELF TO OVERSEE MY STUDIES.
NO, PLEASE, LET ME KEEP DOING IT AS PROMISED!
WORKBOOK
YEAR 1
MATH
HAAAH... QUESTIONS THAT HAVE ANSWERS ARE SO CALMING...
THIS IS MY OASIS...
OKAY. IF IT'S FINE WITH YOU, IT'S FINE WITH ME TOO...

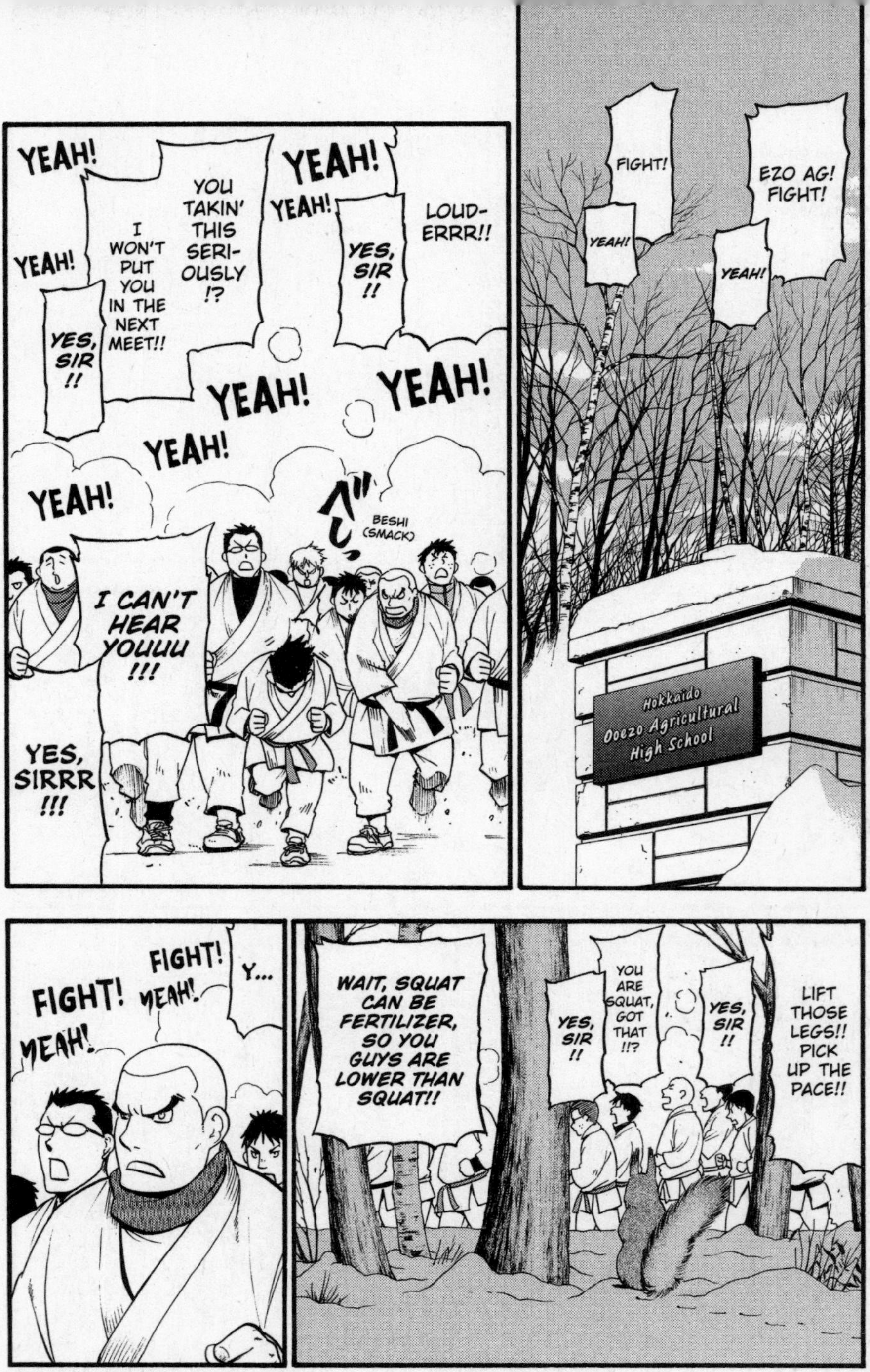
EZO AG! FIGHT!
FIGHT!
YEAH!
YEAH!
Hokkaido Ooezo Agricultural High School
LOUD-ERRR!!
YES, SIR !!
YEAH!
YEAH!
YOU TAKIN' THIS SERI-OUSLY !?
I WON'T PUT YOU IN THE NEXT MEET!!
YEAH!
YEAH!
YES, SIR !!
YEAH!
YEAH!
YEAH!
BESHI (SMACK)
I CAN'T HEAR YOUUU !!!
YES, SIRRR !!!
LIFT THOSE LEGS!! PICK UP THE PACE!!
YES, SIR !!
YOU ARE SQUAT, GOT THAT !!?
YES, SIR !!
WAIT, SQUAT CAN BE FERTILIZER, SO YOU GUYS ARE LOWER THAN SQUAT!!
Y...
FIGHT!
MEAH!
FIGHT!
MEAH!

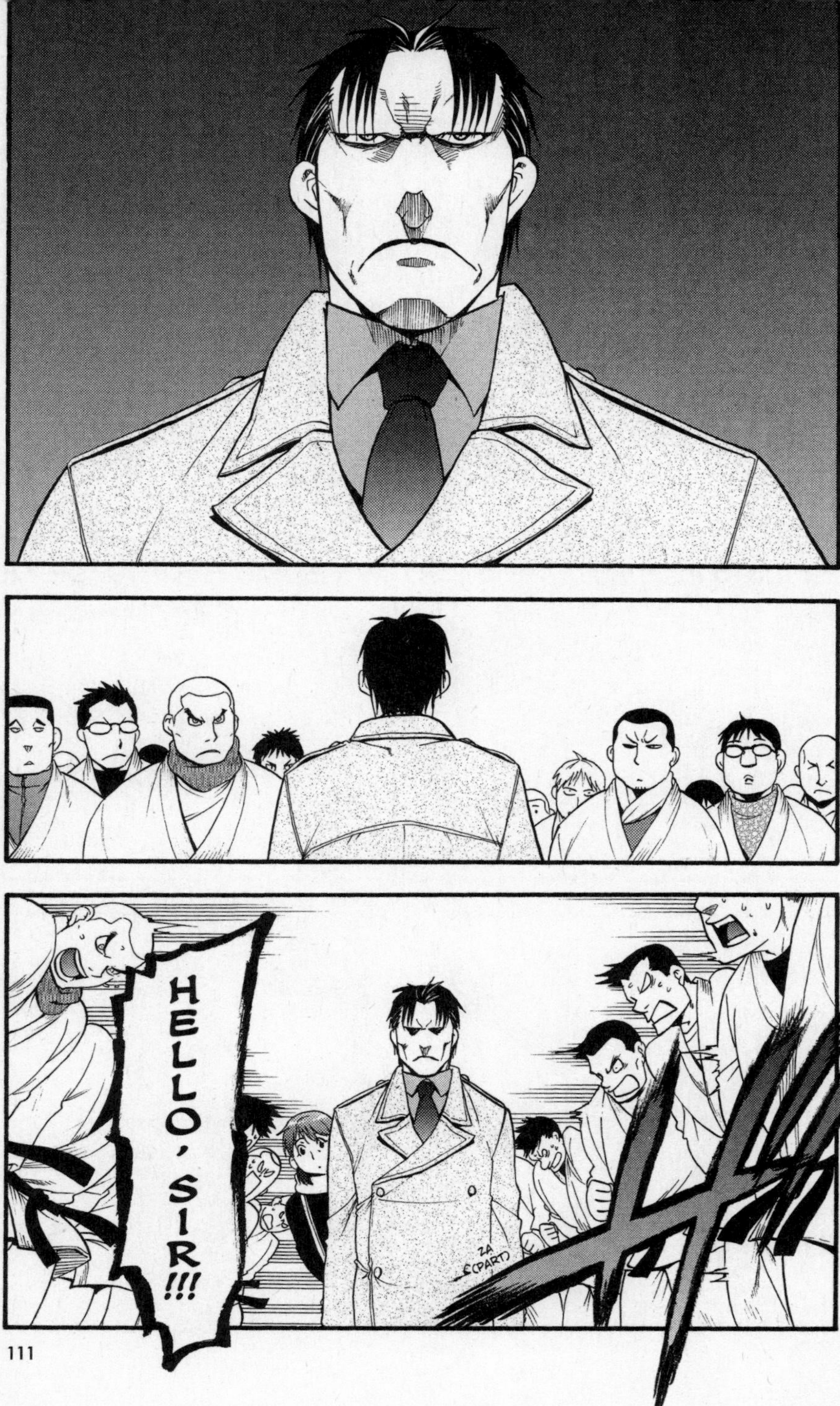
HELLO, SIR!!!
ZA (PART)

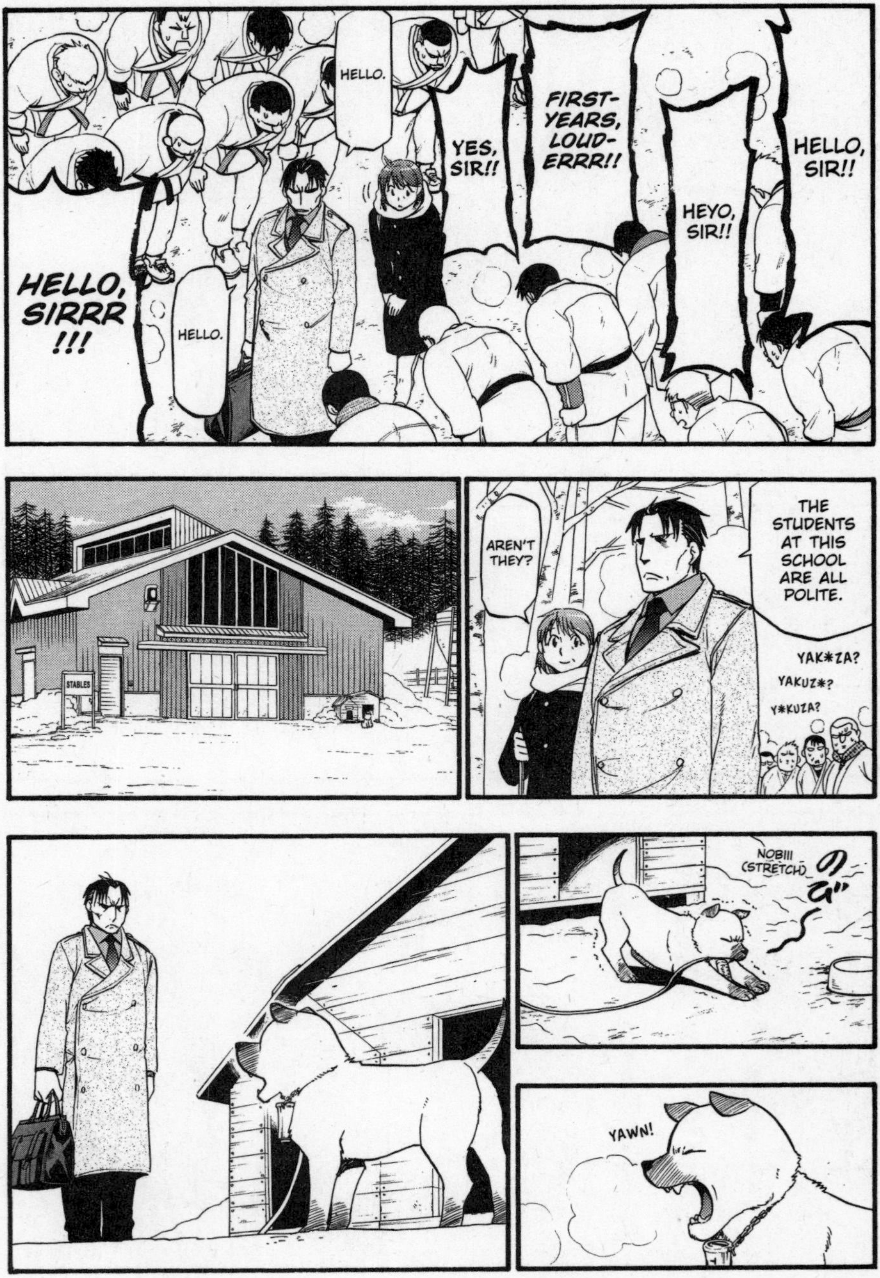
HELLO, SIR!!
HEYO, SIR!!
FIRST-YEARS, LOUD-ERRR!!
YES, SIR!!
HELLO.
HELLO, SIRRR!!!
HELLO.
THE STUDENTS AT THIS SCHOOL ARE ALL POLITE.
AREN'T THEY?
YAK*ZA?
YAKUZ*?
Y*KUZA?
STABLES
NOBIII (STRETCH)
のび
YAWN!

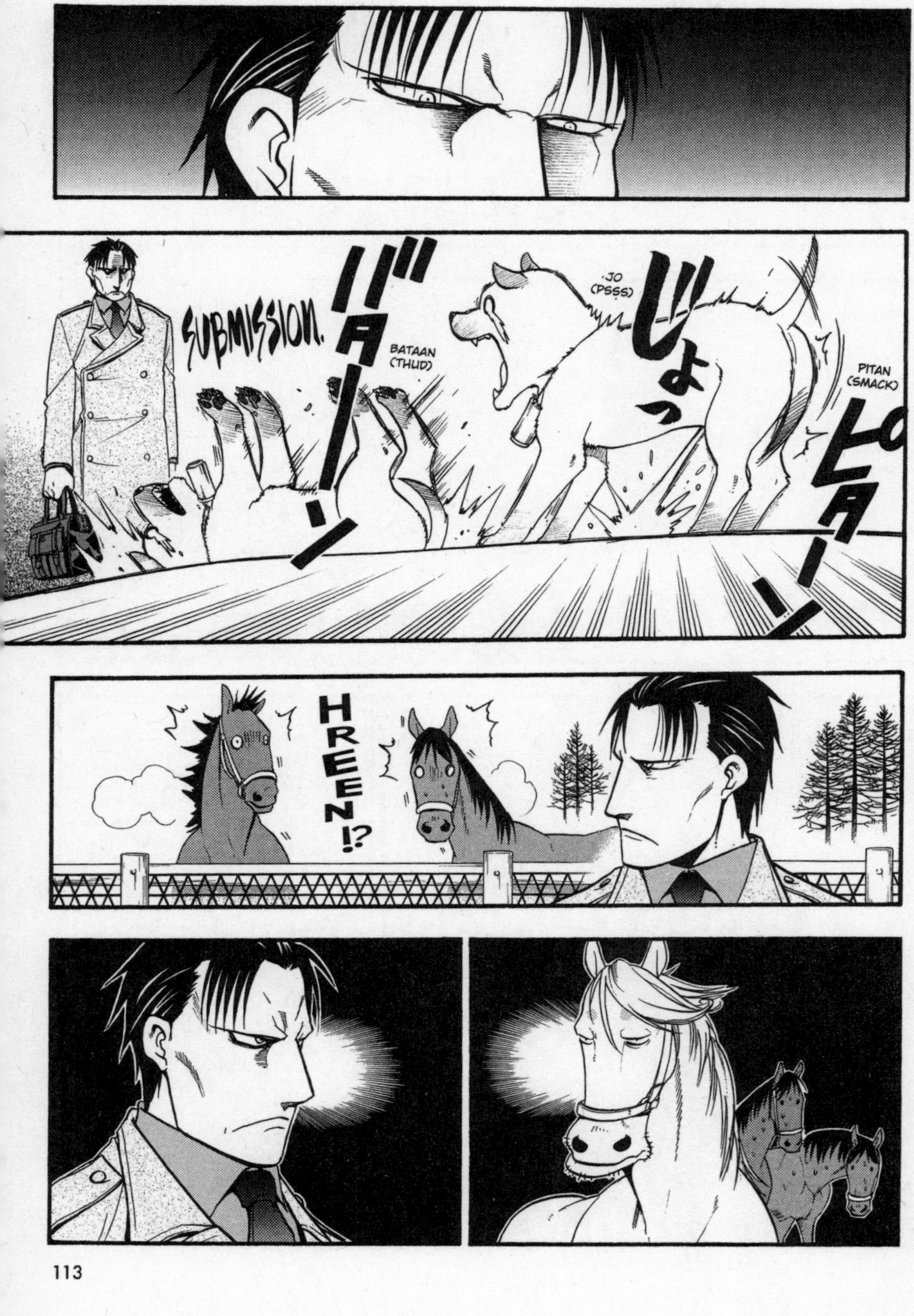
ピターン
PITAN (SMACK)
じょっ
JO (PSSS)
バターン
BATAAN (THUD)
SUBMISSION.
HREEN!?

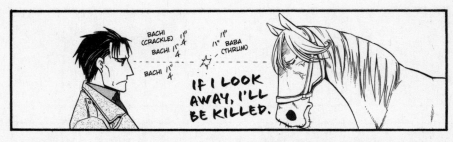

BACHI (CRACKLE) バチ
BACHI バチ
BACHI バチ
バババ BABA (THRUM)
IF I LOOK AWAY, I'LL BE KILLED.
THERE YOU ARE!
MOM!
WE COULD HAVE JUST MET UP AT THE STATION!
SORRY.
SINCE WE WERE ALREADY HERE, I WANTED YOUR DAD TO SEE YOUR SCHOOL TOO.
...THEY AREN'T DOING VEGETABLE SALES OR ANYTHING TODAY?
NOPE.
AND HERE I CAME HOPING FOR YUMMY FOOD...
AH...
しょぼん SHOBON (SULK)
ARF!

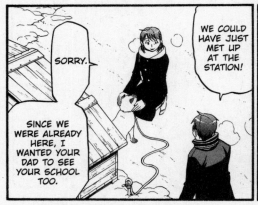

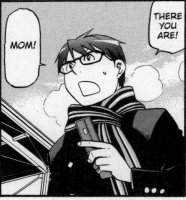

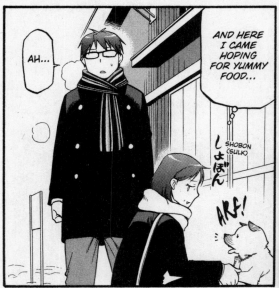

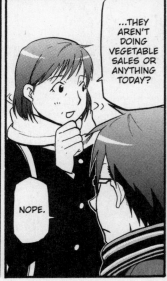

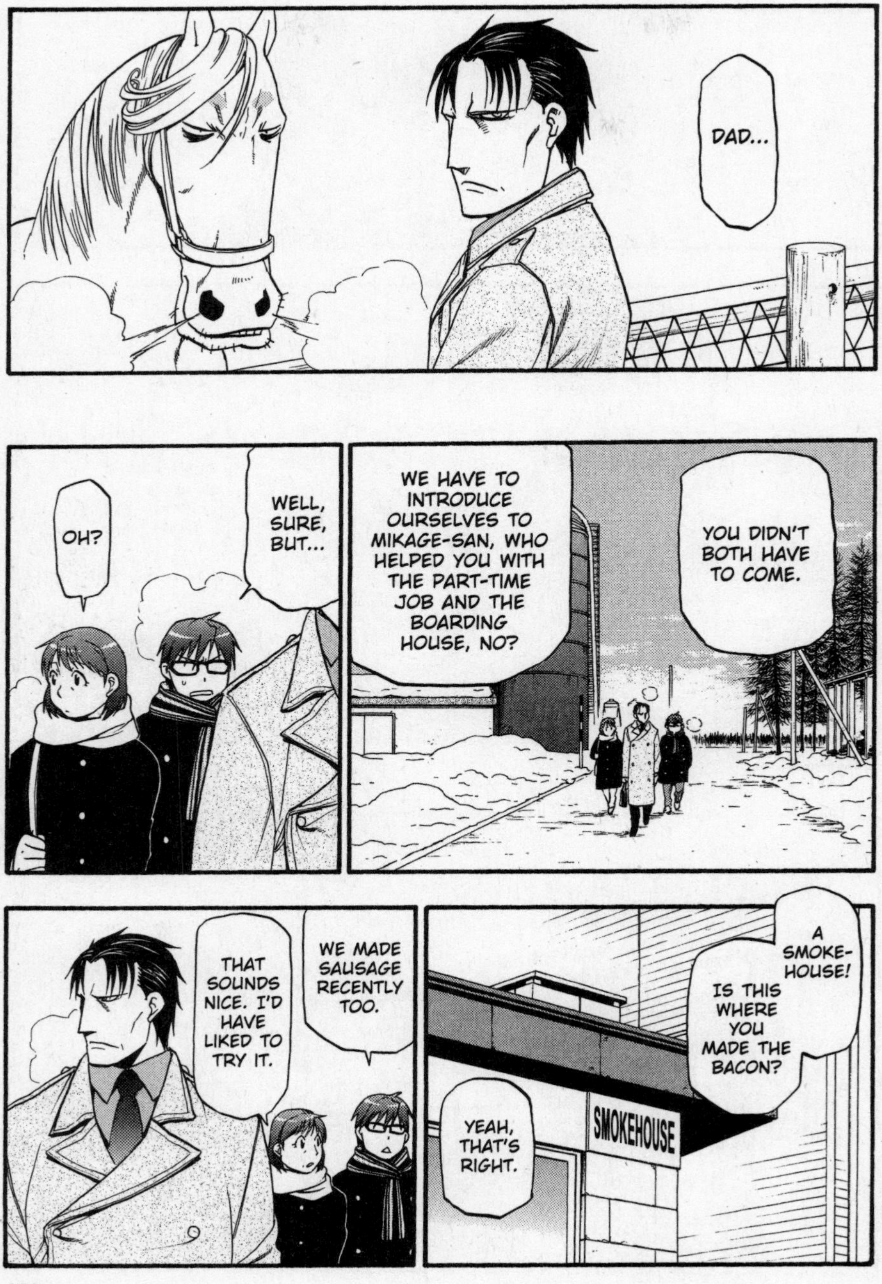
DAD...
YOU DIDN'T BOTH HAVE TO COME.
WE HAVE TO INTRODUCE OURSELVES TO MIKAGE-SAN, WHO HELPED YOU WITH THE PART-TIME JOB AND THE BOARDING HOUSE, NO?
WELL, SURE, BUT...
OH?
A SMOKE-HOUSE!
IS THIS WHERE YOU MADE THE BACON?
SMOKEHOUSE
YEAH, THAT'S RIGHT.
WE MADE SAUSAGE RECENTLY TOO.
THAT SOUNDS NICE. I'D HAVE LIKED TO TRY IT.

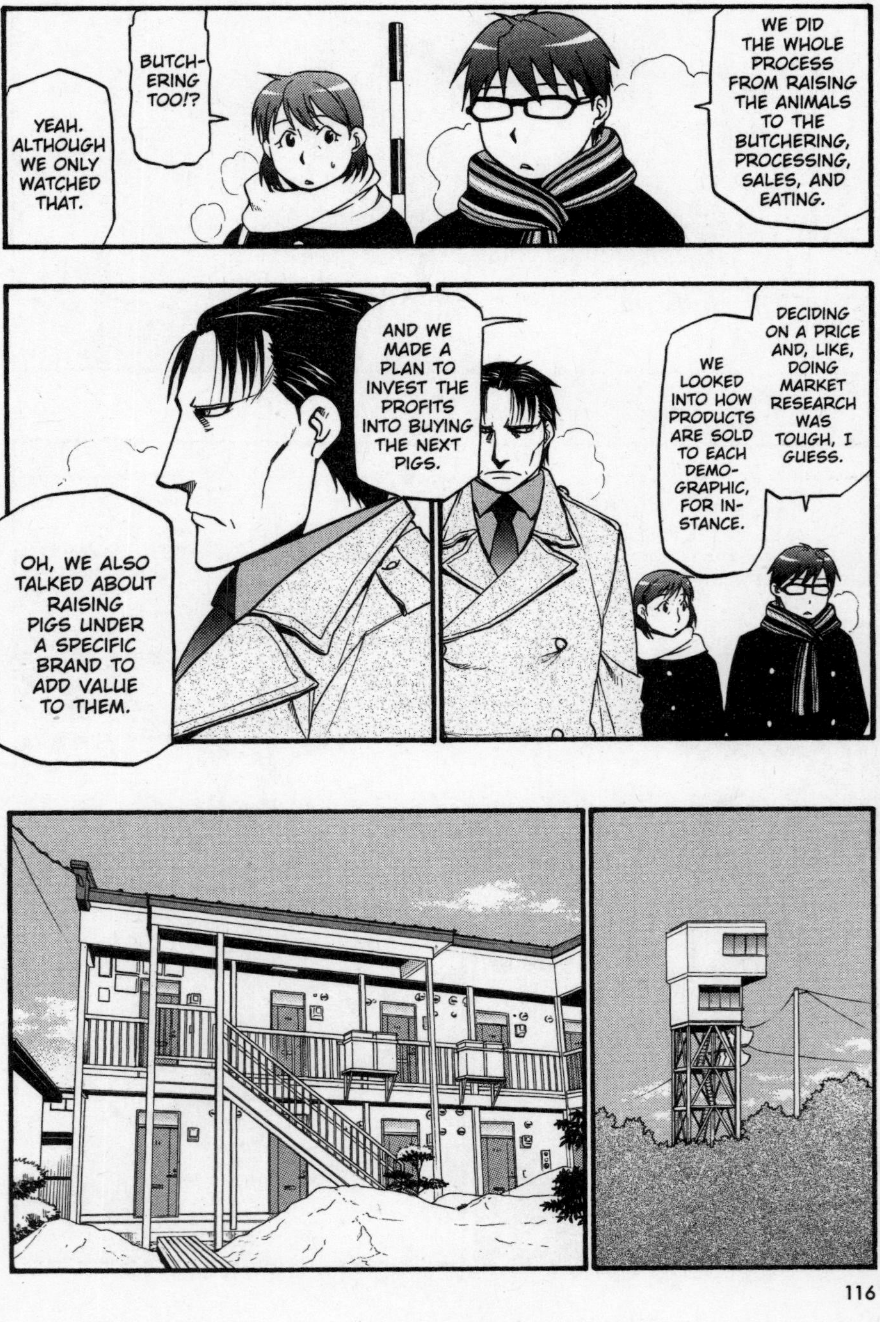
WE DID THE WHOLE PROCESS FROM RAISING THE ANIMALS TO THE BUTCHERING, PROCESSING, SALES, AND EATING.
BUTCH-ERING TOO!?
YEAH. ALTHOUGH WE ONLY WATCHED THAT.
DECIDING ON A PRICE AND, LIKE, DOING MARKET RESEARCH WAS TOUGH, I GUESS.
WE LOOKED INTO HOW PRODUCTS ARE SOLD TO EACH DEMO-GRAPHIC, FOR IN-STANCE.
AND WE MADE A PLAN TO INVEST THE PROFITS INTO BUYING THE NEXT PIGS.
OH, WE ALSO TALKED ABOUT RAISING PIGS UNDER A SPECIFIC BRAND TO ADD VALUE TO THEM.

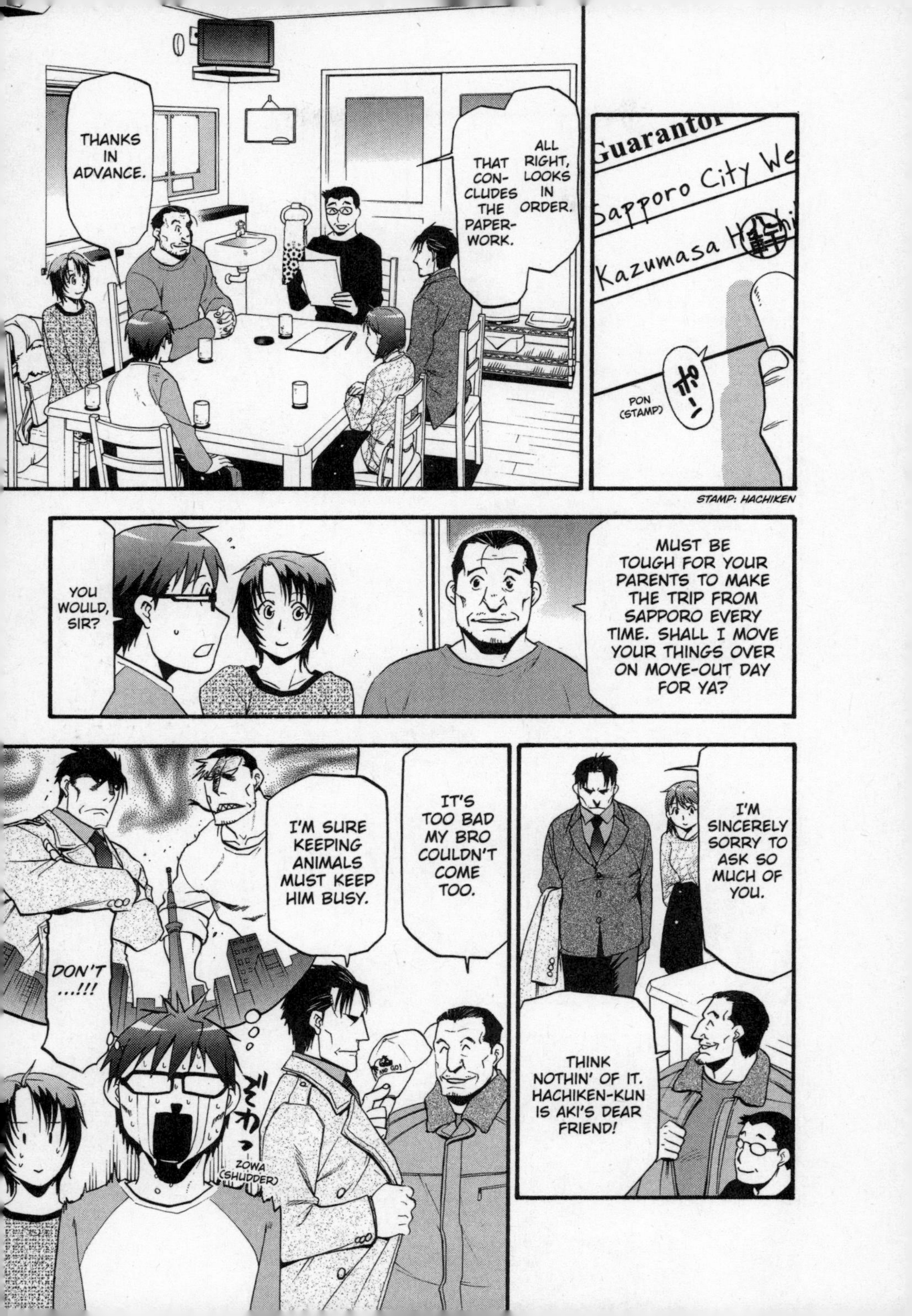
Guarantor
Sapporo City We
Kazumasa H
PON (STAMP)
STAMP: HACHIKEN
ALL RIGHT, LOOKS IN ORDER.
THAT CONCLUDES THE PAPERWORK.
THANKS IN ADVANCE.
MUST BE TOUGH FOR YOUR PARENTS TO MAKE THE TRIP FROM SAPPORO EVERY TIME. SHALL I MOVE YOUR THINGS OVER ON MOVE-OUT DAY FOR YA?
YOU WOULD, SIR?
I'M SINCERELY SORRY TO ASK SO MUCH OF YOU.
THINK NOTHIN' OF IT. HACHIKEN-KUN IS AKI'S DEAR FRIEND!
IT'S TOO BAD MY BRO COULDN'T COME TOO.
I'M SURE KEEPING ANIMALS MUST KEEP HIM BUSY.
DON'T ...!!!
ZOWA (SHUDDER)

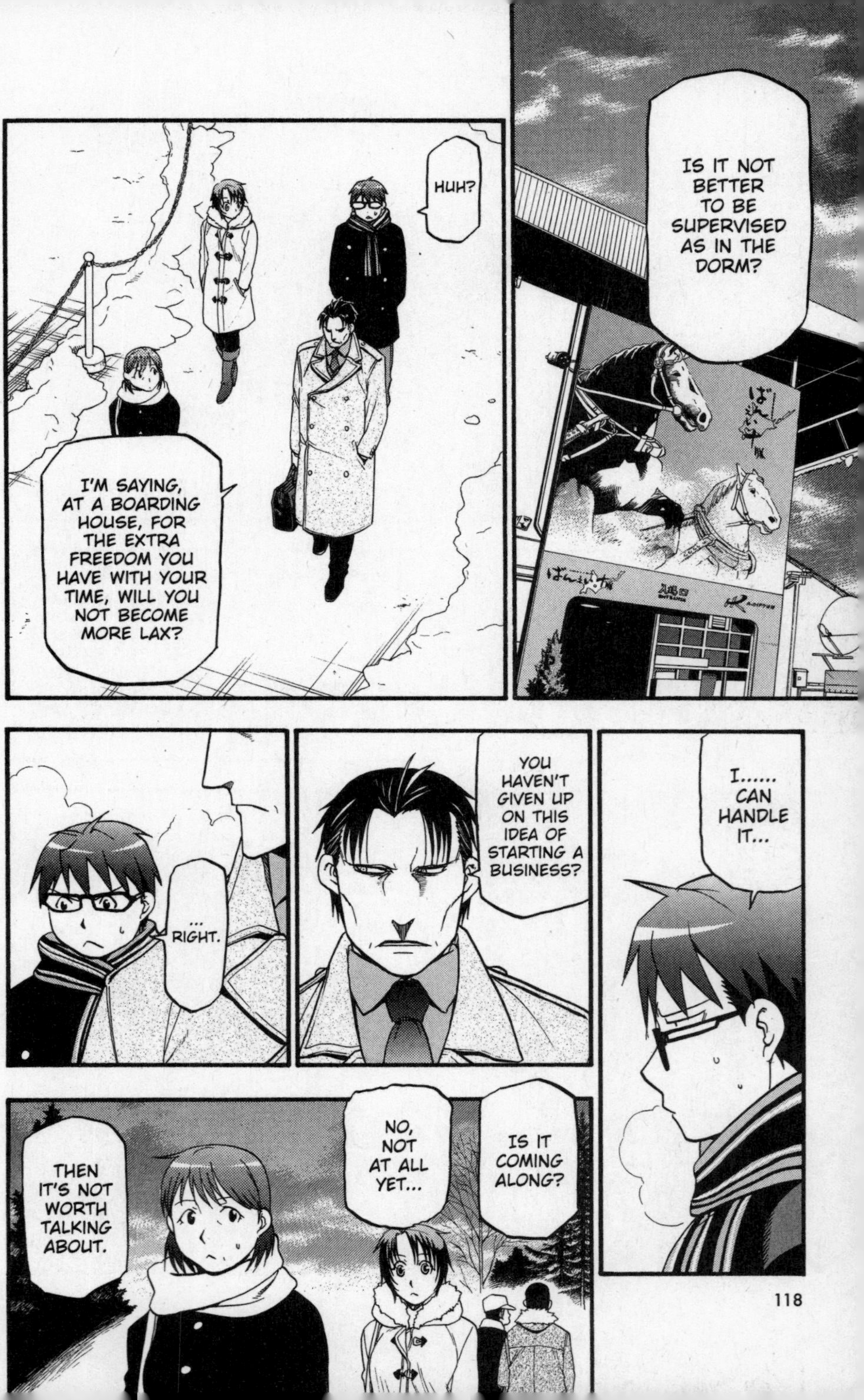
IS IT NOT BETTER TO BE SUPERVISED AS IN THE DORM?
HUH?
I'M SAYING, AT A BOARDING HOUSE, FOR THE EXTRA FREEDOM YOU HAVE WITH YOUR TIME, WILL YOU NOT BECOME MORE LAX?
I...... CAN HANDLE IT...
YOU HAVEN'T GIVEN UP ON THIS IDEA OF STARTING A BUSINESS?
...RIGHT.
IS IT COMING ALONG?
NO, NOT AT ALL YET...
THEN IT'S NOT WORTH TALKING ABOUT.

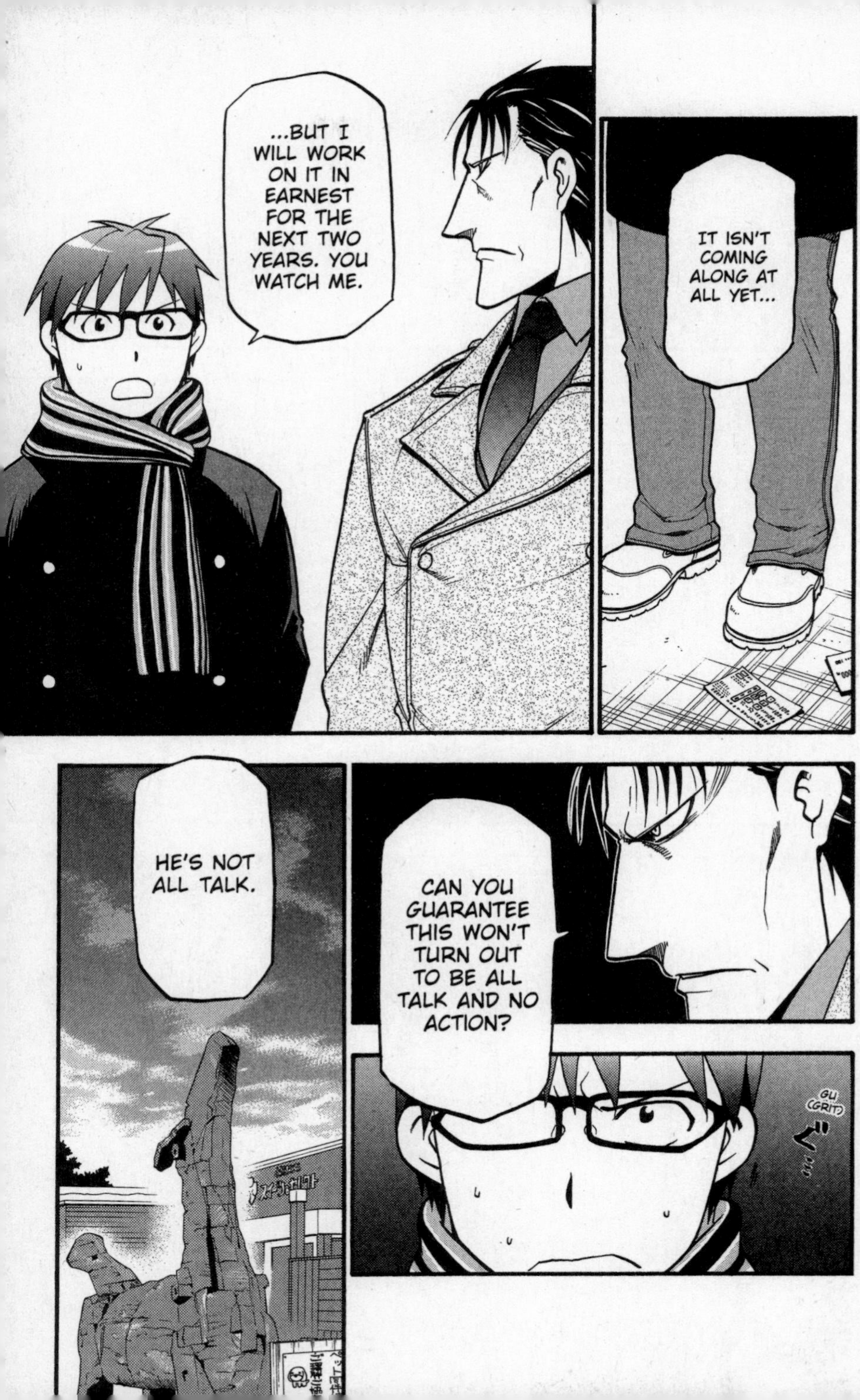
IT ISN'T COMING ALONG AT ALL YET...
...BUT I WILL WORK ON IT IN EARNEST FOR THE NEXT TWO YEARS. YOU WATCH ME.
CAN YOU GUARANTEE THIS WON'T TURN OUT TO BE ALL TALK AND NO ACTION?
GU (GRIT)
HE'S NOT ALL TALK.

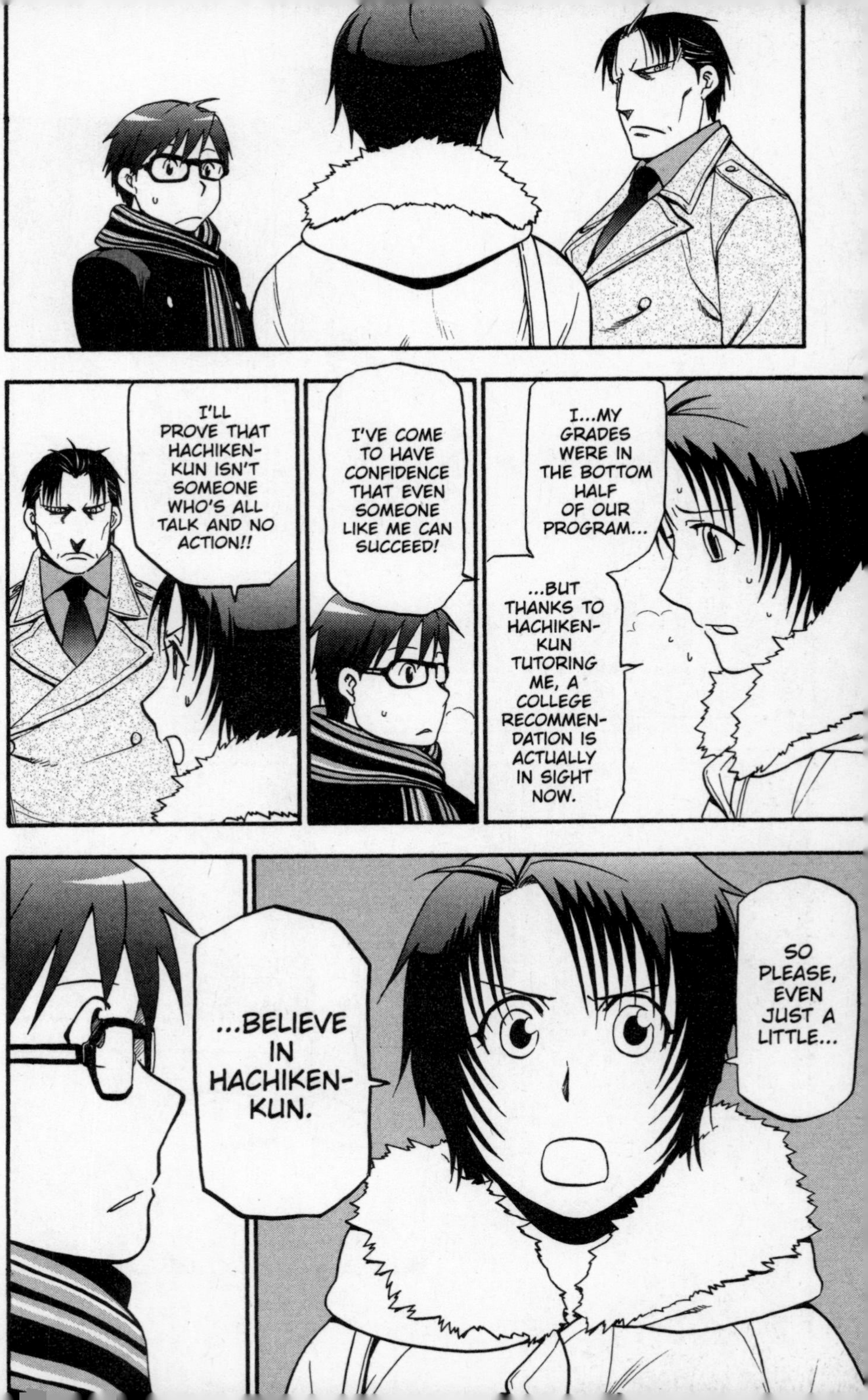
I...MY GRADES WERE IN THE BOTTOM HALF OF OUR PROGRAM...
...BUT THANKS TO HACHIKEN-KUN TUTORING ME, A COLLEGE RECOMMENDATION IS ACTUALLY IN SIGHT NOW.
I'VE COME TO HAVE CONFIDENCE THAT EVEN SOMEONE LIKE ME CAN SUCCEED!
I'LL PROVE THAT HACHIKEN-KUN ISN'T SOMEONE WHO'S ALL TALK AND NO ACTION!!
SO PLEASE, EVEN JUST A LITTLE...
...BELIEVE IN HACHIKEN-KUN.

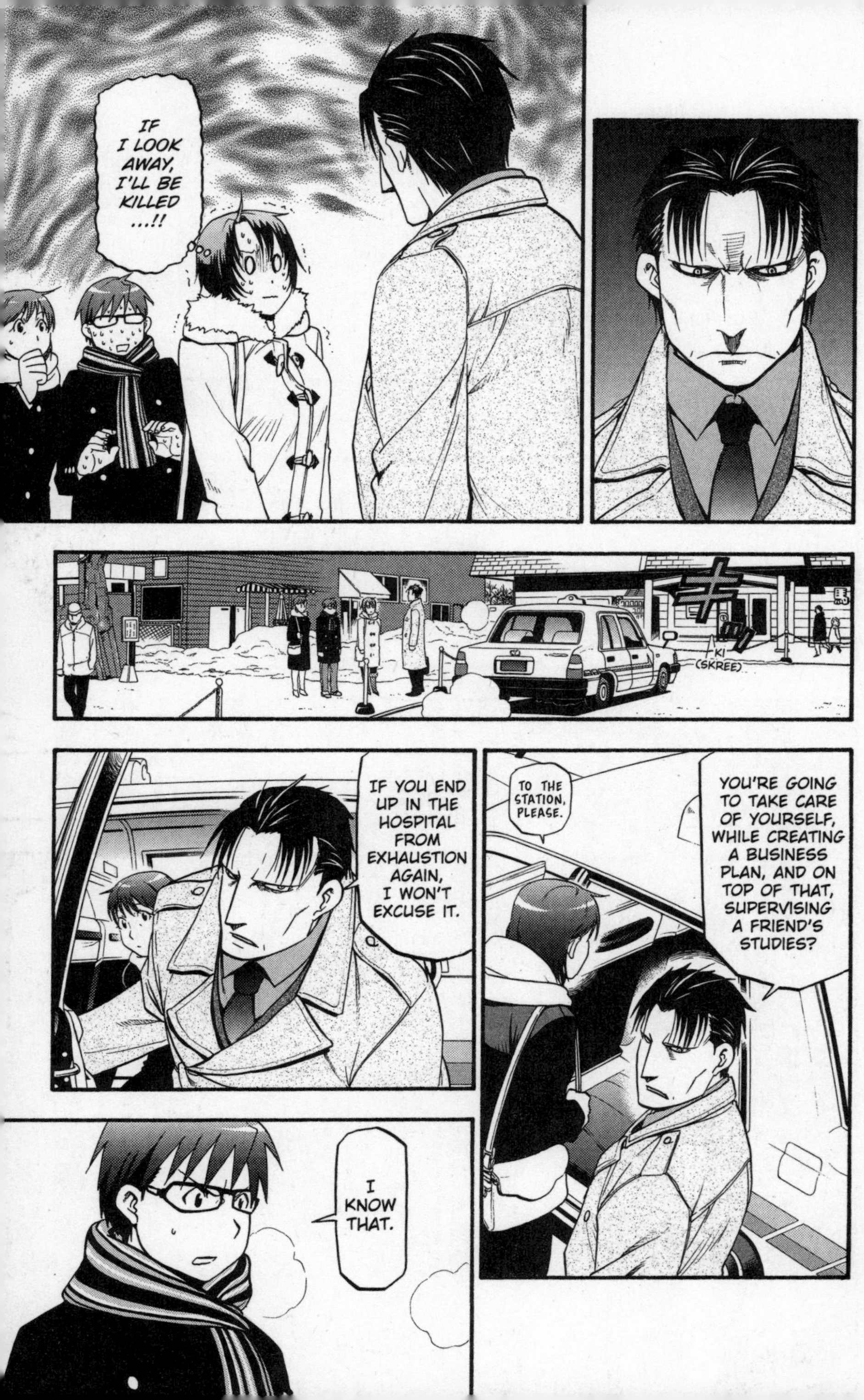
IF I LOOK AWAY, I'LL BE KILLED ...!!
KI (SKREE)
YOU'RE GOING TO TAKE CARE OF YOURSELF, WHILE CREATING A BUSINESS PLAN, AND ON TOP OF THAT, SUPERVISING A FRIEND'S STUDIES?
TO THE STATION, PLEASE.
IF YOU END UP IN THE HOSPITAL FROM EXHAUSTION AGAIN, I WON'T EXCUSE IT.
I KNOW THAT.

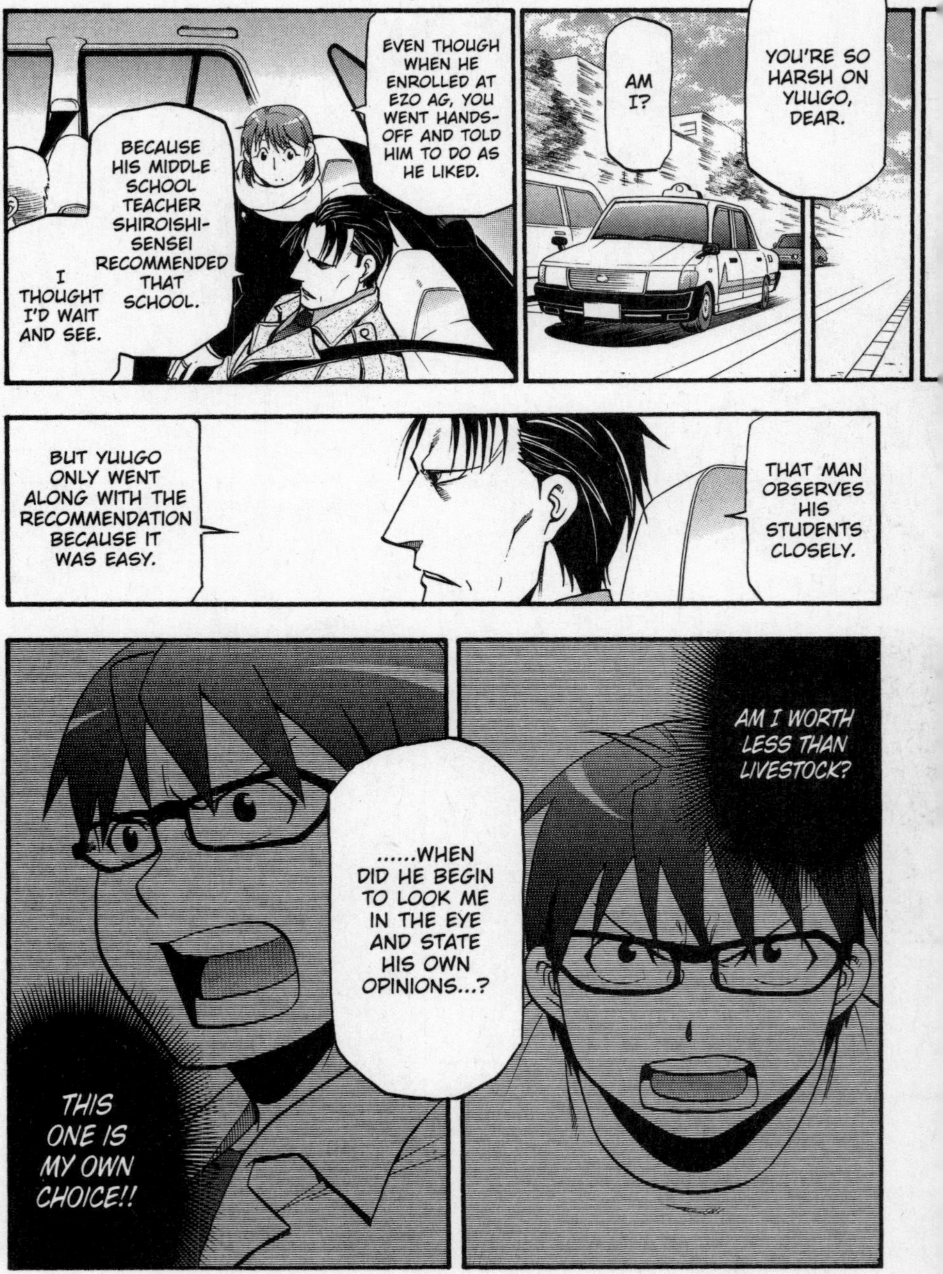
YOU'RE SO HARSH ON YUUGO, DEAR.
AM I?
EVEN THOUGH WHEN HE ENROLLED AT EZO AG, YOU WENT HANDS-OFF AND TOLD HIM TO DO AS HE LIKED.
BECAUSE HIS MIDDLE SCHOOL TEACHER SHIROISHI-SENSEI RECOMMENDED THAT SCHOOL.
I THOUGHT I'D WAIT AND SEE.
THAT MAN OBSERVES HIS STUDENTS CLOSELY.
BUT YUUGO ONLY WENT ALONG WITH THE RECOMMENDATION BECAUSE IT WAS EASY.
AM I WORTH LESS THAN LIVESTOCK?
THIS ONE IS MY OWN CHOICE!!
......WHEN DID HE BEGIN TO LOOK ME IN THE EYE AND STATE HIS OWN OPINIONS...?

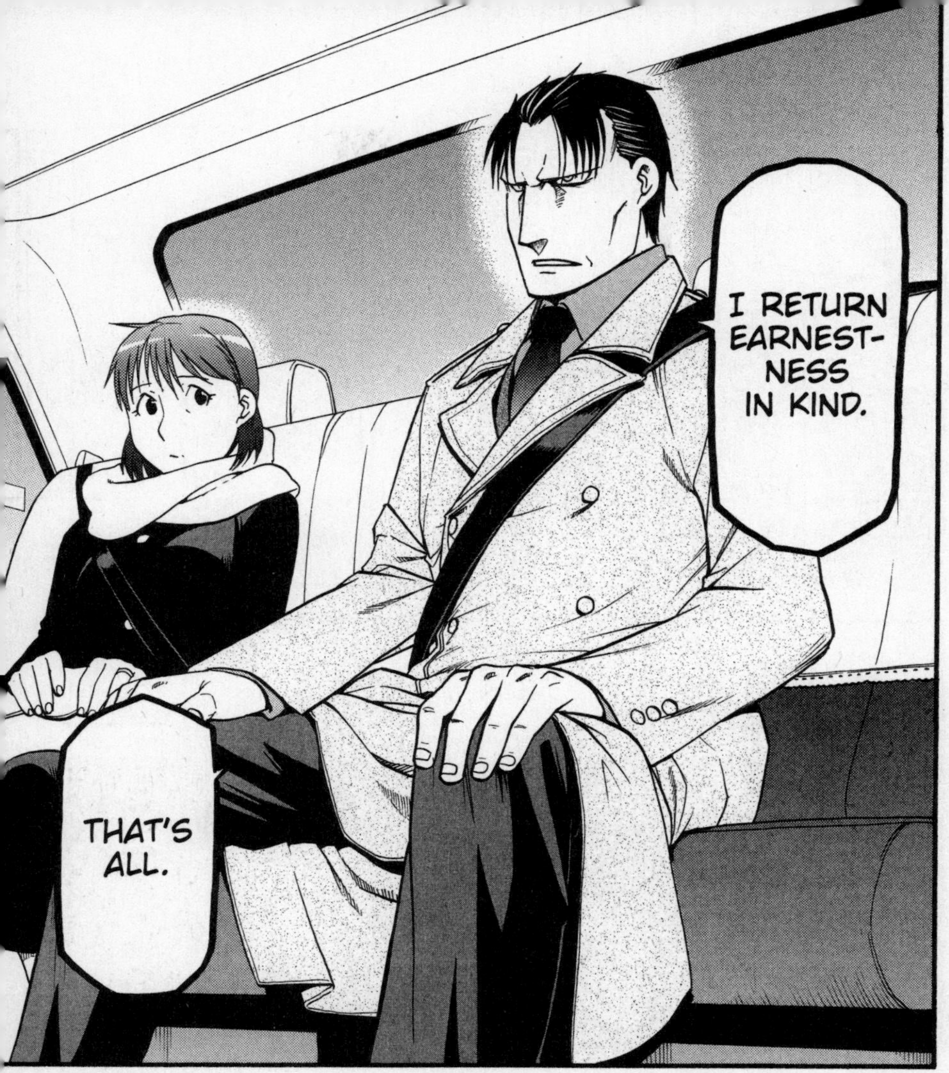
I RETURN EARNEST-NESS IN KIND.
THAT'S ALL.

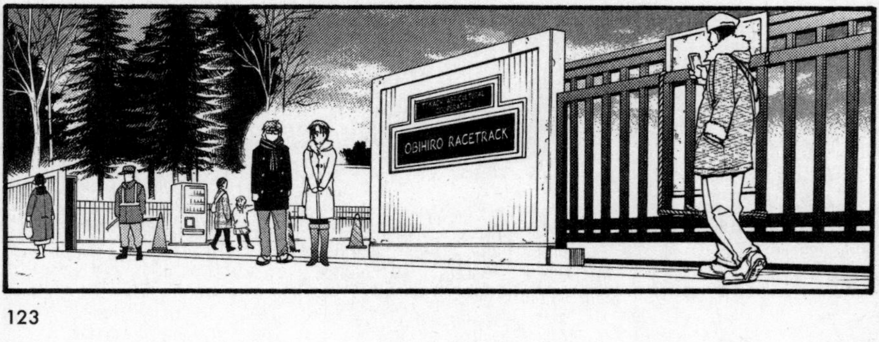
OBIHIRO RACETRACK

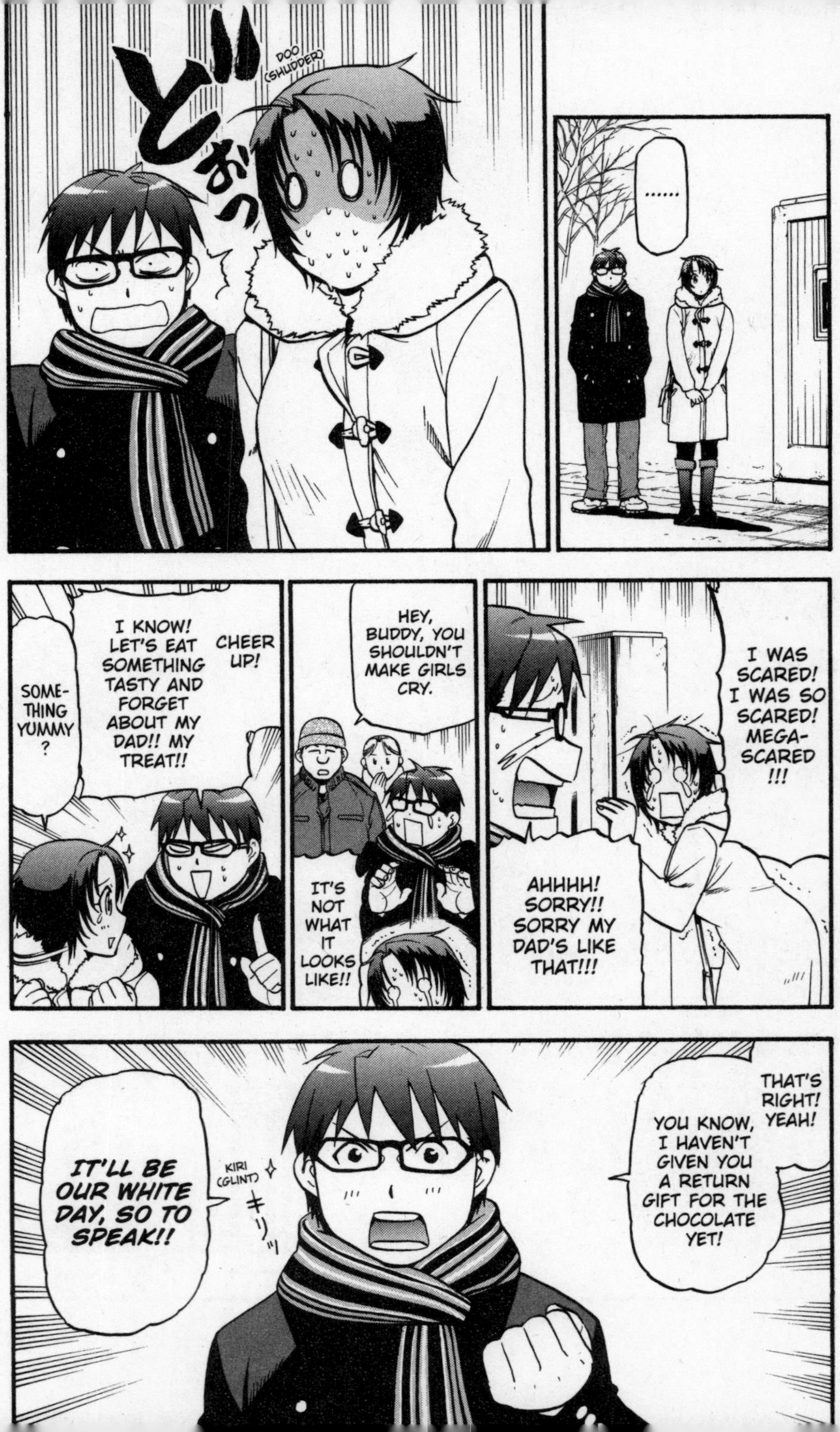
......
DOO (SHUDDER)
どぉっ
I WAS SCARED! I WAS SO SCARED! MEGA-SCARED!!!
AHHHH! SORRY!! SORRY MY DAD'S LIKE THAT!!!
HEY, BUDDY, YOU SHOULDN'T MAKE GIRLS CRY.
IT'S NOT WHAT IT LOOKS LIKE!!
CHEER UP!
I KNOW! LET'S EAT SOMETHING TASTY AND FORGET ABOUT MY DAD!! MY TREAT!!
SOME-THING YUMMY?
THAT'S RIGHT! YEAH!
YOU KNOW, I HAVEN'T GIVEN YOU A RETURN GIFT FOR THE CHOCOLATE YET!
KIRI (GLINT)
キリッ
IT'LL BE OUR WHITE DAY, SO TO SPEAK!!

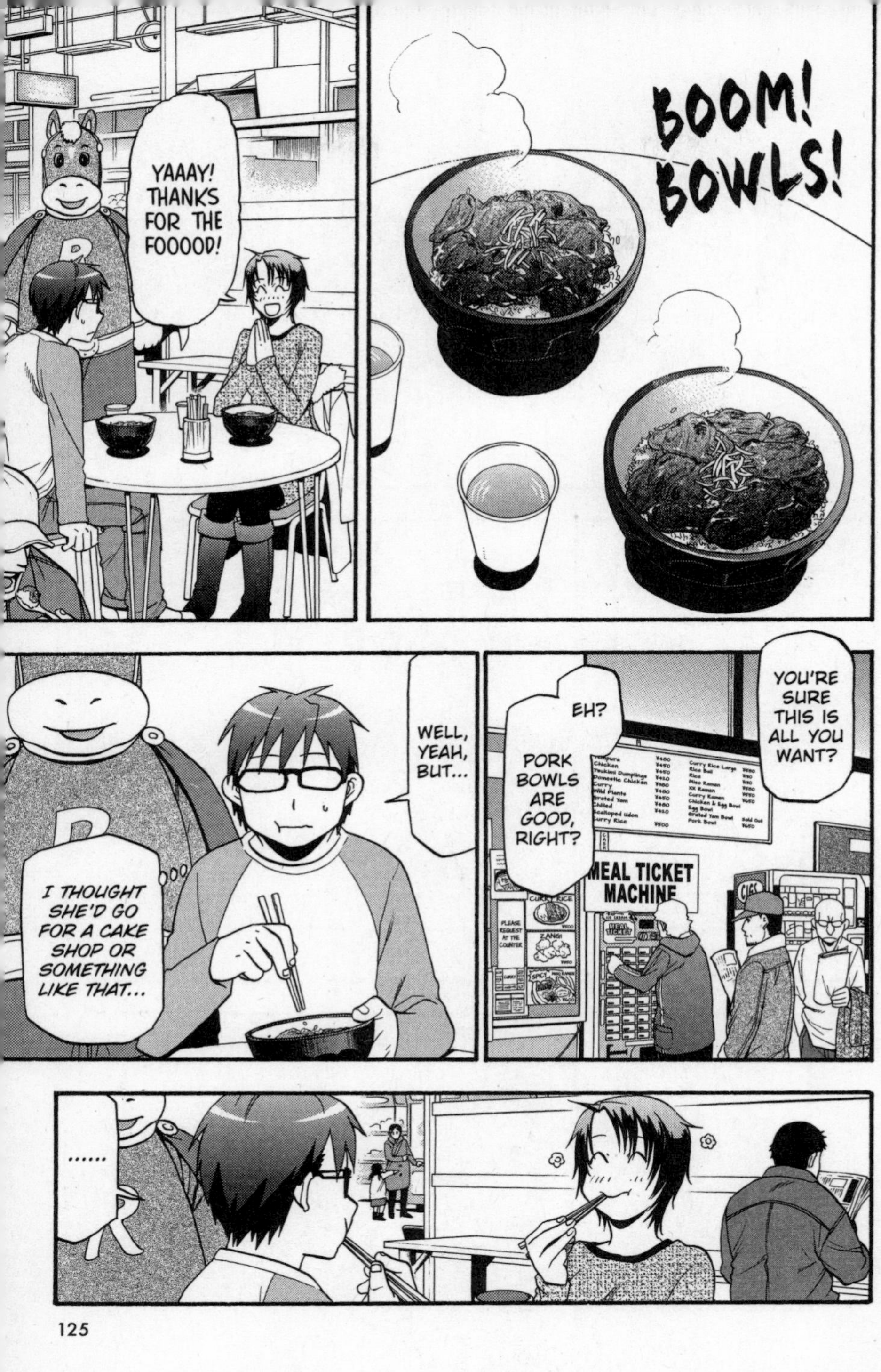
BOOM! BOWLS!
YAAAY! THANKS FOR THE FOOOOD!
YOU'RE SURE THIS IS ALL YOU WANT?
EH? PORK BOWLS ARE GOOD, RIGHT?
MEAL TICKET MACHINE
WELL, YEAH, BUT...
I THOUGHT SHE'D GO FOR A CAKE SHOP OR SOMETHING LIKE THAT...
......

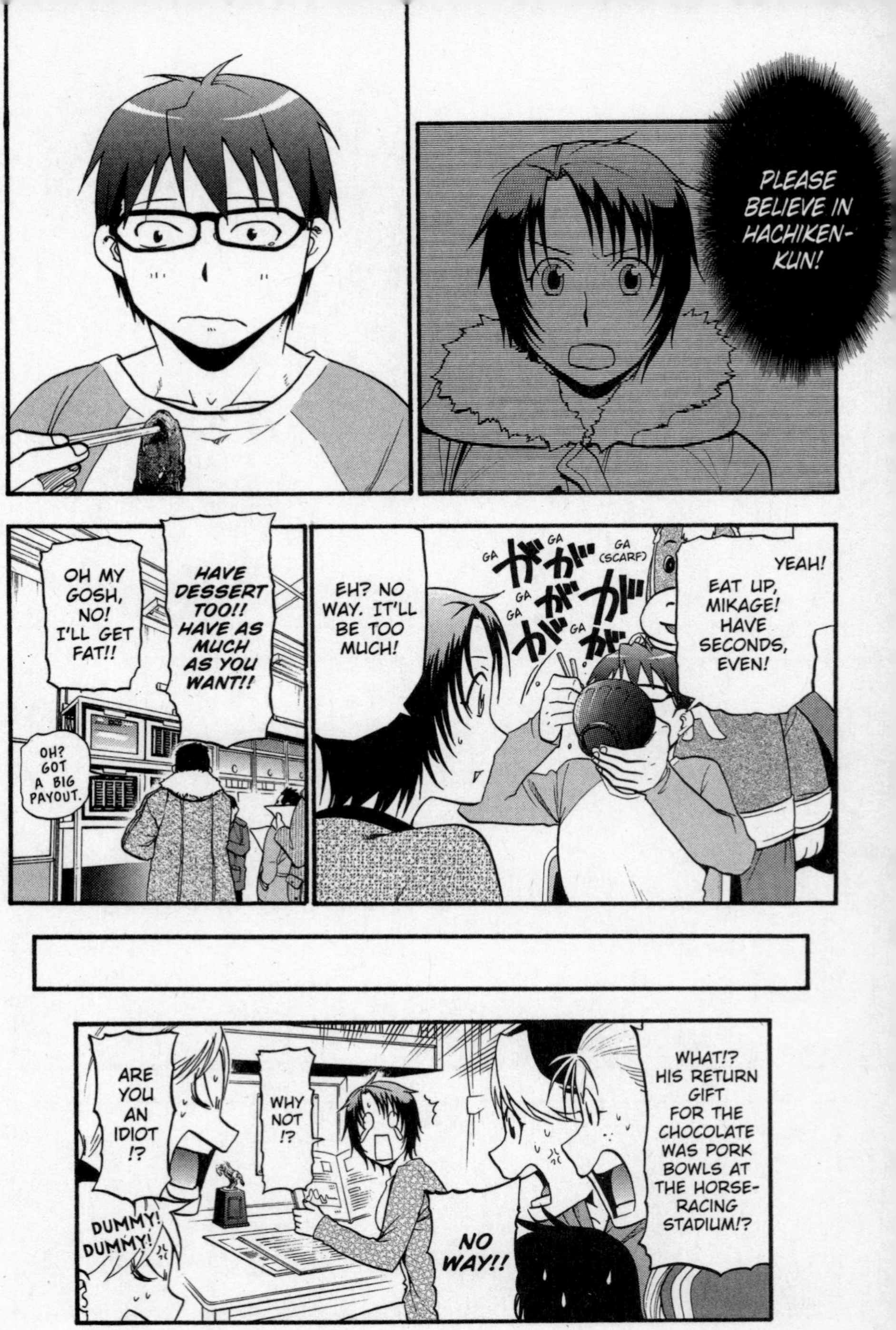
PLEASE BELIEVE IN HACHIKEN-KUN!
YEAH! EAT UP, MIKAGE! HAVE SECONDS, EVEN!
GA GA GA (SCARF) GA GA GA
がががががが
EH? NO WAY. IT'LL BE TOO MUCH!
HAVE DESSERT TOO!! HAVE AS MUCH AS YOU WANT!!
OH MY GOSH, NO! I'LL GET FAT!!
OH? GOT A BIG PAYOUT.
WHAT!? HIS RETURN GIFT FOR THE CHOCOLATE WAS PORK BOWLS AT THE HORSE-RACING STADIUM!?
NO WAY!!
WHY NOT!?
ARE YOU AN IDIOT!?
DUMMY! DUMMY!

Silver Spoon

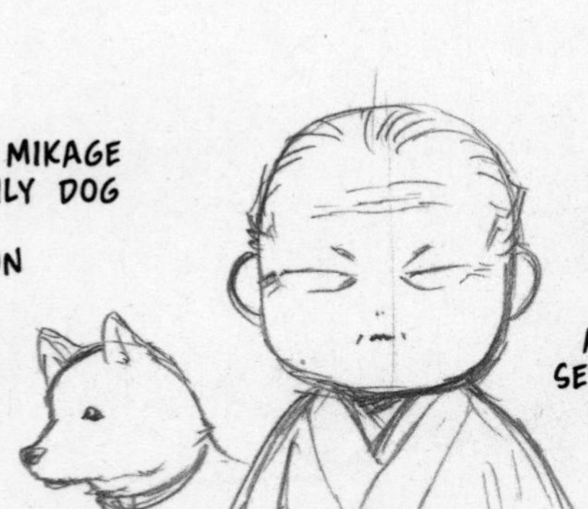
THE MIKAGE FAMILY DOG
TSUN
MIXED-BREED
SHINO MIKAGE
AKI'S GREAT-GRANDMA SETTLED IN HOKKAIDO AS A FRONTIER FARMER

Chapter 95:
Tale of Winter ㉜

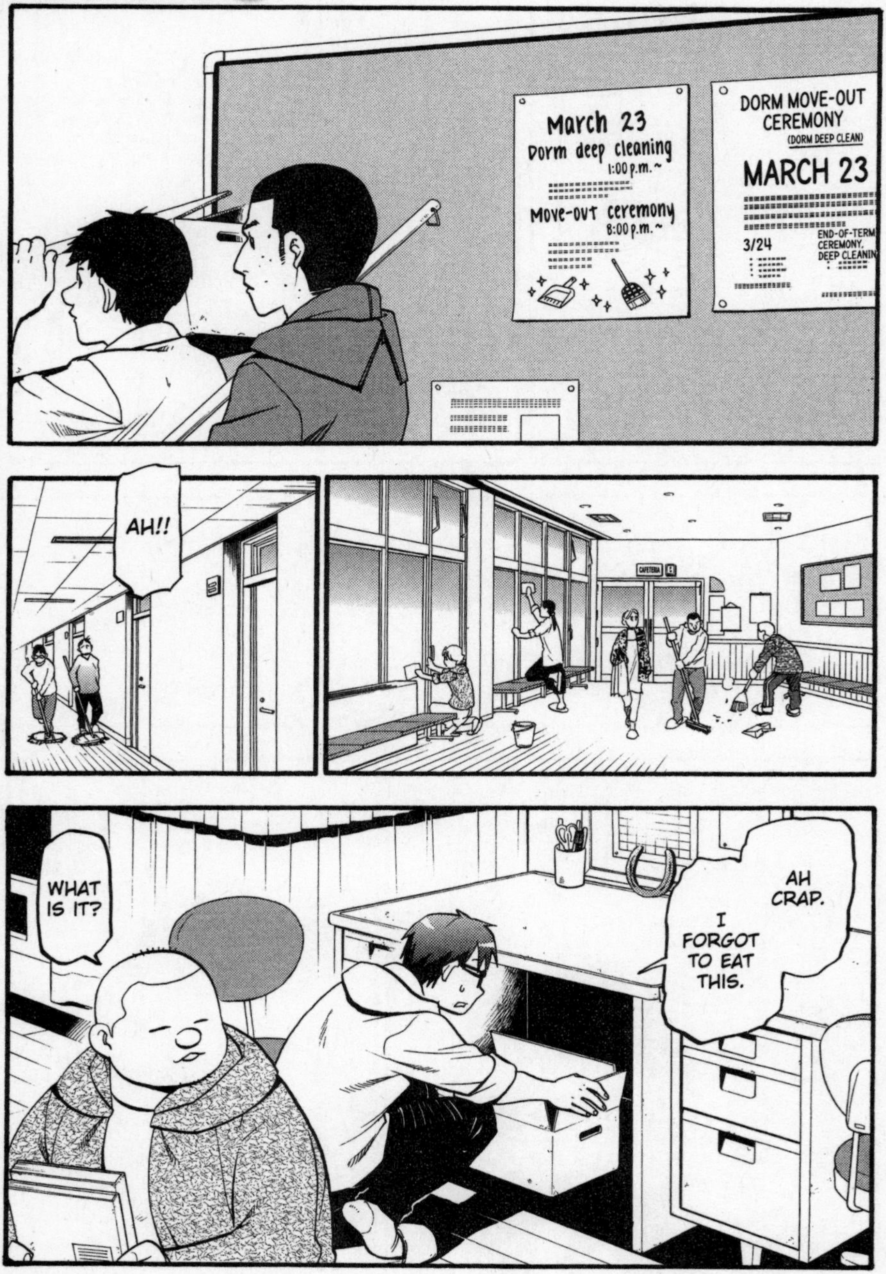

DORM MOVE-OUT CEREMONY
(DORM DEEP CLEAN)
MARCH 23
3/24
END-OF-TERM CEREMONY, DEEP CLEANIN
March 23
Dorm deep cleaning
1:00 p.m. ~
Move-out ceremony
8:00 p.m. ~
CAFETERIA
AH!!
WHAT IS IT?
AH CRAP.
I FORGOT TO EAT THIS.

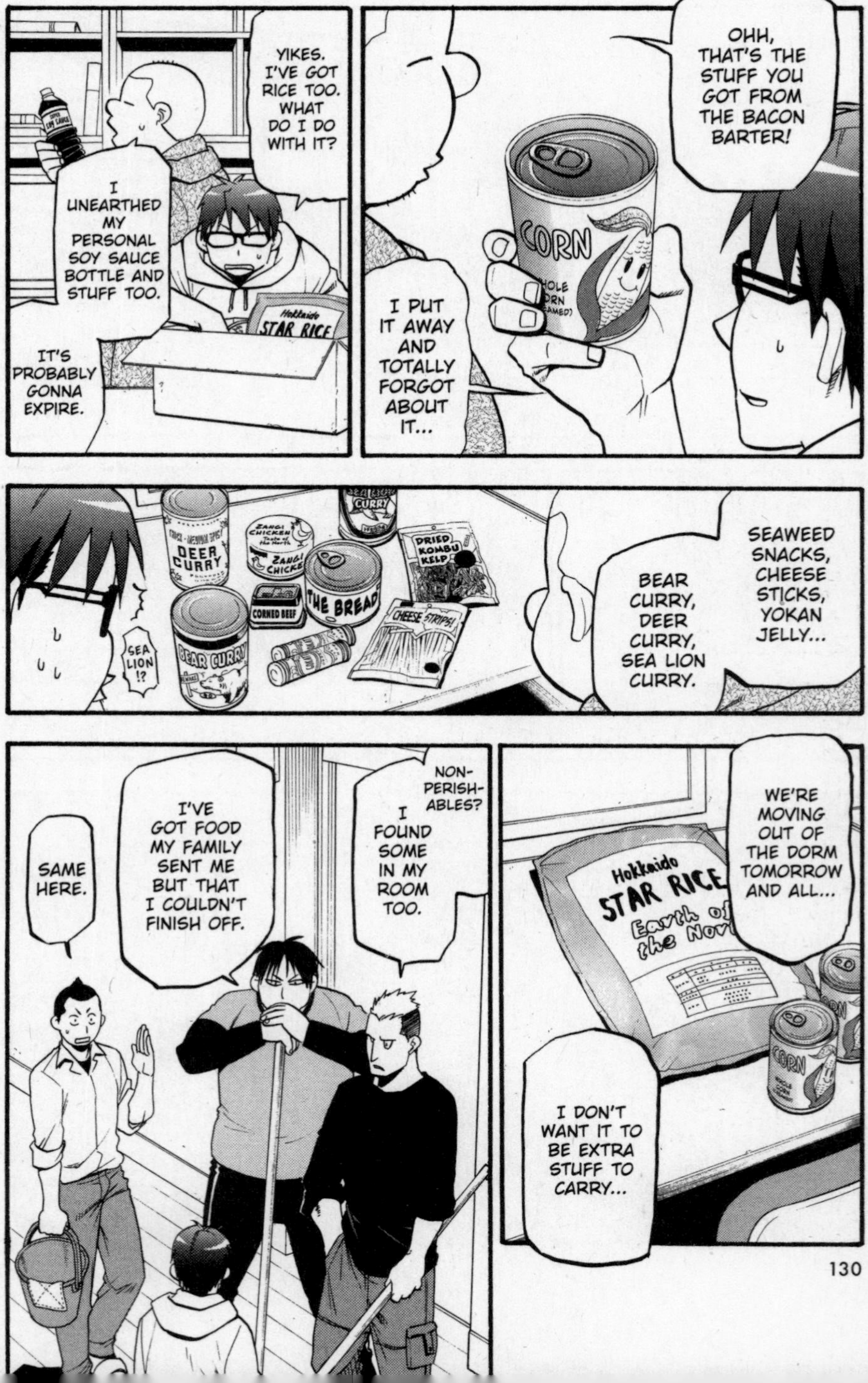
OHH, THAT'S THE STUFF YOU GOT FROM THE BACON BARTER!
CORN
I PUT IT AWAY AND TOTALLY FORGOT ABOUT IT...
YIKES. I'VE GOT RICE TOO. WHAT DO I DO WITH IT?
Hokkaido STAR RICE
I UNEARTHED MY PERSONAL SOY SAUCE BOTTLE AND STUFF TOO.
IT'S PROBABLY GONNA EXPIRE.
SEAWEED SNACKS, CHEESE STICKS, YOKAN JELLY...
BEAR CURRY, DEER CURRY, SEA LION CURRY.
DRIED KOMBU KELP
CHEESE STRIPS!
DEER CURRY
THE BREAD
CORNED BEEF
BEAR CURRY
SEA LION!?
WE'RE MOVING OUT OF THE DORM TOMORROW AND ALL...
Hokkaido STAR RICE
I DON'T WANT IT TO BE EXTRA STUFF TO CARRY...
NON-PERISHABLES?
I FOUND SOME IN MY ROOM TOO.
I'VE GOT FOOD MY FAMILY SENT ME BUT THAT I COULDN'T FINISH OFF.
SAME HERE.

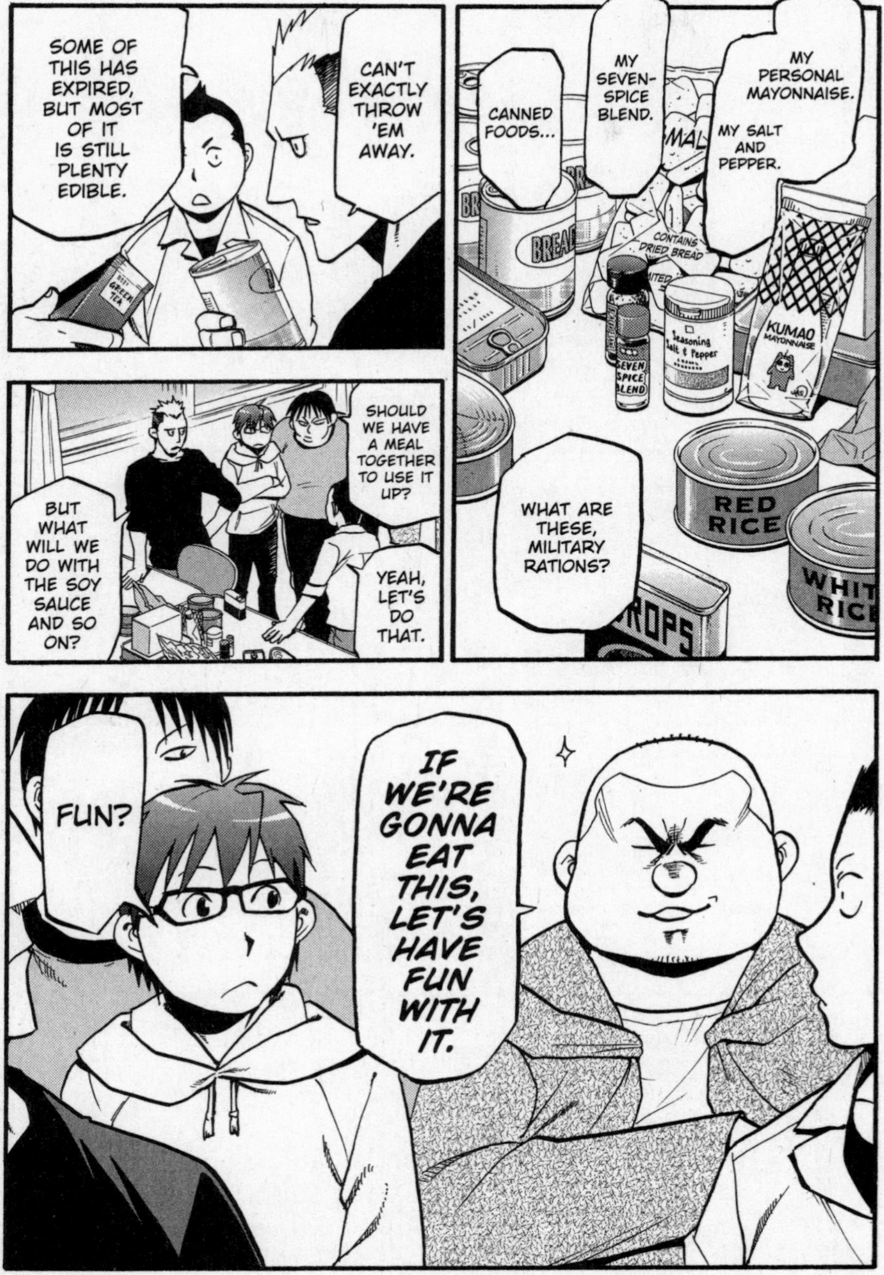
MY PERSONAL MAYONNAISE.
MY SALT AND PEPPER.
MY SEVEN-SPICE BLEND.
CANNED FOODS...
BREAD
CONTAINS DRIED BREAD
KUMAO MAYONNAISE
Seasoning Salt & Pepper
SEVEN SPICE BLEND
RED RICE
WHAT ARE THESE, MILITARY RATIONS?
CAN'T EXACTLY THROW 'EM AWAY.
SOME OF THIS HAS EXPIRED, BUT MOST OF IT IS STILL PLENTY EDIBLE.
GREEN TEA
SHOULD WE HAVE A MEAL TOGETHER TO USE IT UP?
YEAH, LET'S DO THAT.
BUT WHAT WILL WE DO WITH THE SOY SAUCE AND SO ON?
IF WE'RE GONNA EAT THIS, LET'S HAVE FUN WITH IT.
FUN?

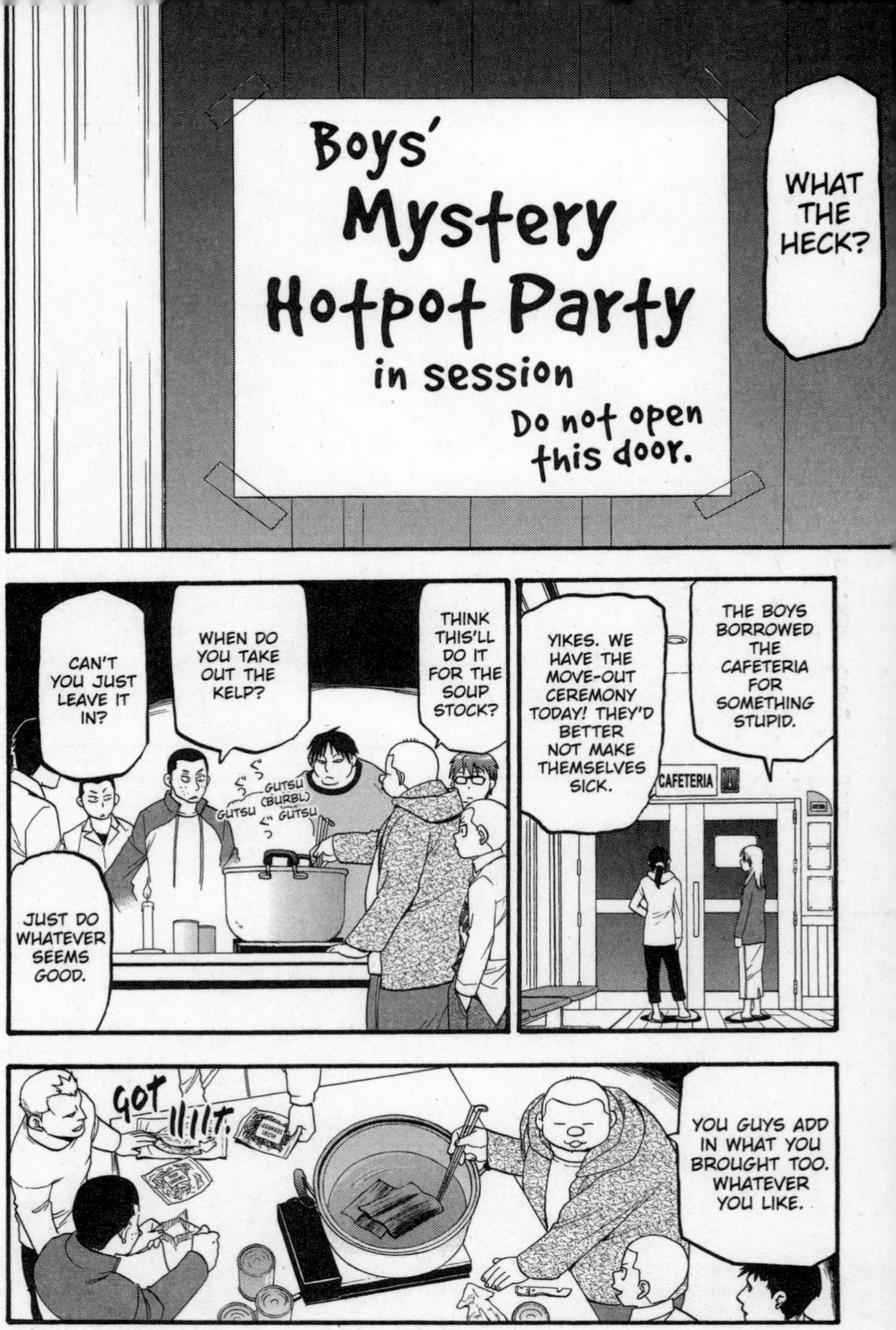
WHAT THE HECK?
Boys' Mystery Hotpot Party in session
Do not open this door.
THE BOYS BORROWED THE CAFETERIA FOR SOMETHING STUPID.
YIKES. WE HAVE THE MOVE-OUT CEREMONY TODAY! THEY'D BETTER NOT MAKE THEMSELVES SICK.
CAFETERIA
THINK THIS'LL DO IT FOR THE SOUP STOCK?
WHEN DO YOU TAKE OUT THE KELP?
CAN'T YOU JUST LEAVE IT IN?
GUTSU GUTSU (BURBL) GUTSU
JUST DO WHATEVER SEEMS GOOD.
YOU GUYS ADD IN WHAT YOU BROUGHT TOO. WHATEVER YOU LIKE.
GOT IIIT.

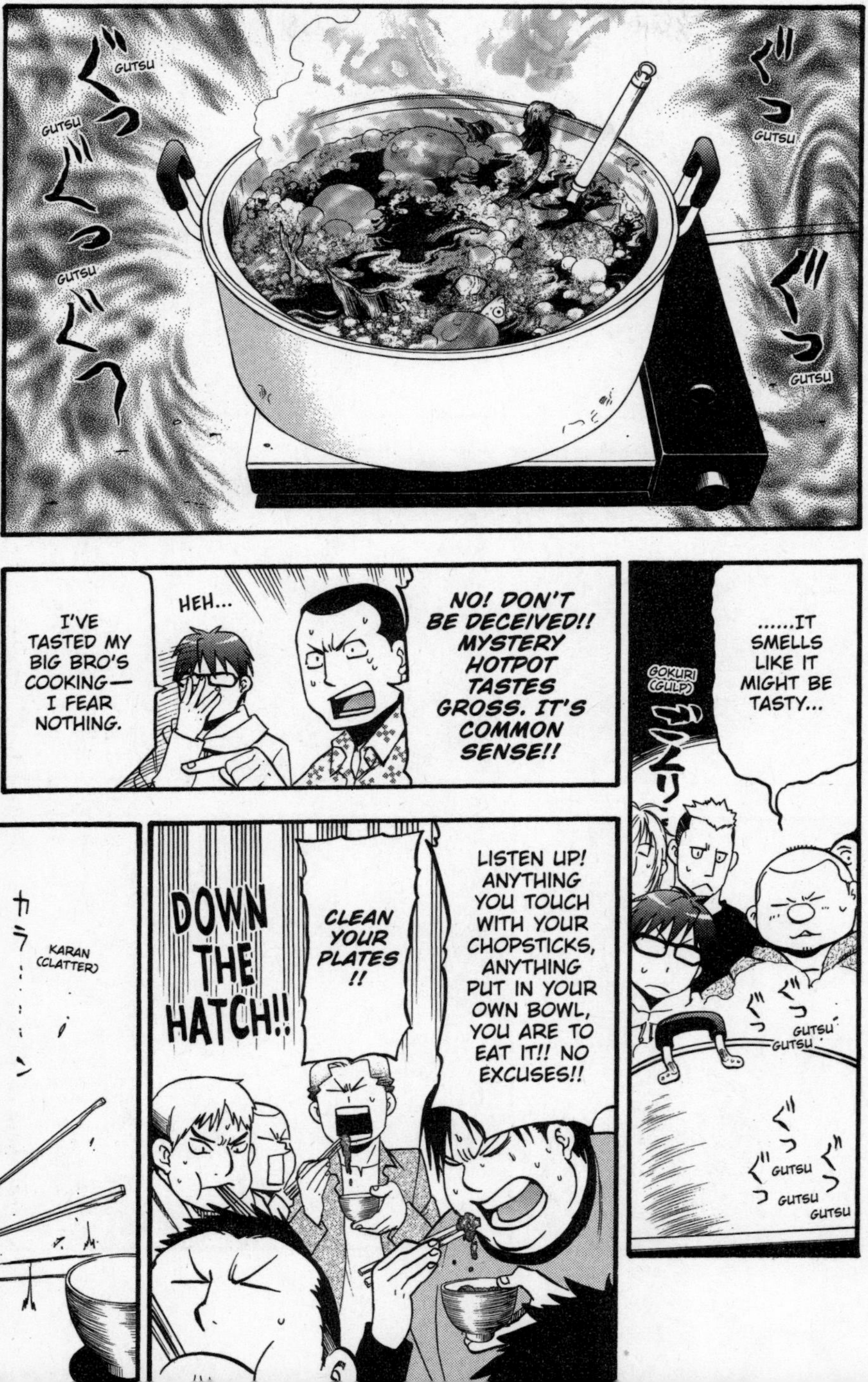
GUTSU
GUTSU
GUTSU
GUTSU
GUTSU
......IT SMELLS LIKE IT MIGHT BE TASTY...
GOKURI (GULP)
GUTSU
GUTSU
GUTSU
GUTSU
GUTSU
NO! DON'T BE DECEIVED!! MYSTERY HOTPOT TASTES GROSS. IT'S COMMON SENSE!!
HEH...
I'VE TASTED MY BIG BRO'S COOKING— I FEAR NOTHING.
LISTEN UP! ANYTHING YOU TOUCH WITH YOUR CHOPSTICKS, ANYTHING PUT IN YOUR OWN BOWL, YOU ARE TO EAT IT!! NO EXCUSES!!
CLEAN YOUR PLATES !!
DOWN THE HATCH!!
KARAN (CLATTER)

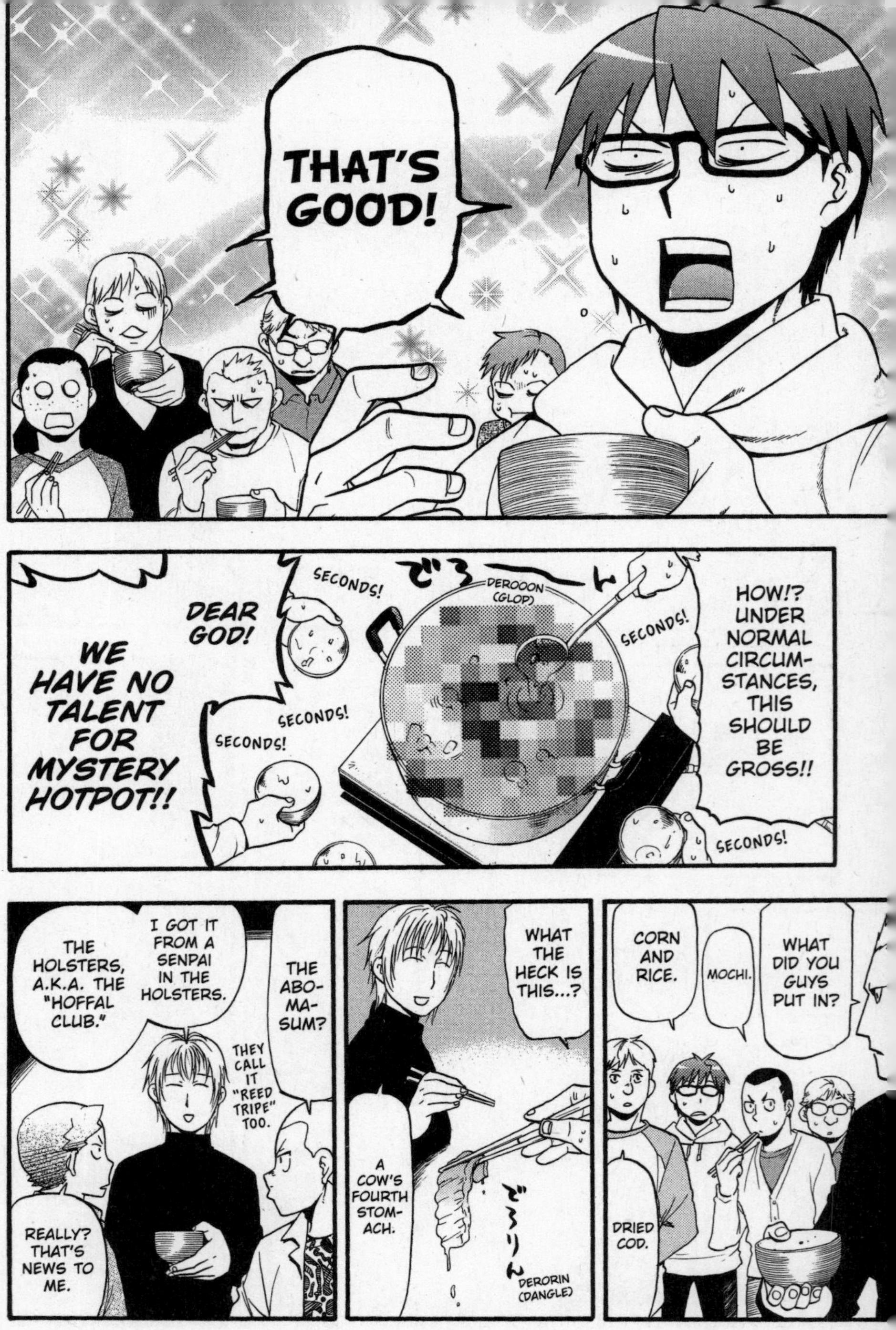
THAT'S GOOD!
HOW!? UNDER NORMAL CIRCUM-STANCES, THIS SHOULD BE GROSS!!
SECONDS!
SECONDS!
でろーーん
DEROOON (GLOP)
SECONDS!
DEAR GOD!
SECONDS!
SECONDS!
WE HAVE NO TALENT FOR MYSTERY HOTPOT!!
WHAT DID YOU GUYS PUT IN?
MOCHI.
CORN AND RICE.
DRIED COD.
WHAT THE HECK IS THIS...?
A COW'S FOURTH STOM-ACH.
でろりん
DERORIN (DANGLE)
THE ABO-MA-SUM?
THEY CALL IT "REED TRIPE" TOO.
I GOT IT FROM A SENPAI IN THE HOLSTERS.
THE HOLSTERS, A.K.A. THE "HOFFAL CLUB."
REALLY? THAT'S NEWS TO ME.

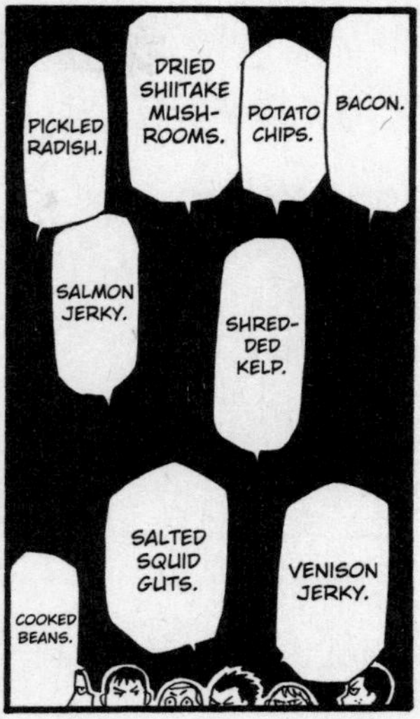
BACON.
POTATO CHIPS.
DRIED SHIITAKE MUSH-ROOMS.
PICKLED RADISH.
SHRED-DED KELP.
SALMON JERKY.
VENISON JERKY.
SALTED SQUID GUTS.
COOKED BEANS.
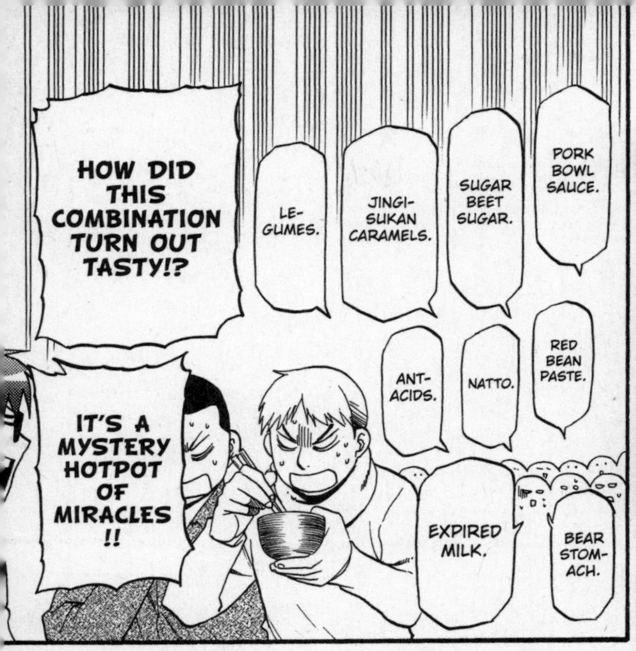
PORK BOWL SAUCE.
SUGAR BEET SUGAR.
JINGI-SUKAN CARAMELS.
LE-GUMES.
HOW DID THIS COMBINATION TURN OUT TASTY!?
RED BEAN PASTE.
NATTO.
ANT-ACIDS.
BEAR STOM-ACH.
EXPIRED MILK.
IT'S A MYSTERY HOTPOT OF MIRACLES!!
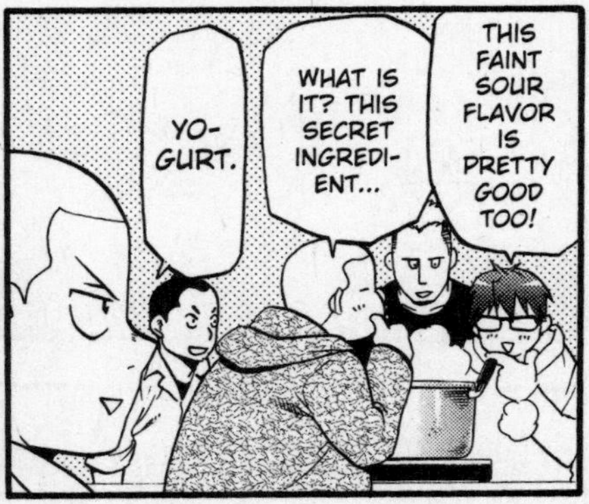
THIS FAINT SOUR FLAVOR IS PRETTY GOOD TOO!
WHAT IS IT? THIS SECRET INGREDI-ENT...
YO-GURT.
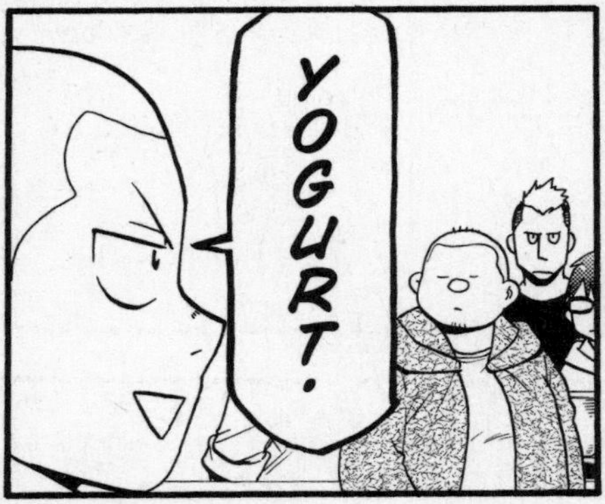
YOGURT!
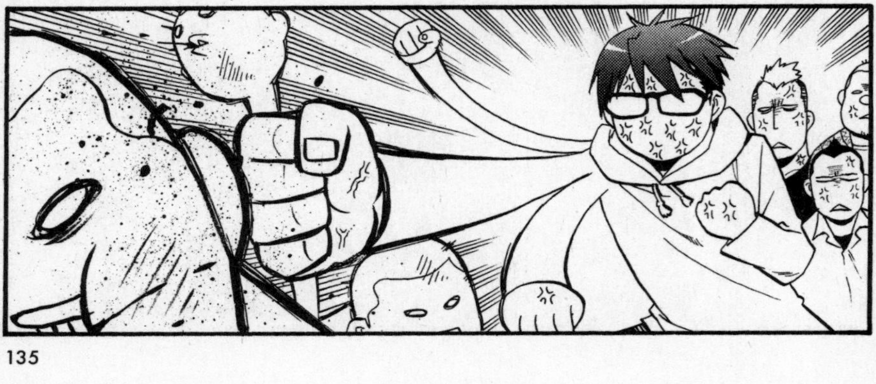

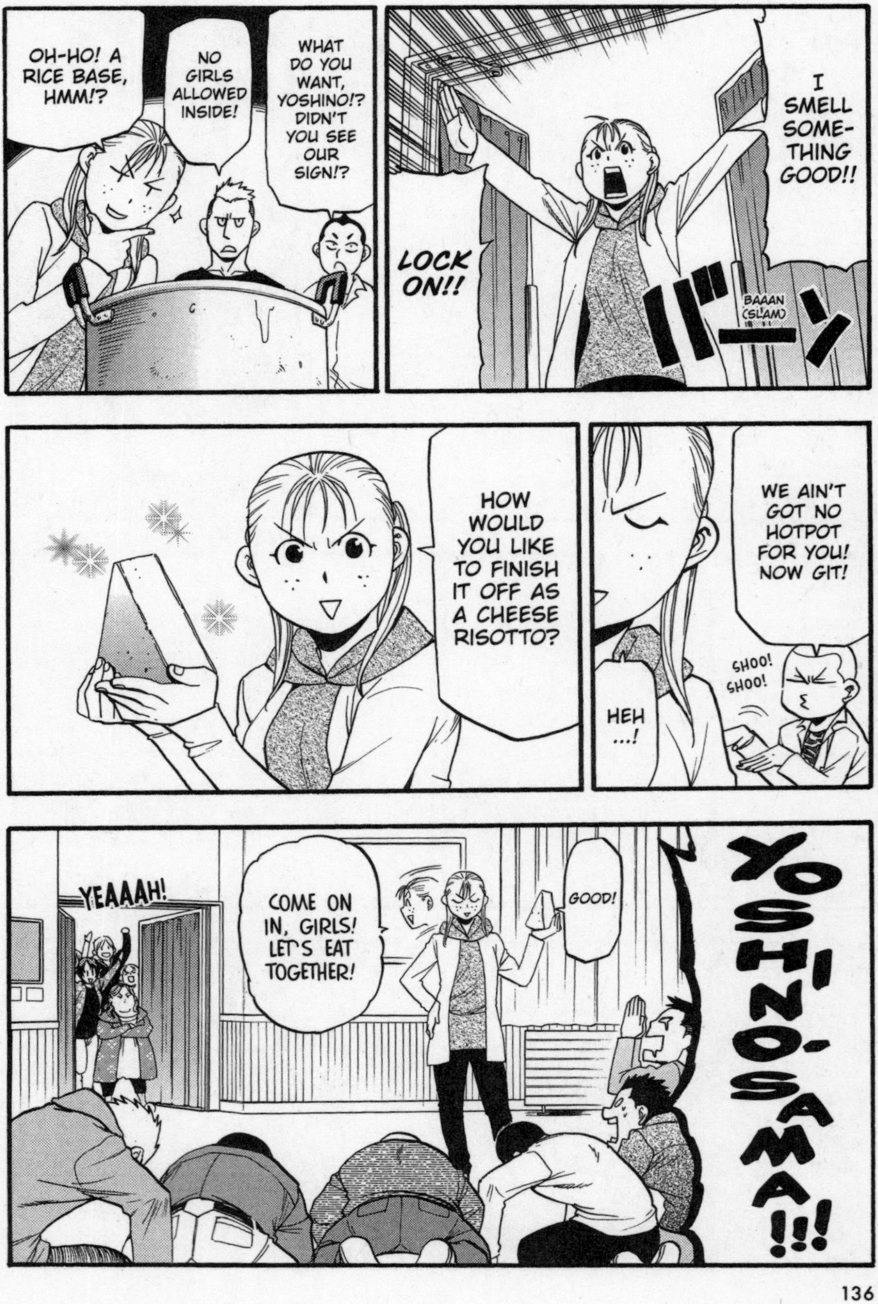
I SMELL SOME-THING GOOD!!
LOCK ON!!
バーン
BAAAN (SLAM)
WHAT DO YOU WANT, YOSHINO!? DIDN'T YOU SEE OUR SIGN!?
NO GIRLS ALLOWED INSIDE!
OH-HO! A RICE BASE, HMM!?
WE AIN'T GOT NO HOTPOT FOR YOU! NOW GIT!
SHOO! SHOO!
HEH ...!
HOW WOULD YOU LIKE TO FINISH IT OFF AS A CHEESE RISOTTO?
YOSHINO-SAMA!!!
GOOD!
COME ON IN, GIRLS! LET'S EAT TOGETHER!
YEAAAH!

Chapter 95: Tale of Winter 32

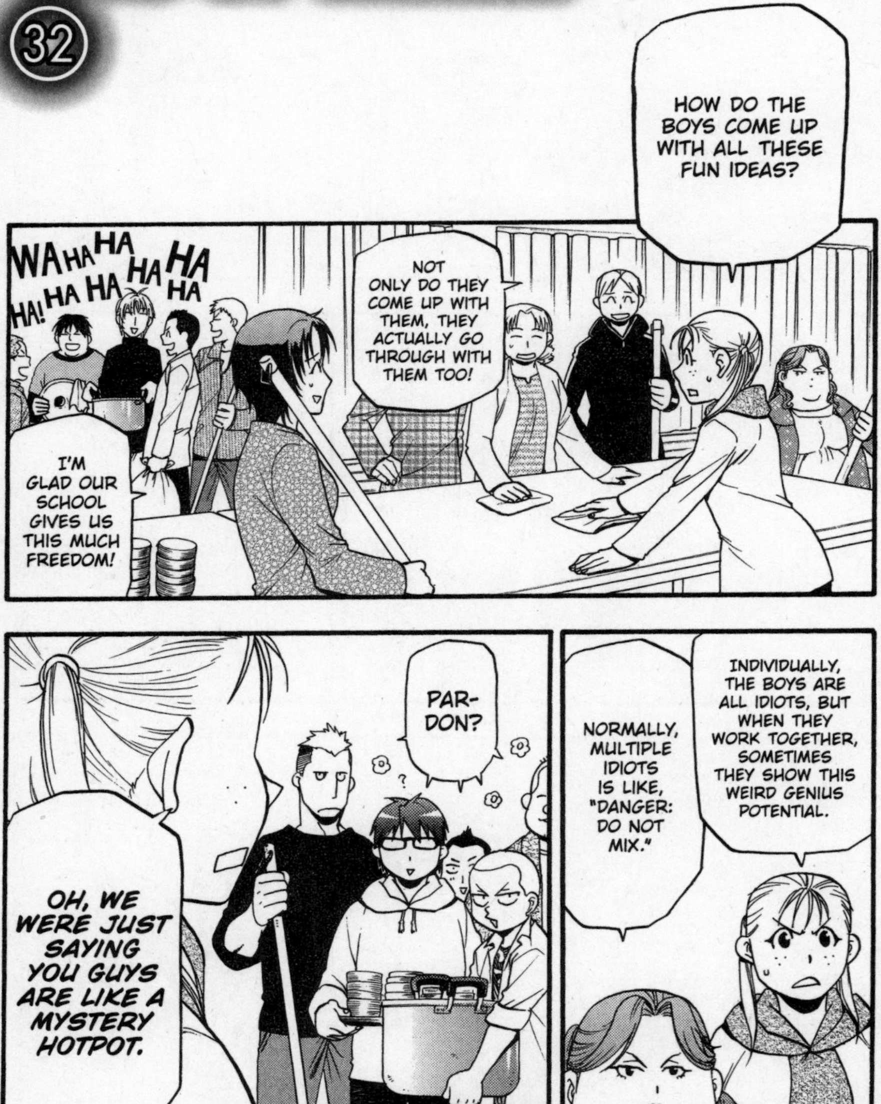
HOW DO THE BOYS COME UP WITH ALL THESE FUN IDEAS?
NOT ONLY DO THEY COME UP WITH THEM, THEY ACTUALLY GO THROUGH WITH THEM TOO!
WAHAHAHA HA! HA HA HA HA HA HA
I'M GLAD OUR SCHOOL GIVES US THIS MUCH FREEDOM!
INDIVIDUALLY, THE BOYS ARE ALL IDIOTS, BUT WHEN THEY WORK TOGETHER, SOMETIMES THEY SHOW THIS WEIRD GENIUS POTENTIAL.
NORMALLY, MULTIPLE IDIOTS IS LIKE, "DANGER: DO NOT MIX."
PAR-DON?
?
OH, WE WERE JUST SAYING YOU GUYS ARE LIKE A MYSTERY HOTPOT.

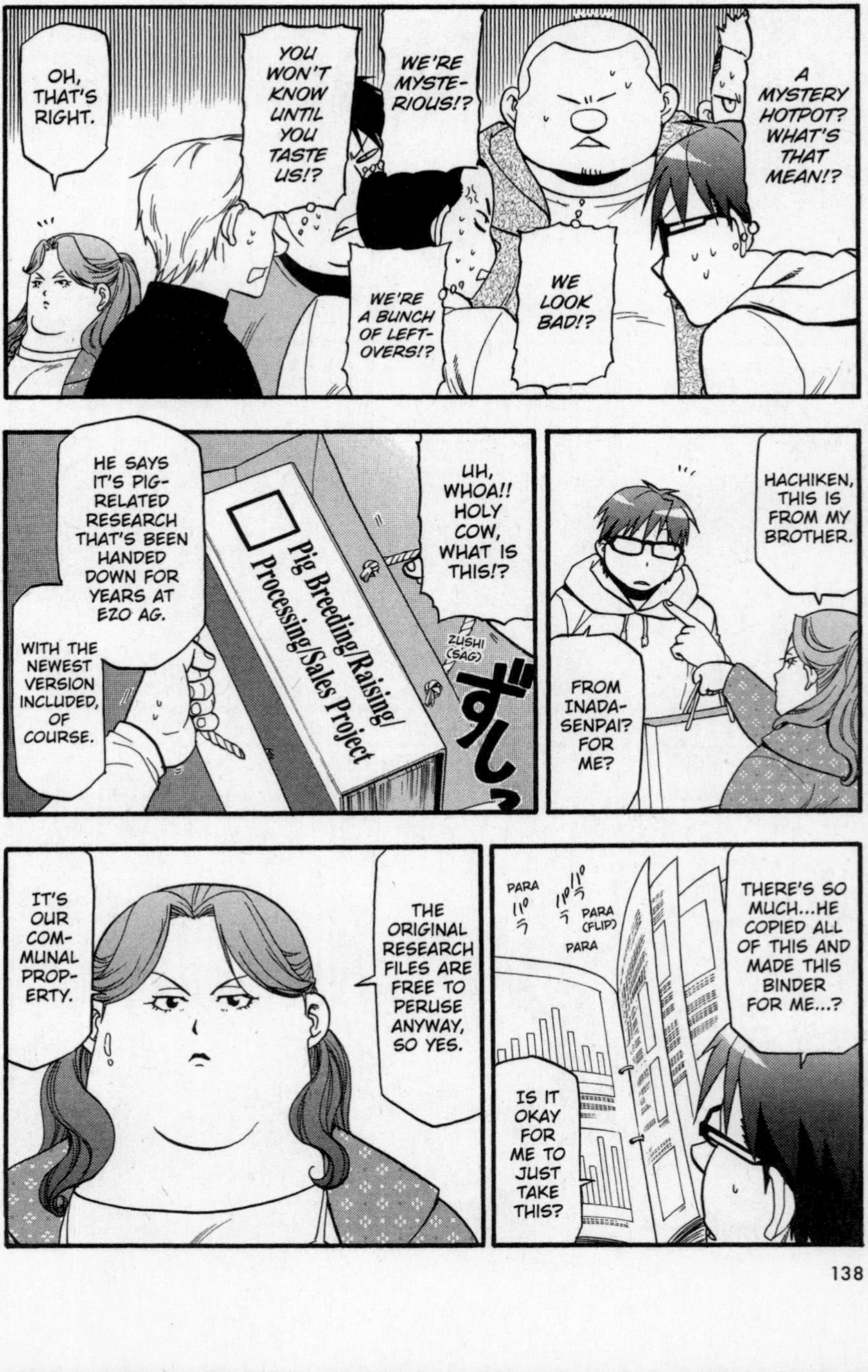
A MYSTERY HOTPOT? WHAT'S THAT MEAN!?
WE'RE MYSTERIOUS!?
WE LOOK BAD!?
YOU WON'T KNOW UNTIL YOU TASTE US!?
WE'RE A BUNCH OF LEFTOVERS!?
OH, THAT'S RIGHT.
HACHIKEN, THIS IS FROM MY BROTHER.
FROM INADA-SENPAI? FOR ME?
UH, WHOA!! HOLY COW, WHAT IS THIS!?
ZUSHI (SAG)
Pig Breeding/Raising/Processing/Sales Project
HE SAYS IT'S PIG-RELATED RESEARCH THAT'S BEEN HANDED DOWN FOR YEARS AT EZO AG.
WITH THE NEWEST VERSION INCLUDED, OF COURSE.
PARA PARA (FLIP) PARA
THERE'S SO MUCH...HE COPIED ALL OF THIS AND MADE THIS BINDER FOR ME...?
IS IT OKAY FOR ME TO JUST TAKE THIS?
THE ORIGINAL RESEARCH FILES ARE FREE TO PERUSE ANYWAY, SO YES.
IT'S OUR COMMUNAL PROPERTY.

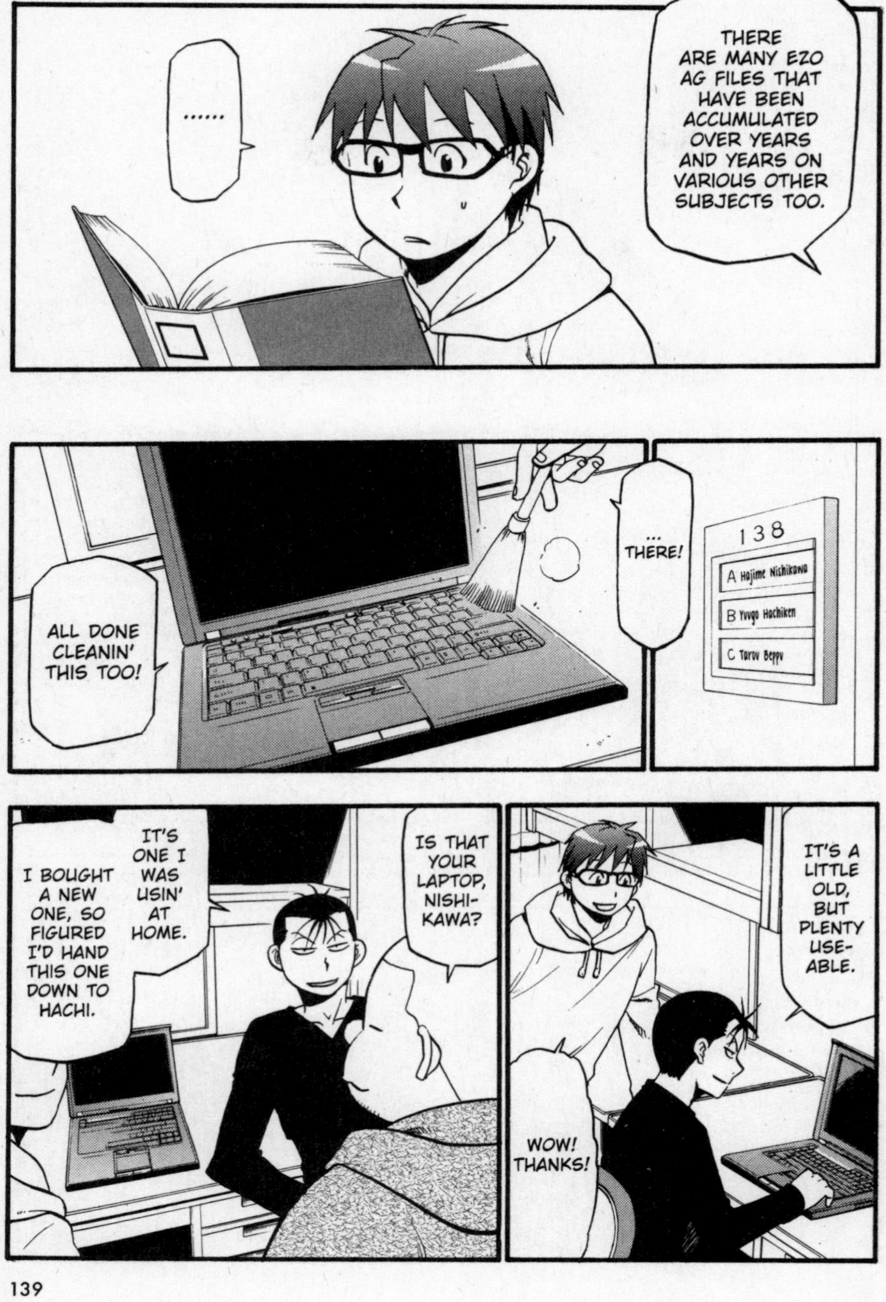
THERE ARE MANY EZO AG FILES THAT HAVE BEEN ACCUMULATED OVER YEARS AND YEARS ON VARIOUS OTHER SUBJECTS TOO.
......
... THERE!
138
A Hajime Nishikawa
B Yuugo Hachiken
C Tarou Beppu
ALL DONE CLEANIN' THIS TOO!
IT'S A LITTLE OLD, BUT PLENTY USE-ABLE.
WOW! THANKS!
IS THAT YOUR LAPTOP, NISHI-KAWA?
IT'S ONE I WAS USIN' AT HOME.
I BOUGHT A NEW ONE, SO FIGURED I'D HAND THIS ONE DOWN TO HACHI.

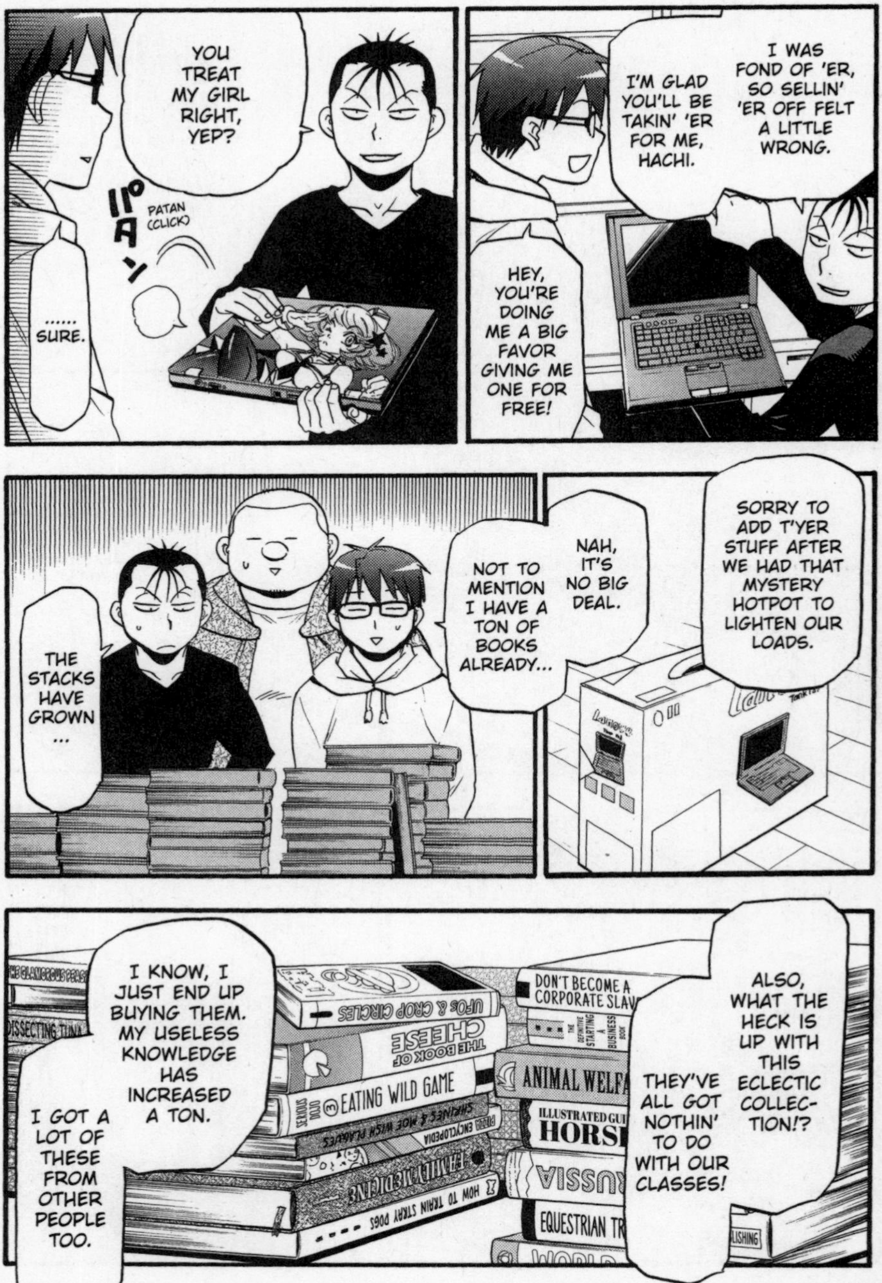
I WAS FOND OF 'ER, SO SELLIN' 'ER OFF FELT A LITTLE WRONG.
I'M GLAD YOU'LL BE TAKIN' 'ER FOR ME, HACHI.
HEY, YOU'RE DOING ME A BIG FAVOR GIVING ME ONE FOR FREE!
YOU TREAT MY GIRL RIGHT, YEP?
パタン
PATAN (CLICK)
...... SURE.
SORRY TO ADD T'YER STUFF AFTER WE HAD THAT MYSTERY HOTPOT TO LIGHTEN OUR LOADS.
NAH, IT'S NO BIG DEAL.
NOT TO MENTION I HAVE A TON OF BOOKS ALREADY...
THE STACKS HAVE GROWN ...
ALSO, WHAT THE HECK IS UP WITH THIS ECLECTIC COLLECTION!?
THEY'VE ALL GOT NOTHIN' TO DO WITH OUR CLASSES!
I KNOW, I JUST END UP BUYING THEM. MY USELESS KNOWLEDGE HAS INCREASED A TON.
I GOT A LOT OF THESE FROM OTHER PEOPLE TOO.
DON'T BECOME A CORPORATE SLAV
THE DEFINITIVE STARTING A BUSINESS BOOK
ANIMAL WELFA
ILLUSTRATED GUI HORS
RUSSIA
EQUESTRIAN TR
UFOs & CROP CIRCLES
THE BOOK OF CHEESE
EATING WILD GAME
SHRINES & MOE WISH PLAQUES
PIZZA ENCYCLOPEDIA
FAMILY MEDICINE
HOW TO TRAIN STRAY DOGS
DISSECTING TUNA

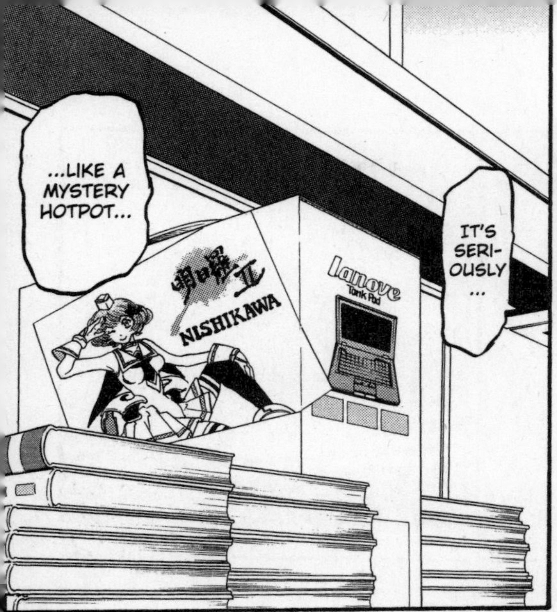
IT'S SERI-OUSLY ...
...LIKE A MYSTERY HOTPOT...
NISHIKAWA
lanove
Tank Pad

STICKER: ASURA II

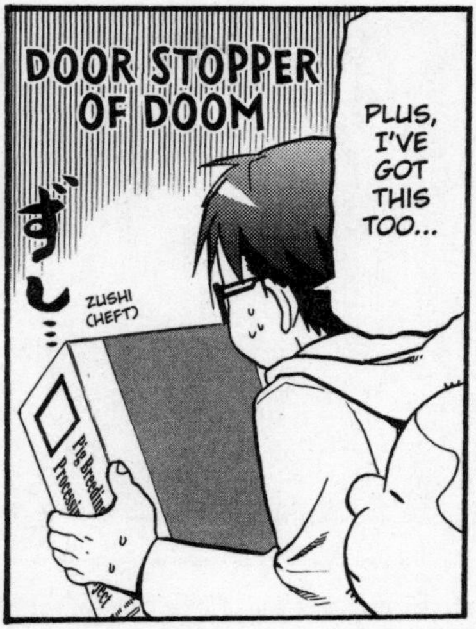
DOOR STOPPER OF DOOM
PLUS, I'VE GOT THIS TOO...
ずし
ZUSHI (HEFT)

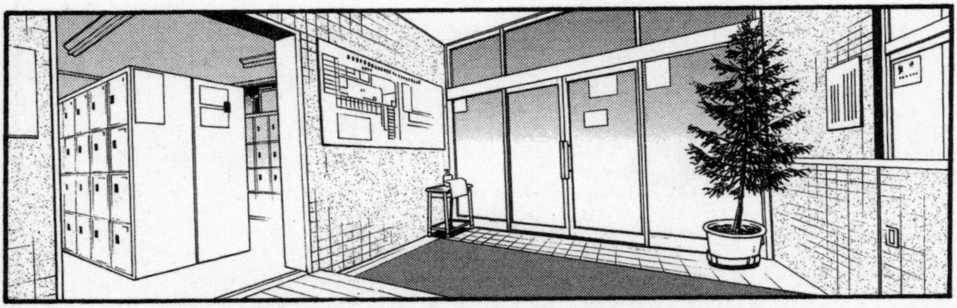

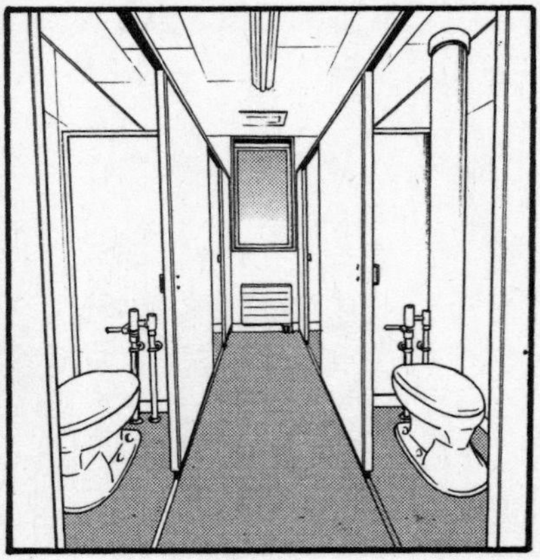

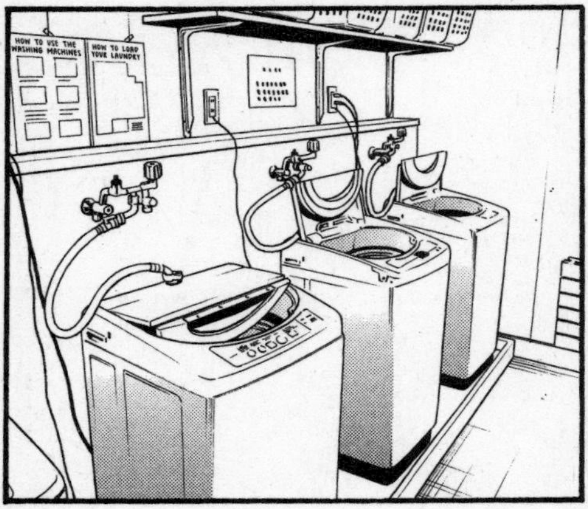
HOW TO USE THE WASHING MACHINES
HOW TO LOAD YOUR LAUNDRY

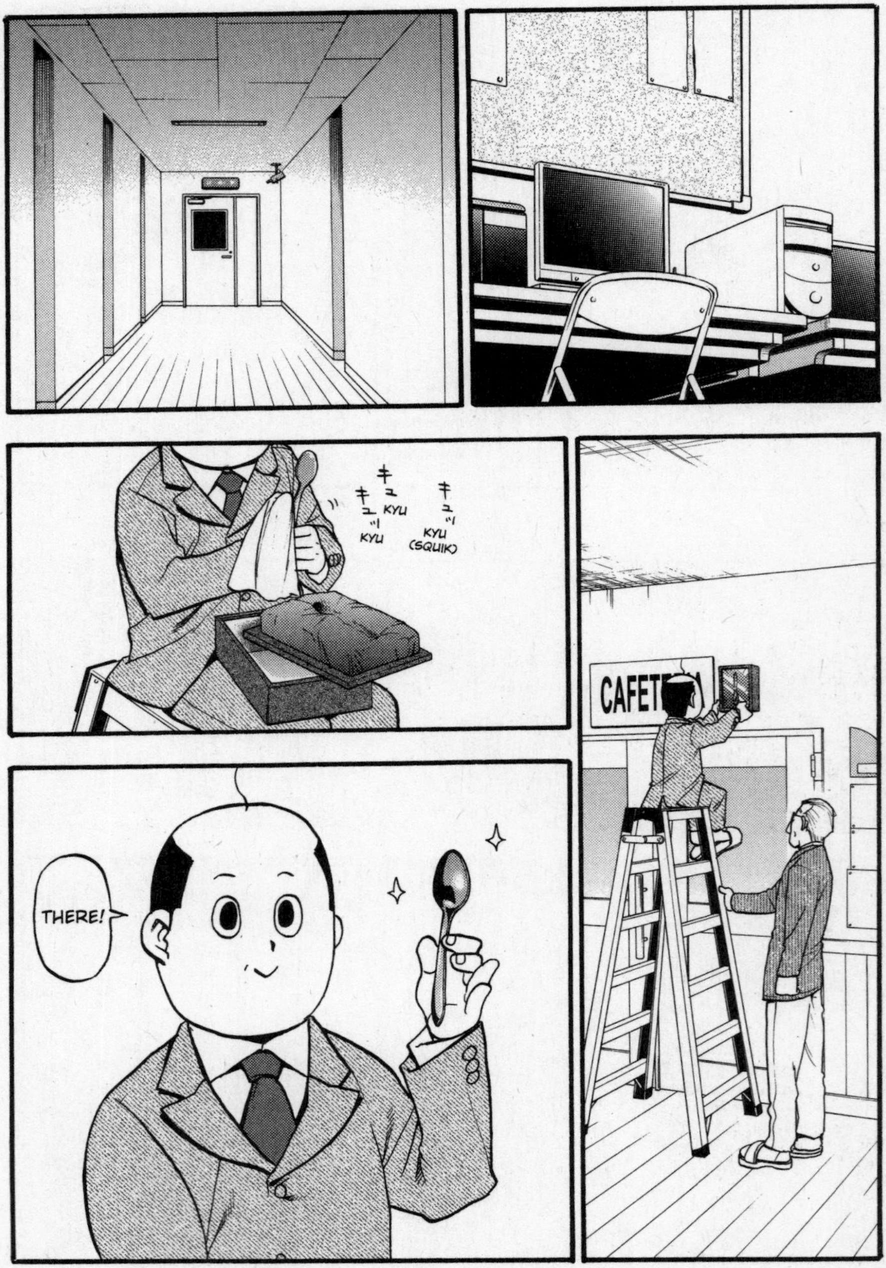
CAFET
キュッ
KYU
(SQUIK)
キュ
KYU
キュッ
KYU
THERE!

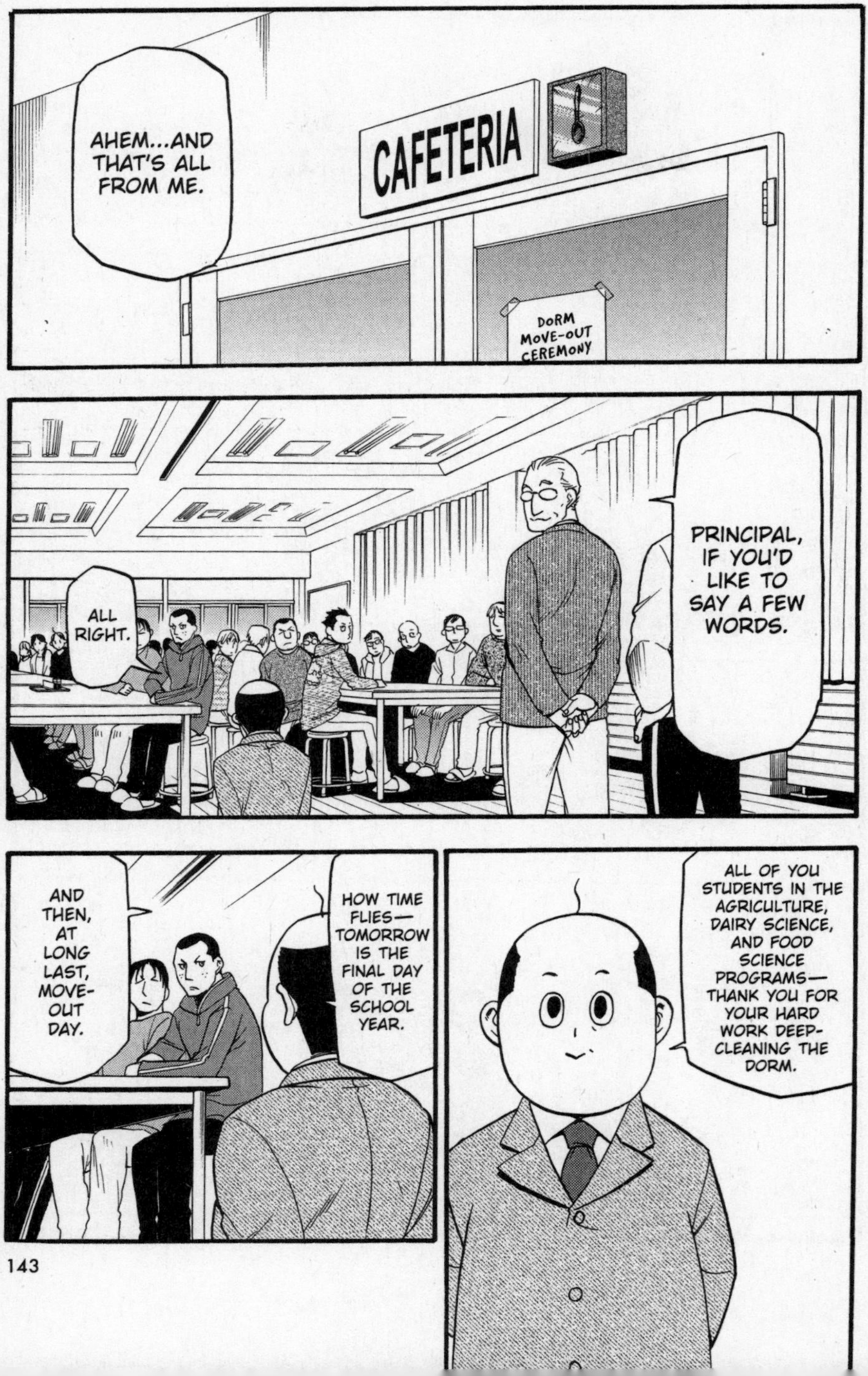
AHEM...AND THAT'S ALL FROM ME.
CAFETERIA
DORM MOVE-OUT CEREMONY
PRINCIPAL, IF YOU'D LIKE TO SAY A FEW WORDS.
ALL RIGHT.
ALL OF YOU STUDENTS IN THE AGRICULTURE, DAIRY SCIENCE, AND FOOD SCIENCE PROGRAMS—THANK YOU FOR YOUR HARD WORK DEEP-CLEANING THE DORM.
HOW TIME FLIES—TOMORROW IS THE FINAL DAY OF THE SCHOOL YEAR.
AND THEN, AT LONG LAST, MOVE-OUT DAY.

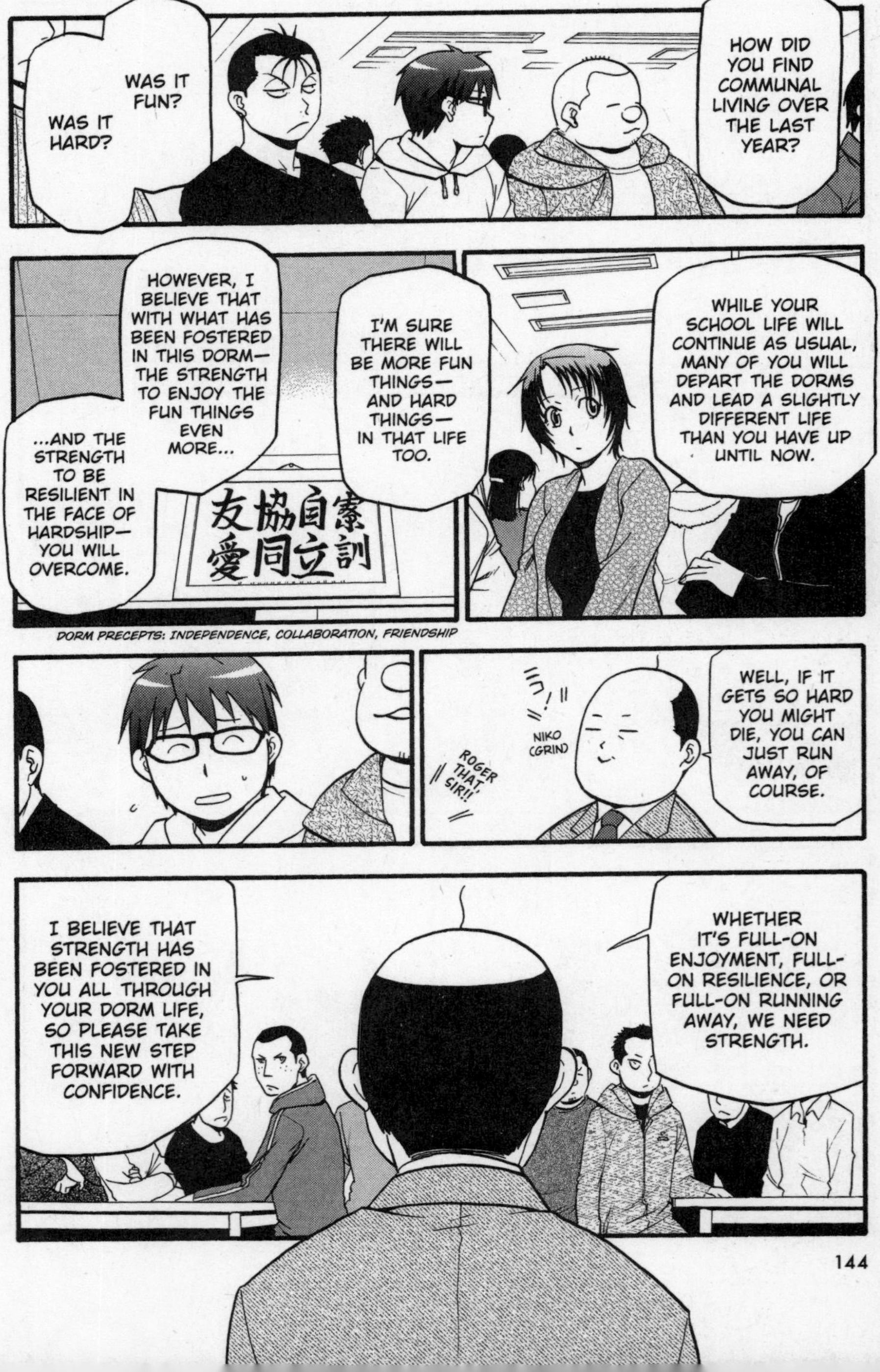
HOW DID YOU FIND COMMUNAL LIVING OVER THE LAST YEAR?
WAS IT FUN?
WAS IT HARD?
WHILE YOUR SCHOOL LIFE WILL CONTINUE AS USUAL, MANY OF YOU WILL DEPART THE DORMS AND LEAD A SLIGHTLY DIFFERENT LIFE THAN YOU HAVE UP UNTIL NOW.
I'M SURE THERE WILL BE MORE FUN THINGS— AND HARD THINGS— IN THAT LIFE TOO.
HOWEVER, I BELIEVE THAT WITH WHAT HAS BEEN FOSTERED IN THIS DORM— THE STRENGTH TO ENJOY THE FUN THINGS EVEN MORE...
...AND THE STRENGTH TO BE RESILIENT IN THE FACE OF HARDSHIP— YOU WILL OVERCOME.
寮訓 自立 協同 友愛
DORM PRECEPTS: INDEPENDENCE, COLLABORATION, FRIENDSHIP
WELL, IF IT GETS SO HARD YOU MIGHT DIE, YOU CAN JUST RUN AWAY, OF COURSE.
NIKO (GRIN)
ROGER THAT, SIR!!
WHETHER IT'S FULL-ON ENJOYMENT, FULL-ON RESILIENCE, OR FULL-ON RUNNING AWAY, WE NEED STRENGTH.
I BELIEVE THAT STRENGTH HAS BEEN FOSTERED IN YOU ALL THROUGH YOUR DORM LIFE, SO PLEASE TAKE THIS NEW STEP FORWARD WITH CONFIDENCE.

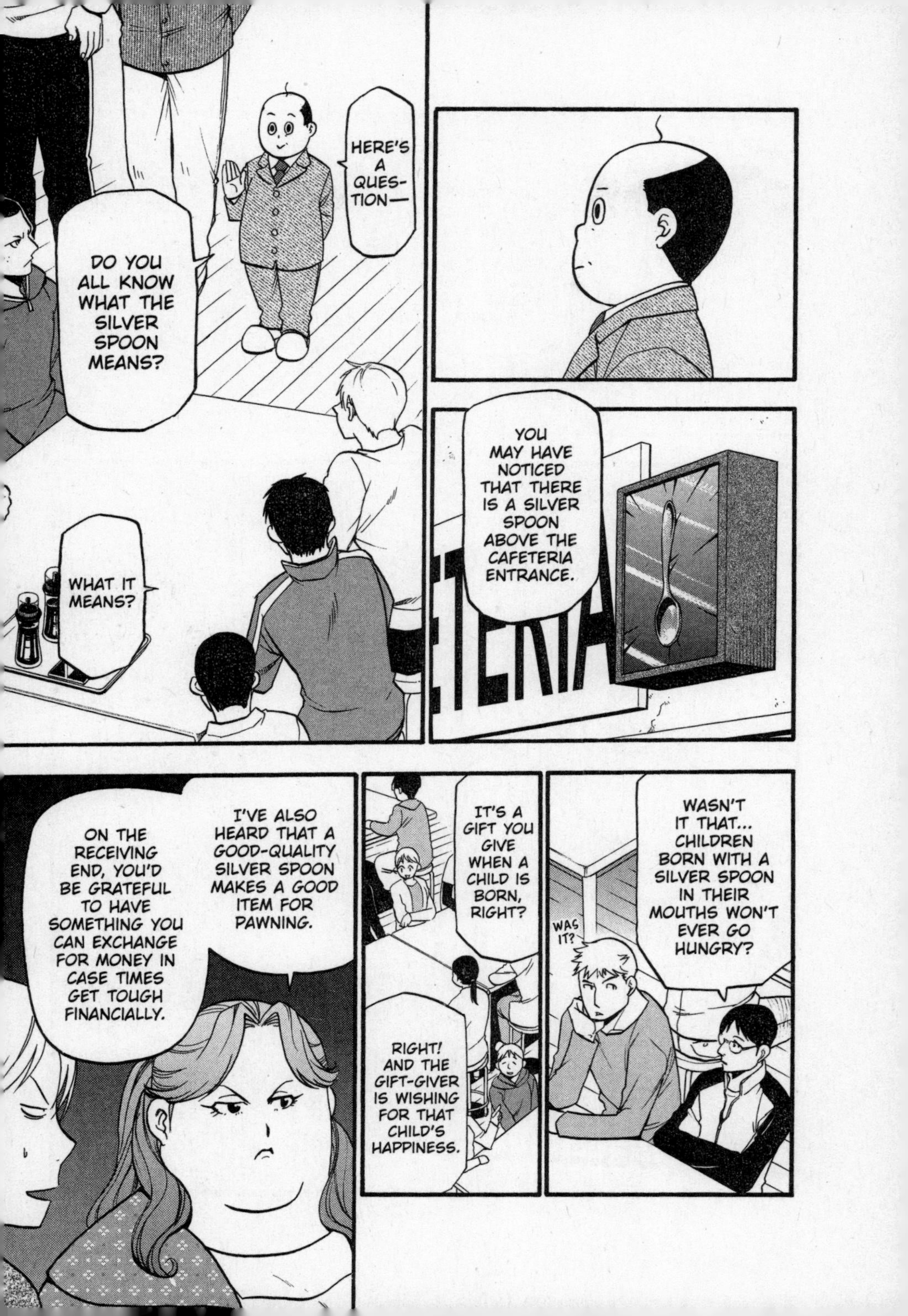
YOU MAY HAVE NOTICED THAT THERE IS A SILVER SPOON ABOVE THE CAFETERIA ENTRANCE.
ETERIA
HERE'S A QUES-TION—
DO YOU ALL KNOW WHAT THE SILVER SPOON MEANS?
WHAT IT MEANS?
WASN'T IT THAT... CHILDREN BORN WITH A SILVER SPOON IN THEIR MOUTHS WON'T EVER GO HUNGRY?
WAS IT?
IT'S A GIFT YOU GIVE WHEN A CHILD IS BORN, RIGHT?
RIGHT! AND THE GIFT-GIVER IS WISHING FOR THAT CHILD'S HAPPINESS.
I'VE ALSO HEARD THAT A GOOD-QUALITY SILVER SPOON MAKES A GOOD ITEM FOR PAWNING.
ON THE RECEIVING END, YOU'D BE GRATEFUL TO HAVE SOMETHING YOU CAN EXCHANGE FOR MONEY IN CASE TIMES GET TOUGH FINANCIALLY.

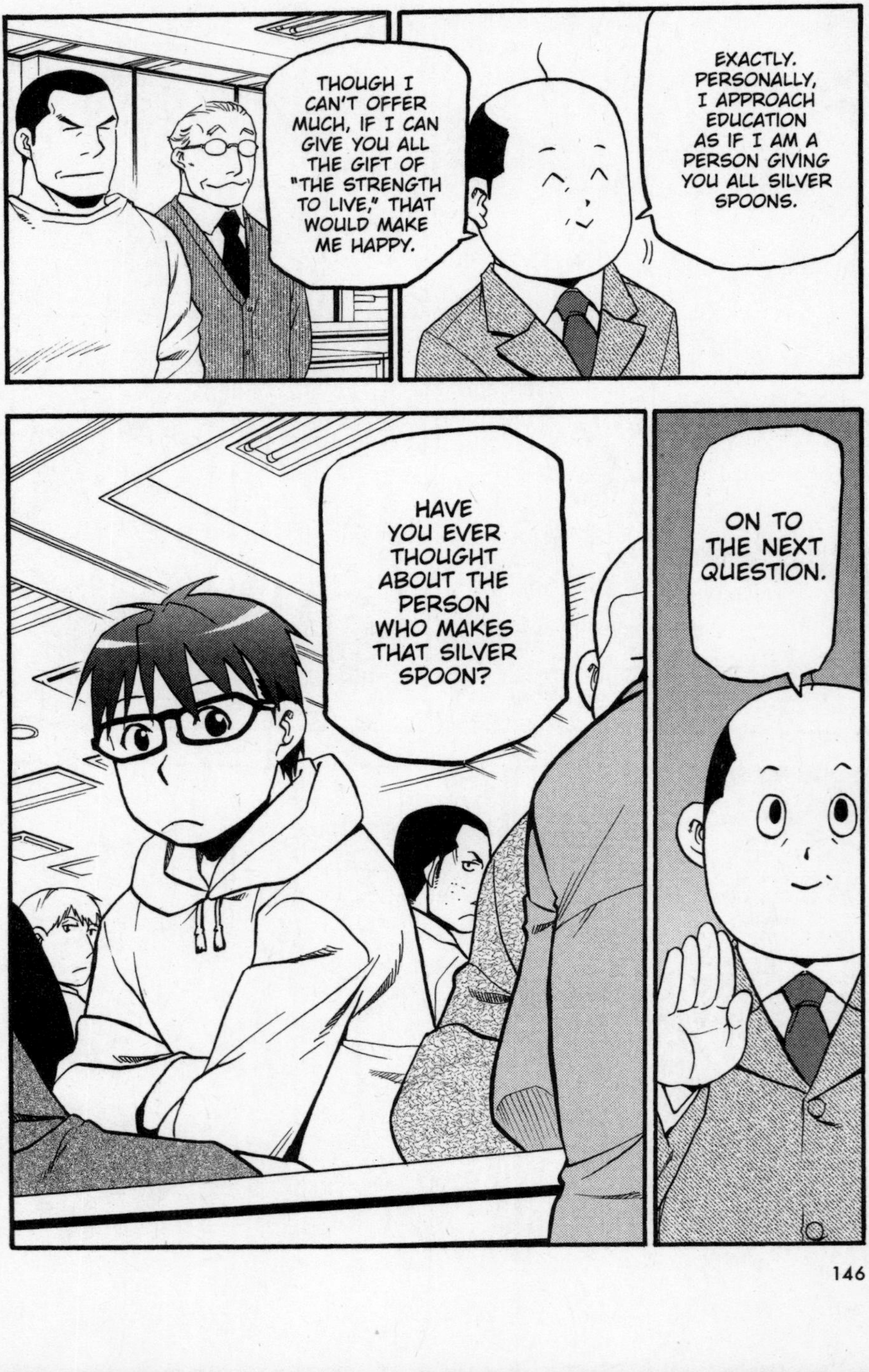
EXACTLY. PERSONALLY, I APPROACH EDUCATION AS IF I AM A PERSON GIVING YOU ALL SILVER SPOONS.
THOUGH I CAN'T OFFER MUCH, IF I CAN GIVE YOU ALL THE GIFT OF "THE STRENGTH TO LIVE," THAT WOULD MAKE ME HAPPY.
ON TO THE NEXT QUESTION.
HAVE YOU EVER THOUGHT ABOUT THE PERSON WHO MAKES THAT SILVER SPOON?

Silver Spoon

MEAT!!

CHIDORI IKEDA

FOOD SCIENCE
PROGRAM FIRST-YEAR

CARNIVOROUS WOMAN
↑ LITERALLY

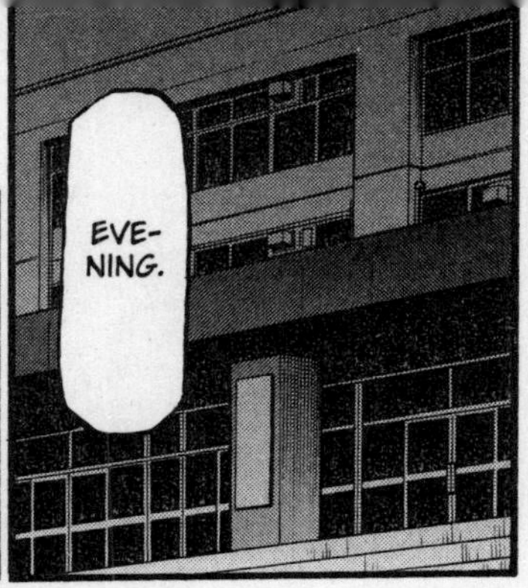
EVE-
NING.

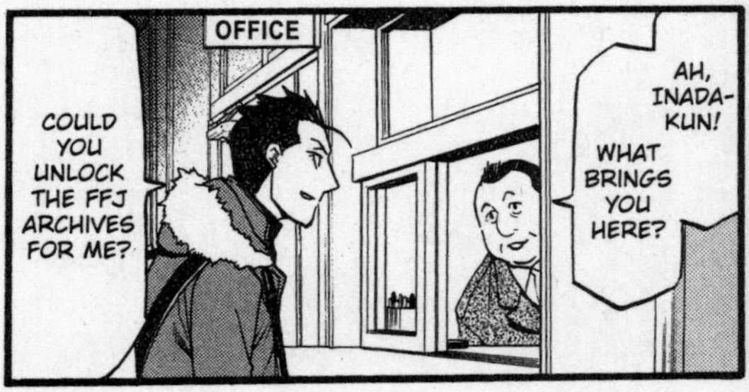
OFFICE
AH, INADA-KUN! WHAT BRINGS YOU HERE?
COULD YOU UNLOCK THE FFJ ARCHIVES FOR ME?

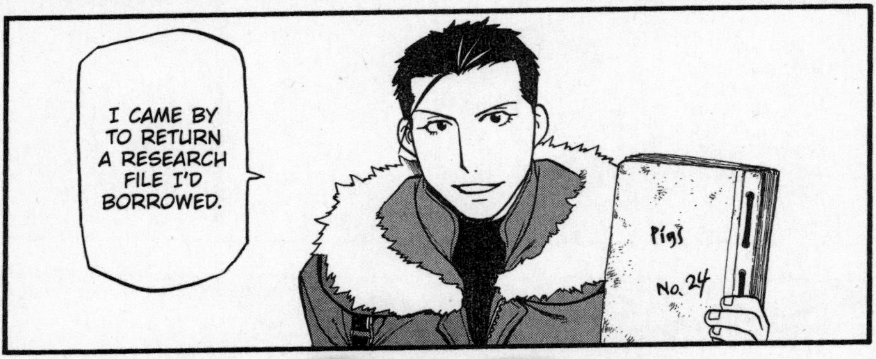
I CAME BY TO RETURN A RESEARCH FILE I'D BORROWED.
Pigs
No. 24

Chapter 96:
Tale of Winter ㉝

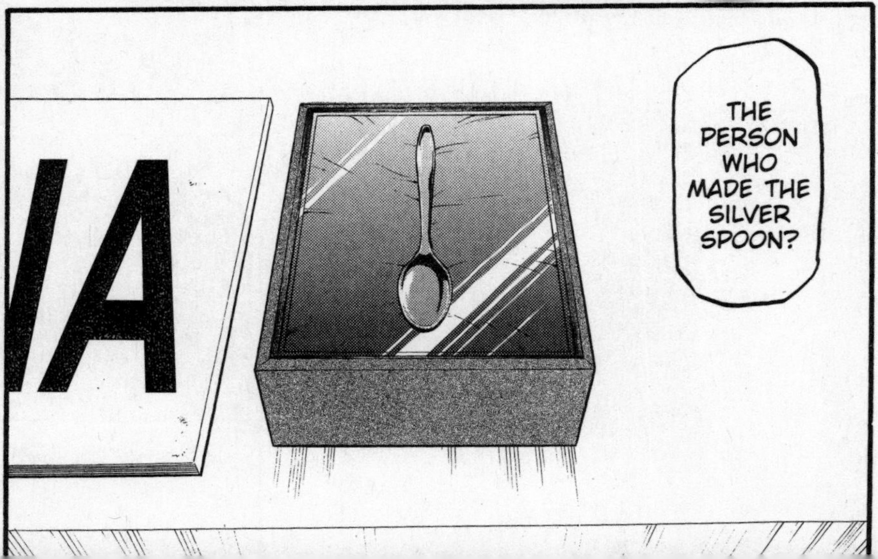
THE PERSON WHO MADE THE SILVER SPOON?

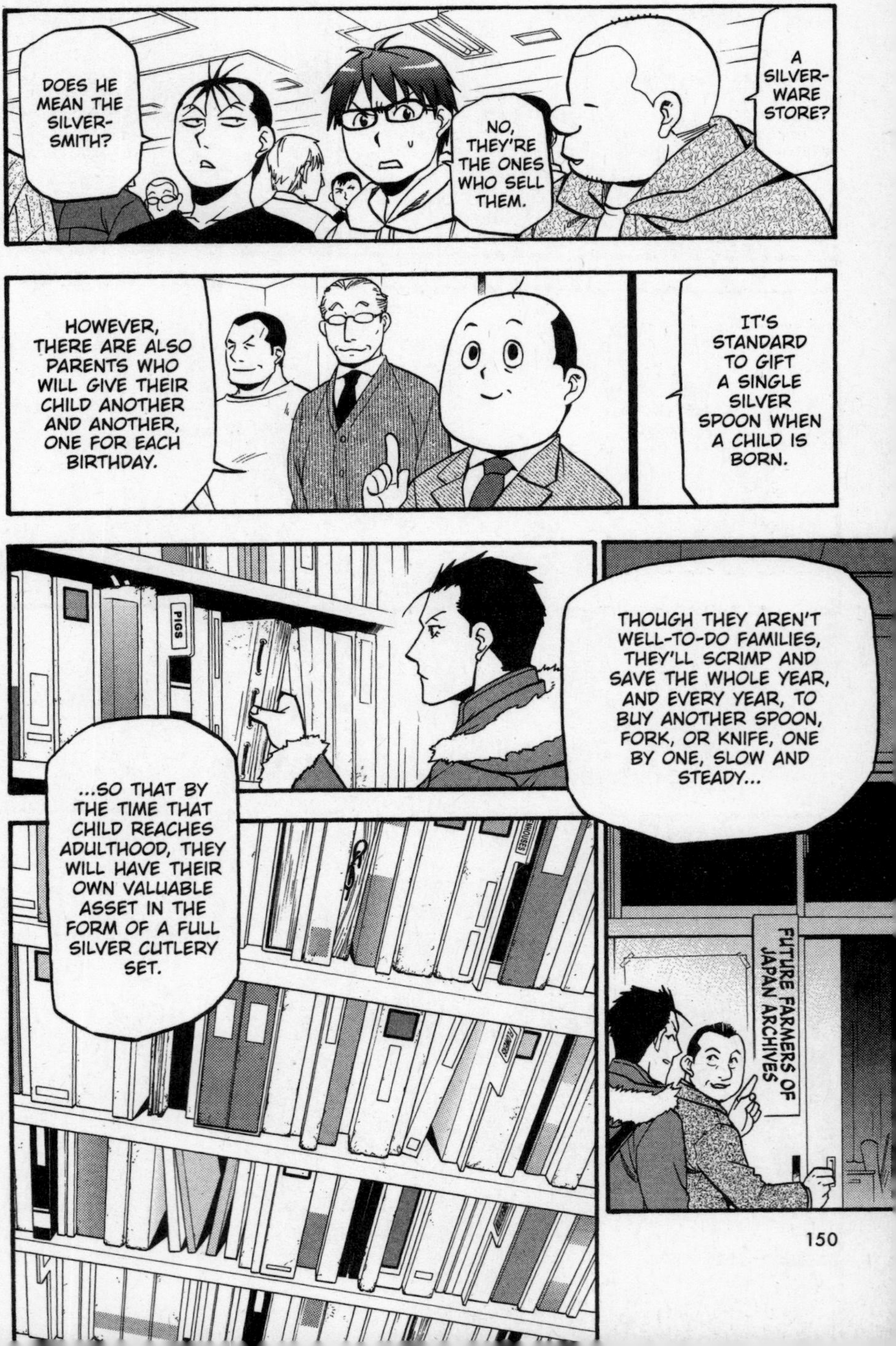
A SILVER-WARE STORE?
NO, THEY'RE THE ONES WHO SELL THEM.
DOES HE MEAN THE SILVER-SMITH?
IT'S STANDARD TO GIFT A SINGLE SILVER SPOON WHEN A CHILD IS BORN.
HOWEVER, THERE ARE ALSO PARENTS WHO WILL GIVE THEIR CHILD ANOTHER AND ANOTHER, ONE FOR EACH BIRTHDAY.
THOUGH THEY AREN'T WELL-TO-DO FAMILIES, THEY'LL SCRIMP AND SAVE THE WHOLE YEAR, AND EVERY YEAR, TO BUY ANOTHER SPOON, FORK, OR KNIFE, ONE BY ONE, SLOW AND STEADY...
PIGS
FUTURE FARMERS OF JAPAN ARCHIVES
...SO THAT BY THE TIME THAT CHILD REACHES ADULTHOOD, THEY WILL HAVE THEIR OWN VALUABLE ASSET IN THE FORM OF A FULL SILVER CUTLERY SET.

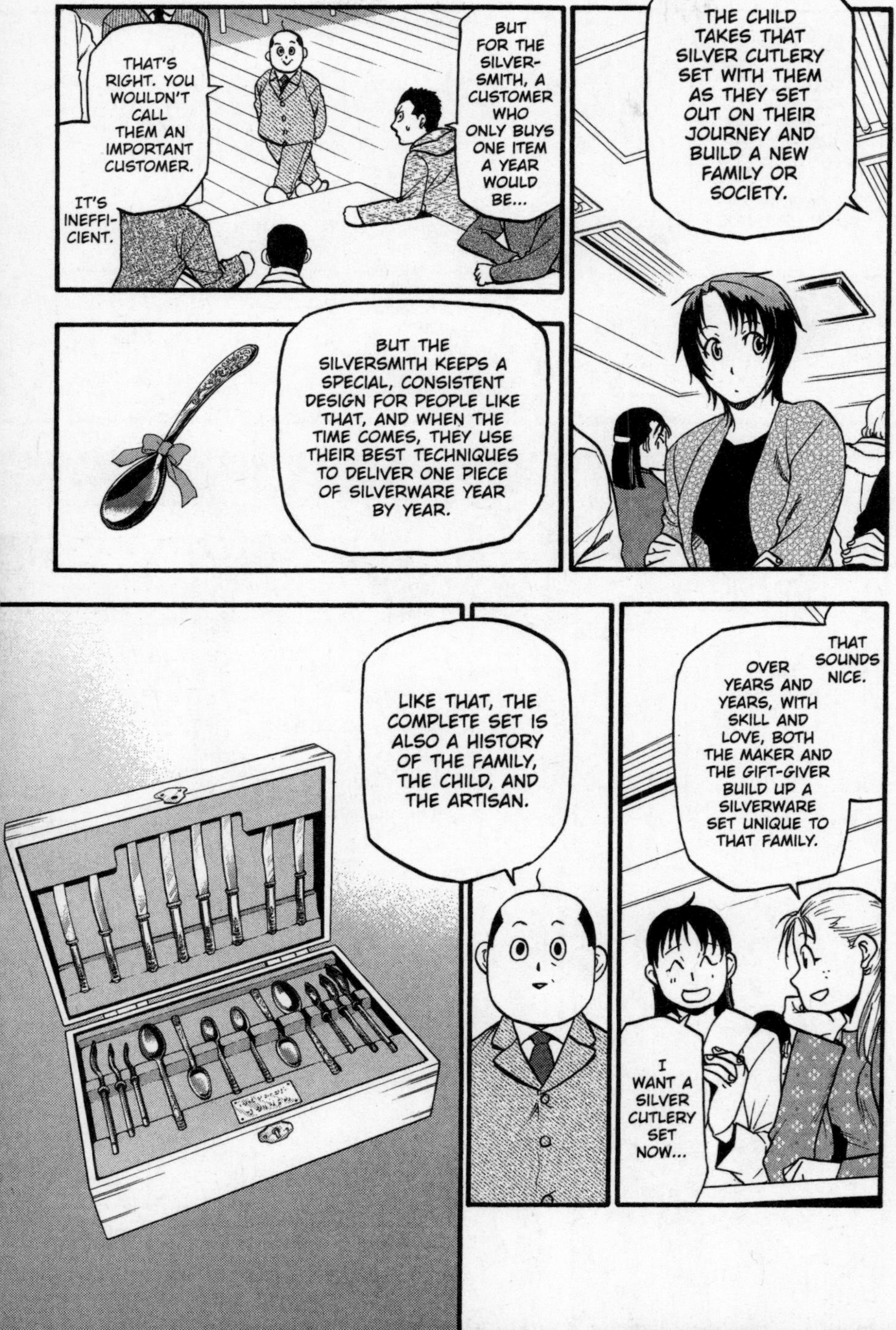
BUT FOR THE SILVER-SMITH, A CUSTOMER WHO ONLY BUYS ONE ITEM A YEAR WOULD BE...
THAT'S RIGHT. YOU WOULDN'T CALL THEM AN IMPORTANT CUSTOMER.
IT'S INEFFI-CIENT.
BUT THE SILVERSMITH KEEPS A SPECIAL, CONSISTENT DESIGN FOR PEOPLE LIKE THAT, AND WHEN THE TIME COMES, THEY USE THEIR BEST TECHNIQUES TO DELIVER ONE PIECE OF SILVERWARE YEAR BY YEAR.
THE CHILD TAKES THAT SILVER CUTLERY SET WITH THEM AS THEY SET OUT ON THEIR JOURNEY AND BUILD A NEW FAMILY OR SOCIETY.
LIKE THAT, THE COMPLETE SET IS ALSO A HISTORY OF THE FAMILY, THE CHILD, AND THE ARTISAN.
OVER YEARS AND YEARS, WITH SKILL AND LOVE, BOTH THE MAKER AND THE GIFT-GIVER BUILD UP A SILVERWARE SET UNIQUE TO THAT FAMILY.
THAT SOUNDS NICE.
I WANT A SILVER CUTLERY SET NOW...

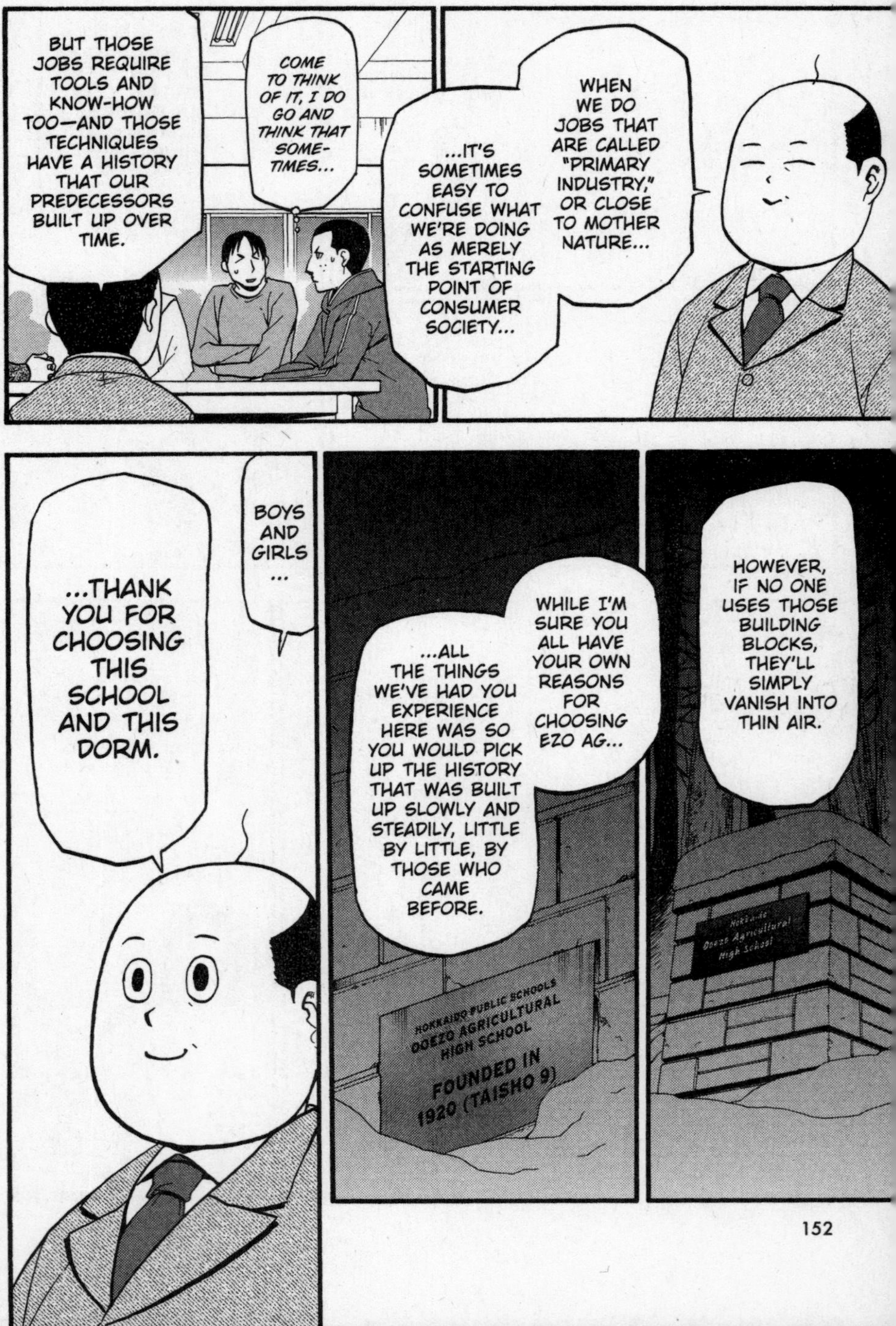
WHEN WE DO JOBS THAT ARE CALLED "PRIMARY INDUSTRY," OR CLOSE TO MOTHER NATURE...
...IT'S SOMETIMES EASY TO CONFUSE WHAT WE'RE DOING AS MERELY THE STARTING POINT OF CONSUMER SOCIETY...
COME TO THINK OF IT, I DO GO AND THINK THAT SOMETIMES...
BUT THOSE JOBS REQUIRE TOOLS AND KNOW-HOW TOO—AND THOSE TECHNIQUES HAVE A HISTORY THAT OUR PREDECESSORS BUILT UP OVER TIME.
HOWEVER, IF NO ONE USES THOSE BUILDING BLOCKS, THEY'LL SIMPLY VANISH INTO THIN AIR.
Hokkaido Ooezo Agricultural High School
WHILE I'M SURE YOU ALL HAVE YOUR OWN REASONS FOR CHOOSING EZO AG...
...ALL THE THINGS WE'VE HAD YOU EXPERIENCE HERE WAS SO YOU WOULD PICK UP THE HISTORY THAT WAS BUILT UP SLOWLY AND STEADILY, LITTLE BY LITTLE, BY THOSE WHO CAME BEFORE.
HOKKAIDO PUBLIC SCHOOLS OOEZO AGRICULTURAL HIGH SCHOOL
FOUNDED IN 1920 (TAISHO 9)
BOYS AND GIRLS...
...THANK YOU FOR CHOOSING THIS SCHOOL AND THIS DORM.

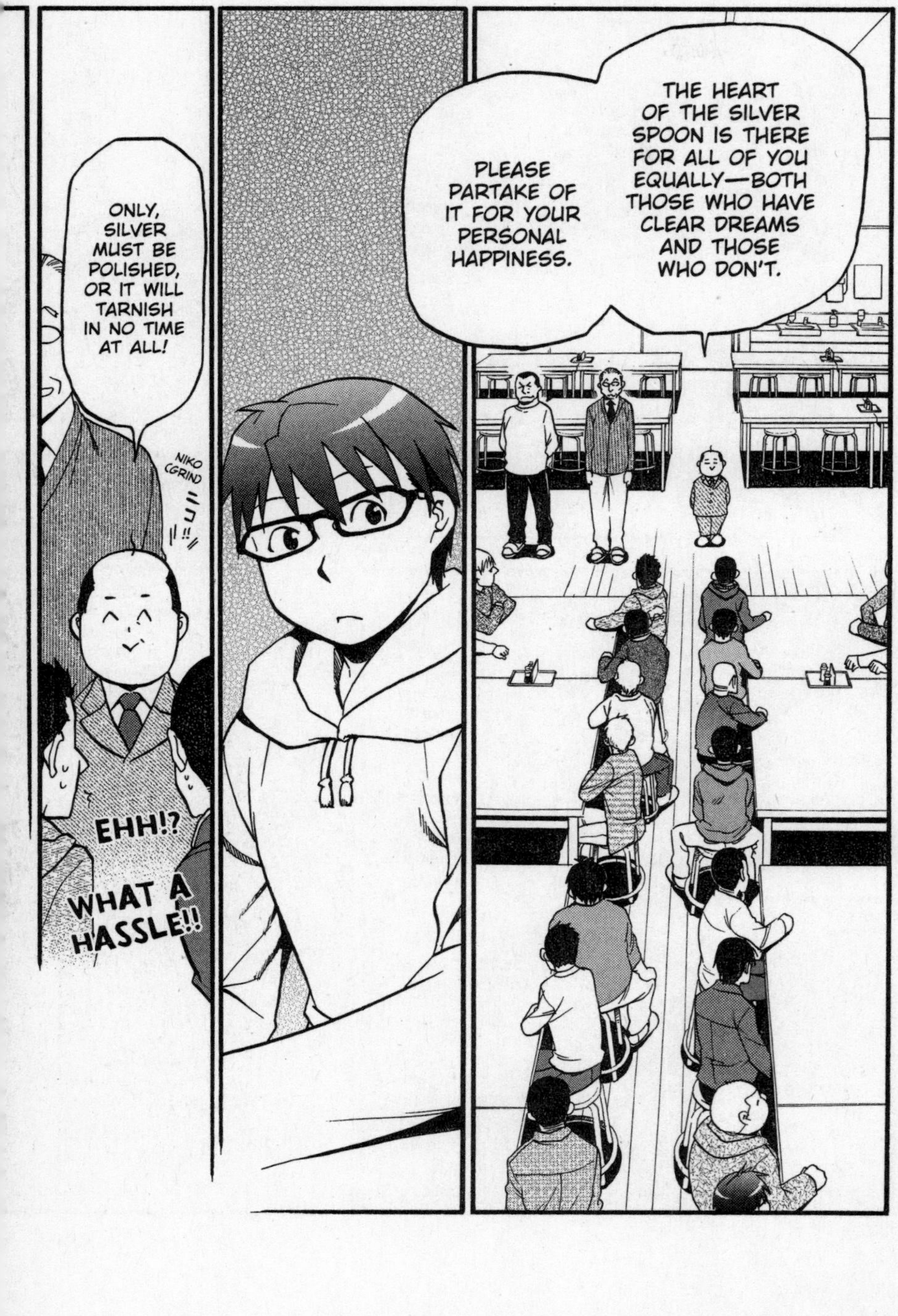
THE HEART OF THE SILVER SPOON IS THERE FOR ALL OF YOU EQUALLY—BOTH THOSE WHO HAVE CLEAR DREAMS AND THOSE WHO DON'T.
PLEASE PARTAKE OF IT FOR YOUR PERSONAL HAPPINESS.
ONLY, SILVER MUST BE POLISHED, OR IT WILL TARNISH IN NO TIME AT ALL!
NIKO (GRIN)
EHH!?
WHAT A HASSLE!!

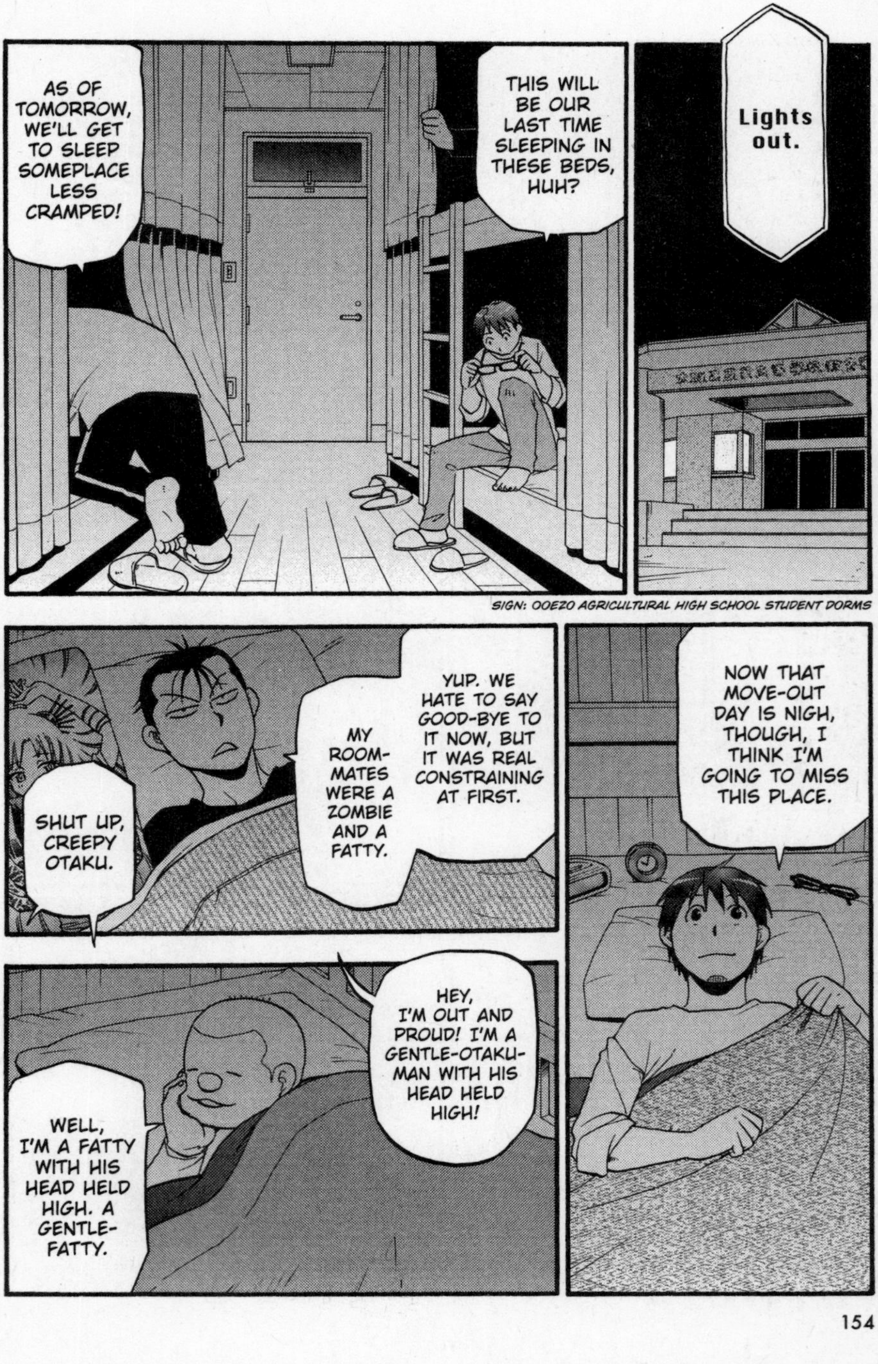
Lights out.
THIS WILL BE OUR LAST TIME SLEEPING IN THESE BEDS, HUH?
AS OF TOMORROW, WE'LL GET TO SLEEP SOMEPLACE LESS CRAMPED!
SIGN: OOEZO AGRICULTURAL HIGH SCHOOL STUDENT DORMS
NOW THAT MOVE-OUT DAY IS NIGH, THOUGH, I THINK I'M GOING TO MISS THIS PLACE.
YUP. WE HATE TO SAY GOOD-BYE TO IT NOW, BUT IT WAS REAL CONSTRAINING AT FIRST.
MY ROOM-MATES WERE A ZOMBIE AND A FATTY.
SHUT UP, CREEPY OTAKU.
HEY, I'M OUT AND PROUD! I'M A GENTLE-OTAKU-MAN WITH HIS HEAD HELD HIGH!
WELL, I'M A FATTY WITH HIS HEAD HELD HIGH. A GENTLE-FATTY.

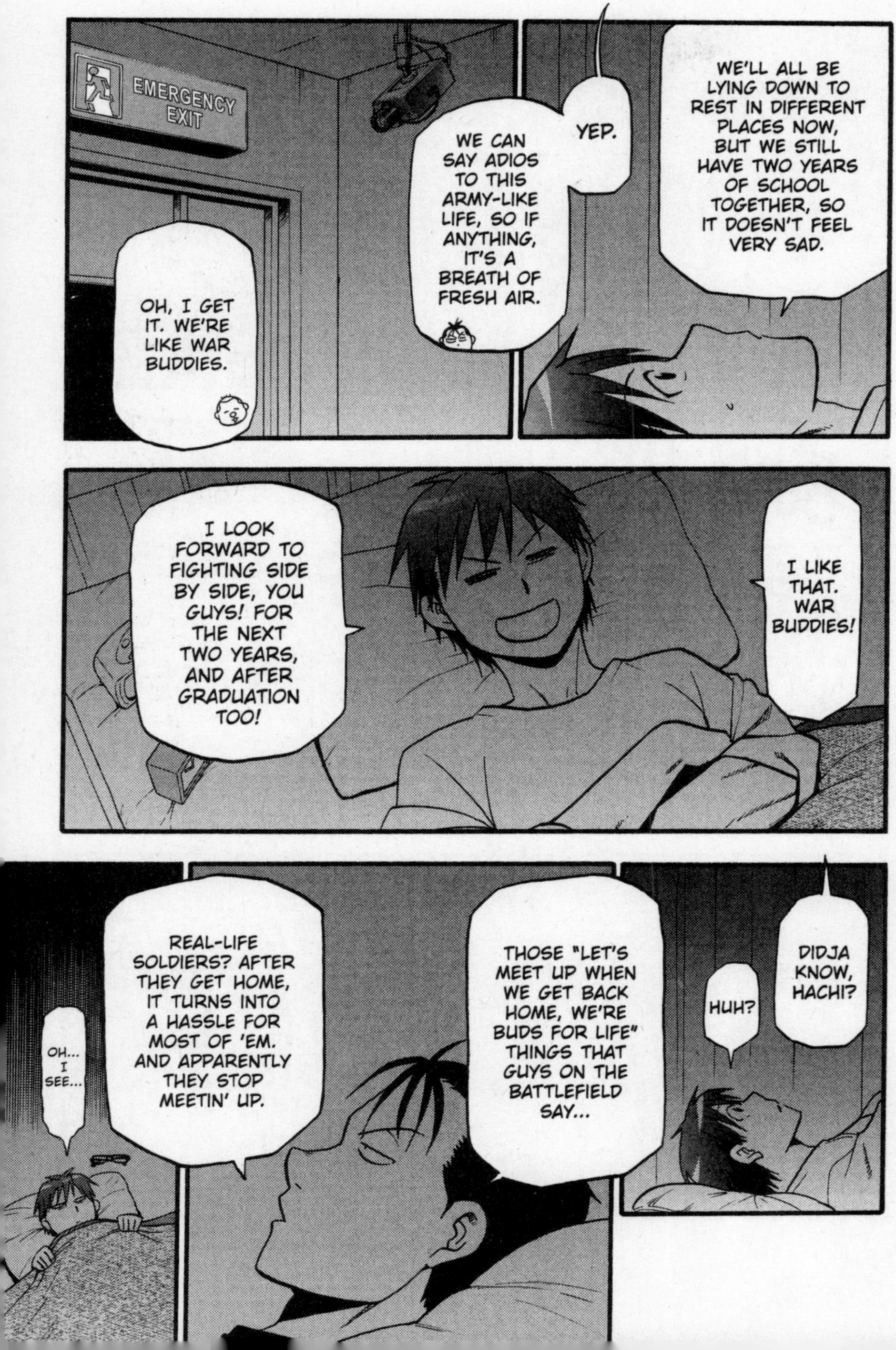
WE'LL ALL BE LYING DOWN TO REST IN DIFFERENT PLACES NOW, BUT WE STILL HAVE TWO YEARS OF SCHOOL TOGETHER, SO IT DOESN'T FEEL VERY SAD.
YEP.
WE CAN SAY ADIOS TO THIS ARMY-LIKE LIFE, SO IF ANYTHING, IT'S A BREATH OF FRESH AIR.
EMERGENCY EXIT
OH, I GET IT. WE'RE LIKE WAR BUDDIES.
I LIKE THAT. WAR BUDDIES!
I LOOK FORWARD TO FIGHTING SIDE BY SIDE, YOU GUYS! FOR THE NEXT TWO YEARS, AND AFTER GRADUATION TOO!
DIDJA KNOW, HACHI?
HUH?
THOSE "LET'S MEET UP WHEN WE GET BACK HOME, WE'RE BUDS FOR LIFE" THINGS THAT GUYS ON THE BATTLEFIELD SAY...
REAL-LIFE SOLDIERS? AFTER THEY GET HOME, IT TURNS INTO A HASSLE FOR MOST OF 'EM. AND APPARENTLY THEY STOP MEETIN' UP.
OH... I SEE...

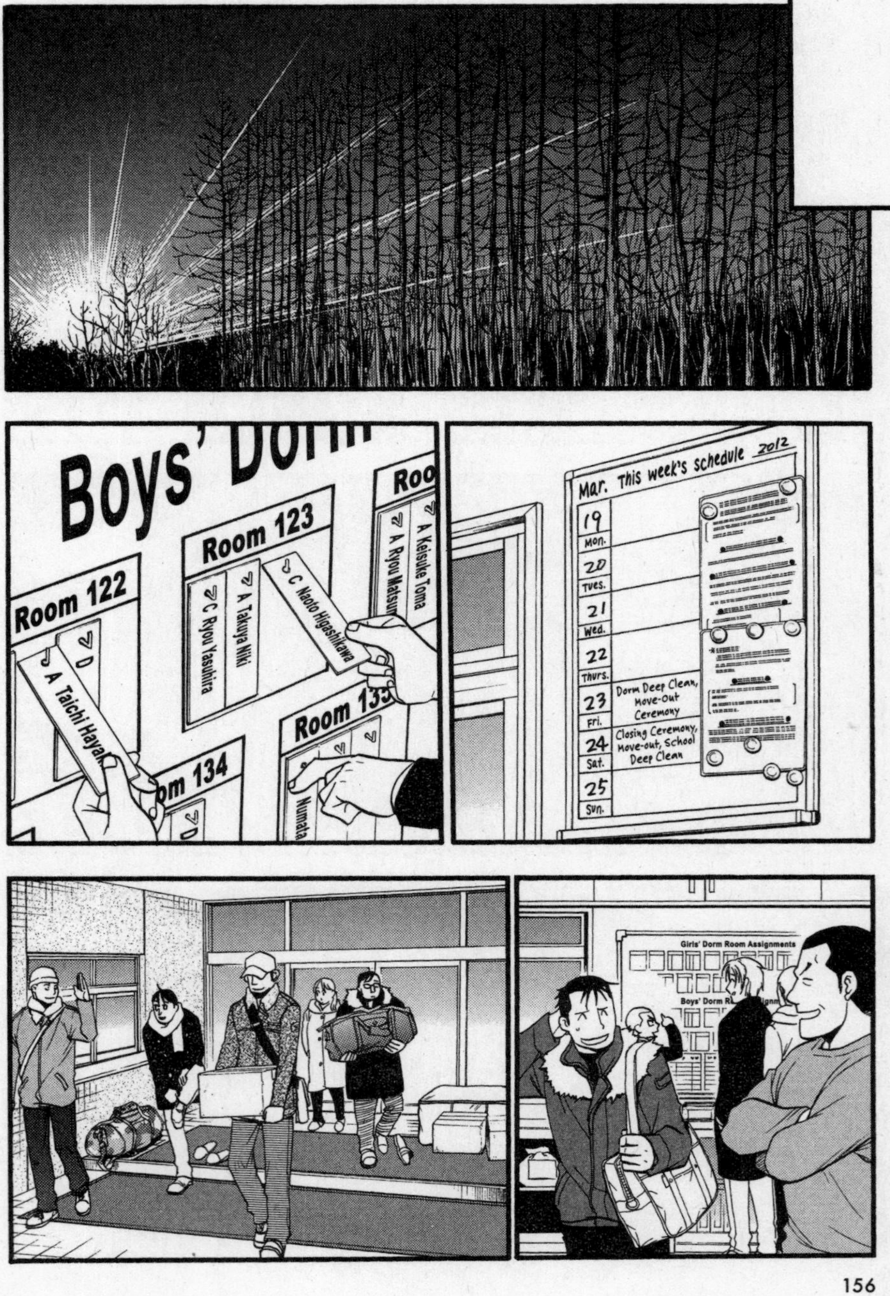
Mar. This week's schedule 2012
19 Mon.
20 Tues.
21 Wed.
22 Thurs.
23 Fri. Dorm Deep Clean, Move-Out Ceremony
24 Sat. Closing Ceremony, Move-out, School Deep Clean
25 Sun.
Boys'
Room 123
C Naoto Higashikawa
A Takuya Niki
C Ryou Yasuhira
A Keisuke Toma
Room 122
A Taichi
D
Numata
Girls' Dorm Room Assignments

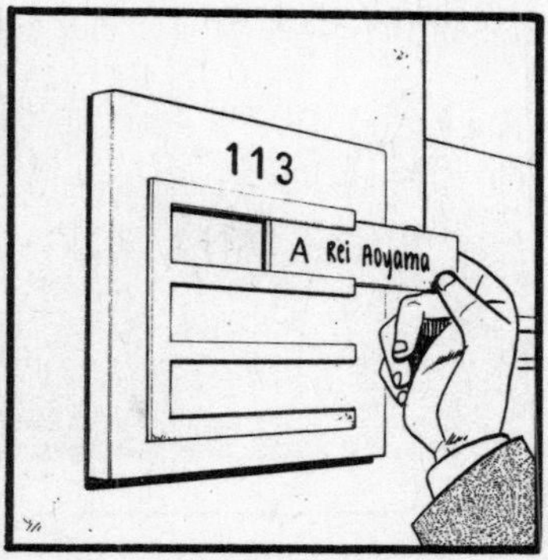
113
A Rei Aoyama

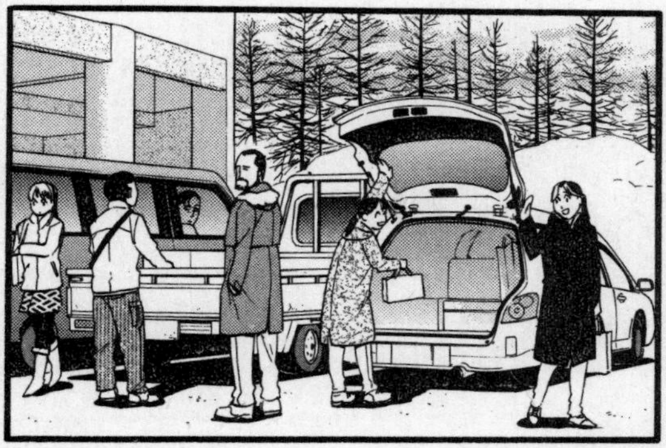

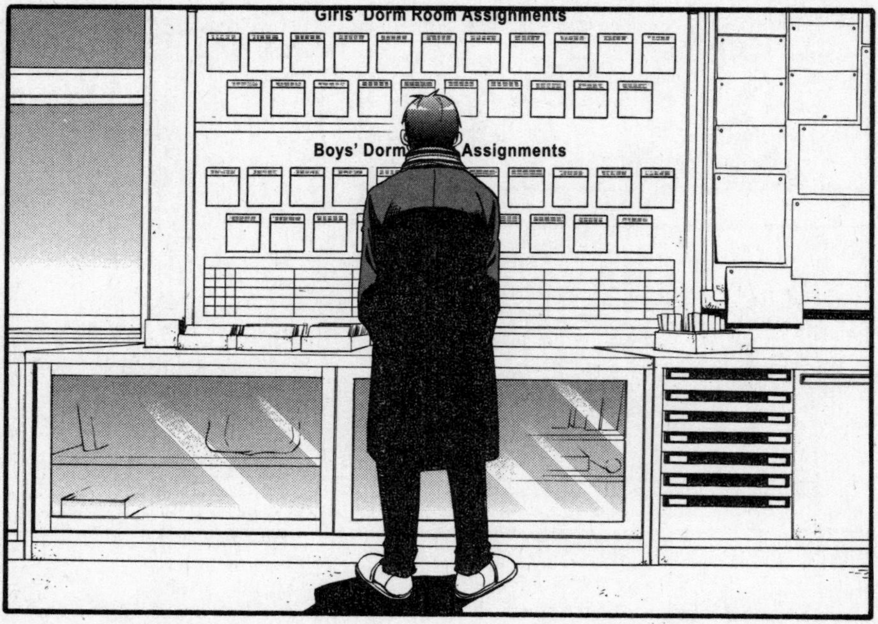
Girls' Dorm Room Assignments
Boys' Dorm
Assignments

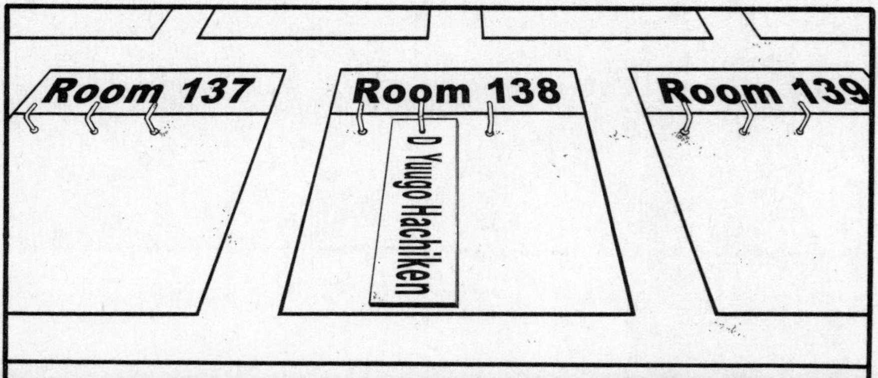
Room 137
Room 138
D Yuugo Hachiken
Room 139

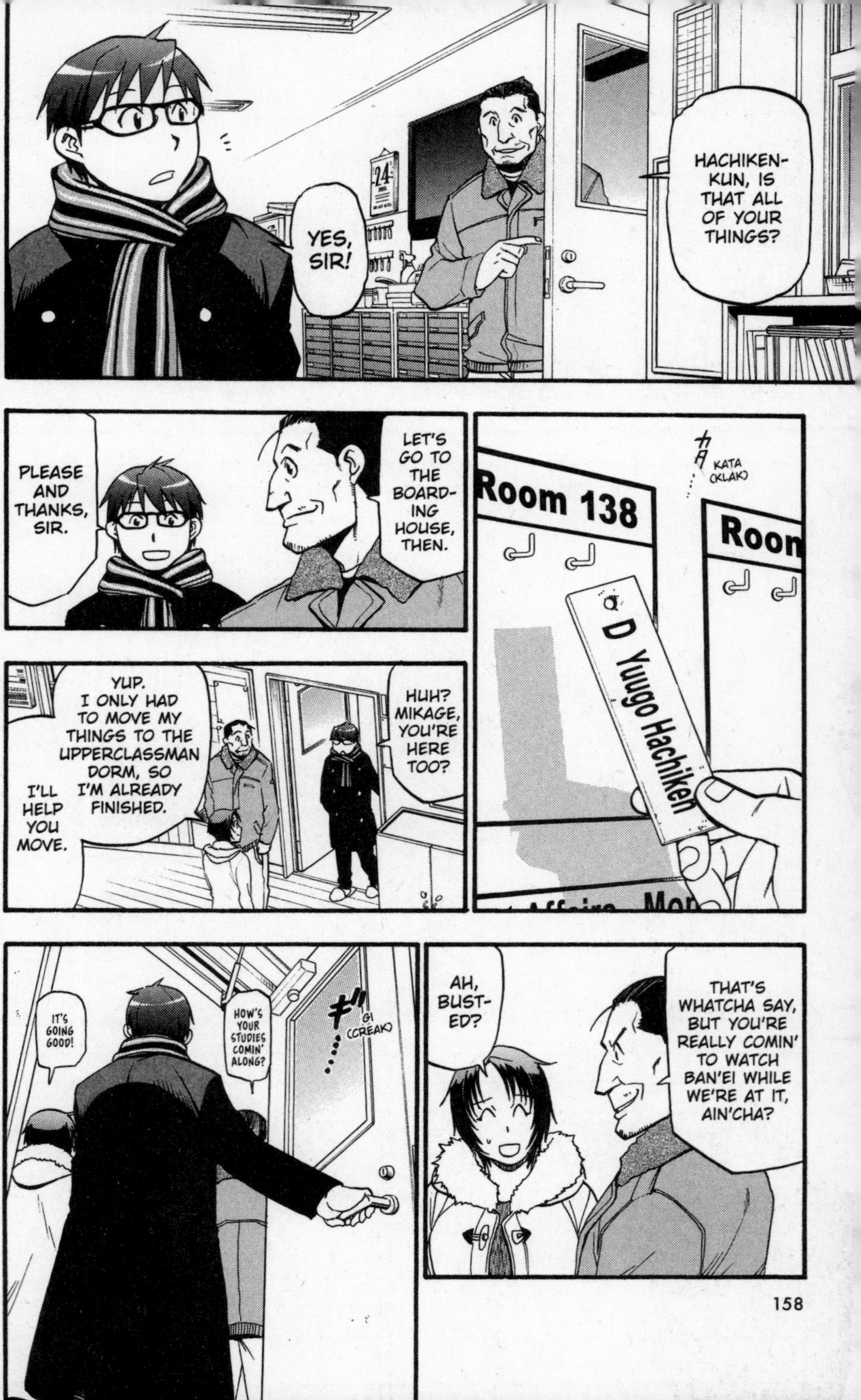
HACHIKEN-KUN, IS THAT ALL OF YOUR THINGS?
YES, SIR!
カタ
KATA (KLAK)
Room 138
D Yuugo Hachiken
LET'S GO TO THE BOARDING-HOUSE, THEN.
PLEASE AND THANKS, SIR.
HUH? MIKAGE, YOU'RE HERE TOO?
YUP. I ONLY HAD TO MOVE MY THINGS TO THE UPPERCLASSMAN DORM, SO I'M ALREADY FINISHED.
I'LL HELP YOU MOVE.
THAT'S WHATCHA SAY, BUT YOU'RE REALLY COMIN' TO WATCH BAN'EI WHILE WE'RE AT IT, AIN'CHA?
AH, BUSTED?
ギ
GI (CREAK)
HOW'S YOUR STUDIES COMIN' ALONG?
IT'S GOING GOOD!

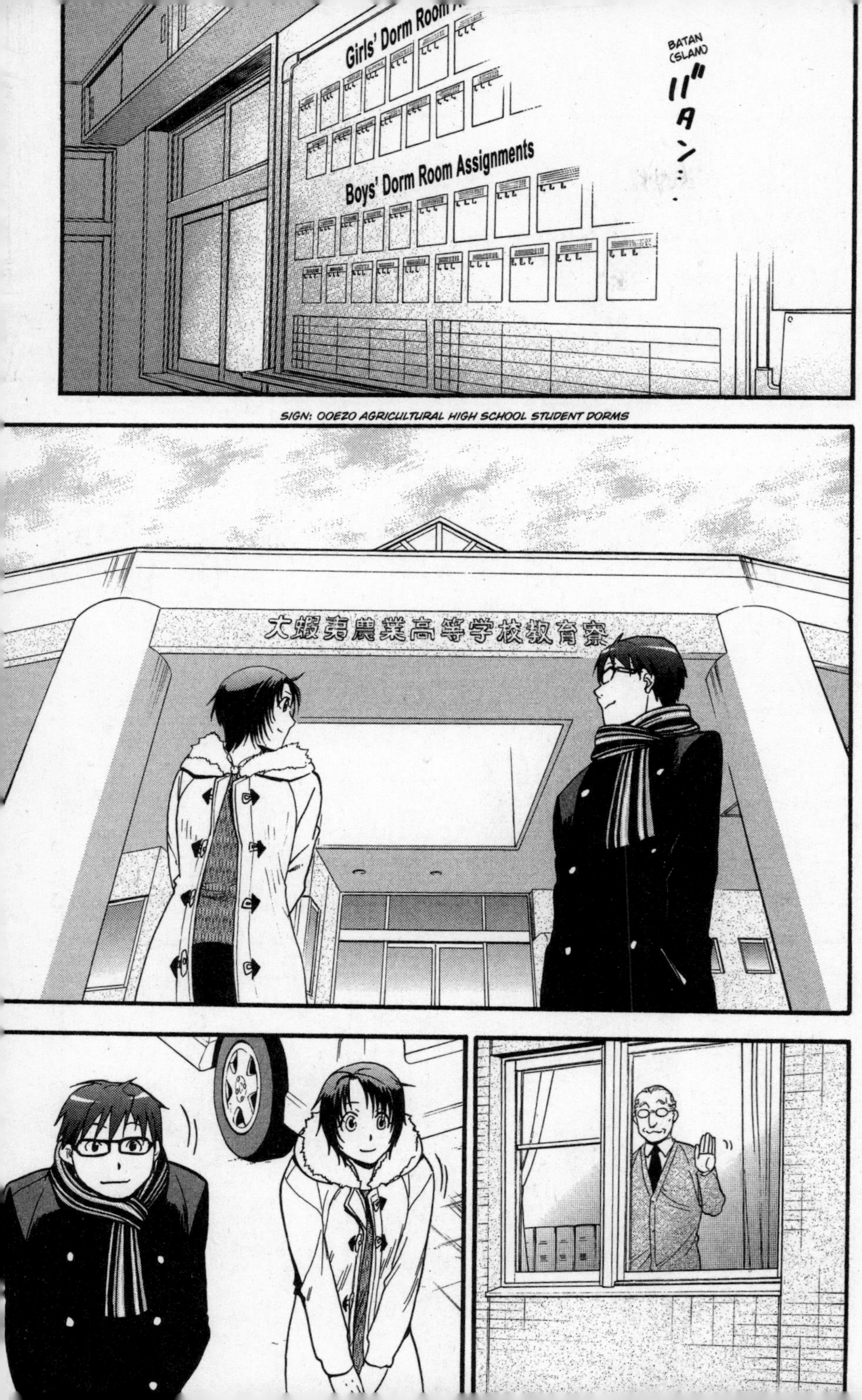
BATAN (SLAM)
バタン…
Girls' Dorm Room A
Boys' Dorm Room Assignments
SIGN: OOEZO AGRICULTURAL HIGH SCHOOL STUDENT DORMS
大蝦夷農業高等学校教育寮

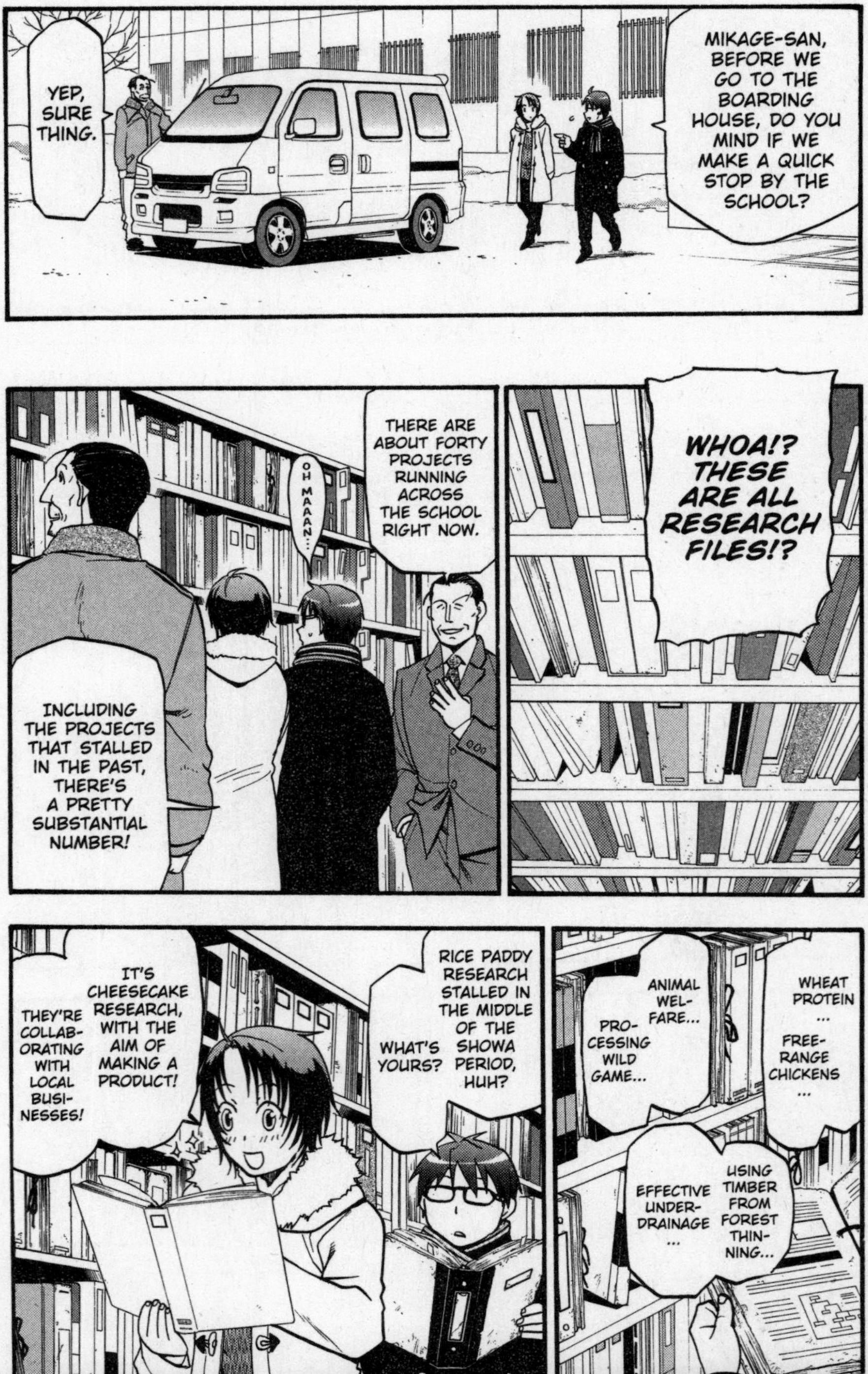
MIKAGE-SAN, BEFORE WE GO TO THE BOARDING HOUSE, DO YOU MIND IF WE MAKE A QUICK STOP BY THE SCHOOL?
YEP, SURE THING.
WHOA!? THESE ARE ALL RESEARCH FILES!?
THERE ARE ABOUT FORTY PROJECTS RUNNING ACROSS THE SCHOOL RIGHT NOW.
OH MAAAN...
INCLUDING THE PROJECTS THAT STALLED IN THE PAST, THERE'S A PRETTY SUBSTANTIAL NUMBER!
WHEAT PROTEIN ...
FREE-RANGE CHICKENS ...
ANIMAL WEL-FARE...
PRO-CESSING WILD GAME...
USING TIMBER FROM FOREST THIN-NING...
EFFECTIVE UNDER-DRAINAGE ...
RICE PADDY RESEARCH STALLED IN THE MIDDLE OF THE SHOWA PERIOD, HUH?
WHAT'S YOURS?
IT'S CHEESECAKE RESEARCH, WITH THE AIM OF MAKING A PRODUCT!
THEY'RE COLLAB-ORATING WITH LOCAL BUSI-NESSES!

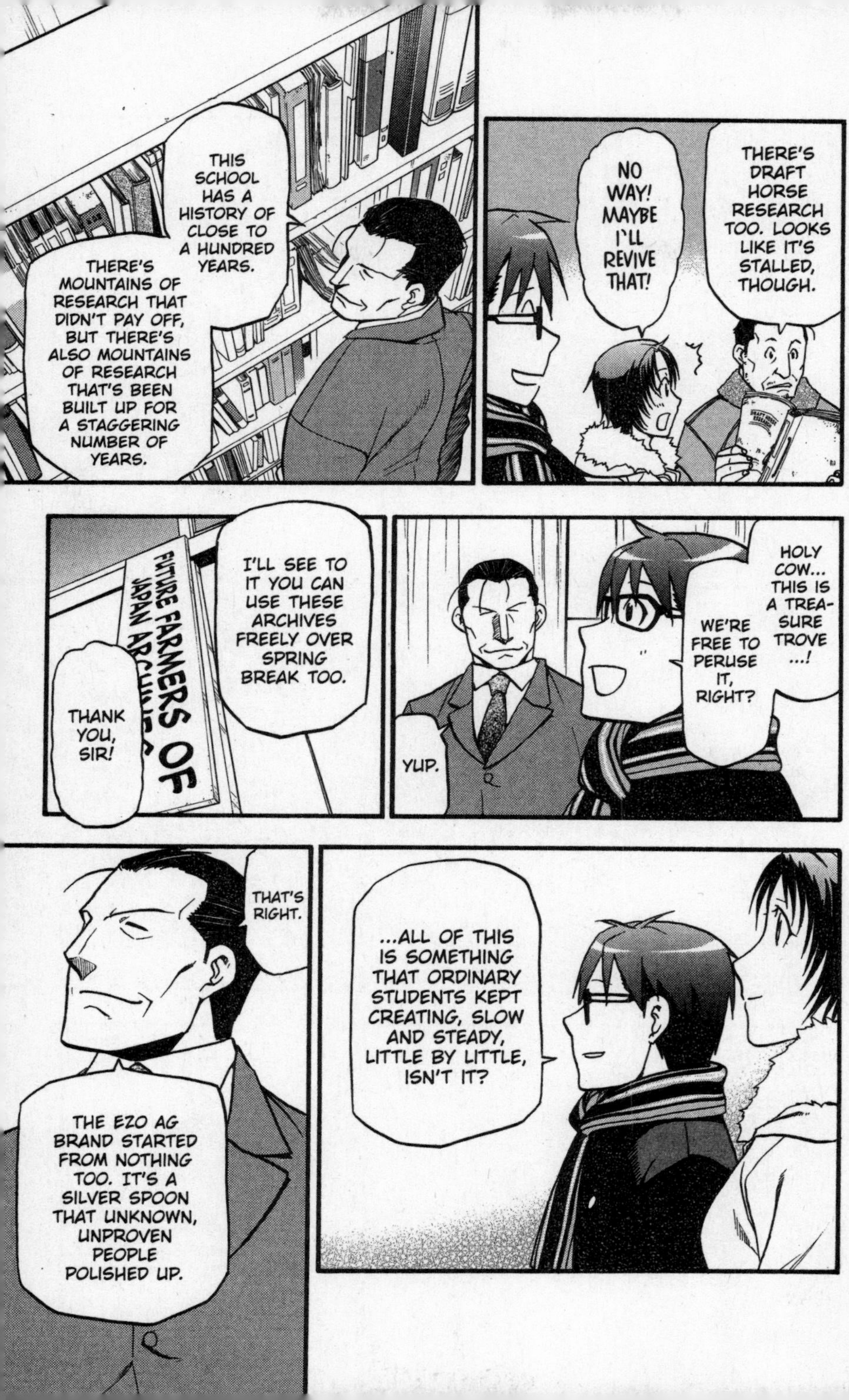
THERE'S DRAFT HORSE RESEARCH TOO. LOOKS LIKE IT'S STALLED, THOUGH.
NO WAY! MAYBE I'LL REVIVE THAT!
THIS SCHOOL HAS A HISTORY OF CLOSE TO A HUNDRED YEARS.
THERE'S MOUNTAINS OF RESEARCH THAT DIDN'T PAY OFF, BUT THERE'S ALSO MOUNTAINS OF RESEARCH THAT'S BEEN BUILT UP FOR A STAGGERING NUMBER OF YEARS.
HOLY COW... THIS IS A TREASURE TROVE...!
WE'RE FREE TO PERUSE IT, RIGHT?
YUP.
I'LL SEE TO IT YOU CAN USE THESE ARCHIVES FREELY OVER SPRING BREAK TOO.
FUTURE FARMERS OF JAPAN ARCH
THANK YOU, SIR!
...ALL OF THIS IS SOMETHING THAT ORDINARY STUDENTS KEPT CREATING, SLOW AND STEADY, LITTLE BY LITTLE, ISN'T IT?
THAT'S RIGHT.
THE EZO AG BRAND STARTED FROM NOTHING TOO. IT'S A SILVER SPOON THAT UNKNOWN, UNPROVEN PEOPLE POLISHED UP.

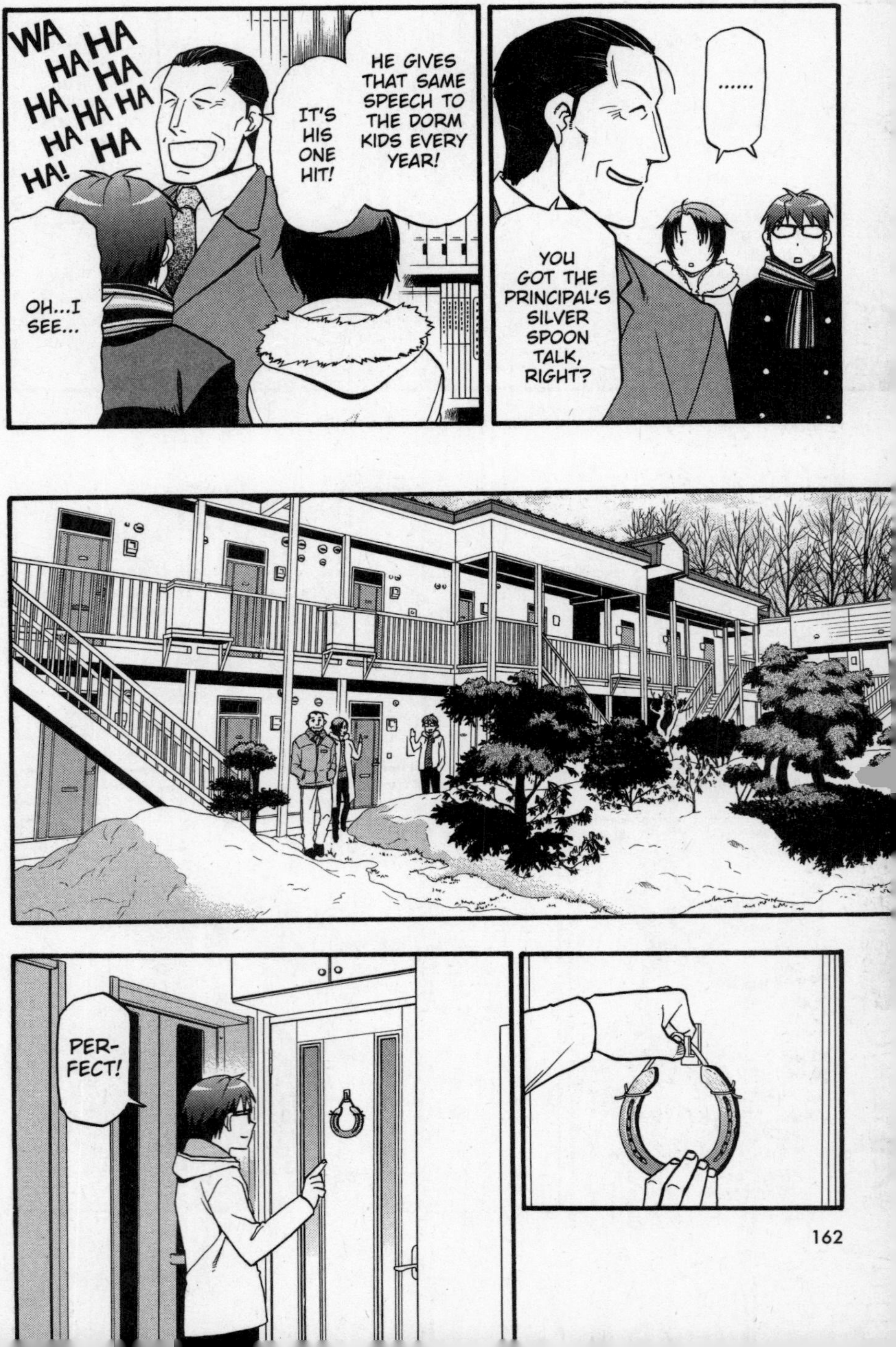
......
YOU GOT THE PRINCIPAL'S SILVER SPOON TALK, RIGHT?
HE GIVES THAT SAME SPEECH TO THE DORM KIDS EVERY YEAR!
IT'S HIS ONE HIT!
WA HA HA HA HA HA HA HA HA HA!
OH...I SEE...
PER-FECT!

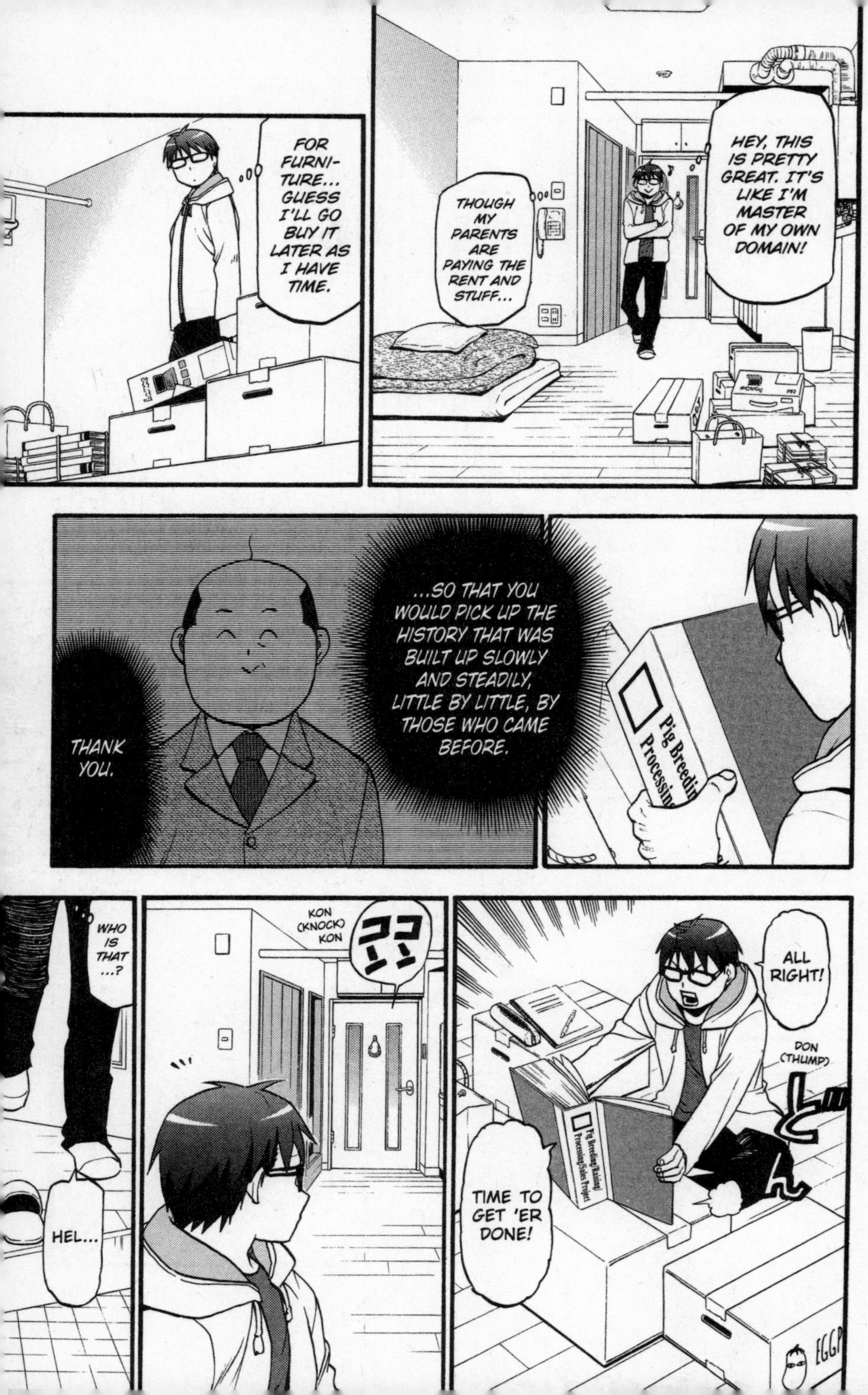
HEY, THIS IS PRETTY GREAT. IT'S LIKE I'M MASTER OF MY OWN DOMAIN!
THOUGH MY PARENTS ARE PAYING THE RENT AND STUFF...
FOR FURNI-TURE... GUESS I'LL GO BUY IT LATER AS I HAVE TIME.
Pig Breeding Processing
...SO THAT YOU WOULD PICK UP THE HISTORY THAT WAS BUILT UP SLOWLY AND STEADILY, LITTLE BY LITTLE, BY THOSE WHO CAME BEFORE.
THANK YOU.
ALL RIGHT!
DON (THUMP)
Pig Breeding/Raising/Processing/Sales Project
TIME TO GET 'ER DONE!
EGGP
KON (KNOCK) KON
HEL...
WHO IS THAT ...?

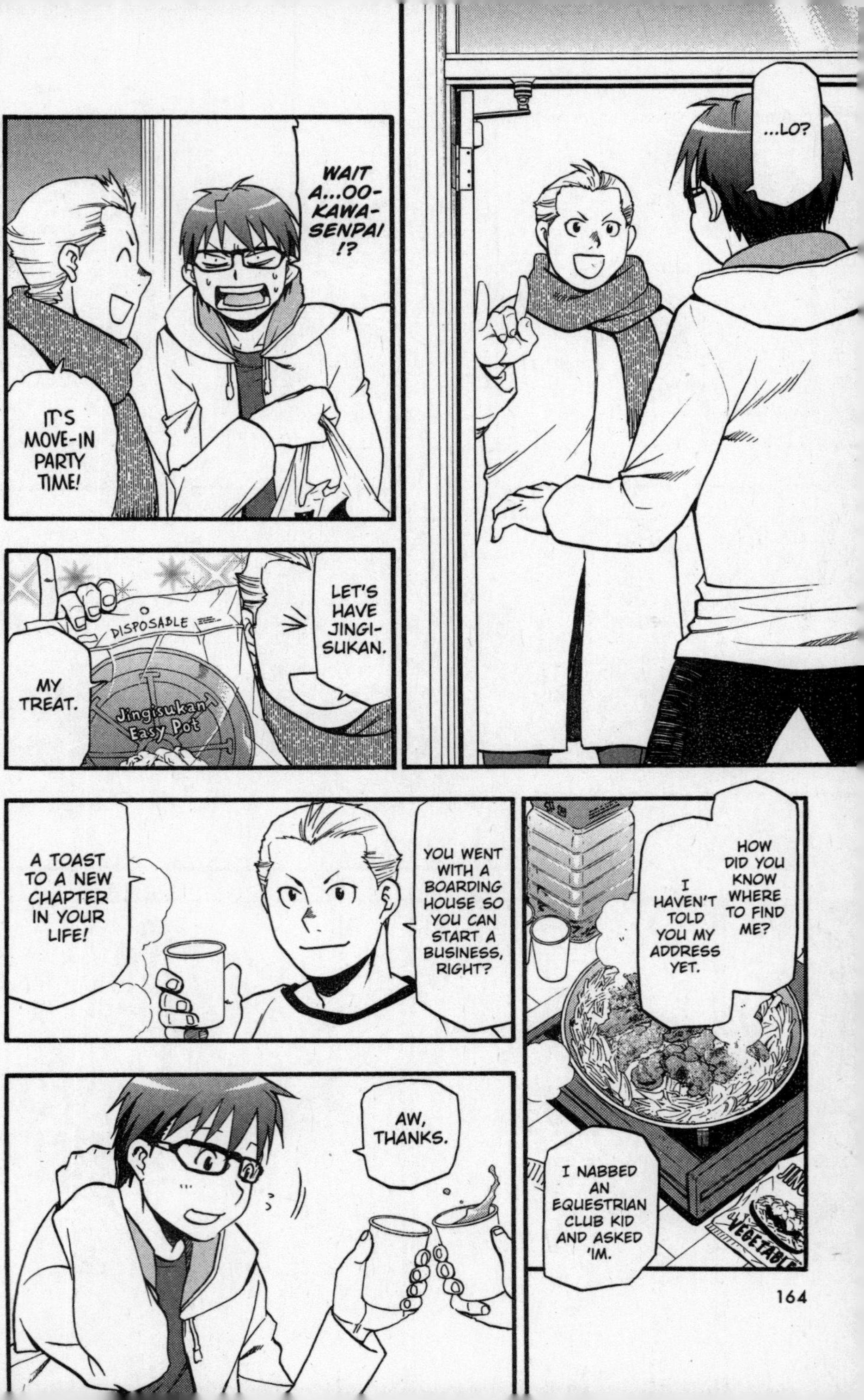
...LO?
WAIT A...OO-KAWA-SENPAI!?
IT'S MOVE-IN PARTY TIME!
LET'S HAVE JINGI-SUKAN.
MY TREAT.
DISPOSABLE
Jingisukan Easy Pot
HOW DID YOU KNOW WHERE TO FIND ME?
I HAVEN'T TOLD YOU MY ADDRESS YET.
I NABBED AN EQUESTRIAN CLUB KID AND ASKED 'IM.
VEGETABLE
YOU WENT WITH A BOARDING HOUSE SO YOU CAN START A BUSINESS, RIGHT?
A TOAST TO A NEW CHAPTER IN YOUR LIFE!
AW, THANKS.

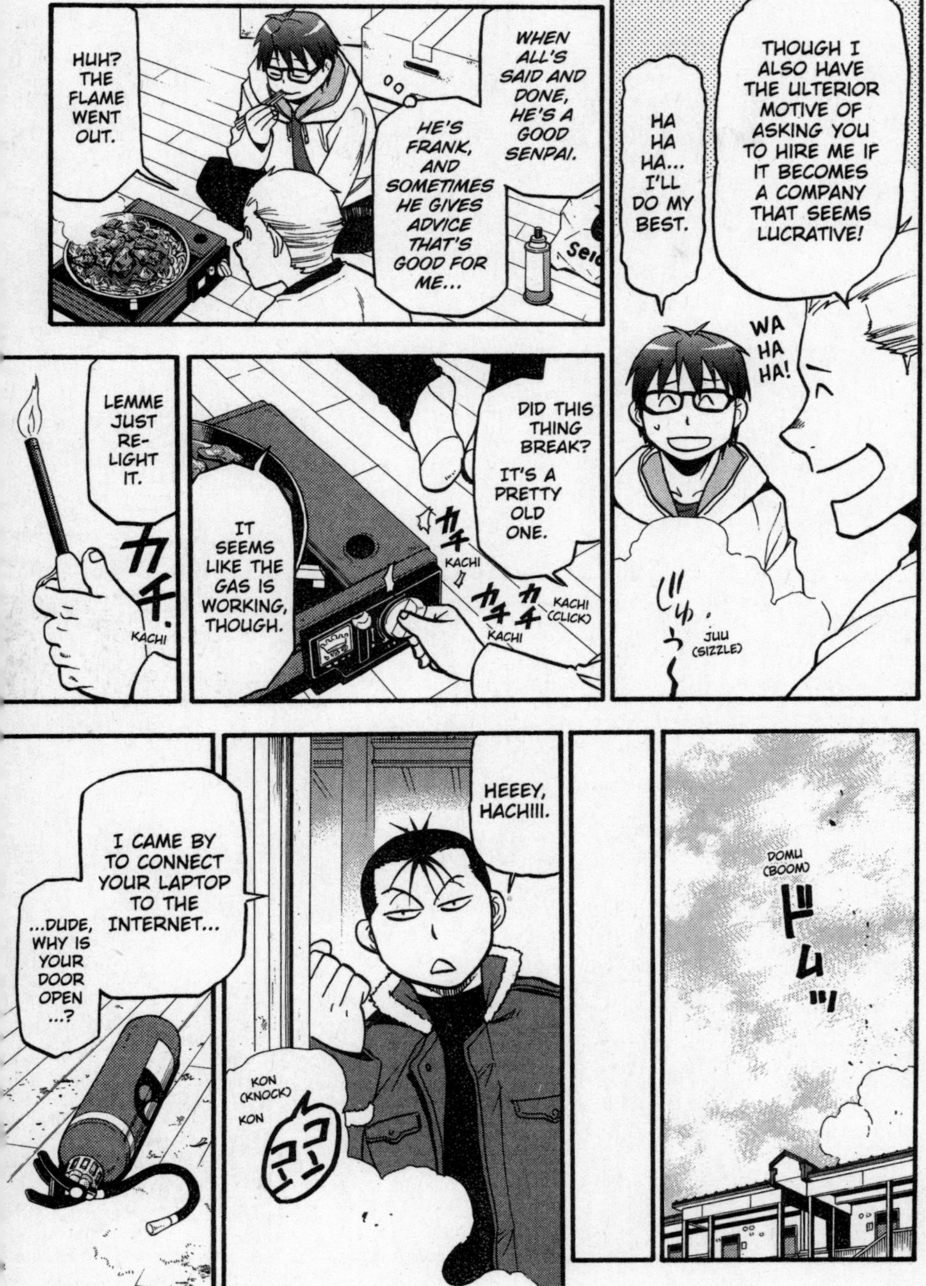
THOUGH I ALSO HAVE THE ULTERIOR MOTIVE OF ASKING YOU TO HIRE ME IF IT BECOMES A COMPANY THAT SEEMS LUCRATIVE!
HA HA HA... I'LL DO MY BEST.
WA HA HA!
じゅう
JUU (SIZZLE)
WHEN ALL'S SAID AND DONE, HE'S A GOOD SENPAI.
HE'S FRANK, AND SOMETIMES HE GIVES ADVICE THAT'S GOOD FOR ME...
HUH? THE FLAME WENT OUT.
DID THIS THING BREAK?
IT'S A PRETTY OLD ONE.
カチ
KACHI
カチカチ
KACHI (CLICK)
KACHI
IT SEEMS LIKE THE GAS IS WORKING, THOUGH.
LEMME JUST RE-LIGHT IT.
カチ
KACHI
ドムッ
DOMU (BOOM)
HEEEY, HACHIIII.
コンコン
KON (KNOCK)
KON
I CAME BY TO CONNECT YOUR LAPTOP TO THE INTERNET...
...DUDE, WHY IS YOUR DOOR OPEN ...?

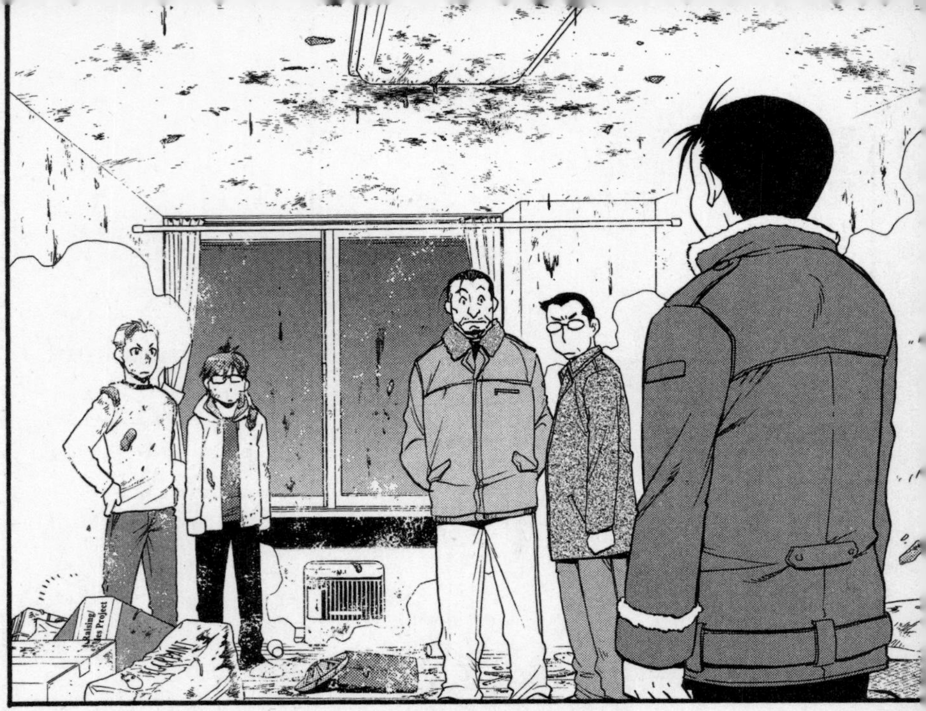

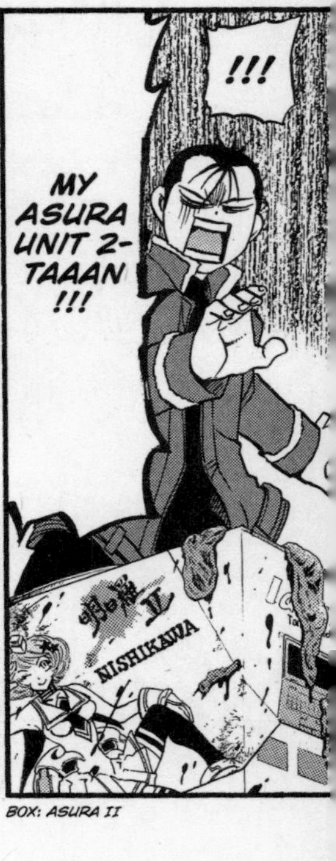
!!!
MY ASURA UNIT 2-TAAAN!!!
NISHIKAWA

BOX: ASURA II

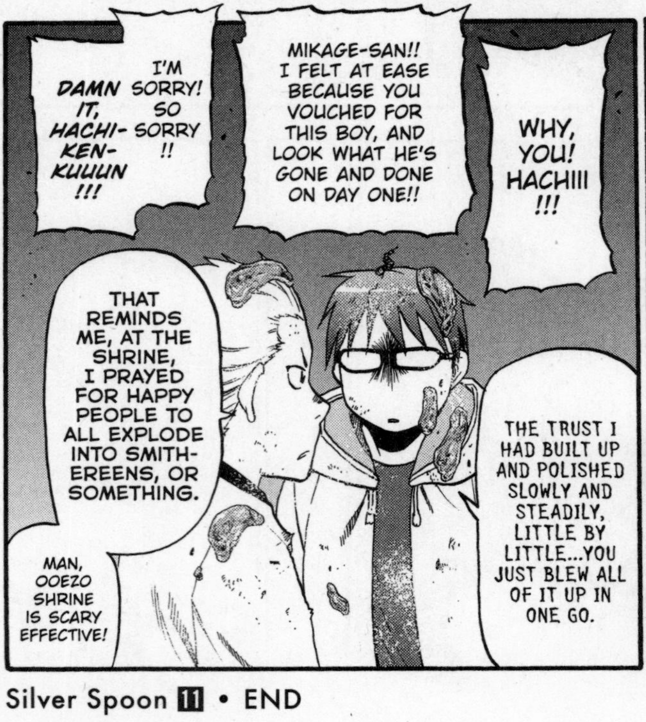
WHY, YOU! HACHIII!!!
MIKAGE-SAN!! I FELT AT EASE BECAUSE YOU VOUCHED FOR THIS BOY, AND LOOK WHAT HE'S GONE AND DONE ON DAY ONE!!
I'M SORRY! SO SORRY!!
DAMN IT, HACHI-KEN-KUUUN!!!
THE TRUST I HAD BUILT UP AND POLISHED SLOWLY AND STEADILY, LITTLE BY LITTLE...YOU JUST BLEW ALL OF IT UP IN ONE GO.
THAT REMINDS ME, AT THE SHRINE, I PRAYED FOR HAPPY PEOPLE TO ALL EXPLODE INTO SMITH-EREENS, OR SOMETHING.
MAN, OOEZO SHRINE IS SCARY EFFECTIVE!

Silver Spoon 11 • END

Silver Spoon

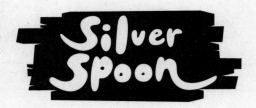

February 14

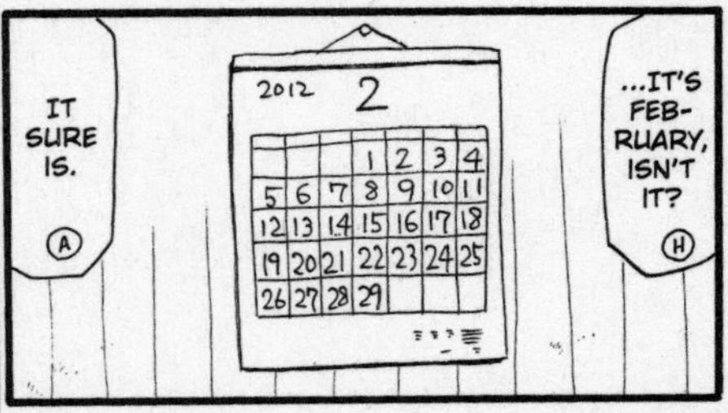
...IT'S FEBRUARY, ISN'T IT?
H
2012 2
IT SURE IS.
A

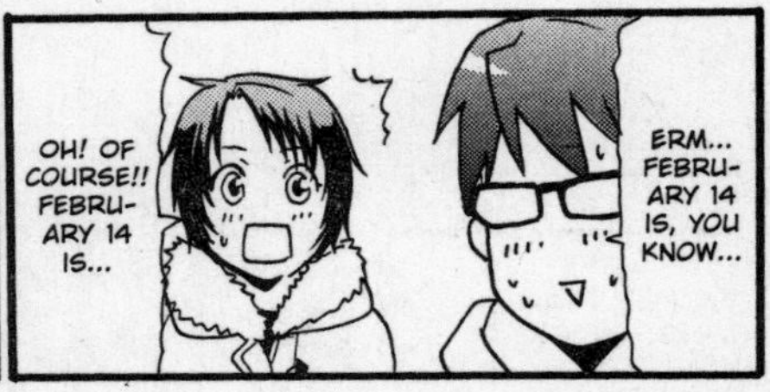
ERM... FEBRUARY 14 IS, YOU KNOW...
OH! OF COURSE!! FEBRUARY 14 IS...

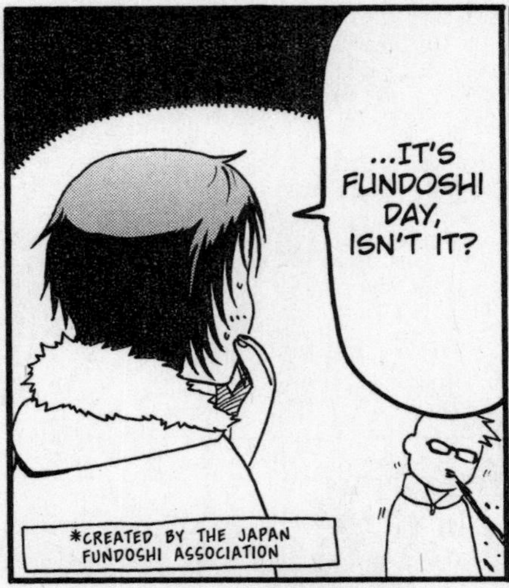
...IT'S FUNDOSHI DAY, ISN'T IT?
*CREATED BY THE JAPAN FUNDOSHI ASSOCIATION

Commercial Spirit

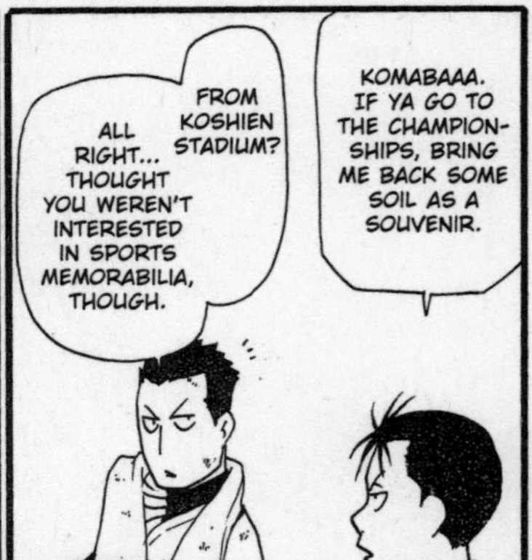
KOMABAAA. IF YA GO TO THE CHAMPIONSHIPS, BRING ME BACK SOME SOIL AS A SOUVENIR.
FROM KOSHIEN STADIUM?
ALL RIGHT... THOUGHT YOU WEREN'T INTERESTED IN SPORTS MEMORABILIA, THOUGH.

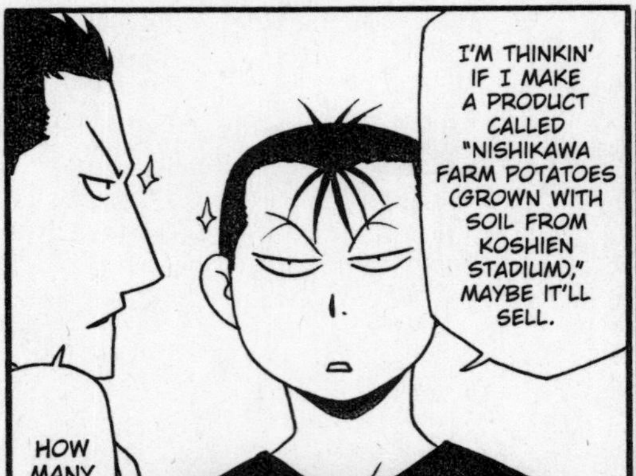
I'M THINKIN' IF I MAKE A PRODUCT CALLED "NISHIKAWA FARM POTATOES (GROWN WITH SOIL FROM KOSHIEN STADIUM)," MAYBE IT'LL SELL.
HOW MANY TONS D'YA NEED?

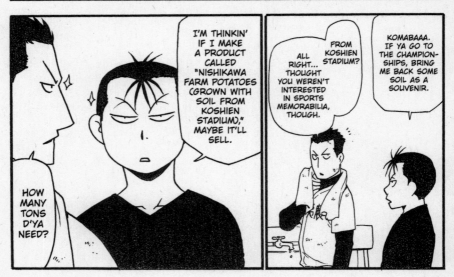

Cow Shed Diaries:
"At the Filming of the Film Adaptation" Chapter (Part 2)

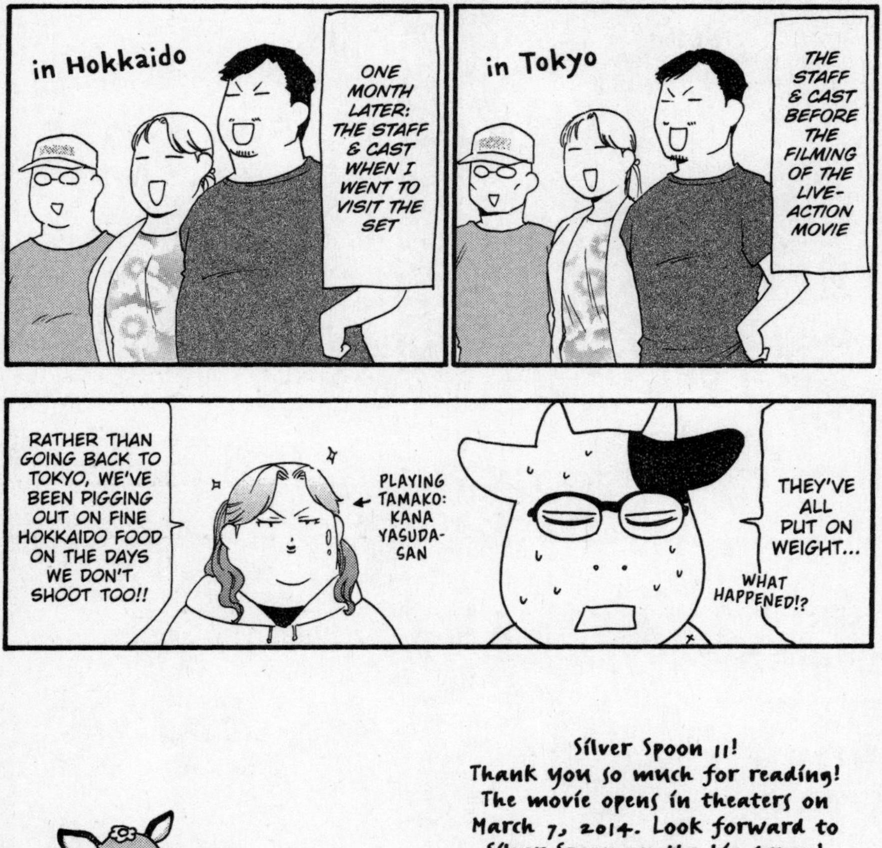
in Tokyo
THE STAFF & CAST BEFORE THE FILMING OF THE LIVE-ACTION MOVIE
in Hokkaido
ONE MONTH LATER: THE STAFF & CAST WHEN I WENT TO VISIT THE SET
THEY'VE ALL PUT ON WEIGHT...
WHAT HAPPENED!?
PLAYING TAMAKO: KANA YASUDA-SAN
RATHER THAN GOING BACK TO TOKYO, WE'VE BEEN PIGGING OUT ON FINE HOKKAIDO FOOD ON THE DAYS WE DON'T SHOOT TOO!!

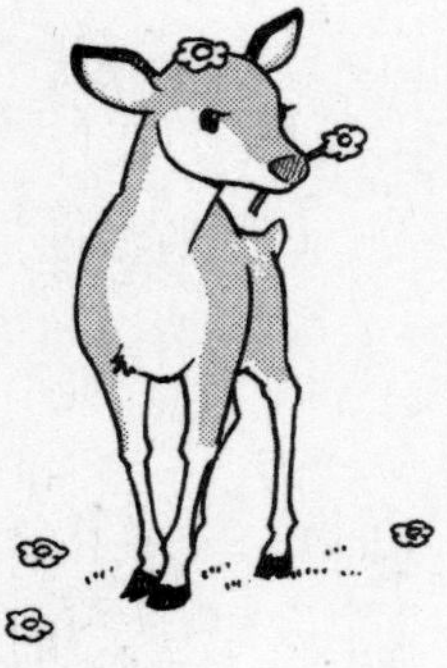

Silver Spoon 11!
Thank you so much for reading!
The movie opens in theaters on
March 7, 2014. Look forward to
Silver Spoon on the big screen!

あらかわひろむ
Hiromu Arakawa

~ Special Thanks ~
All of my assistants,
Everyone who helped with collecting material, interviews, and consulting,
My editor, Mr. Tsubouchi, Mr. Yamada

AND YOU!!

NEXT......

And so the seasons change...

...and Hachiken's second spring arrives—

STABLE 1
STABLE 2

SNOW FEST
TREAT
TREAT FUND

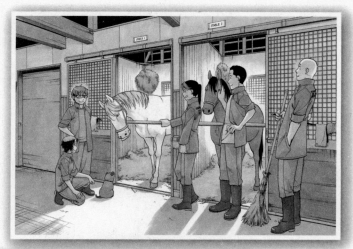

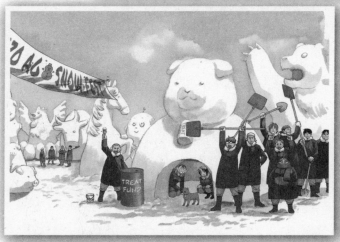

Silver Spoon 12 coming December 2019!!

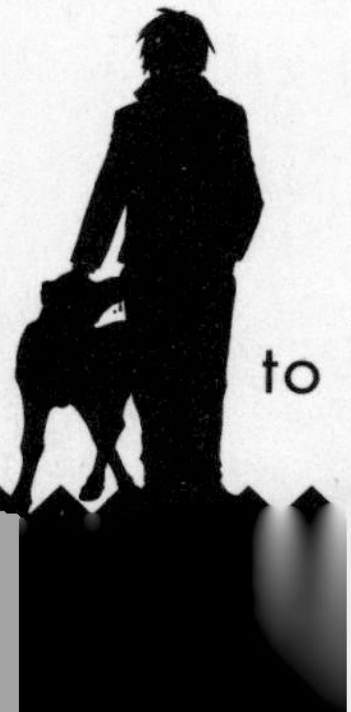

to be continued......

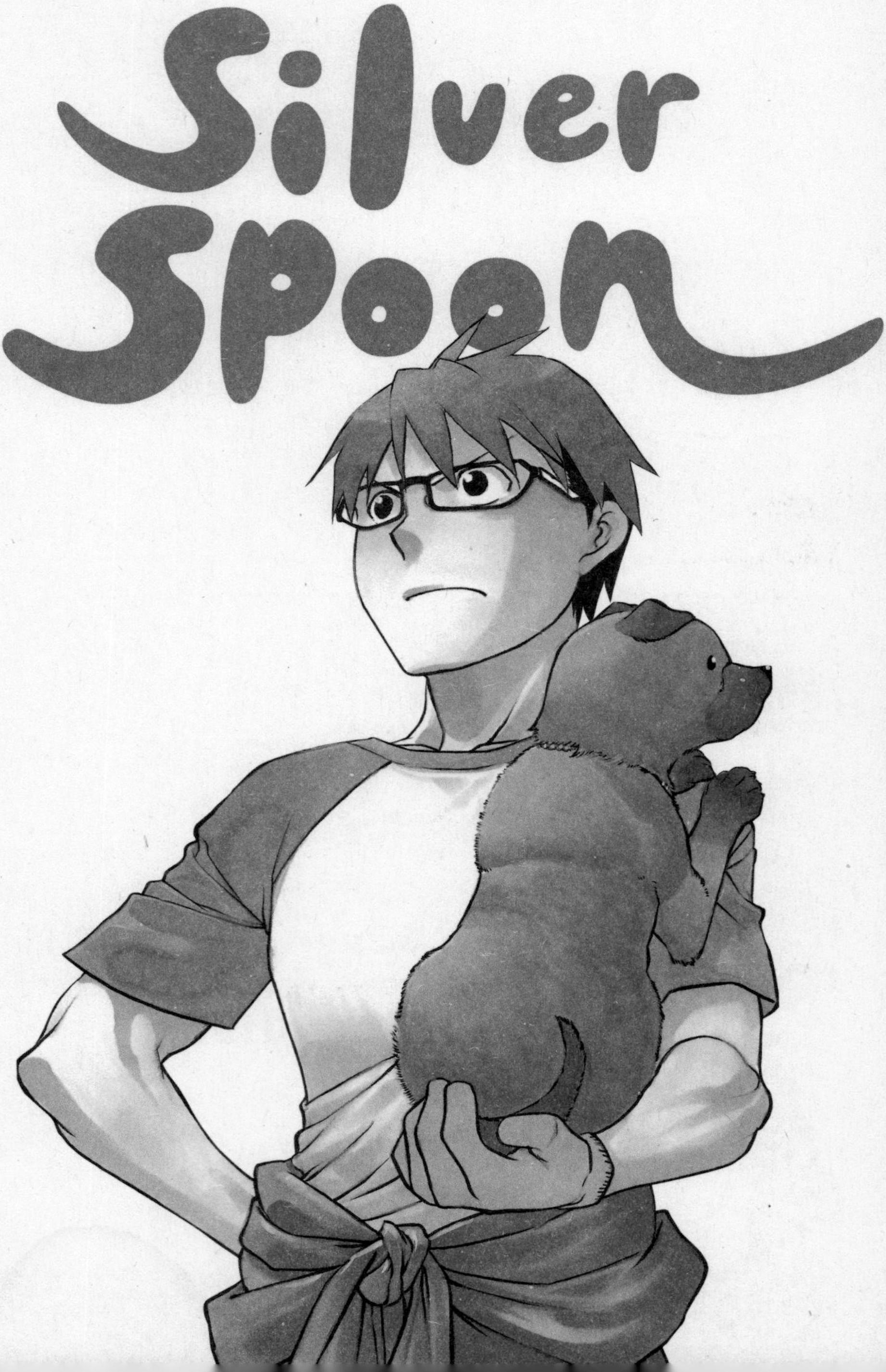
Silver
Spoon

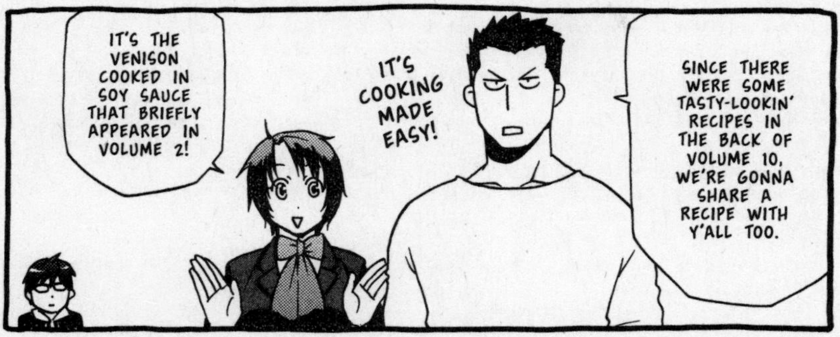
SINCE THERE WERE SOME TASTY-LOOKIN' RECIPES IN THE BACK OF VOLUME 10, WE'RE GONNA SHARE A RECIPE WITH Y'ALL TOO.
IT'S COOKING MADE EASY!
IT'S THE VENISON COOKED IN SOY SAUCE THAT BRIEFLY APPEARED IN VOLUME 2!

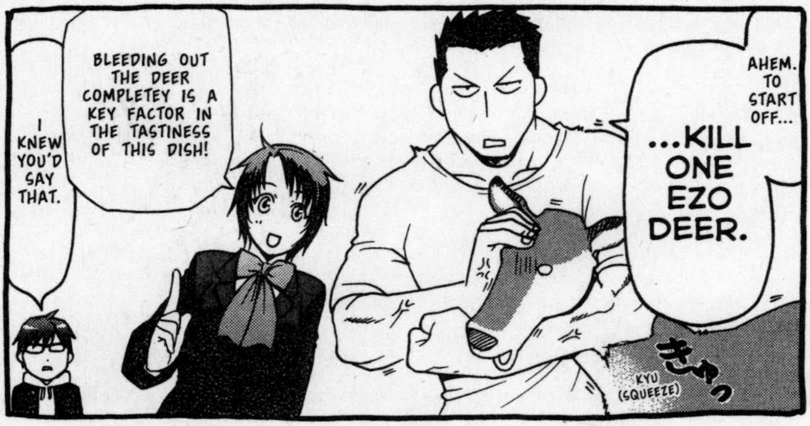
AHEM. TO START OFF...
...KILL ONE EZO DEER.
KYU (SQUEEZE)
BLEEDING OUT THE DEER COMPLETEY IS A KEY FACTOR IN THE TASTINESS OF THIS DISH!
I KNEW YOU'D SAY THAT.

Translation Notes

Common Honorifics

no honorific: Indicates familiarity or closeness; if used without permission or reason, addressing someone in this manner would constitute an insult.

-san: The Japanese equivalent of Mr./Mrs./Miss. If a situation calls for politeness, this is the fail-safe honorific.

-sama: Conveys great respect; may also indicate the social status of the speaker is lower than that of the addressee.

-kun: Used most often when referring to boys, this honorific indicates affection or familiarity. Occasionally used by older men among their peers, but it may also be used by anyone referring to a person of lower standing.

-chan: An affectionate honorific indicating familiarity used mostly in reference to girls; also used in reference to cute persons or animals of either gender.

-sensei: A respectful term for teachers, artists, or high-level professionals.

-niisan, nii-san, aniki, etc.: A term of endearment meaning "big brother" that may be more widely used to address any young man who is like a brother, regardless of whether he is related or not.

-neesan, nee-san, aneki, etc.: The female counterpart of the above, *nee-san* means "big sister."

Currency Conversion

While conversion rates fluctuate, an easy estimate for Japanese Yen conversion is ¥100 to 1 USD.

Page 21
Death by sawing (*nokobiki*) was a form of capital punishment by decapitation employed during Japan's Warring States Period.

Page 26
If you saw Oomori-senpai's name in Japanese, you wouldn't be surprised by how big he is—his given name is written with only the kanji character for "big," and the same character is also used in his family name.

Page 27
The National Center Test for University Admissions is a standardized test used by public (and some private) universities in Japan. It's administered only once annually and competition is fierce. Some schools use only the Center Test as an entrance exam, but others have a second exam of their own and/or additional essays and interviews.

Page 29
Aki and Sakae are giving out *giri choco* ("obligation chocolate")—inexpensive Valentine's Day chocolate given to classmates, friends, or coworkers that don't have the romantic connotations of the more expensive or more elaborate *honmei choco* ("heartfelt chocolate") given to one's crush or romantic partner.

Page 30
White Day is March 14, on which men are expected to give women a return gift for the chocolate they received on Valentine's Day.

Page 36
A NEET is someone who is "Not in Education, Employment, or Training." Technically, Ookawa-senpai is not a NEET at this point, unless he graduates without lining up a job...

Page 64
Nishikawa's "Time for us to play it cool" line is referencing the line "Time for Speedwagon to play it cool" spoken by the character Speedwagon in *JoJo's Bizarre Adventure*, when Speedwagon elects not to interrupt a touching moment between Jonathan Joestar and his love interest, Erina.

Page 117
In Japan, *hanko* (personal seal stamps) are used in lieu of signatures on paperwork.

Page 130
Yokan is a thick, jellied dessert, usually in a block shape, made of red bean paste, agar, and sugar.

Page 132
Mystery hotpot (called *"yami nabe,"* which literally means "hotpot in the dark") is a party/game in which each person brings a random ingredient to add to a hotpot, after which the group dares to eat the doomed concoction. It's done in the dark so you don't see what you're getting!

Page 134
Mochi is a glutinous, sticky rice cake.

Aikawa's original joke is that the Holsters are also known as the "organ meat club." The Holstein Club's full name in Japanese is *"horusutain-bu,"* which is normally shortened to *"horu-bu,"* and the word for "organ meats" in Japanese is *"horumon."* Playing off of the *horu/horu* connection, Aikawa says the club is also called the *"horumon-bu."*

Page 135
Jingisukan is a Hokkaido mutton dish.

Page 141
Nishikawa's Asura II picture resembles the girls of *Kantai Collection,* a game and multimedia franchise featuring anthropomorphized WWII warships.

Page 150
Future Farmers of Japan (*Nougyou kurabu* or *Nou-ku* for short, literally "Agriculture Club") is a real-life youth organization that holds national competitions for students in agricultural high schools.

Page 160
The Showa period refers to the time from 1926 to 1989.

Page 161
The Japanese school year begins in April. For Hachiken and friends, spring break is the vacation between school years.

Pages 168
Fundoshi are a traditional male undergarment/loincloth, now mainly used for festival costumes. The Japan Fundoshi Association really did create Fundoshi Day, based on possible pronunciations of the numbers in the date 2/14: *fun* (2) *do* (10) *shi* (4).

Silver Spoon

Silver Spoon 11

HIROMU ARAKAWA

Translation: **Amanda Haley** Lettering: **Abigail Blackman**

This book is a work of fiction. Names, characters, places, and incidents are the product of the author's imagination or are used fictitiously. Any resemblance to actual events, locales, or persons, living or dead, is coincidental.

GIN NO SAJI SILVER SPOON Vol. 11
by Hiromu ARAKAWA
© 2011 Hiromu ARAKAWA
All rights reserved.
Original Japanese edition published by SHOGAKUKAN.
English translation rights in the United States of America, Canada, the United Kingdom, Ireland, Australia and New Zealand arranged with SHOGAKUKAN through Tuttle-Mori Agency, Inc.

English translation © 2019 by Yen Press, LLC

Yen Press
150 West 30th Street, 19th Floor
New York, NY 10001

Visit us at yenpress.com
facebook.com/yenpress
twitter.com/yenpress
yenpress.tumblr.com
instagram.com/yenpress

First Yen Press Edition: October 2019

Yen Press is an imprint of Yen Press, LLC.
The Yen Press name and logo are trademarks of Yen Press, LLC.

The publisher is not responsible for websites (or their content) that are not owned by the publisher.

Library of Congress Control Number: 2017959207

ISBN: 978-1-9753-2766-8

10 9 8 7 6 5 4 3 2 1

WOR

Printed in the United States of America